ON THE
RECORD

**ALSO BY
ANNA HARWELL CELENZA**

*Jazz Italian Style: From its Origins in
New Orleans to Fascist Italy and Sinatra*

The Cambridge Companion to Gershwin

Music and Human Flourishing

CHILDREN'S BOOKS

Bach's Goldberg Variations

Beethoven's Heroic Symphony

Duke Ellington's Nutcracker Suite

Gershwin's Rhapsody in Blue

Haydn's Farewell Symphony

Mussorgsky's Pictures at an Exhibition

Saint-Saëns's Danse macabre

Vivaldi's Four Seasons

ON THE RECORD

MUSIC THAT CHANGED AMERICA

Anna Harwell Celenza

· · · · ·

W. W. Norton & Company

Independent Publishers Since 1923

Copyright © 2026 by Anna Harwell Celenza

All rights reserved
Printed in the United States of America
First Edition

For information about permission to reproduce selections from this book, write to
Permissions, W. W. Norton & Company, Inc., 500 Fifth Avenue, New York, NY 10110

For information about special discounts for bulk purchases, please contact
W. W. Norton Special Sales at specialsales@wwnorton.com or 800-233-4830

Manufacturing by Lake Book Manufacturing
Book design by The Cosmic Lion
Production manager: Lauren Abbate

Library of Congress Control Number: 2025044676

ISBN: 978-1-324-00499-8

W. W. Norton & Company, Inc.
500 Fifth Avenue, New York, NY 10110
www.wwnorton.com

W. W. Norton & Company Ltd.
15 Carlisle Street, London W1D 3BS

Authorized EU representative:
EAS, Mustamäe tee 50, 10621 Tallinn, Estonia

1 2 3 4 5 6 7 8 9 0

For my husband, Chris, whose love and support accompanied the writing of every word.

Contents

Preface	xi
1 ▪ Land of the Free, Home of the Brave	1
2 ▪ The Unanswered Question	27
3 ▪ The Search for an American Sound	51
4 ▪ Saving the American Landscape	73
5 ▪ Witness for the Prosecution	95
6 ▪ A New Vision for America	117
7 ▪ America's Secret Sonic Weapon	139
8 ▪ There's a Place for Us . . . Somewhere	161
9 ▪ What's Going On?	187
10 ▪ Sonic Shift: When Politics Changed Music	211
11 ▪ Under African Skies	233
12 ▪ Who Tells Our Story?	259
Acknowledgments	279
Notes	283
Credits	315
Index	319

Preface

May 23, 2024. A crowd has gathered at Homewood Field for the annual commencement ceremony at Johns Hopkins University. It's a gray, rainy morning, and the celebratory mood that usually accompanies such an event is darkened by a cloud of anxiety. It has been a stressful semester. Student protests over the Israeli–Palestinian conflict have rattled campus, and as I take my place on stage among my faculty colleagues, I wonder if there will be more disruptions.

At the front of the dais sit six leaders from the realms of business, politics, the sciences, and the arts who are being awarded honorary doctorates. Among them is US Senator Mitt Romney, who has been asked to give the keynote address. As Romney begins his speech, which emphasizes the value of public service and family commitments over professional accomplishments, a cacophony of honking horns, piercing sirens, and angry shouts filters into the stadium from outside. Romney continues speaking, seemingly unfazed by the demonstration.

At the conclusion of Romney's speech, Ron Daniels, the university president, approaches the podium. As if on cue, a group of protestors inside the stadium unfurl a homemade banner—"FREE PALESTINE DIVEST FROM OCCUPATION"—and begin chanting through megaphones: "Let Gaza live! Let Gaza live!" Daniels stands silent for a moment, waiting for this second demonstration to end. When it doesn't, he motions to one of the honorary guests on stage and makes an unexpected request:

> It is with the greatest hope and aspiration that I look to our extraordinary graduate today, Dr. Stevie Wonder. And I say: We have a piano. We have a microphone. Do you think there's any chance? Because we would love to hear from you today.

As the crowd releases a jubilant roar, Wonder flashes his inimitable smile and makes his way to the keyboard. "Show me the money!" he jokes as he begins improvising on a familiar tune. The protestors continue chanting, but with each musical phrase, their shouts grow less forceful. As Wonder continues to play, he intermittently offers a few insights that put the current political situation in context:

> I was thinking, coming up here, that we have a lot of differences that people talk about. And there are those who will say that we are too different to make a connection. But truly, music has made the connection since the beginning of time: sound. So, I want to use your voice, your spirit, to let the sound of unity, of coming together, for the meaning of ending all wars forever, all over this world that we live in.

The audience breaks out in applause. The protestors, now silent, drop their banner. Wonder continues:

> I also want to say that we all have something in common, every single one of us. And we cannot exist without this that we have in common. We all have to breathe. We cannot exist without breathing. We all have to have the chance to eat. So, I say that we must care about this planet that we live on. Don't take it for granted.

Wonder then sings three songs: "The Secret World of Plants," "You Are the Sunshine of My Life," and "I Just Called to Say I Love You." As one attendee later noted online: "What I came here for: To see my cousin graduate from a high tier university. What I got: A Stevie Wonder mini-concert. Unreal!"

I was in the throes of writing the final chapters of this book when I witnessed Wonder's surprise performance, and I will admit that my perception of the event was likely colored by my own preoccupations at the time. Nonetheless, as I watched the performance and saw its effect on others, I was struck by Wonder's enduring ability to harness the political power of music. His remarks underscored the importance of empathy. His choice of songs channeled themes of universality, hope, and compassion. And for just a moment, the societal tensions of the previous weeks seemed to fade away.

As a singer-songwriter, Wonder has spent the whole of his career engaging in political causes. His song "Happy Birthday" was composed in support of creating a federal holiday in honor of Martin Luther King Jr. Similarly, "It's Wrong (Apartheid)" called out the injustices of government-sponsored racial segregation in South Africa. Wonder has advocated for the rights of people with disabilities. He has raised awareness about climate change and environmental issues. He has supported global hunger relief, AIDS awareness, and various campaigns for peace. So, it should come as no surprise that many of the political issues he has engaged with over the years are similar to those that make an appearance in this book.

On the Record: Music that Changed America offers a political history of the United States through a musical lens. It highlights an array of musical works by American composers that sparked debates in the halls of Congress, and it explores the many ways in which music, perhaps more than any other art form, has given voice to those who might otherwise have gone unheard.

Hundreds of musical compositions and popular songs have been written in response to American politics. Stevie Wonder's "Happy Birthday," "It's Wrong (Apartheid)," and "The Secret World of Plants" are good examples. But only a few dozen works have actually *instigated* change in Congress. *On the Record: Music that Changed America* focuses on these compositions: works that altered the way politicians think about the world around them; music that influenced important changes in domestic and foreign policy; compositions that left an indelible mark on American culture.

Each chapter in *On the Record: Music that Changed America* references a specific piece of legislation that arose in response to one or more musical compositions. These range from debates over national identity and immigration policy to decisions about intellectual property, the environment, race relations, foreign policy, and the future of American democracy. The chapters are arranged chronologically, according to the composition date of the work discussed. Most chapters cover a time span of several decades, since many of these compositions live on in the public consciousness. Over time, they have transformed, and this process of transformation has added layers of new meaning and significance. Consequently, this book unfolds in episodes rather than following a straightforward storyline. The chapters often overlap in time, revealing how many of these compositions have intersected with one another and together shaped American politics.

In each chapter I seek to reframe, reconsider, and in some cases refute previous assumptions about the intersection of music and politics in the United States. My aim is not just to describe these works, but to illustrate their effectiveness as agents of political change. By presenting fresh hearings of compositions from a range of genres and styles, I hope to offer a clearer sense of why music matters in American politics. In some chapters, I also explore how politics has changed music. What happens in Congress affects the arts community in more fundamental ways than most people realize. Widely ranging political decisions have been made over the past half century that have directly influenced how music is produced, preserved, and perceived by audiences in the United States and abroad. Some of the changes have been for the good. Others, not so much.

I deeply value all the compositions discussed in this book. These are works that have inspired me intellectually, and over the course of my career I have spent countless hours listening to them and discussing them with students and colleagues. These works have benefited me spiritually, too. They have helped me understand my place in the world, both as a music lover and as an American. Consequently, one of my goals in writing *On the Record* is to instill in readers a belief in the power of art. These are works that should be studied closely and performed often. Each tells a story about the ideals and aspirations that, for better or worse, influenced political debate and eventually changed America.

Transformative compositions do not exist in a cultural vacuum; they gain strength and significance by interacting with the mutable world around them. Learning about the music that has influenced American politics, for good and for bad, can teach us a great deal about our past. But even more importantly, discovering music's power to activate change can help us listen more attentively to the present world around us.

ON THE RECORD

LAND OF THE FREE, HOME OF THE BRAVE

On March 3, 1931, the congressional act that designated "The Star-Spangled Banner" the official national anthem of the United States was signed into law by President Herbert Hoover. Eighty-five years later, on a cool, late summer evening in 2016, quarterback Colin Kaepernick sparked a nationwide debate when he refused to stand during a performance of that anthem.

Kaepernick's team, the San Francisco 49ers, were hosting the Green Bay Packers in a pre-season game at Levi Stadium. The 49ers lost, 21 to 10, but that wasn't why some fans burned their Kaepernick jerseys. "If you don't love our country, get the [expletive] out," posted one man on Twitter. Another pondered the quarterback's motives: "He feels oppressed making $126 million?" But as Kaepernick later explained, his protest wasn't personal, it was symbolic. He wanted Americans to take the anthem's message seriously. He wanted them to pay attention to the racial injustices that continue to plague American society. "I am not going to stand up to show pride in a flag for a country that oppresses black people and people of color," he said. "To me, this is bigger than football, and it would be selfish on my part to look the other way."

Kaepernick wasn't protesting the national anthem. He was protesting the performance of a public ritual—the standing up, hand over heart, during a performance of "The Star-Spangled Banner." When Kaepernick took a knee, he forced Americans to think about what that ritual is supposed to mean. He posed the question: Is America really "the land of the free and the home of the brave?"

Race anxiety pervades much of American history, and the nation's music history is no exception. Kaepernick was not the first to protest the ritual now associated with the singing of "The Star-Spangled Banner." Since its origins during the War of 1812, the song has been a symbol of both victory and protest. Although the anthem's soaring melody and heroic lyrics solidified early its reception as a symbol of patriotic uplift, concerns about inequality—racial, gender, and economic—have arisen time and again during the anthem's evolution. Even the lyrics have been in flux, as various Americans have attempted to shape its message to their own worldview. The ritual we now associate with performances of "The Star-Spangled Banner" is a relatively recent development, a change set in motion by the US Congress during the Great Depression in an effort to unite an economically and politically fractured society.

Like much American music from the early nineteenth century, "The Star-Spangled Banner" is a contrafactum—a song created by exchanging one set of lyrics with another without substantial change to the melody. The author of the new set of lyrics was Francis Scott Key (1779–1843), a young lawyer from Georgetown whose family had arrived in America nearly a century earlier. Key's family had aristocratic British origins, and his father, a lawyer and regional judge, saw to it that his son was well educated and well connected.

Key penned the lyrics to "The Star-Spangled Banner" in September 1814 in celebration of the US defeat of the British in the Battle of Baltimore, one of the last military confrontations in the War of 1812. We tend to forget that this war began as an act of US aggression. General William Hull invaded Canada to expand our nation's territory. In response, Britain entered the conflict in defense of Canada. By the time the Battle of Baltimore took place in 1814, British troops had already decimated numerous cities along the East Coast, including Washington, DC. Baltimore was the nation's third largest city and one of its most important ports. If the British could take Baltimore, many then believed, it would mean the end of US independence.

Several hours before the battle commenced, US military leaders sent

Key to speak with British Rear Admiral George Cockburn (set to lead the British attack by sea) about an exchange of military prisoners. Key was hoping to dissuade Cockburn from attacking. Instead, he found himself sequestered by British troops on a boat anchored just outside Baltimore harbor, where he watched the progress of the ensuing strike.

On September 13, amid a fierce storm, Cockburn launched an attack with more than 1,500 rockets, their fiery trails screeching through the air before exploding overhead and raining shells and shrapnel on the Americans below. The assault lasted long into the night. Then, just after sunrise, on September 14, the bombing stopped. "The awful stillness and suspense were unbearable," Key remembered. As the smoke cleared, Key noticed that the fort's storm flag, a small banner flown during inclement weather, was still flying. This was a hopeful sign, an indication that US troops had not surrendered. As Key later described it, he watched as the fort's storm flag was lowered and a massive garrison flag, forty-two feet in length, was raised in its place. As a private named Isaac Munroe explained in a letter to a friend a few days later, when the victory flag was hoisted, "our morning gun was fired . . . 'Yankee Doodle' played . . . and we all appeared in full view of [our] formidable and mortified enemy."

The reference to "Yankee Doodle" is telling. Although the melody appears to have originated in fifteenth-century Holland, the lyrics known as "Yankee Doodle" were penned by a British soldier in 1755 to ridicule colonial Americans. In typical US fashion, however, Americans embraced the song with pride and regularly used its melody for contrafacta mocking the British. One such song, titled "The Battle of Baltimore," gives a blow-by-blow description of the military encounter. Despite its thirteen verses—yes thirteen!—this song was hastily written after the battle, around the same time Key penned the words to what is now known as "The Star-Spangled Banner."

A handwritten draft of Key's original lyrics still exists. From the beginning, he envisioned his piece as a victory song. The first two verses recap the dramatic events of the battle, the last two criticize the British and justify war. Key tweaked his text over the next few days, still sequestered in the harbor. By the time the British departed on September 16, Key had completed a final draft, which he delivered to a local newspaper, the *Baltimore Patriot & Evening Advertiser*, the following day. The song, originally titled "The Defence of Fort M'Henry," was quickly printed and distributed as a broadside. Like most broadsides at the time, no musical notation accompanied the lyrics. Instead, performers were instructed to sing Key's text to the melody of a preexisting tune called "To Anacreon in Heaven."

"To Anacreon in Heaven" is a British song composed in the early 1770s as the "constitutional song" of an aristocratic gentleman's club in London called the Anacreontic Society. The founders named their club in honor of Anacreon, a Greek lyric poet from the fifth century BC best known for his verses celebrating love and wine in equal measure. The song, with lyrics by Ralph Tomlinson (1744–78) and music by John Stafford Smith (1750–1836), was performed at each club meeting to mark the commencement of the evening's jovial post-dinner activities. As a contemporary chronicler named R. J. S. Stevens explained, "the greatest levity and vulgar obscenity, generally prevailed" at these gatherings "without any shame whatever . . . till the Society broke up, which was generally very late." Stevens notes that a ritual had developed around the singing of the song. Although the verse proper was sung by a soloist, the two-line refrain that concluded each verse was sung in unison by club members. A look at the opening verse gives a sense of the overall effect.

> *Solo:*
> To Anacreon in Heav'n, where he sat in full Glee,
> A few Sons of Harmony sent a Petition,
> That he their Inspirer and Patron would be;
> When this answer arriv'd from the Jolly Old Grecian:
> "Voice, Fiddle, and Flute,
> No longer be mute,
> I'll lend you my Name and inspire you to boot.
> *Unison:*
> And, besides I'll instruct you, like me, to entwine
> The Myrtle of Venus with Bacchus's Vine."

As the refrain clearly states, the men of the Anacreontic Society sought a patron who would guide them in their pursuit of women and wine. Not the most noble of aspirations. Nonetheless, herein lies the origin of America's national anthem.

In 1796, Stafford Smith published a sophisticated arrangement of "To Anacreon in Heaven" that made use of four-part harmony and a series of call-and-response passages. This version proved popular in the United States, where it was sung by glee clubs up and down the East Coast. By the time Key graduated from St. John's College in Annapolis in 1796, "To Anacreon in Heaven" had become a popular tune for contrafacta. For example, in 1798, the melody served as the basis for one of the nation's first campaign songs, "Adams and Liberty." Gone are all references to women and wine. The lyrics sound more like a stump speech. They praise the country's founding fathers, promote free trade, and denounce the French for the economic and social instability their decade-long revolution was fomenting around the world. Key was a supporter of Adams's bid for the presidency, and as such he no doubt sang "Adams and Liberty" countless times. By 1800, the tune had become strongly connected with American politics. So, it should come as no surprise that Key used it when composing songs linked to heroic patriotism.

The first was a song written in 1805 to honor two close friends, Stephen Decatur Jr. (1779–1820) and Charles Stewart (1778–1869), who had just returned from North Africa, where they had been fighting pirates in the Barbary Coast War. A celebratory dinner was held at McLaughlin's Tavern in Georgetown, where, as various newspapers reported, Key's new "Song" was performed to the tune "To Anacreon in Heaven."

> When the warrior returns, from the battle afar,
> To the home and the country he nobly defended,
> O! warm be the welcome to gladden his ear,
> And loud be the joy that his perils are ended:
> In the full tide of song let his fame roll along,
> To the feast-flowing board let us gratefully throng,
> Where, mixed with the olive, the laurel shall wave,
> And form a bright wreath for the brows of the brave.

Fun trivia fact: the third verse of this song marked the first time in the English language that the term "star-spangled" was used to describe the American flag.

When Key returned to the tune in 1814, he used four verses to tell the story of the Americans' defense of Fort McHenry. The first, we all know. It recounts the battle and poses the question: "Does that star-spangled banner yet wave?" Verse two confirms that it indeed does. Verse three is dedicated to disparaging the British, "whose blood has washed out their foul footsteps' pollution." For two centuries, this verse has caused controversy because of the violence directed not only toward the British but also toward their collaborators: "No refuge could save the hireling or slave, / From the terror of flight or the gloom of the grave." Today, this line evokes horrific images of the countless African Americans who suffered under the injustices of slavery. But in 1814, the reference was often interpreted differently. "Hireling" referred to the German mercenaries Britain employed during the War of 1812. "Slave" was interpreted in various ways by nineteenth-century listeners. Some gleaned a reference to those who had escaped enslavement and fought on the side of the British. Others thought the term referred to the British indentured servants forced to fight as repayment for their debts. Key never clarified his intentions with this verse, but his personal stance on the rights of African Americans were clear. Although he sought to uphold the rights of free blacks as the US district attorney in Washington, DC (a position he held from 1833 until 1841, after being appointed by then President Andrew Jackson), he also used his office to fight abolitionists and defend the rights of slaveholders. Like his parents before him, Key was a slaveholder himself, and once described those of African descent as "a distinct and inferior race of people."

Key's concluding verse asserts that the US is a "heav'n rescued land" and praises "the power that hath made and preserved us a nation." It glorifies war as the cost of liberty: "Then conquer we must, when our cause it is just / And this be our motto—'In God is our trust.'"

Several months after the publication of "In Defence of Fort M'Henry" as a broadside, a Baltimore publisher named Thomas Carr issued a new version of the song, now titled "The Star-Spangled Banner," with music for piano and optional flute. By this point, the lyrics had been published in countless newspapers, from Boston to New Orleans. Carr's sheet music version gives the first clear indication of how the anthem was originally performed. Written in 6/4 time, the music is marked "con spirito"—to be sung at a brisk pace "with spirit." The optional flute part was a nod toward the song's militaristic origins. Since the sixteenth century, the flute had been widely used on the battlefield in Europe and later in the US.

This early publication of "The Star-Spangled Banner" contains the label "a patriotic song," and for many the lyrics, at least, were patriotic. But the tune, with its lilting, waltz-like meter, felt somehow inappropriate. You couldn't really march to it. And how could a tune you can't march to serve as a symbol of America's military power? In 1816, a New York composer and publisher named James Hewitt attempted to rectify the problem by composing new music for Key's lyrics. Hewitt's version adhered to a steady 2/4 beat, which made it perfect for marching, but not so perfect for singing. The new meter made the lyrics sound stilted and clunky, and the elimination of the original soaring melody destroyed the song's emotional uplift.

As the nineteenth century progressed, various other patriotic songs vied for attention in the American consciousness. One of the most popular was "Hail, Columbia," a tune that presents the president as the nation's unifying symbol. "Hail, Columbia," as we know it today, came into being in 1798, and, like "Adams and Liberty," it celebrated John Adams, the second US president. The instrumental music, composed in 1789 by a Philadelphia music teacher named Philip Phile, was originally titled "The President's March" and was written in celebration of George Washington's first inauguration and republished in honor of his second inauguration. Five more years passed, however, before a Philadelphia lawyer named Joseph Hopkinson gave the tune lyrics, which he published as "The Federalist Song" in honor of Adams. Like Key, Hopkinson was an avid Federalist who came from a well-connected family. His father had been a signer of the Declaration of Independence, and for many Americans, this lineage added an air of respectability to the song, making it a more appropriate choice than "The Star-Spangled Banner" for important public occasions. The fact that both the words *and* music were written by Americans only added to its popularity. Nonetheless, "Hail, Columbia" had its drawbacks. To begin with, the song's bland lyrics and plodding melody pale in comparison to the dramatic emotion of "The Star-Spangled Banner." Although "Hail, Columbia" is easy to sing, there's nothing in it that sparks a sense of hallowed glory or soaring freedom. Given that the song's unifying symbol is the president, some deemed it too political for a national anthem. Critics warned that rallying the nation around a president could be dangerous if that leader turned tyrannical. Looking back at our nation's recent history, we can see just how prescient these critics were.

"My Country 'Tis of Thee" was another popular political song of the era. Here the lyrics weren't a problem: the song's unifying symbol is the concept of liberty. But like "The Star-Spangled Banner," "My Country 'Tis of Thee" is a contrafactum based on a British tune, in this case "God Save the King." "Yankee Doodle" was also popular, and some suggested that, with appropriate lyrics, it might fill the patriotic need at public ceremonies. (If Benjamin Franklin could suggest a turkey as the national bird, why not "Yankee Doodle" as a national song?) All of this is to say that by the 1830s, there were numerous songs in circulation that were regularly referred to as America's "national air" or "patriotic song." But it was "The Star-Spangled Banner," more than any other, that served as an important vehicle for protest over the next few decades.

As the nineteenth century progressed, singing "The Star-Spangled Banner" became the musical equivalent of waving the national flag. Consequently, interest groups across the political spectrum rewrote the lyrics to fit their own agendas. Abolitionists, especially, viewed the song as a target and drew attention to the contradiction between the song's lyrics and the realities of American society. In one parody of the song called "The Patriot's Banner," the symbolic refrain was subtly edited: "'Tis the star-spangled banner, while it doth wave / O'er the land no more free—'tis the home of the slave!"

Abolitionist indignation at the song was no doubt enflamed by Key himself. In 1836, a race riot broke out in Washington, DC after a white mob attacked a well-known free black restaurant owner. By this point, nearly 30 percent of the city's black population was free, and this angered those who believed that the capital had become a sanctuary for runaway slaves. Believing that abolitionists from the north were riling things up, Key sought, as the city's attorney general, to crack down on the free speech of anti-slavery protesters. In the ensuing case, *U.S. v. Reuben Crandall,* Key prosecuted a New York physician residing in Georgetown for possessing abolitionist pamphlets. The trial drew national attention as Key posed a provocative question: Did the property rights of slaveholders take precedence over the free speech rights of those advocating for the abolition of slavery? As if that weren't enough, in the same year the House of Representatives adopted a series of "gag rules" that automatically tabled all anti-slavery petitions, effectively silencing any discussion on the matter. This action sparked outrage among individuals like E. A. Atlee, who viewed the suppression of debate as a direct attack on the First Amendment. In 1844 Atlee published "A New Version of the National Song," which shone a spotlight on the violent horrors of slavery:

> Oh, say do you hear, at the dawn's early light
> The shrieks of those bondmen, whose blood is now streaming
> From the merciless lash, while our banner in sight
> With its stars mocking freedom, is fitfully gleaming?
> Do you see the backs bare? Do you mark every score
> Of the whip of the driver trace channels of gore?
> And say, doth our star-spangled banner yet wave
> O'er the land of the free, and the home of the brave?

As time passed, references to "The Star-Spangled Banner" were used to promote a variety of viewpoints, not all of them palatable. Between 1847 and 1854, Justin Jones of Boston published "a racist, nativist newspaper" called *The Star-Spangled Banner*, wherein he spewed hatred for immigrants, especially Irish Catholics and those of African descent. Jones also published a series of popular dime novels that further tied his racist ideas to national symbols like the flag. By the 1850s, the anti-Catholic nativism and racial discrimination promoted by Jones invigorated a secret fraternal organization called the Order of the Star-Spangled Banner, which spread across the northeast.

Despite the appropriation of "The Star-Spangled Banner" by various groups, ranging from suffragists to teetotalers and capitalists, Key's original version of the song continued to sell well and was often coopted by presidential campaigns. For example, when William Henry Harrison ran for office in 1840, eight different parodies of "The Star-Spangled

Banner"—including one called "The Harrison Banner"—were published in a promotional songbook. In mounting Lincoln's presidential campaign in 1860, the Republican Party linked their candidate to the "star-spangled" symbol with the campaign song "Lincoln and Liberty":

Then up with our banner so glorious,
The star-spangled red-white-and-blue,
We'll fight till our flag is victorious,
For Lincoln and Liberty too!

Other verses in "Lincoln and Liberty" raised the call for racial equality:

Come all you true friends of the nation
Attend to humanity's call
Oh aid of the slaves' liberation
And roll on the liberty ball

We'll finish the temple of freedom
And make it capacious within
That all who seek shelter may find it
Whatever the hue of their skin.

This was a position that did not sit well with many pro-slavery states. Between December 1860 and April 1861, eleven of them seceded from the US, and from this point on "The Star-Spangled Banner" took on new meaning. As William Porcher Miles, a South Carolina congressman in the new Confederate States of America (CSA) explained, although many Southerners still maintained an "attachment to the Stars and Stripes . . . it is manifest that, in inaugurating a new government, we cannot retain the flag of the government from which we have withdrawn." This also required the abandonment of the song that praised it. In the South, songs like "Dixie" and "The Bonnie Blue Flag" rose to prominence, while new songs like "Farewell to the Star-Spangled Banner" (1860) and "Adieu to the Star-Spangled Banner Forever" (1861) were published and distributed as CSA propaganda.

In reaction to what was seen in the North as a treasonous act, the abolitionist poet Oliver Wendell Holmes Sr. penned a new verse for "The Star-Spangled Banner" that praised the end of slavery and castigated the Confederates for their desecration of the flag:

When our land is illumined by Liberty's smile,
If a foe from within strikes a blow at her glory,
Down, down with the traitor who dares to defile
The flag of her stars and the page of her story!
By the millions unchained when our birthright was gained,
We will keep her bright blazon forever unstained!
And the Star-Spangled Banner in triumph shall wave
While the land of the free is the home of the brave!

Northerners embraced "The Star-Spangled Banner" as a symbol of their support for the Union cause. As *Dwight's Musical Journal* reported in 1861, it appeared "at concerts, declaimed with fiery energy by accomplished singers, in the streets and in the public meetings by the sonorous tones of brass bands, often sung in spontaneous chorus by all who had heart to feel or voice to sing." Northern publishers printed elaborate editions of "The Star-Spangled Banner" featuring colorful illustrations in support of the war effort.

As the war raged on, "The Star-Spangled Banner" and "Dixie" rose to prominence as the unofficial anthems of the North and South respectively, the irony of which cannot be overlooked. Whereas "The Star-Spangled Banner" was composed by a former slaveholder whose descendants sided with the South, "Dixie" was penned by an antislavery Northerner named Daniel Decatur Emmett. Emmett premiered the song, in blackface, with his band, Bryant's Minstrels, as part of a vaudeville show in New York in 1859. One year later, the song was incorporated into a minstrel show in New Orleans and quickly spread in popularity across the South. In February 1861, "Dixie" was performed in Richmond as part of Jefferson Davis's inauguration ceremony as president of the Confederacy. From that point on, "Dixie" was deemed the "National Anthem of Secession."

The South's abandonment of "The Star-Spangled Banner" only heightened fervor for the song in the North, where the war accelerated the commercialization of patriotism. Spring 1862 marks the first time "The Star-Spangled Banner" was performed at a professional baseball game. That same year, a publisher named James Homer Kennedy released *Star-Spangled Banner Poems, Consecrated to the Union and Liberty*. In his preface, Kennedy claimed that the purpose of his collection was to "fire your patriotism, invigorate your loyalty, and help you kindle a bonfire to Freedom." But the true motive of his publication was revealed on the inside cover, where Kennedy laid out his distribution scheme: he sought "Patriotic local agents" who would "pay cash" for bulk orders and then distribute his "Patriotic Work among our half million and upward Soldiers." Other businesses came up with similar "patriotic" advertising campaigns. Some created their own limited-edition, Star-Spangled Banner mementos, which were regularly advertised as "special offers" in a wide range of commercial products, from soaps and cereals to a potent cough syrup containing a mix of "cannabis, chloroform and alcohol."

During Lincoln's reelection campaign in 1864, he relied on "The Star-Spangled Banner" again, as did his Democratic rival, George McClellan, who created a stir when he noted that his running mate, George Pendleton, was the son-in-law of Francis Scott Key. When the war finally ended one year later, symbolic public performances of "The Star-Spangled Banner" took place in both the South and the North. Sallie Putnam, a dismayed citizen of Richmond, noted the effective use of the song by Union soldiers when they took control of the Confederate capital on April 3. As Northern troops entered the city, she recalled, "the strains of an old, familiar tune floated in the air—a tune that, in days gone by, was wont to awaken a thrill of patriotism. But now only the most bitter and crushing recollections awoke within us, as upon our quickened hearing fell the strains of 'The Star-Spangled Banner.' For us, it was a requiem for buried hopes." That same day, the song was also performed in New York City. As a bystander explained, when the news arrived that Richmond had fallen to Union forces, people filled the streets in celebration: "Never before did I hear cheering that came straight from the heart, that was given because people felt relieved by cheering and hallooing ... These were spontaneous and involuntary and of vast magnetizing power. They sang... 'The Star-Spangled Banner,' repeating the last two lines of Key's song over and over, and with a massive roar from the crowd and a unanimous wave of hats at the end of each repetition."

Music has a way of healing cultural wounds. After the war, "The Star-Spangled Banner" was performed regularly at public events in the North and the South, where it became a tool for unification. For example, at Georgetown University, students from the North and the South who had fought in the war returned to campus in 1865 and, after learning of President Lincoln's assassination, joined forces and performed "The Star-Spangled Banner" as part of the president's funeral procession in an effort to "still those passions which rage within our breasts." And at the Great National Peace Jubilee, held in Boston in 1869, the bandleader Patrick Gilmore led a performance of "The Star-Spangled Banner" arranged for organ, orchestra, military band, drum corps, bells, cannon, and a chorus of 10,000. Three years later, at the World's Peace Jubilee and International Music Festival, he led an expanded performance with 2,000 instrumentalists and a chorus of 20,000!

Rituals around the performance of "The Star-Spangled Banner" became regularized around this time. For example, on July 26, 1889, the Secretary of the Navy designated "The Star-Spangled Banner" as the official tune to be played at the raising of the flag, and issued instructions for proper behavior during performances: "All persons present, belonging to the Navy" should "face towards the colors and salute as the ensign reaches the peak or truck in hoisting.... When the ensign leaves the deck or rail all sentries shall salute and remain at a salute until the band ceases to play the national air."

The military salute referenced above was essentially the same one used today. Few Americans realize that there once was also a popular civilian salute that was used at public events like baseball games. Called the Bellamy salute, it was introduced in schools in the 1890s by Francis Bellamy (1855–1931), a Christian socialist who is best known for authoring the Pledge of Allegiance in 1892. As Bellamy explained, the salute, to be used for the Pledge of Allegiance and the singing of "The Star-Spangled Banner," involved raising the right hand, palm down, in a straight-arm salute pointing toward the flag. Although the Bellamy salute remained a popular element of flag rituals across the US for nearly four decades, Americans discontinued its use in the 1930s when Benito Mussolini and Adolf Hitler began using it for their own Fascist and Nazi ceremonies.

By the turn of the century, "The Star-Spangled Banner" had become an important national symbol. As music critic Louis C. Elson noted in 1899: "If an American were asked the name of his national anthem, he would probably pass by the rollicking 'Yankee Doodle' and the bombastic 'Hail, Columbia' and acknowledge only 'The Star-Spangled Banner.'" Colonel Nicholas Smith of Wisconsin agreed: "Of all the songs inspired by patriotism . . . 'The Star-Spangled' probably has the firmest hold on the American people."

This preference for "The Star-Spangled Banner" over other songs was especially strong among immigrant communities, who began singing the anthem in various translations: German, Swedish, Czech, and Spanish, to name just a few. Abroad, "The Star-Spangled Banner" signaled American identity; Giacomo Puccini incorporated it into *Madame Butterfly* (1904) to define the national spirit of the opera's leading man, Navy Lieutenant B[enjamin] F[ranklin] Pinkerton. Still, there were those in the US who objected to the anthem's militaristic tone, and at the turn of the century two new songs appeared that offered a contrasting view of American identity: "America the Beautiful" (1893) by Katharine Lee Bates, and "Lift Every Voice and Sing" (1900) by the brothers James Weldon Johnson and John Rosamond Johnson.

Bates was an English professor at Wellesley College, and in 1893 she traveled to Colorado Springs, where the sweeping view from Pikes Peak moved her to write a poem that eventually became "America the Beautiful." The first verse, loved by many, celebrates the beauty of the nation's natural wonders. The later verses juxtapose the nation's idealistic potential against the flawed reality of everyday life. A similar sentiment is found in the Johnson brothers' "Lift Every Voice and Sing."

As James Weldon Johnson explained, "Lift Every Voice and Sing" was originally composed in 1900 for a celebration of Abraham Lincoln's birthday hosted by the Edwin M. Stanton School in Jackson, Florida. Sensing the significance of the day, Johnson, who at the time was principal of the school, set pen to paper:

I got my first line: Lift ev'ry voice and sing. Not a startling line; but I worked along grinding out the next five. When, near the end of the first stanza, there came to me these lines:

> *Sing a song full of the faith that the dark past has taught us.*
> *Sing a song full of the hope that the present has brought us.*

As Johnson explained, these words were pivotal, "the spirit of the poem." They captured the essence of the historical moment by acknowledging the past and setting a path for the future. This was an era marked by the government's abandonment of Lincoln's promise of Reconstruction. Just four years earlier, the Supreme Court had upheld the doctrine of "separate but equal" in *Plessy v. Ferguson*. The Stanton School was large for the time, nearly 500 students. It was also segregated. "The spirit of the poem had taken hold of me," Johnson explained. "I finished the stanza and turned it over to Rosamond" so that he could begin composing the music.

When the song was complete, Rosamond "sent a copy of the manuscript to our publishers [Joseph W. Stern and Edward B. Marks] in New York, requesting them to have a sufficient number of mimeographed copies made for the use" at the Stanton School celebration. Stern and Marks supplied the Johnson brothers with their requested copies. They also submitted the music for copyright under the publisher's name, Jos. W. Stern & Co., and in doing so ensured that they, not the Johnson brothers, controlled all publishing and performance rights for "Lift Every Voice and Sing."

The copy of the music submitted by Stern and Marks in 1900 is still held at the Library of Congress. The music is "respectfully dedicated to Booker J. [sic] Washington" and identified as a "National Hymn for the Colored People of America." This information was likely included on the manuscript copy of the song the Johnson brothers sent to Stern and Marks. Booker T. Washington had been invited to speak at the Stanton School celebration, and the arrangement for four-part chorus and piano adheres to the arrangement performed there.

Several months later, a devastating fire ripped through Jacksonville and destroyed thousands of buildings, including the Stanton School and the Johnson brothers' home. With little left other than the shirts on their backs, the Johnson brothers moved to New York and "went on with other work." At this point, "both the song and the occasion passed out of our minds," Johnson later explained. "But the school children of Jacksonville kept singing the song; some of them went off to other schools and kept singing it; some of them became schoolteachers and taught it to their pupils. Within twenty years the song was being sung in schools and churches and on special occasions throughout the South and in some other parts of the country."

The song's spontaneous popularity is not surprising, given its uplifting, unifying message:

> *Lift every voice and sing*
> *Till earth and heaven ring,*
> *Ring with the harmonies of Liberty . . .*

This first verse calls for a unified march toward progress. It communicates a sense of optimism and joy:

> *Let our rejoicing rise*
> *High as the listening skies,*
> *Let it resound loud as the rolling sea.*

The second verse serves as a reminder of the dark past:

> *Stony the road we trod,*
> *Bitter the chastening rod,*
> *Felt in the days when hope unborn had died . . .*

It acknowledges the sorrow and violent suffering that African Americans have struggled to overcome:

> *We have come over a way that with tears has been watered,*
> *We have come, treading a path through the blood of the slaughtered.*

The third and final verse confronts future struggles, which must be met with courage and faith in God:

Keep us forever in the path, we pray . . .
Shadowed beneath Thy hand,
May we forever stand.
True to our God,
True to our native land.

"Lift Every Voice and Sing" emerged at a pivotal moment in history, as Jim Crow laws took hold and African Americans grappled with questions of identity and belonging. The song steadily rose in popularity and, for many, offered a meaningful alternative to traditional patriotic anthems like "The Star-Spangled Banner," which carried painful associations with slavery.

One of the young students who grew up singing "Lift Every Voice and Sing" was the artist–activist Amiri Baraka. As Baraka explains, "Lift Every Voice and Sing" served a symbolic role at "dances, conventions, meetings, etc." It was featured "at soirees . . . a benefit for the NAACP or Urban League, or the black community hospital, or my grandfather's black republican meetings," and with each chorus, Baraka noted, he "felt black angels hovering invisibly, rah-rahing the proceedings."

> The song had a blossoming beauty to it. The words began to deepen in me over the years. What my consciousness had grasped as literal meaning was also given a heavier gravity by the emotional opening the words carried with them.

As Baraka explains, the song was especially important in the formation of African American youth. It showed "that there was a beauty to us, a dignity, a strength, untouched by the acknowledged Ugly American national oppression, its robbery, denial of rights, slander, repression, violence, murder." It revealed "that we existed independent of that, somehow, that our 'humanity' was as real as we were, and could not be damaged by the devil himself."

Author James Thomas Jackson also remembered singing "Lift Every Voice and Sing." He was first introduced to the song by his high school music teacher, "who was a beautiful black rebel in her own right." And as he explains, she always had them sing "Lift Every Voice and Sing" before

"The Star-Spangled Banner." But they had to be careful. "She tried to get us to sing it softly if she thought [the white faculty members] were anywhere near, but her efforts always failed terribly." This was because "Francis Scott Key's lyrics" were "not in the same league with the Johnson Brothers' soul-ensnaring bombast":

> *Sing a song full of the faith that the dark past has taught us*
> *Sing a song full of the hope that the present has brought us*
> *Facing the rising sun, of our new day begun,*
> *Let us march on, til victory – is won.*

One of the things that made "Lift Every Voice and Sing" so popular was its history—the circumstances under which it had been written and first performed. It was linked indelibly to Black History lessons in African American schools. As Imani Perry has explained: "It was a song that resisted the dominant society's depiction and treatment of black Americans. It was a song of fortitude, not hope, and the intimacy of the black community rather than the dashed dream of interracial unity through integration."

The Johnson brothers' publisher made the most of the song's growing popularity. In 1920, Marks bought out Stern and renamed the company Edward B. Marks Music Co. He then renewed the copyright for "Lift Every Voice and Sing" in his own name and published a new edition, this time for solo voice and piano. Marks published a wide range of music by some of the most important African American composers of the early twentieth century. In addition to the Johnson brothers, he worked with James Reese Europe, Lucky Roberts, Bert Williams, Eubie Blake, and Scott Joplin. "Lift Every Voice and Sing" was arguably one of the most important publications of Marks's career.

As "Lift Every Voice and Sing" grew in popularity among African Americans, many white communities sought to control the rituals surrounding "The Star-Spangled Banner." Not surprisingly, Baltimore was the first to do so. In 1916, Layton F. Smith, a member of the Sons of the American Revolution, petitioned the Baltimore City Council to pass a law regulating performances of the "Star-Spangled Banner." Smith was distressed by the way that popular music had begun to influence how the song was performed—in his words, he did not approve of "the ragtime mutilation of 'The Star-Spangled Banner.'" Claiming to speak for everyone, he argued:

> We do not believe that it ["The Star-Spangled Banner"] should be set to jig time, as has been done by one popular comedian. We do not believe that a few strains from it should be introduced in an indiscriminate medley every time an American soldier or an American warship is shown on the screen in a moving picture house.

In response to Smith's petition, the Baltimore City Council passed an ordinance that required "musicians, performers, or other persons" to stand while performing the anthem. The fine for failing to do so was upward of $100—a sizeable sum. Over the next five years, other communities across the US passed similar laws, including cities in Colorado, Massachusetts, Michigan, Minnesota, and New Mexico.

In defining its place on the global stage, a country generally adopts three symbolic emblems: a flag, an official seal, and a national anthem. As the United States contemplated its entrance into World War I, it had only two of these: the flag, with its recognizable stars and stripes, and the Great Seal, featuring an eagle, which was established by Congress in 1782. Ever since the Civil War, Congress had been unable to agree on an appropriate national anthem. Although a string of bills and joint resolutions had been put forward during the early twentieth century to legislate a national anthem into existence, none passed, which gladdened musicians like John Philip Sousa, who believed that an anthem should be chosen spontaneously by the people, not through legislation. "Though Congress is a powerful body," he explained, "it cannot make people sing what they don't want to sing." Eventually, President Woodrow Wilson took matters into his own hands. In 1916, he signed an executive order designating "The Star-Spangled Banner" as "the national anthem of the United States" for all military ceremonies. World War I had been raging in Europe for several years, and Wilson realized that the US would eventually have to send troops overseas. The nation needed an anthem, a symbol of strength and unity. But which version of "The Star-Spangled Banner" should be used? To solve this problem, Wilson commissioned a group of five musicians, including Sousa, to decide on a standard version of the song. The commission generally agreed that Key's lyrics should be retained, with one exception. Since Great Britain was no longer an enemy of the US, the committee decided that Key's third verse, with its derision of the British, should be removed. When US troops crossed the Atlantic in 1917, the official service version of "The Star-Spangled Banner" that they took with them did not include references to "the hireling or slave."

Wilson's executive order transformed "The Star-Spangled Banner" into a litmus test for American loyalty. For example, in April 1917 a British newspaper reporter named Frederick S. Boyd was beaten by an angry crowd when he and two suffragists refused to stand while "The Star-Spangled Banner" was played by a dance band at Rector's restaurant in New York City.

"The Star-Spangled Banner" also became a regular feature at orchestra concerts, especially those including music by German composers. Conductors were expected to begin each concert with a performance of the "The Star-Spangled Banner." Those who refused were often fired, or at the very least called out in public for refusing to perform the song. In an editorial for the *New York Times*, former president Theodore Roosevelt made it clear what he thought of such conductors: "Any man who refuses to play 'The Star-Spangled Banner' in this time of national crisis," he declared, "should be forced to pack up and return to the country he came from."

President Wilson encouraged these nationalistic displays through music. "The man who disparages music as a luxury and non-essential is doing the nation an injury," he stated. "Music now, more than ever before, is a national need." Even his daughter Margaret got involved and made a recording of the song to raise money for the Red Cross.

One week before Wilson declared war on Germany, he established the Committee on Public Information, a propaganda effort that used performances of "The Star-Spangled Banner" to sell Liberty Bonds and boost military recruitment. Wilson also added a new facet to the Independence Day ceremonies on July 4, 1918, when he asked all foreign-born Americans to pledge loyalty to the United States. This act was symbolized by a ceremony at Mount Vernon, where representatives of thirty-three national ethnic organizations laid a wreath on George Washington's grave while the Irish tenor John McCormack sang "The Star-Spangled Banner."

African Americans were not included in these ceremonies. Since his inauguration, Wilson had made a point of segregating not only Washington DC, but the nation as a whole. Nonetheless, African Americans volunteered to fight overseas. In fact, the first American heroes of World War I were the 369th, a regiment of black Harlem musicians led by James Reese Europe nicknamed the Harlem Hellfighters, who fought alongside French troops on the front line. When the war concluded and American troops returned home, race relations in the United States grew even more divisive. Lynchings and race riots plagued the nation, so much so that 1919 was dubbed the Red Summer. It was not lost on black audiences when pianist James P. Johnson blended "Dixie" with "The Star-Spangled Banner" that summer during performances of his "Imitators' Rag." The growing sense of inequality and separation also contributed to the NAACP's decision that year to designate "Lift Every Voice and Sing" as the Negro National Anthem. The point wasn't to replace "The Star-Spangled Banner," but rather to add another voice—a voice of their own—to the public rituals of American life. In 1921, the Edward B. Marks Music Co. renewed its copyright for "Lift Every Voice and Sing."

As African Americans embraced their own unifying hymn, other groups pushed back against Wilson's executive order institutionalizing "The Star-Spangled Banner." Kitty Cheatham, a popular performer of children's music, published a pamphlet in 1917 titled "A Protest in Defense of Children" that decried "the mental poison of hatred, autocracy, fear, [and] animality" brought on by "The Star-Spangled Banner." Others objected to the song's glorification of war, especially those who argued that the US should stay out of conflicts overseas. When Prohibition went into effect in 1920, temperance societies protested the origins of the anthem's tune: "All the perfumes of Araby cannot eliminate the taint of booze from the black past of that tune," complained a teetotaler to the *New York World*, going so far as to speculate "that certain difficult intervals in the song were intended to be filled with hiccups."

On Flag Day in 1922, Warren Harding made history with the first national radio broadcast delivered by a president. The broadcast came from Fort McHenry, which Harding had decided to designate as a "sacred shrine of American patriotism." In keeping with the theme, Harding referred to "The Star-Spangled Banner" as an "invocation" to the flag and an expression of "militant Americanism." According to Harding, no other song "has, even for a moment, threatened the throne which 'The Star-Spangled Banner' occupies as the royal anthem of American patriotism."

The Christian Scientist Augusta Stetson saw things differently. In 1922 she began running ads in daily newspapers declaring the anthem a hate-filled screed born of drunken debauchery. These ads sparked countless debates, which only increased in 1924, when the Olympics introduced the ritual of performing national anthems during medal ceremonies. That year, two national anthem bills were debated in Congress. Both failed, but the sides were clearly drawn. As Maryland Republican John Hill noted, the fight for "The Star-Spangled Banner" had become personal. It wasn't just about a song anymore; it was a fight for American ideals. Hill claimed that "to throw mud on the national anthem" was "the same thing as throwing mud on the American flag and mud on the memory of the men who, when they were buried, had that 'Star-Spangled Banner' in their minds when the bugle blew taps over them." Violence erupted. John Martin, who belonged to a conservative group called the Bureau for American Ideals, declared that it was "sacrilegious" to remain seated during "The Star-Spangled Banner," and he recommended that those who didn't rise should be "shook up" then "knocked down and made to get up again."

Between 1911 and 1929, over forty bills and joint resolutions were introduced in the House and Senate aiming to legislate a national anthem into existence; none passed. It wasn't until the nation was fractured by the Great Depression that a resolution on the matter was reached. On October 29, 1929—Black Tuesday—Wall Street collapsed, wiping out billions of dollars and devastating thousands of investors. Five days later, Robert L. Ripley of "Ripley's Believe It or Not!" ran an edition of his syndicated cartoon that stated: "Believe It or Not, America has no national anthem." Ripley noted how ironic it was that instead "the U.S.A (being a dry country) has been using—without authorization—a vulgar old English drinking song" for official occasions. The cartoon caused a wave of negative press. In response, Ripley encouraged readers to write to their congressmen instead of to him. Five million Americans followed his advice, and, in 1930, Representative John Linthicum of Maryland secured a hearing with the Judiciary Committee. There, he implored his colleagues to pass H.R. 14, claiming that, more than ever before, the nation "needed a national song to give expression to its patriotism." The bill passed the House on April 21, 1930. Eleven months later, it passed the Senate. On March 3, 1931, President Herbert Hoover signed it into law.

The new law did not specify an official text or musical arrangement for "The Star-Spangled Banner." The language was purposefully vague, leaving room for creative arrangements and interpretations. This vagueness had an important consequence. When Congress declared "The Star-Spangled Banner" the national anthem, the tune and its lyrics were already in the public domain, according to copyright law. If Congress had selected a specific version or arrangement of the tune or lyrics, then publishers would have had to seek permission from the government before publishing the song or copyrighting alternate arrangements of it for profit.

The open copyright status of "The Star-Spangled Banner" enabled it to grow and transform. It could be performed in any public venue, or on any recording, in any version, without threat of copyright infringement. Such was not the case for "Lift Every Voice and Sing." As Johnson noted in a 1935 interview, he believed "Lift Every Voice and Sing" projected a message that "could represent the nation," not just African Americans. But this was not to be. In the 1930s, right around the time "The Star-Spangled Banner" was signed into law, Edward B. Marks, the publisher of "Lift Every Voice and Sing," thwarted dissemination of the song by demanding high fees for reprint and recording rights. Marks was white, and, like most publishers in the 1920s, he retained copyright for the works he released by black composers. Consequently, performances of "Lift Every Voice and Sing" went underground and remained limited to black communities well into the 1950s, when the work finally entered the public domain.

Once free of its publisher's control, "Lift Every Voice and Sing" slowly expanded from a hymn of faith and resilience in black schools and churches into a national symbol of unity and progress. This change began in the 1950s, when the song took on increased political significance as an anthem for resistance and hope during the civil rights movement. As the NAACP continued to promote "Lift Every Voice and Sing" as a unifying symbol in the struggle for equality, Martin Luther King Jr. began invoking the song's lyrics in his speeches. "Lift Every Voice and Sing" became a regular component at marches, rallies, and commemorations.

As the nation began reckoning with civil rights victories and ongoing racial disparities in the 1970s, "Lift Every Voice and Sing" began to be recognized beyond the black community. Churches in a wide range of denominations began including the song in their official hymnals, and public schools began incorporating the song into their curricula. This last change was prompted by President Gerald Ford's official recognition of Black History Month in 1976. "Lift Every Voice and Sing" also began expanding its reach into the world of entertainment. Kim Weston sang it to an audience of 100,000 at the historic Watts Stax concert in 1972. In 1990, Melba Moore released an all-star version featuring Anita Baker, Dionne Warwick, and Stevie Wonder. In 2008, jazz vocalist René Marie sparked debate when she performed the lyrics of "Lift Every Voice and Sing" to the tune of "The Star-Spangled Banner" at a civic event in Denver, Colorado. Twelve years later, Jon Batiste included "Lift Every Voice and Sing" as a countermelody in his instrumental rendition of "The Star-Spangled Banner." That performance was featured at the NBA's post-Covid reopening, and since then, "Lift Every Voice and Sing" has become a staple at major sporting events. The NFL, for instance, has featured the song in pregame performances at the Super Bowl since 2020—partially in response to the racial justice concerns raised by Colin Kaepernick in 2015.

The Black Lives Matter movement played a major role in the expanded recognition of "Lift Every Voice and Sing." Over the last decade, artists from a range of genres performed the song to great effect. Mezzo-soprano Denyce Graves delivered a stirring rendition of the hymn at the opening ceremonies of the National Museum of African American History and Culture in 2016. And in 2018, Beyoncé's performance at Coachella resonated deeply with a new generation of listeners, many of whom were hearing the song for the first time. Since then, viral social media performances have kept the song's message alive. And as its presence in public life has grown, so have conversations about the song's significance, most notably in the halls of Congress.

On January 13, 2021, Representative James E. Clyburn introduced H.R. 301, a bill that proposed to designate "Lift Every Voice and Sing" as the national hymn of the United States. In February 2022, the Subcommittee on the Constitution, Civil Rights, and Civil Liberties held a public hearing to discuss the history and cultural importance of the song. Two months later, the House Judiciary Committee held a markup session and voted 26 to 11 in favor of putting the bill up for a vote. Although H.R. 301 was placed on the House calendar on June 7, it never made it onto the floor for final passage. While many lawmakers saw the bill as an opportunity to recognize black history and national unity, others questioned the necessity of designating another national song alongside "The Star-Spangled Banner."

It's been nearly a century since Congress's acknowledgment of "The Star-Spangled Banner" put it front and center in the American consciousness and solidified the civic ritual of performance that has grown up around it. In the decades since then, this ritual—standing, hand over heart, while facing the flag—and the political message it claims to communicate, have turned "The Star-Spangled Banner" into a vehicle for both patriotism and protest. As debate over "Lift Every Voice and Sing" continues in Congress in the years to come, we will see if it succumbs to a similar fate.

THE UNANSWERED QUESTION

On September 11, 1959, Congressman Donald J. Irwin of Connecticut stood at the podium of the House of Representatives and announced, with great enthusiasm, a musical performance that had recently taken place in the Soviet Union. "Mr. Speaker, just less than a month ago the New York Philharmonic, directed by Leonard Bernstein, gave Moscow one of the most exciting, tradition-shattering concerts the Soviet capital has seen in recent musical history."

The concert in question was part of "a significant first step in the improvement of mutual understanding" between the United States and the Soviet Union. And as Representative Irwin explained, the highlight of the evening was the "rousing demand by the cheering, stomping, clapping throng for a repeat performance of an unusual little piece by one of the first American composers of modern ideas, Charles Ives."

This "unusual little piece" was *The Unanswered Question*, a contemplative work composed in 1908 that "had never been heard in the Soviet Union." As Irwin explained, America's respect for this composition, and its composer, was long overdue.

> I am delighted, Mr. Speaker, that Charles Ives is, at long last, beginning to receive the recognition he so richly deserves.

> It is to be regretted that such recognition comes after his death... the recognition that here is an authentic American genius, in all probability one of the greatest composers America has produced.

Music history lessons are not common occurrences in the House of Representatives, but Irwin thought it important to highlight Ives as both a "native of Connecticut" and a national icon. "America should learn more about its own composers," he claimed. "And it is hoped that the recognition accorded Charles Ives in Moscow several weeks ago... becomes contagious." He concluded his speech with a final declaration: "All America should learn to enjoy and love the music of Charles Ives—a great American composer who had a full measure of the gift of compassion and laughter, and translated them into music."

I like to think that Charles Ives would have appreciated the recognition he received in the House of Representatives on September 11, 1959. A patriot at heart, he spent decades as a businessman and activist trying to strengthen the nation's democratic policies. Much to his surprise and disappointment, these efforts had little to no effect. Instead, it was his work as a composer that eventually changed America.

The first sign of the musical talent Representative Irwin would later extol in Congress occurred on February 17, 1892, when the seventeen-year-old Ives made his way to the organ loft of the First Methodist Church in Brewster, New York, and performed a piece identified in the program as "Variations on a National Hymn." Ives had composed the work the year before, and the "national hymn" referenced in the program was not "The Star-Spangled Banner," as some in the audience might have assumed, but rather "America," another contrafactum composed during the nineteenth century. The lyrics to "America" were written in 1831 by a seminary student from New England named Samuel Francis Smith, who set them to the British tune "God Save the King." Ives's choice of "America" as the basis for his composition wasn't surprising. For him, the nation's spirit was rooted not in militaristic battles but in the promise of "liberty" and "freedom," the beauty of "woods and templed hills," and his own New England heritage. The fact that "America" was a song built on a British melody did not bother him. In his hometown of Danbury, Connecticut (just a few miles from Brewster), most of the residents were descended from English immigrants.

Ives was already well known locally as a music prodigy when he took his seat at the organ that day. At age fourteen, he had become the youngest salaried organist in Connecticut and was hailed as "a musical genius" with a promising future by the *Danbury Evening News*. The theme-and-variations structure used in his "Variations on a National Hymn" was ideal for showing off his talent. As Ives noted, he considered the piece "partly serious and partly in fun." He wasn't particularly interested in writing music to build community. Instead, he approached composition as a solitary art—a means of contemplating the world around him. Ives was not composing music *for* America; he was composing music *about* America. This reflectiveness was clearly displayed in his performance of the variations, published many years later as *Variations on "America."*

Variations on "America" is a collage of the music Ives regularly encountered as a boy in Danbury, a commentary of sorts on American society, and a series of contrasts—each distinct, yet part of a unified whole. The work opens dramatically with a royal fanfare full of joyful grandeur and brooding anticipation. The theme itself is a slow, solemn hymn, quite at home in the venue where Ives first performed it. The variations that follow draw on different facets of New England music culture. The first evokes a Fourth of July celebration with an explosive display of virtuosic fireworks. The second features the meanderings of barbershop harmonies, followed by what sounds like a drunken interlude. The third variation takes on the guise of a calliope, pumping out a playful march at the county fair. A minor-key polonaise typical of a parlor concert appears next, followed by another dissonant interlude. The final variation draws on the syncopated rhythms of ragtime. Here, Ives spared no effort. The music is physically demanding, with arms and legs, hands and feet, all moving in different directions. Ives once told a friend that playing the final variation was "almost as fun as playing baseball." Most importantly, *Variations on "America"* reflected Ives's unquenchable thirst for experimentation—a trait that would distinguish his work.

Ives inherited his experimental streak from his father, George Ives, Danbury's leading musical figure and a former Union bandmaster who had survived Gettysburg—a rare fate among the town's Civil War soldiers.

The war's ideals were woven into the family's identity. Charles's grandparents on his father's side had long fought for the abolition of slavery, and he would proudly recall how his grandmother once rescued a fugitive slave. After the war, the family sponsored the education of Henry Anderson Brooks, a young African American boy George had befriended when his regiment was in Virginia. Though these events preceded Charles's birth, they shaped his upbringing, instilling in him a deep sense of pride in the struggle for justice. In May 1880, when Charles was just five, he accompanied his father to the dedication ceremony of Danbury's Civil War monument. A reporter for the local newspaper was struck by the child's reverent manner: "the little son of G. E. Ives, dressed in national colors, sat in front and saluted the colors"—i.e., the flag.

After the Civil War, George Ives studied music theory with a private tutor in New York before returning to Danbury, where he conducted various bands, including an all-girl brass band, church choirs, and theater orchestras. George gave music lessons to local children, performed as a pick-up musician with touring minstrel shows, and played his bugle and fiddle at solemn ceremonies and local dances. As a *New York Herald* article published in 1890 explained, "all Danbury loves music" and George Ives "has probably done more for instrumental music than any other man" in town. Still, locals considered George an eccentric. He was best known for his music experiments, which ran the gamut from trying to capture the sound of a thunder crash on the piano to having Charles sing in one key while he accompanied him in another. The physics of sound fascinated George, and he was especially intrigued by the way sound changes as it moves through space. One of his most famous experiments, remembered fondly by Charles, involved the use of two marching bands "brought together in cacophonous conflict." George stationed the bands on opposite sides of Danbury's central square and, at his signal, sent them marching in opposite directions, each playing a different tune. George and Charles stood in the middle, taking note of how the music clashed and the pitches bent and expanded as the two bands drew closer, passed one another, and then marched away. On another occasion, George asked his son to wait at the edge of a pond while he went to the other side. He then took out his cornet and played a melody while Charles gauged the effect of distance on the tone. The memory of that sound, a cornet receding into an echoing distance, stayed with Charles the rest of his life.

George Ives encouraged Charles to listen closely to the "music" around him—be it the whack of a baseball bat, the roar of a crowd, or the rapturous strains of congregants singing at a late summer camp meeting. This was the era before recorded sound, and community music-making was the wellspring of Charles Ives's early training. Under his father's tutelage, he composed a wide range of works that reflected the types of music he heard in Danbury: fiddle tunes, church anthems, parlor music, and marches. George taught Charles that music wasn't measured by its beauty or charm. Instead, the value of music lay in its ability to reflect the society that created it. At its best, music challenged audiences to listen in new ways, to hear what often went unheard. This was the motivation behind Ives's *Variations on "America"*, and when he played it that day in the Brewster Methodist Church, his father delighted in its raucous rhythms and dissonant harmonies. George Ives was proud of what his son had accomplished. He was also painfully aware that his son's performance confused most of the other listeners sitting around him. As Charles noted many years later, his father advised him not to play *Variations on "America"* too often in church, since "it made the boys laugh."

Charles came from a long line of Yale alumni. His great-grandfather Isaac Ives had been the first in the family to attend Yale. After graduating in 1785 he settled in Danbury, where he set up shop as a lawyer. Since then, all Ives men had pursued careers in either law or business. Even George, the black sheep of the family, was eventually forced to conform. In 1891, he grudgingly accepted a job as a teller at the Danbury Savings Bank, which had been founded by his father decades earlier. George had fallen on hard times financially and was weary of the hand-to-mouth existence of a small-town musician. Fearing that his son would follow in his footsteps, he advised Charles to avoid a career in music. "Father felt that a man could keep his music-interest stronger, cleaner, bigger, and freer, if he didn't try to make a living of it," Ives later explained. His father warned him that being a professional musician required too many artistic sacrifices, such as being expected to "weaken" to the desires of the public, to "go 'ta ta' for money." Pursuing a career in music was fine, "assuming a man lived by himself and with no dependents." But if one hoped to marry and raise a family, George Ives explained, then he would have no choice but to sell out. "How can he let the children starve on his dissonances?"

Charles moved into his dorm room at Yale in September 1894. Six weeks later, he was called back to Danbury. His father, only forty-nine, had died unexpectedly from a stroke. For the first time in his life, Charles heard a great silence. Although he attended the funeral and went through the familial rituals expected of him, he never fully recovered from the loss or reached a sense of closure. Memories of his father haunted him the rest of his life.

Once back at Yale, Ives set off on his own path. He cared little for his course work and only applied himself in American literature and music classes. His literature courses were taught by William Lyon Phelps, a young, charismatic lecturer who shared Ives's love of baseball. Under Phelps's tutelage, Ives became enthralled by the works of Ralph Waldo Emerson, Nathaniel Hawthorne, Henry David Thoreau, and the Alcotts (Amos Bronson and Louisa May). He found in their works a reverence for individualism and nature that felt authentically American. Emerson, especially, became a role model. His promotion of Transcendentalism, a distinctly American philosophy rooted in the act of discovery, fascinated Ives. The Transcendentalists criticized society for its unthinking conformity, and they urged their readers to find, in Emerson's words, "an original relation to the universe." In his literature courses, Phelps encouraged Ives to resist the dictate of European models and turn instead to the experimental spirit of America's own authors. The message Ives received in his music courses, however, was notably different.

Ives studied composition with Horatio Parker, a musician who in many ways was the exact opposite of Ives's father. Whereas George Ives had been experimental, Parker revered tradition above all else. Whereas George had promoted American band music, Parker preferred the sound of an orchestra and chorus. This contrast in taste was rooted in the diverse training each man had received. While George had developed his musical skills in regimental bands on the battlefield, Parker, like most "serious" American composers of his generation, had trained in Europe and strongly believed that the future of American music should be built on European models. Ives chafed under Parker's regimen but nonetheless learned a great deal in his courses. As a teacher, Parker emphasized traditional compositional practices. Ives spent countless hours laboring through counterpoint and orchestration exercises, and, under Parker's guidance, he composed symphonies, art songs, and string quartets. But Ives never abandoned writing music for himself. In his spare time he went his own way, composing lighthearted songs for friends and experimental works that drew on his father's influence. As he noted many years later: "Parker was a composer and widely known, and Father was not a composer and little known—but from every other standpoint I should say that Father was the greater man."

Ives once described art as "not about something that happens" but rather "the *way* something happens." His four-minute soundscape *Yale–Princeton Football Game* is a perfect example. The piece was inspired by a game Ives attended on November 20, 1897, when the Yale Bulldogs beat the Princeton Tigers 6–0 in a bitter ground game. Ives's composition focuses on the highlight of the contest, when Yale quarterback Charles deSaulles zigzagged fifty-five yards down the field on a fourth down for the winning touchdown. The piece has no central theme or melody. Instead, it is a collage of sound effects and noises from the crowd. In his score, Ives labeled the entrance of each new sonic element, from the well-known cheers ("Brek-ek-ek-ex, Ko-ax, Ko-ax" and "Rah, Rah, Yale") and college songs ("Hold the Fort," "Hy-can nuck-a-no," and "Harvard Has Blue Stocking Girls") to the action on the field ("Fat Guards, pushing, grunting;" "First Down;" "Run around left end: loss;" "Dodging tackle;" "Close formation: Wedge;" "Last Down;" "Run Around Right;" and "Touchdown"). A referee's whistle marks the end of each down. The work concludes with the echo of Yale's pep band marching off into the distance.

In addition to football, Ives took an interest in business and politics at Yale. In 1896, he composed a campaign song for presidential candidate William McKinley titled "William Will." Ives's support of McKinley wasn't surprising; all the Ives men had been Republicans. McKinley promised to bolster the economy by implementing high tariffs on foreign imports, guaranteeing industrial growth, and controlling inflation by sticking to the gold standard. All these issues appealed to Ives:

What we want is Honest Money,
Good as gold and pure as honey,

Every dollar sound and true.
What we want is full protection,
And we'll have it next election,
For low tariff and low wages make us blue.

"William Will" is an upbeat song, designed to please a broad audience. It was Ives's first publication, and it proved popular during the campaign. On November 1, 1896, a New York City event dubbed the Sound Money Parade featured hundreds of businessmen, lawyers, and clergymen marching in formation up Broadway in support of McKinley. As they passed through the streets, they chanted slogans and sang campaign songs, among them Ives's "William Will." In January 1897, "William Will" and Ives's *Intercollegiate March* were both performed by "The President's Own" Marine Band at McKinley's inauguration as president.

After graduation, Ives moved to New York City, where he lived with a few Yale friends in an apartment they jokingly called "poverty flats." Ives had been popular in college. As a member of Delta Kappa Epsilon and Wolf's Head, one of Yale's prestigious secret societies, he had bonded with members of America's elite class. His nickname at Yale was Dasher, since he was always dashing from one activity to the next. His tendency to keep busy continued in New York, where a cousin, Robert Granniss, got him a job at the Charles H. Raymond Agency, a division of the Mutual Life Insurance Company. To supplement his salary, Ives secured a part-time position as organist at the Central Presbyterian Church. He was clearly contemplating a career in music, despite his father's advice. As the years passed, however, Ives grew frustrated with the creative constraints of being a church musician and, as he later described it, "resigned as a nice organist and gave up music" in 1902.

Of course, Ives did not actually give up music. Rather, he abandoned the obligations that came with being a public musician and committed himself more fully to pursuing music as an introspective activity focused on experimentation. By day, Ives worked hard at his job as a clerk in the actuary department, where he gained a broad knowledge of the insurance industry. By night and on weekends, he socialized with friends or worked alone on his compositions. For several years, Ives seemed relatively content. But all that changed in 1905, when a series of catastrophic events changed his outlook on life and his approach to composition.

The first involved his work at Mutual Life. In 1905, Senator William W. Armstrong convinced the New York legislature to launch an investigation that sought to root out corruption in the insurance industry. The findings transformed business practices and resulted in the criminal indictment of several upper-level executives, among them Ives's cousin Robert Granniss, his boss, Charles Raymond, and the President of the Mutual Life Insurance Co., Richard A. McCurdy. Ives was too low on the totem pole to be ensnared in the investigation, but he nonetheless witnessed its devastating effects, and the stress of the situation affected his health.

In 1906, Ives suffered the first of several heart attacks. He was only thirty-two, and the health scare shook him to his core. Spurred by memories of his father's premature passing, Ives slipped into a state of deep depression and turned to music in search of solace. It was during this dark period that he wrote the first draft of what would become his most famous composition.

The Unanswered Question is a deep exploration of life's meaning. Composed for strings, four flutes, and offstage trumpet, the work is relatively short—around seven minutes—but incredibly powerful. It begins almost inaudibly with the strings playing a cycle of ethereal chords at an excruciatingly slow tempo. As Ives later explained, these represent the eternal passage of time, "the silences of the Druids, who know, see and hear nothing." Over this harmonious background a lone trumpet emerges with an angular five-note theme, full of longing. This is "The Perennial Question of Existence," Ives explained. The trumpet poses its question seven times. The flutes offer unsatisfying responses to the first six queries, each time with more dissonance and a greater sense of frustration. They represent the "Fighting Answerers" who attempt, unsuccessfully, to make sense of the world. When the trumpet plays its theme the final time, the flutes fail to respond. The question hangs in the air, unanswered, as the strings—"The Silences"—slowly fade away into "Undisturbed Solitude."

After Ives completed the first draft of *The Unanswered Question*, he slipped it into a drawer, where it lay for many years. Ives did not compose the work for an audience. The music was too personal, too painful. It was a private meditation in response to the eternal question Why: Why are we here? What is our purpose? And, most importantly for Ives at the time: Why must we die? The offstage trumpet represents an obvious link to his father's cornet, which also featured in a song Ives composed at around the same time titled "Remembrance" or "The Pond." The lyrics, also by Ives, consist of a single line: "A sound of a distant horn, O'er shadowed lake is borne—my father's song."

Composing *The Unanswered Question* was therapeutic for Ives. The work is not emotional, or sensual, or compositionally complex. Rather, it is philosophical—three planes of sound in a static universe. Like Transcendentalism, *The Unanswered Question* places the intuitive and spiritual above the empirical. It reveals that even though finding a definitive answer to the perennial question of existence is not possible, the pursuit of such knowledge is what gives life meaning. When Ives completed the work, which he later noted was "sometime before July 1908," it was unlike anything he, or anyone else in the world, had ever composed.

Working on *The Unanswered Question* helped Ives put things in perspective and move forward with his life. He went back to his job and then married a young nurse, fittingly named Harmony, who shared his interest in Transcendentalism and showed unwavering faith in his talents as a composer and businessman. Although Ives was horrified by the way his colleagues' misdeeds had impacted the general public's view of the insurance industry, he believed he could reform it. So, on January 1, 1907, Ives joined forces with John Myrick, an associate from work, and founded a new agency, Ives & Co., which became Ives & Myrick two years later. The company prospered. Within a few years, it was one of the largest agencies of its kind in the United States.

Ives was the ideas man in the company. His health scare, combined with his years of experience working in an actuary department (which involves predicting mortality probabilities over the long run), helped Ives view human life in broad, universal terms, from birth to death. He came up with sales pitches, developed the first-ever training curriculum for new agents, and developed the formulae (based on income and household expenses) used to determine the amount of insurance an individual needed. This approach was new in the insurance industry—developing custom-made policies designed to offer financial stability and security. In essence, Ives invented estate planning—not just for the wealthy, but more importantly for laborers and the middle class. As he explained to his employees time and again, selling insurance strengthened democracy because it offered a way of protecting the vulnerable from falling into economic ruin. Ives also promoted these ideas to customers in the pamphlets and advertising copy he penned, quoting Emerson and extolling the social virtue of life insurance. As Ives later explained, one of his central goals in business was to instill in "the soul and mind" of his "fellow man, the responsibility of meeting his obligations." Eventually, this would also become one of his central goals as a composer.

Ives often talked about leveling the playing field in the insurance industry. "To an insurance man," he wrote, "there *is* an 'average man,' and he is humanity." In his advertising copy for insurance policies, Ives often spoke of "human life values." Here he was referring to both the monetary value of a human life—an essential component of insurance—and, more importantly, "the humanistic and spiritual values people live by." He once explained that his business experience showed him "tragedy, nobility, meanness, high aims, low aims, brave hopes, great ideals, no ideals," and that "the finer sides of these traits were not only in the majority but in the ascendency." Simply put, Ives was optimistic about the future. He brought a social justice mentality into the insurance business, and, in the years that followed, attempted to do the same in his music and in the realm of politics.

An example of Ives's synthesis of social justice and music can be found in a piece for orchestra that he began in 1911, called "Black March." Like *The Unanswered Question*, it is a contemplation, a stream-of-consciousness commentary on the state of things, in this case, the country's memory of the Civil War and American race relations. During a walk on Boston Common he encountered Augustus Saint-Gaudens's monument to Robert Gould Shaw and the Massachusetts 54th Regiment and was moved by the dramatic scene. The monument shows Colonel Robert Shaw, the son of abolitionists, and his men, the nation's first African American regiment, as they march into battle. Frederick Douglass had lobbied Lincoln for the admittance of African Americans into the Union Army, and his sons, Lewis and Charles, eventually joined the 54th Regiment. Lincoln consented to black troops, but only on the condition that the regiments remain segregated and be led by white commanders. The effect of Lincoln's decision is clearly visualized in Saint-Gaudens's monument. Shaw is on horseback, elevated above his men, with his back straight and his eyes on the horizon. The men of the 54th occupy the space below, trudging valiantly toward battle.

Ives was likely reminded of his father as he gazed up at Colonel Shaw, but it was the soldiers who fueled his imagination. For these men, the stakes were higher and the fight more difficult. Saint-Gaudens depicted them as weary, but strong. They lean forward, shifting their center of gravity as if climbing a hill. These are troops walking in formation, left, right, left, right. In "Black March," Ives captured the same sense of movement, the same sense of resolute heroism in the face of interminable struggle.

The piece begins, like *The Unanswered Question*, with slow-moving chords in the strings. In this case, however, the effect is more psychological than philosophical. The lush orchestral tone, with its warm dissonances, evokes a sense of dreamlike memory as snatches of Civil War-era tunes emerge and fade away. A few minutes into the piece, one hears the entry of a military drumbeat, no doubt inspired by the young drummer leading the troops in Saint-Gaudens's sculpture. Ives included an explanatory note in the score: "Often when a mass of men march uphill, there is an unconscious slowing up. The drum seems to follow the feet, rather than the feet the drum."

Ives described "Black March" as "emblematic of the fight against slavery." The central melody is a collage of motifs from several tunes that were popular in the 1860s and during Ives's youth. Two of these, "The Battle Cry of Freedom" and "Marching through Georgia," refer specifically to the war and were sung by Civil War veterans like Ives's father. George F. Root wrote "The Battle Cry of Freedom" to boost recruitment in 1862, when Union morale was especially low. "Marching Through Georgia," by Henry Clay, memorializes General Sherman's March to the Sea in 1864, when Union soldiers captured Savannah. The lyrics, written from the point of view of a Union soldier, tell of marching through Confederate territory, freeing the enslaved, and encountering Southern Unionist men happy to see the stars and stripes of the US flag.

The other pair of tunes referenced in "Black March"—"Massa's in de Cold Ground" (1852) and "Old Black Joe" (1860)—were composed by Stephen Foster (1826–64). The first, written in dialect and intended for the minstrel stage, describes the sorrow of plantation slaves over the death of their master. The second, sung in first person and published as a parlor song, reflects the wistful memories of an elderly black man as he faces death. To most twenty-first-century listeners, the racial stereotypes in Foster's songs create discomfort. But in the years leading up to the Civil War, Foster's songs were received by many in the North as sympathetic to the plight of the enslaved. Foster lived in Pittsburgh and New York his entire life and was strongly pro-Union. In 1855, Frederick Douglass observed the virtue of Foster's "Ethiopian songs," noting that they "can call forth a tear as well as a smile. They awaken the sympathies for the slave, in which anti-slavery principles take root and flourish." Later, during Ives's childhood, Foster's songs enjoyed a resurgence as Tin Pan Alley publishers released new editions and singers, both black and white, regularly performed them in theaters and concert halls. In 1903, W. E. B Du Bois commented on "Old Black Joe" specifically, noting that it was different from the "debasements and imitations" found in "Negro 'minstrel' songs and . . . contemporary 'coon' songs." Du Bois contended that as a songwriter, Foster was "distinctively influenced by the slave songs" and at times "incorporated whole phrases of Negro melody." Whether this last statement is accurate or not, it illuminates the cultural context of Ives's use of Foster's tunes. The songs evoked the emotions shown in the faces of Saint-Gaudens's soldiers: sorrow over the death of their colonel (Shaw died in battle), longing for loved ones, and courage in the face of death. Ives found in Foster's songs a distinctive "sadness for the slaves." In an effort to clarify the underlying message of his composition, Ives penned a poem, which he eventually published as a preface to the score:

> Moving – Marching – Faces of Souls!
> Marked with generations of pain,
> Part-freers of a Destiny,
> Slowly, restlessly – swaying us on with you
> Towards other Freedom . . .

You images of a Divine Law
Carved in the shadow of a saddened heart –
Never light abandoned –
Of an age and of a nation.

Above and beyond that compelling mass
Rises the drum-beat of the common heart
In the silence of a strange and
Sounding afterglow
Moving – Marching – Faces of Souls!

"Black March" was an attempt to compose a work that reflected on the past while looking to the future. As Ives's poem reflects, the struggle of African Americans during the Civil War was a haunting memory that rose like "the drum-beat of the common heart" in the nation's consciousness. But the struggles were far from over, and there was still much to do "towards other Freedom." "Black March" marked a shift in Ives's political philosophy, and during the years that followed he attempted to influence what he viewed as a flawed political process. Ives became interested in giving voice to the people, in making sure that all Americans could contribute to the political process. He believed that by empowering every American, the nation would finally rid itself of the social ills brought on by prejudice and greed. In short, he became a committed advocate for direct democracy.

The central goal of direct democracy is to empower voters, enabling them to bypass politicians when it comes to approving or revoking laws, electing senators, or nominating political candidates. In the early twentieth century, the concept of legislation coming directly from the people was familiar to those, like Ives, who grew up in New England towns governed by town meetings. For the rest of America, however, the concept was strange. The United States is one of only a few western industrial democracies without the possibility of a national referendum on any issue. Instead, federal change occurs through the legislative process of Congress or by executive order from the president. Ives believed this political structure undermined the voice of the people, and he saw direct democracy as a solution.

Direct democracy became a campaign issue during the contentious presidential election of 1912. Theodore Roosevelt, who had served as president from 1901 to 1908 as a Republican, challenged his successor, the Republican incumbent William Howard Taft, in the primaries. When the party stuck with Taft as their nominee, Roosevelt ran under the banner of the new Progressive Party, effectively splitting the Republican vote. The Democratic nominee, Woodrow Wilson, took full advantage of the situation. Both Wilson and Roosevelt supported direct democracy; Taft opposed it. This troubled Ives, so much so that he abandoned the Republican Party and actively began to promote the idea that Americans would be better off voting on the issues instead of along party lines. "It is discouraging for thinking persons," he wrote, "to go to the polls and find nothing on the ballots but a mass of names and party emblems staring dumbly up at them." He vented his frustration with a sarcastic campaign song, "Vote for Names," that offered some cynical advice: "After trying hard to think what's the best way to vote I say: Just walk right in and grab a ballot with the eyes shut and walk right out again." The music, little more than strident banging on the piano, perfectly reflected Ives's growing frustration with American politics.

Wilson handily defeated Taft and Roosevelt, and within a year the Seventeenth Amendment to the Constitution was enacted, which introduced a facet of direct democracy into the election process. By changing just a few key words, senators would no longer be "chosen by the Legislature" but instead "elected by the people" in a statewide vote. But that wasn't enough for Ives. He wanted citizens to inform decisions on the national level, and to express his point of view he composed "The Masses," a song for chorus and orchestra that captured the intensifying political wave that Ives believed was about to crest. The lyrics, clear and simple in their message, resemble a protest chant. The accompaniment, full of trudging, cacophonous chords, propels the thunderous call to action.

The Masses! The Masses! The Masses have toiled,
Behold the works of the World!
The Masses are thinking,
Whence comes the thought of the World!
The Masses are singing,

> *Whence comes the Art of the World!*
> *The Masses are yearning,*
> *Whence comes the hope of the World.*
> *The Masses are dreaming,*
> *Whence comes the visions of God!*
> *God's in His Heaven,*
> *All will be well with the World!*

Ives's song did not change America. The ideal world he envisioned in "The Masses" never came to fruition. Instead, the injustices Ives witnessed in the world around him only intensified as reports of a devastating war overseas began to dominate the news. At first, Ives objected to the idea of the US going to war in Europe, but by the time Wilson committed troops to the effort, his attitude had changed. A turning point occurred on May 7, 1915, when the *Lusitania* sank, and Ives witnessed an episode of communal mourning while standing on a train platform in Manhattan's financial district:

> Leaving the office and going uptown about 6 o'clock, I took the Third Avenue "L" at the Hanover Square Station. As I came on the platform, there was quite a crowd waiting for the trains, which had been blocked lower down, and while waiting there, a hand-organ, or hurdy-gurdy was playing on a street below. Some workmen sitting on the side of the tracks began to whistle the tune, and others began to sing or hum the refrain. A workman with a shovel over his shoulder came on the platform and joined in the chorus, and the next man, a Wall Street banker with white spats and a cane, joined in it, and finally it seemed to me that everybody was singing this tune, and they didn't seem to be singing for fun, but as a natural outlet for what their feelings had been going through all day long. There was a feeling of dignity all through this. The hand-organ man seemed to sense this and wheeled the organ nearer the platform and kept it up fortissimo.... Then the first train came and everybody crowded in, and the song eventually died out, but the effect on the crowd still showed. Almost nobody talked—the people

acted as though they might be coming out of a church service. In going uptown, occasionally little groups would start singing or humming the tune.

As Ives went on to explain, that tune was the popular gospel hymn "The Sweet By-and-By." In the weeks that followed, Ives transformed his experience on the platform into a short orchestral sketch titled "From Hanover Square North, at the End of a Tragic Day, the Voice of the People Again Arose." As in "Black March," Ives used excerpts from various songs as a means of depicting the scene and characterizing its participants. In addition to the hymn, he included an Anglican Te Deum, Alexander Ewing's "Jerusalem, The Golden," and Foster's "Massa's in de Cold Grave" and "My Old Kentucky Home." The mix of tunes reflected the racial and economic mix of the singers on the train platform and the various perspectives of sorrow that Ives joined together in an effort to project a unified national voice.

Ives saw World War I as a global fight for democracy, and he wrote several songs to support the troops. "In Flanders Field" and "Tom Sails Away" reflect the tragedy of war and the virtue of personal sacrifice, while the rousing march "He is There!" calls for "a world where we all may have a say." Ives grew so committed to the war effort that he volunteered for the YMCA's ambulance service in France, but health problems prevented him from serving. In 1918, he suffered another serious heart episode and was diagnosed with diabetes. This was in an era before insulin treatment, and the diagnosis forced Ives to cut back dramatically on his daily activities. He began to work mostly from home—by then a country house in Redding, Connecticut—and he assessed, once again, his priorities in life. In the decade that followed, Ives recommitted himself, in both words and music, to the ideals and values of American democracy as he envisioned them. In Ives's mind, the time had come for him to voice his opinions—to engage more actively in the world around him as an activist–composer. He wanted to effect change.

Ives's first step was to author and advocate publicly for a new amendment to the Constitution. Emboldened by the ratification of the Nineteenth Amendment in 1920, which gave women the right to vote, Ives proposed a Twentieth Amendment that would enable the national electorate (black and white, male and female) to vote directly on substantive policy issues. Determined to engage directly with those figures he saw as the nation's power brokers, Ives wrote letters to prominent politicians and sent editorials to national newspapers and magazines. He even printed five thousand flyers at his own expense, with the intention of distributing them at the Republican and Democratic national conventions. Nevertheless, each attempt to stimulate debate ended in failure. Adding to Ives's frustration with the status quo was Warren G. Harding's landslide victory in the 1920 presidential election. Harding, a Republican, promised voters a "return to normalcy." Ives saw it as a repudiation of everything America had fought for overseas, a rejection of the Democrats' global vision and commitment to the League of Nations. Ives vented his frustration, as he often did, in music. The result was a bitter protest song titled "Nov. 2, 1920" or "The Election."

Ives described the song as a "soliloquy," written from the point of view "of an old man whose son lies in 'Flanders Fields.'" Wondering if the war was fought in vain, the old man calls out his countrymen for their apathy and notes how "some who stayed home are beginning to forget . . . the pocketbook [and] certain little things talked loud and noble [i.e., Harding's campaign promises] have gotten in the way." The lyrics lay bare the ills of the US political process: "too many readers go by the headlines," "party men [i.e., politicians] . . . muddle up the facts," and "a good many citizens voted as grandpa always did or thought a change for the sake of change seemed natural enough." Ives blames "prejudice and politics" for what he sees as the nation's turn in the wrong direction. Underlying it all is the nation's greed and complacency. "We've got enough to eat," claims a cynical electorate, "to hell with ideals!"

Up to this point, Ives had not attempted in any serious way to publish his music. His regular process was to work on a composition for a few weeks or months and then stash it away. Now and then, he would perform a song for friends or colleagues or pay a theater orchestra to sight-read a work in progress, but generally he kept his music to himself. As his political advocacy increased, however, so too did his desire to influence American concert music. Why did European composers still dominate conservatories and concert halls in the United States? Hadn't the time come for Americans to revere their own composers? Ives pondered these questions while on a rest cure in Asheville, North Carolina. The ever-increasing resurgence of his health problems had ignited within him a sense of urgency to change the status quo. In 1919, he completed one of his most challenging compositions, Piano Sonata No. 2, subtitled "Concord, Mass., 1840–1860." He then wrote a small book, *Essays Before a Sonata*, which served the dual purpose of describing the various movements of the sonata (each dedicated to one of his favorite authors: Emerson, Hawthorne, the Alcotts, and Thoreau) and laying out his political and philosophical ideology. By 1920, Ives was a wealthy man. He no longer feared that his family would "starve on his dissonances." Consequently, he set to work on a scheme to get his sonata and *Essays* into the hands of America's most powerful curators of culture.

First, he compiled a list of possible recipients of his musical efforts. He consulted *Who's Who in America* and purchased the subscription list of the weekly trade magazine *Musical Courier*. From these he gathered a list of roughly two hundred influential musicians, composers, and music critics—the gatekeepers of American musical culture.

The next step was finding a publisher. Ives reached out to G. Schirmer, the nation's most revered music press. In addition to publishing a popular series of canonical works called "Schirmer's Library of Musical Classics," the publisher ran its own engraving and printing plant and published the *Musical Quarterly*, America's oldest academic music journal. Schirmer agreed to publish Ives's sonata under the condition that the composer cover all production and publication costs. Ives spared no expense. The paper quality, binding, and printing were all top-of-the-line. For his book of essays, Ives contracted with the Knickerbocker Press under a similar set of conditions. Both editions were complete by the beginning of 1921, and Ives promptly shipped them out to composers, performers, conductors, and music scholars across the United States. Most didn't know what to make of the two volumes they received. A few published their impressions of the sonata and its accompanying essays, but most remained silent. Undiscouraged, Ives tried again a year later with another publication, aptly titled *114 Songs*, which included all the songs he had composed over the years—from college ditties to sentimental ballads and political tunes. His song "The Masses," now retitled "The Majority" (no doubt with the aim of separating his ideology from the recently founded Communist Party USA), served as the volume's opening number. This choice was intentional. Ives described it as a challenge to those who dared to criticize him. If the gatekeepers of culture didn't like his songs, Ives supposedly didn't care. As he explained it, the time had come for him to "clean house," to put his ideas "on the line" for "all to see." Ives included annotations to some of the songs, describing the inspiration behind them and/or their connection to his political philosophy. He ordered 1,000 copies of *114 Songs*—five times the number of his sonata and essays. In addition to sending them to those who had received the earlier publications, he advertised the song collection in newspapers and music journals, offering a complimentary copy to anyone who wrote and requested one. Several of the songs found their way onto recital programs over the course of the decade, but in general Ives's efforts had little impact on the world around him. American politics grew more divisive, and voter suppression increased as a crescendo of materialism and racism swept the decade along, culminating in 1929 with the collapse of the stock market.

Financially, Ives was fine. He had invested his money wisely. Physically and psychologically, however, he was spent. Ives retired from the insurance business on January 1, 1930 and soon found himself struggling emotionally. Depressed by the bread lines, unemployment, and class warfare plaguing the nation, he lost the will to compose new music and sought refuge in revisiting works from the past, among them *The Unanswered Question*. Ives's worldview had changed noticeably since he composed it. The "Perennial Question of Existence" no longer concerned just his own suffering but rather the suffering of the nation, of humanity altogether. Ives revised his piece accordingly. He altered a pitch slightly in each query from the trumpet, creating a greater sense of angst and urgency, and intensified the combative nature of the "Fighting Answerers" by adding more dissonance to the flutes. Ives revised other works as well, organizing them into groups which he referred to as orchestral sets. The most famous of these, Orchestral Set No. 1, he subtitled "Three Places in New England." The first movement, "The St. Gaudens in Boston Common," was a revision of his original "Black March." In addition to the new title and expanded orchestration, Ives added the Christian hymn "Jesus Loves Me" to his sonic depiction of the 54th Regiment. The second and third movements are "Putnam's Camp, Redding Connecticut" and "The Housatonic at Stockbridge."

Toward the end of the decade, Ives finally began to see the fruits of his labor—not politically, but musically. A new generation of young composers and conductors took an interest in his work. In 1939, his *Concord Sonata* was premiered by American pianist John Kirkpatrick, who later became a scholar of Ives's work. Bernard Herrmann, then an up-and-coming film composer, noticed his music as well. Herrmann perceived a cinematic quality in Ives's sense of musical space, and Ives's emotive dissonances and sound effects influenced the music of the famous shower scene in *Psycho* (1960). The composer who had the greatest impact on Ives's legacy, however, was Henry Cowell, who visited the aging composer regularly at his home in Redding and sifted through piles of unpublished manuscripts. Cowell was determined to realize a canon of great American works, and he envisioned Ives as one of the founding fathers. Their friendship began in 1927, when Cowell established *New Music*, a journal committed to promoting the work of contemporary composers. Ives offered Cowell financial support for many years, and in return Cowell helped organize a recording of Ives's *Concord Sonata* by Columbia Records in 1945.

After World War II, interest in Ives's work accelerated quickly. Elliott Carter, who had been a recipient of Ives's publications a quarter century earlier, organized the first "all-Ives" concert in 1946, at Columbia University's McMillin Theater; the performers were all students from Julliard. Various works were on the program—a selection of songs, Ives's Third Symphony, Second String Quartet, Second Violin Sonata, and the tone poem *Central Park in the Dark*—but the piece that had the greatest impact on the rapt audience was *The Unanswered Question*. In the program, Ives identified the work as "a contemplation of a serious matter" and outlined in detail the importance of each sonic element. Coming on the heels of World War II, many in the audience no doubt heard in the piece a response to the horror humanity had recently witnessed. *The Unanswered Question* urged listeners to reflect on the past and contemplate their place in the world moving forward.

The concert at Columbia solidified Ives's reputation as a founding father of American concert music. Paul Henry Lang, the noted music critic for the *Saturday Review*, labeled Ives a legend after hearing his works performed. The Pulitzer Prize Committee honored his Third Symphony with the nation's most coveted music award. But it was the composer Lou Harrison who best described the significance of Ives's music. Harrison understood what drove Ives as a composer, and he put it into words better than Ives himself ever managed to do. In an article published in the November 1946 issue of *Listen*, he laid out plainly how Ives's music might one day change America:

> I suspect that the works of Ives are a great city, with public and private places for all, and myriad sights in all directions... In the not-too-distant future it may be that we will enter this city and find each in his own way his proper home address, letters from the neighbors, and indeed all of a life, for who else has built a place big enough for us, or seen to it that all were equally and justly represented?
>
> Such is the work of Ives. And if we here, in the United States, are still really homeless of the mind, it is not because men have not spent their hearts and spirit building that home... but simply because we refuse to move in.

In the decades that followed, *The Unanswered Question* became Ives's most programmed composition. The work was added to the curriculum of the nation's conservatories and music schools, and, one by one, young American composers visited the "great city" built by Ives. For John Adams, one of the most prominent composers of the last half century, *The Unanswered Question* offered a key to national healing. In 2001, Adams was commissioned by the New York Philharmonic to compose a work in response to the 9/11 terrorist attacks. Adams's first instinct was to decline the commission, on the grounds that the nation's suffering was still too raw to capture in music. But then he remembered the power of *The Unanswered Question*: "9/11 and all the loss of those people, of any people... from such a sudden act *is* an unanswered question," Adams noted. "I realized right up front that the public did not need any more images... It didn't need some tasteless dramatization of the events in music and text." What was needed most was a space "where you can go and be alone with your thoughts." The result was *On the Transmigration of Souls*, a work that superimposes prerecorded street sounds and the reading of victims' names over a live performance by chorus and orchestra. As Adams later explained, *The Unanswered Question* offered him a path forward as he composed. "It's there. It's a ghost in the background... and then, every once in a while, these clouds... disperse for a second and you'll just get a glimpse of the Ives *Unanswered Question*, as if it's just playing all the way through the piece."

Like Ives's composition, *On the Transmigration of Souls* is neither emotional nor sensual. Rather, it is philosophical in tone. And as a nod to Ives, Adams inserted a lone trumpet, rising high and then receding into an echoing distance, asking once again the unresolvable question: "Why?"

THE SEARCH FOR AN AMERICAN SOUND

■ ■ ■ ■ ■

On October 27, 1998, President Bill Clinton signed the Sonny Bono Copyright Term Extension Act. Named in honor of Representative Bono, who died several months before the bill became law, the new legislation expanded by twenty years the copyright protection afforded to composers, writers, and visual artists in the United States.

One might assume, given the legislation's title, that Bono was a catalyst in the writing of the legislation. Before being elected to the House of Representatives in 1994, Bono had spent four decades as a singer-songwriter, most notably as part of the pop duo Sonny and Cher. But the version of the bill Bono had supported never made it to a vote in the Senate. Instead, it was Senator Orrin Hatch of Utah who first proposed the Copyright Term Extension Act in 1995 and saw it through to its completion. Hatch was an amateur musician, but he had no skin in the game when it came to extending the profits made from artistic creations. Instead, he was motivated by the lobbying efforts of two major forces in the entertainment world, namely the Disney Corporation and the Gershwin Family Trust. Both were concerned about the looming end to their lucrative copyrights: Mickey Mouse in 2003, and *Rhapsody in Blue* in 2004.

When Hatch presented the legislation to his colleagues, he began with a brief history of copyright law:

> In 1790, the first Congress set the maximum term of copyright protection at 28 years... In 1831, we extended that period by 14 years... In 1909, the major copyright reform act of the era extended the maximum term of copyright to 56 years... Most recently, the Copyright Act of 1976 fundamentally altered the way in which we measure copyright by protecting works throughout the life of their creator plus an additional 50 years.

As Hatch explained, the overhaul of copyright law in 1976 was done to align the copyright of all new works with "the prevailing international standard of protection." For works published before 1976, the copyright extended to 75 years after the initial publication date. But this was still not adequate, argued Hatch:

> Mr. President, this legislation matters, and it matters to some of the most distinguished members of America's cultural and artistic community. If we examine the significance of this legislation just in the area of popular music alone, I believe we will see its importance.

"Just two months ago," he noted, George Gershwin's "Swanee," a song "still widely performed in theaters and through media around the world... fell into public domain." And even more troubling: "Within the next few years, if Congress does not act to adopt legislation such as that which I introduce today," other works would soon lose protection, most notably *Rhapsody in Blue* by George Gershwin.

When reporters reached out to Marc Gershwin, a nephew of the composer and co-trustee of the Gershwin Family Trust, he did not hesitate to defend his family's interests. "The monetary part is important," he admitted, but even more important was protecting the integrity of great American works like *Rhapsody in Blue*: "If works of art are in the public domain, you can take them and do whatever you want with them... Someone could turn *Porgy and Bess* into rap music," for example.

The Sonny Bono Copyright Term Extension Act was not the first time Congress referenced *Rhapsody in Blue* in debates over copyright. On August 6, 1935, when George Gershwin was still alive, Senator Robert F.

Wagner of New York cited Gershwin's music as evidence of why an extension of copyright protection was unnecessary. Great American works, like *Rhapsody in Blue*, were part and parcel of the nation's identity. "Who does not know... the genuine genius of *Rhapsody in Blue*?" he asked. "The rhapsody will live as long as American music."

So, what is it, one may ask, that makes *Rhapsody in Blue* so American? Many historians, and even Gershwin himself, regularly answered that question with a description of the music's origins.

On January 3, 1924, George Gershwin was shooting pool with his good friend B. G. "Buddy" DeSylva at the Ambassador Billiard Parlor on Broadway and 52nd Street. His older brother, Ira, was perusing the *New York Tribune* when he came across the notice of an upcoming concert and began to read aloud. According to the article, the bandleader Paul Whiteman had organized a "concert to be given at Aeolian Hall, Tuesday afternoon, February 12," whose alleged purpose was to answer a single question: "What is American Music?" Stars of the concert hall—"Sergei Rachmaninoff, Jascha Heifetz, Efrem Zimbalist, and Alma Gluck"—had been selected for "a committee of judges," and "the leading musical critics of the United States" were expected as well. The concert would feature a wide range of works, "from blues to symphonies," by American composers, most notably "George Gershwin, who is at work on a jazz concerto."

Upon hearing that last line, George dropped his pool cue. He had talked informally with Whiteman about composing a new piece, but they had never settled on a date. Yet there it was, in black and white, for all to see. As Gershwin later confessed, he was panic-stricken at first. With less than six weeks until the event, he didn't know where to begin. In the days that followed, he set to work devising melodies for his new composition but struggled with the overall structure of the piece. Adding to his stress was the fact that he was soon expected in Boston for performances of his latest musical, *Sweet Little Devil*. It was during the trip north, Gershwin later explained, when everything fell into place:

> It was on the train, with its steely rhythms, its rattle-ty bang that is so often stimulating to a composer, that I suddenly heard—even saw on paper—the complete construction of the Rhapsody, from beginning to end. No new themes came to me,

but I worked on the thematic material already in my mind and tried to conceive of the composition as a whole. I heard it as sort of a musical kaleidoscope of America—of our vast melting pot, of our incomparable national pep, our blues, our metropolitan madness.

Over the next few weeks, Gershwin completed his famous *Rhapsody in Blue*, which was premiered at Whiteman's concert. The audience went wild, and critics embraced the work as an American masterpiece. *Rhapsody in Blue* had captured the mechanistic beat of modern life, with its soaring skyscrapers, roaring automobiles, and pulsating rhythms. With a single composition, Gershwin had answered the probing question: "What is American music?"

This is the story often told about the iconic composition that turned the twenty-five-year-old Gershwin into an international celebrity. It's a great tale that highlights the protagonist's innate talent and willingness to face a challenge and come out on top. If only it were that simple—but, as with most origin stories, there is more to the making of *Rhapsody in Blue* than what is generally chronicled in history books. Despite some journalists' claims at the time, Gershwin did not definitively answer the question: "What is American music?" Rather, he took the first step in the promotion of an "American sound" for both commercial profit and, eventually, corporate branding.

The son of working-class Jewish immigrants from Russia, Gershwin was a product of multicultural New York. Born in 1898—the same year New York was officially defined by its five boroughs: Manhattan, Brooklyn, Queens, the Bronx, and Staten Island—Gershwin witnessed the opening of the city's subway system, the growth of its iconic skyline, and the birth of the modern music industry. In his youth, Gershwin regularly explored various parts of the city, which was populated by nearly five million inhabitants, 40 percent of whom were foreign-born, like his parents. Gershwin also witnessed the burgeoning of New York's African American population, from roughly 60,000 in 1900 to over 300,000 the year *Rhapsody in Blue* premiered. Although segregation kept most African Americans confined to a handful of neighborhoods, by the 1920s the most prominent of these, Harlem, had become an internationally recognized cultural hub. Eager to imbibe as wide an array of musical influences as possible, Gershwin familiarized himself with the various music traditions the city had to offer, from the European classics of Carnegie Hall to the Yiddish theater songs and klezmer tunes of the Lower East Side, the music of Tin Pan Alley and Broadway, and the ragtime and jazz of Harlem. Each of these traditions contributed to his education. According to Gershwin, growing up in New York exposed him to the voice of the American soul:

> It spoke to me on the streets, in school, at the theater ... Old music and new music, forgotten melodies and the craze of the moment, bits of opera, Russian folk songs, Spanish ballads, chansons, ragtime ditties combined in a mighty chorus in my inner ear. And through and over it all I heard, faint at first, loud at last, the soul of this great America of ours.

Gershwin's career as a professional musician began in 1914, when he was hired as a song plugger by the Jerome H. Remick Music Company. The primary duty of a song plugger was to demonstrate and promote (i.e., plug) sheet music to aspiring musicians and theater directors. The job required formidable skills at the piano, a clear voice, and most importantly a magnetic personality—all talents that Gershwin possessed. Although taking the job meant dropping out of high school, the salary—fifteen dollars a week—was too good to pass up. Gershwin became the primary breadwinner for his family.

Tin Pan Alley—28th Street between Fifth and Sixth Avenues, where New York's major music publishers were found—was where Gershwin learned to compose. The name, legend has it, referred to the loud clattering—like a bunch of tin pans—created by the numerous song pluggers demonstrating the most recent hits in the salesroom of each publishing house. By the time Gershwin arrived in 1914, Tin Pan Alley represented the hub of America's popular music industry, and it gave Gershwin a hands-on overview of the nation's latest musical trends. By day, he pitched new songs to vaudeville stars and served as a rehearsal accompanist for revues and musicals. By night, he visited Harlem nightclubs and performed at private soirées on the Upper West Side. Within a year, he was writing songs himself.

Tin Pan Alley produced three basic categories of music: ballads (generally slow, sentimental songs), dance tunes (most notably those with syncopated rhythms), and novelty songs (comedic pieces). Gershwin tried his hand at writing music in each category. He had a talent for tapping into what attracted audiences, and he realized quickly that the key to making it in the popular music industry was to appeal to a growing sense of national pride and cultural independence. This was especially true in the years leading up to World War I. Gershwin worked with various lyricists early on, including Irving Caesar, Buddy DeSylva, and eventually his older brother, Ira. The first song the Gershwin brothers penned together, "The Real American Folk Song (is a Rag)" (1917), was a manifesto of sorts in its claim that the "creative vein" and "native strain" that distinguishes every nation is its folk music, and that in America, the distinctive element "is a rag."

Ragtime was one of the first African American genres to appeal to listeners across socio-economic, ethnic, and cultural barriers. Its global appeal, first made obvious with Scott Joplin's performances in 1893 at the Chicago World's Fair, led to a commercialization of the form and the addition of lyrics. Often categorized as "novelty songs" in Tin Pan Alley catalogues, rags generally poked fun at ethnic stereotypes, from Jews and Germans to Italians and African Americans. Gershwin's songs touched on all these ethnicities, but it was "Swanee" (1919), a blackface number made famous by Al Jolson, that launched his career as a composer. The lyrics, written by Irving Caesar, depict a black man longing for his "Mammy" and life in the antebellum South. It's an expansive, up-tempo parody of Stephen Foster's "Old Folks at Home" (1851), distinguished by its mix of minstrelsy, exoticism, and ragtime.

As Gershwin explained to a reporter shortly after the song's release, "Swanee" was calculated to be a commercial success. His goal was to "represent the soul of the country" by combining "the romance" of the South with the "business" instincts of the North. But there was more to the story. Gershwin composed "Swanee" during the Red Summer of 1919, one of the most violent periods of racial conflict in US history. The term was coined by James Weldon Johnson, who experienced the uprisings while working as a field secretary for the NAACP. In an attempt to quell the violence, Johnson organized peaceful protests, many of which incorporated the singing of uplifting songs like his own "Lift Every Voice and Sing."

The escalation of anti-black violence that rocked the nation in 1919 was exacerbated by a variety of post-World War I social tensions, including an economic slump and a shortage of jobs and affordable housing in major cities. All summer, newspapers across the country reported on the violence, which involved at least thirty-eight white-on-black riots and the lynching of more than fifty black men. The NAACP responded to the violence by declaring "Lift Every Voice and Sing" the Negro National Anthem. Gershwin capitalized on the moment by composing "Swanee." Written to appeal to the audiences flocking to Broadway after the war, Gershwin's "Swanee" perpetuated an ethnic stereotype made popular during the early years of the Great Migration: that of the homesick black man. It was a stereotype Gershwin turned to time and again, and it served as a central plot device in his first major composition exploring the juxtaposition of classical music and jazz: his one-act opera *Blue Monday*.

Blue Monday premiered as part of the musical revue *George White's Scandals of 1922*. Like most revues of the 1920s, White's were elaborate stage productions designed for upper-class white audiences. They were episodic in structure (alternating between music performances, dance numbers, and comedy sketches) and featured a mix of chorus girls in revealing costumes and irreverent dissections of current events. Although a serious one-act opera might seem out of place in such a production, Gershwin's *Blue Monday* was included as a "scandalous" response to the recent blockbuster success of the first Broadway musical to be written, produced, and performed entirely by African Americans—*Shuffle Along* (1921), by Eubie Blake and Noble Sissle.

Shuffle Along launched the careers of numerous legendary performers, including Josephine Baker, Adelaide Hall, Florence Mills, Fredi Washington, and Paul Robeson. The show drew enthusiastic crowds and received glowing reviews from the press. James Weldon Johnson praised it for legitimizing the African American musical, demonstrating to producers and theater managers that audiences were not only willing, but eager, to pay to see black performers on Broadway. Gershwin attended multiple performances of *Shuffle Along*, taking note of how the composers integrated jazz into a work for the stage. He got to know several of the musicians in the orchestra, including William Grant Still, and he reached out to Will Vodery, the composer who orchestrated *Shuffle Along*, and asked if he would do the same for *Blue Monday*. Vodery accepted the commission, and on his copy of the final score, he labeled Gershwin's *Blue Monday* "Opera à la Afro-American." Whereas *Shuffle Along* was a lighthearted comedy featuring jazz and an African American cast, *Blue Monday* was envisioned as an operatic tragedy in blackface.

Set in a basement café in Harlem, *Blue Monday*'s plot revolves around an explication of each character's hopes and desires: Joe, a gambler, wants to return home to visit his mother; Vi (Joe's lover) wants Joe; Tom, a singer, wants Vi's attention. The climax comes when Tom deviously tells Vi that Joe has received a telegram from another woman. In response, Vi shoots Joe in a jealous rage, only to discover afterward that the telegram was from his sister. The opera concludes with Joe calling out in anguish for his mother as he dies in Vi's embrace.

Blue Monday received mixed reviews. The problem wasn't the music, which was generally praised, but rather the placement of such a tragic work within the context of a revue. Charles Darnton, writing in the *New York World*, called *Blue Monday* "the most dismal, stupid, and incredible black-face sketch that has probably ever been perpetrated" and suggested that the show would have been better if Vi had killed the entire cast and then turned the gun on herself. Although *Blue Monday* was cut from the show after the New York premiere, it nonetheless led to greater things for Gershwin. Paul Whiteman, the music director for *Blue Monday*, was impressed by Gershwin's ability to merge disparate styles—opera, jazz, Broadway dance tunes, and melodrama—into a cohesive work. As Gershwin later explained, it was his "association with Whiteman in this show" that led to "Paul's asking me to write a composition for his first jazz concert." Gershwin is referring to the commission of *Rhapsody in Blue*. As a conductor and entrepreneur, Whiteman was interested in developing an "American" sound for the concert stage that rivaled European models. It was this interest that motivated him to commission a jazz concerto—what became *Rhapsody in Blue*—for his inaugural "Experiment in Modern Music" concert in 1924.

Much has been written about this concert, which took place in New York's Aeolian Hall on February 12, Lincoln's birthday. The choice of date was no coincidence; Lincoln had politically united America's North and South, and Whiteman hoped to unite America's black (jazz) and white (European concert music) cultures. The concert was presented as a history of jazz from its origins in the South to its integration with the symphonic traditions of the North. The concert began with what Whiteman dubbed a "primitive" performance of the first piece ever recorded by a jazz band, "Livery Stable Blues," and evolved, step by step, to the "elevated," jazz-infused concert music epitomized by the Paul Whiteman Orchestra. Gershwin's *Rhapsody in Blue* marked the end point in Whiteman's teleology—the final product of his modern "Experiment." As Whiteman later explained, his goal in organizing the concert was not to glorify the origins of jazz (which he defined as "barbaric . . . jungle cacophony") but rather to "reform" (i.e., whitewash) it by commissioning works from composers like Gershwin:

> All the years that I was playing jazz, I never stopped wanting to go into concert halls and in some measure remove the stigma of barbaric strains and jungle cacophony from jazz. I felt George could write the thing I needed. Something that would show that jazz had progressed. Something that would illustrate that it was a great deal more than savage rhythm. Something that would give expression to what I was seeking to bring out.

Despite Whiteman's intentions, *Rhapsody in Blue* is not jazz. Rather, it is a symphonic work that makes use of characteristics associated with jazz, namely syncopated rhythms, blue notes, and jazz band instruments. Written originally for piano and Whiteman's Palais Royal Orchestra, it is episodic in nature and structured around five closely related themes, each based on a blues scale. There is a stylistic dualism in *Rhapsody in Blue*, between the ensemble playing foxtrot-inspired themes featuring jazz instruments and the soloist at the piano who, using techniques and devices associated with European concert music, responds to those themes. This dualism has led some to describe the work as a concerto, and in many ways this designation is fitting, since the work is built on exchanges between the solo piano and orchestra. But Gershwin labeled his composition a rhapsody, a musical genre perfected in the nineteenth century by composers like Johannes Brahms and Franz Liszt. The word comes from the ancient Greek *rhapsōidos*, which refers to a reciter of epic poetry, what we now call a rhapsode or rhapsodist. In antiquity, rhapsodes traveled from town to town giving recitations of Homeric poetry and improvised linguistic performances that highlighted the history and valor of a region's people. Virtuoso performer-composers referenced this tradition in the nineteenth century when they created instrumental rhapsodies meant to highlight the musical characteristics of a specific nation and its people. The *Hungarian Rhapsodies* by Liszt serve as standout examples. When Gershwin chose to compose a rhapsody, he was referencing this nationalist attribute. In fact, he originally titled his work *American Rhapsody*; it was his brother, Ira, who recommended the name *Rhapsody in Blue*, on the grounds that it was more evocative.

Gershwin's goal in composing the piece was to capture the various ethnic characteristics he heard on the streets of New York. The opening clarinet passage references klezmer music, just as the wa-wa trumpets are a nod to jazz. Simply put, *Rhapsody in Blue* is a collision of cultures in sonic form—a thrilling evocation of the urban soundscape of 1920s' America. It was noticeably different from anything else on the bill that night, and the public loved it. *Rhapsody in Blue* was also warmly received by Gershwin's Tin Pan Alley and musical theater colleagues. But in the realm of concert music, many composers and critics—most notably Aaron Copland, George Antheil, and Virgil Thomson—dismissed *Rhapsody in Blue* for its episodic structure and lack of thematic development. Gershwin was also criticized for not orchestrating the work himself. That task had been assigned to Whiteman's arranger, Ferde Grofé. Gershwin took all these criticisms in stride. Due to popular demand, Whiteman's "Experiment" was soon repeated at Carnegie Hall and then taken on a national tour. Gershwin was featured on the cover of *Time* magazine on July 20, 1925—the first American composer to enjoy such an honor—and within a year netted roughly $250,000 in royalty payments. *Rhapsody in Blue* turned Gershwin into an international star, and an up-and-coming performer named Edward Kennedy "Duke" Ellington took notice.

In music history books, Gershwin and Ellington are rarely discussed in tandem. Some might assume from existing discussions of their music that they came from different generations. Yet Ellington was born in 1899, just seven months after Gershwin. And their musical upbringings were not as different as one might think. As pianists, both were well versed in the works of European composers like Beethoven, Chopin, Dvořák, and Liszt, and Americans like Scott Joplin, Stephen Foster, and James P. Johnson. The rare discrepancy was Gershwin's connection to klezmer music, a tradition to which Ellington was not exposed in his youth.

Ellington was born in Washington DC, where he was raised in the privileged, middle-class black neighborhood near Howard University called Uptown (now known as Shaw). At the turn of the century, Washington was home to the largest black urban community in the United States, and Howard University served as an intellectual hub. Black-owned businesses flourished in Uptown during Ellington's youth. The federal government also offered career opportunities, as civil servants and social workers, to the city's black residents. Ellington's maternal grandfather was a policeman, and his father ran a catering business that included the White House among its clients. As a young man, Ellington was raised to value a well-rounded education that embraced European and American literature, the fine arts, and—most importantly—African American culture, with a strong emphasis on black world history. He was influenced by the accomplished role models in his parents' circle: doctors, lawyers, entrepreneurs, and Howard University professors. Encouraged by his parents and confident in his own talent and potential, Ellington was inspired from an early age to achieve greatness.

Like Gershwin, Ellington did not study music formally in school, instead learning what he needed from those around him. His first piano teacher, a woman aptly named Marietta Clinkscales, gave Ellington a foundation in classical concert works and technique. This was supplemented by concerts at Howard University, where he heard European classics and the works of black composers like Clarence Cameron White and Will Marion Cook. At home, his mother supplemented this repertoire with nostalgic Victorian parlor songs, and at church he was exposed to hymns and spirituals. Ellington grew up a short walk from U Street, Uptown's central entertainment district. In local venues like Frank Holliday's Poolroom and the Poodle Dog Café, he tried his hand at ragtime and Tin Pan Alley tunes. At the Howard Theatre and True Reformer's Hall, he attended performances by out-of-town acts, including James Reese Europe's Clef Club Orchestra and the cast of *Shuffle Along*. Most influential on the young Ellington were the large-scale historical pageants that celebrated black history. In 1911, he attended the sweeping allegorical work *The Evolution of the Negro in Picture, Song and Story* at Howard University, and four years later, he saw *The Star of Ethiopia* at the American Legion Ballpark. Written by W. E. B. Du Bois, this magisterial work, which required hundreds of musicians and dancers, lasted three and a half hours and encapsulated "10,000 years of the history of the Negro race," from ancient Egypt to the dawn of the twentieth century. The production featured a mix of music, from Verdi's *Aida* to contemporary works by pioneering black composers like Bob Cole, J. Rosamond Johnson, and Samuel Coleridge-Taylor.

Ellington composed his first tune, "Poodle Dog Rag," around 1915. Over the next couple of years he performed regularly at local venues, and by 1919 he was managing his own band, the Duke's Serenaders. They played all sorts of gigs: private soirées in the homes of the Washington elite, charity events for local causes, college parties in Georgetown, and embassy balls. Despite these successes, Ellington wanted out. The Washington of his youth was slowly slipping away. By the early 1920s, Jim Crow policies had firmly taken root in the nation's capital.

Ellington first took note of these transformations at age fifteen, when he witnessed the devastating changes wrought by President Woodrow Wilson's administration. Wilson had promised fair treatment for African Americans in his 1912 campaign, but, once elected, he oversaw the segregation of federal offices, from the treasury and post office to the navy. Photographs became mandatory for all federal job applications, which led to increased levels of racial discrimination and unemployment. When confronted about these changes by black leaders like W. E. B. Du Bois and William Monroe Trotter, Wilson noted with condescension that avoiding "friction" was his primary motivation. "Segregation is not a humiliation," he said, "but a benefit, and ought to be so regarded by you gentlemen."

The enforcement of Jim Crow practices in the nation's capital led to a rise in race-related violence. In 1919, Ellington witnessed the horrific violence of the Red Summer, when white mobs terrorized Uptown for five long days. When the fighting finally ended, fifteen people were dead and over 150 were injured. The final straw for Ellington, however, came in 1922, at the dedication of the Lincoln Memorial. While veterans of the Confederate Army were given seats of honor, black attendees were banned from sitting in front of the monument and were escorted instead by armed soldiers, when necessary, to a fenced-off "colored section." Adding insult to injury, the lone black speaker, educator Robert Russa Moton, was barred from sitting on the dais with the other presenters, who were white. Within the span of a single decade, Ellington had witnessed the deterioration of opportunities for aspiring black men in the nation's capital. So, like many others of his generation, he headed north for a promised land called Harlem. "It was New York that filled our imagination," Ellington explained. "We were awed by the never-ending roll of great talents there, and songwriting, in jazz and theatre, in dancing and comedy.... Harlem, to our minds, did indeed have the most glamorous atmosphere. We had to go there."

Ellington quickly established himself in New York. Like Gershwin, he frequented the city's music clubs, attended rent parties in Harlem, and sold his first song on Tin Pan Alley. Unlike Gershwin, he formed a band of his own and soon snagged a steady engagement at the Kentucky Club, on West 49th Street between Seventh Avenue and Broadway. "It was a good place for us," Ellington explained, "because it stayed open all night and became a rendezvous for all the big stars and musicians on Broadway after they got through working." This included George Gershwin, Ferde Grofé, and Fred Astaire. "Paul Whiteman came often, and he always showed his appreciation by laying a big fifty-dollar bill on us." After their regular sets, Ellington and his band worked the late-night crowd by taking requests: "We sang anything and everything—pop songs, jazz songs, dirty songs, torch songs, Jewish songs." When Ellington and his orchestra transferred to the swanky Cotton Club in Harlem a few years later, his fans followed.

Always awake to what was new, Ellington took note when Whiteman presented his first Experiment in Modern Music, and in the months that followed, he tried to crack the code of Gershwin's success. This is documented by two transcriptions of *Rhapsody in Blue* in the Duke Ellington Collection at the Smithsonian Museum of American History. Like many composers before him, Ellington knew that the best way to learn how a composition works is to study it closely, note by note, and in 1926 he created a musical response, a multithemed work for piano solo titled *Rhapsody Jr.* that borrowed a classical theme ("Spring Song") by Felix Mendelssohn and melded it with his own newly composed melodies. This early work, with its ninth and augmented chords, whole-tone melodies, and parallel triads, marks Ellington's first response to Gershwin's *Rhapsody in Blue*. Others soon followed. "Swanee River Rhapsody," for example, was composed as the finale for *The Blackberries of 1930* revue at the Cotton Club. Gershwin named it one of his favorite Ellington tunes. No wonder: it riffed on both Gershwin and Stephen Foster. One year later, Ellington composed *Creole Rhapsody*, his most direct response to Gershwin's *Rhapsody in Blue*. As Ellington explained to a reporter, his aim was to offer "an authentic record of my race written by a member of it." He recorded *Creole Rhapsody* twice in 1931, first for the popular label Brunswick, then six months later for the classical label Victor. Both times, the recording took up two full sides of a 78 rpm disc. The only other nonclassical recording to carry the same honor, up to that point, was the Whiteman–Gershwin recording of *Rhapsody in Blue*.

Ellington's *Creole Rhapsody*, especially the revised and extended Victor version, responds subtly to the question posed by Whiteman in 1924: What is American music? Like *Rhapsody in Blue*, *Creole Rhapsody* is episodic. But Ellington draws more deeply than Gershwin did on the musical traditions of black Americans: ragtime, the blues, and spirituals. Like Gershwin, Ellington marks the opening with a clarinet. But instead of the klezmer wail from *Rhapsody in Blue*, Ellington offers the warm-sugar tone of a New Orleans clarinet playing an undulating countermelody to the band's syncopated, train-like motive. Barney Bigard, the clarinetist on the recording, was a native of New Orleans who identified as Creole, a term referring to the mixed-race culture of the region. In a similar manner, Ellington's first piano interlude references the stride piano style of James P. Johnson. And the two strains of twelve-bar blues that follow, played by the full ensemble, are introduced by a direct quote from *Rhapsody in Blue*—the famous opening clarinet glissando. It's as if Ellington is reminding listeners of Gershwin's work and saying, "Now let me show you what some *real* blues sounds like." About midway through the piece, on the Victor recording, a third theme appears, languid and dreamy, played first by muted trumpet and a chorus of saxophones, then trombone, and finally piano and clarinet. In all three iterations, a shadow of melancholy tints the mood, and occasionally, in the saxophone accompaniment, one hears echoes of a black church choir. As the work draws to a close, Bigard again quotes snippets from *Rhapsody in Blue* before a final, heroic version of the languid theme is carried above the band by tenor saxophone.

Creole Rhapsody marked a new era in Ellington's work as a composer. As he later explained, it was "the seed from which all kinds of extended works . . . later grew." Ellington had cracked the code of his own distinctive sound, which he often referred to as "the Negro idiom." Those in the know heard it and quickly understood the commentary Ellington was making with his various Gershwin references: *Rhapsody in Blue* was an attempt at the American sound, but Ellington's response suggested that it wasn't the final answer.

Creole Rhapsody led to greater exposure and commissions for Ellington. A famous press photo from 1932 shows Paul Whiteman smiling broadly as Ellington hands him a copy of the score. In the years that followed, Whiteman commissioned Ellington to compose additional extended works: *Blue Bells of Harlem*, for his eighth Experiment in Modern Music Concert, and *Blutopia*. The success of *Creole Rhapsody* also led to an offer by Paramount in 1934 to star in an upcoming film, a musical mystery titled *Murder at the Vanities*. This was a big step for Ellington— the first time he and his orchestra would share the screen with white actors *not* in blackface. As Ellington's contract reveals, Paramount had designed a special scene for him, a revue act within the film titled "Ebony Rhapsody." In it, Ellington would appear as a modern-day virtuoso–composer, the twentieth-century American equivalent of Franz Liszt.

As the scene opens, we see the nineteenth-century Liszt (played by Eric Lander) seated at the piano, playing his Hungarian Rhapsody No. 2 and singing along: "Someday, the finest orchestra will play my rhapsody . . ." A few phrases later, his prediction comes true. A modern-day orchestra appears and continues playing Liszt's tune. As the music progresses, Ellington and his musicians deftly insert themselves into the ensemble, adding jazz licks between phrases until the conductor (Homer

Boothby) and orchestra stomp off the stage. Ellington and his orchestra then transform Liszt's music into an Ebony Rhapsody, which brings great pleasure to the dozens of young women, both black and white, who appear on stage and dance with great abandon. This is all well and good, until it's not. The scene ends abruptly when the original conductor returns with a "prop machine gun" and mows down everyone on stage with a barrage of bullets. The whole scene had been pitched to Ellington as a humorous classical-versus-jazz commentary. But when Ellington saw the final product, he discovered, much to his dismay, that the basic narrative of the scene had been drastically altered.

Firstly, the name of Ellington's number had been changed from "Ebony Rhapsody" to "Rape of a Rhapsody." This was indicated by the printed program shown on screen at the beginning of the scene. The program divides the scene into three parts: "The Rhapsody" featuring Eric Lander as Liszt, "The Rape" played by "Duke Ellington and His Band," and "The Revenge" carried out by "Homer Boothby and Company." Clearly, there was more going on here than a harmless classical-versus-jazz commentary. Instead of appearing as masters of American music, Ellington and his orchestra became the unwitting victims of a metaphorical lynching.

It should be noted that when *Murder at the Vanities* premiered in 1934, Congress was embroiled in a heated debate over two newly proposed anti-lynching laws (more about this in chapter 5). Ellington's scene in *Murder at the Vanities* was edited to capitalize on the situation, but at what cost? "Rape of the Rhapsody" belittled Ellington and his music, and for the rest of his career he excluded the film from his list of silver screen appearances. Years later, in an unpublished poem, he reflected on the distortion of his image:

And was the picture true
Of you? The camera eye in focus . . .
Or was it all a sorry bit
Of ofay hocus-pocus?

How then, this picture
They have drawn?

*It can't be true
That all you do . . .
Is dance and sing
And moan!*

*Harlem! For all her moral lurches
Has always had
LESS cabarets than churches!*

*Who draped those basement dens
With silk, but knaves and robbers
And their ilk?
Who came to prostitute your art
And gave you pennies
For your part . . .
And ill-repute?*

*Who took your hunger
And your pain,
Outraged your honor
For their gain?*

*Who put the spotlight
On your soul
And left you rotting
In the hole
These strangers dug!*

Shortly after the premiere of *Murder at the Vanities*, Ellington demanded restitution, insisting that his image as a serious composer be rectified. In response, Paramount produced a new film, a masterpiece in miniature titled *Symphony in Black*. The title was a rebuttal, of sorts, to Gershwin's *Rhapsody in Blue*. If Gershwin could write a jazz-infused rhapsody about the white man's experience in New York, Ellington could write a symphony about the black experience.

Symphony in Black was shot at Paramount's Astoria studios in New

York roughly seven months after the release of *Murder at the Vanities*. Subtitled "A Rhapsody of Negro Life," the nine-minute film depicts "the History of the Negro in American Society." Duke Ellington composed all the music, the only actors were members of his band, and the film featured Billie Holiday in her first screen appearance.

Symphony in Black opens with the image of an anonymous hand placing a letter in a mail slot labeled "Duke Ellington Studio." The letter is from an organization called The National Concert Bureau. It reads: "Just a reminder that the world premiere of your new symphony of Negro Moods takes place two weeks from today. I trust that work on the manuscript is nearing completion so that you may soon start rehearsals." Gershwin had six weeks to compose his rhapsody; in *Symphony in Black*, Ellington accomplishes the task in just two. In the next shot, the camera looks over Ellington's shoulder at the score he is writing out in pencil. The camera then cuts to a shot of the composer in profile, from head to toe. He's dressed elegantly, working at the piano on his new creation. The camera zooms in on the title of the work: "Symphony in Black." From this point on, shots of Ellington composing are intercut with scenes of the full orchestra in performance and a series of pantomime dramatizations based on the music. Each scene change represents a single movement, of which there are four: 1) "The Laborers"; 2) "A Triangle: Dance, Jealousy, Blues"; 3) "A Hymn of Sorrow"; and 4) "Harlem Rhythm."

The first movement, "The Laborers," links the steady pulse of the traditional work song to contemporary men toiling away at blue-collar jobs in a basement and on a loading dock. As with each movement of *Symphony in Black*, the music is presented first, in the concert hall by the Ellington Orchestra, before the scene cuts away to a visual explication of the music's reference to black culture—in this case, physical labor. Each drumbeat coordinates perfectly with the movement of the workers on screen, who are shoveling coal and hoisting bales.

The second movement, "Triangle," reveals the exhilaration, jealousy, and suffering associated with love. The suffering, portrayed by a young Billie Holiday singing "Lost My Man Blues," is introduced by Barney Bigard on clarinet. As in *Creole Rhapsody*, he plays the distinctive glissando from Gershwin's *Rhapsody in Blue*, reminding listeners that the blues in Gershwin's American sound came from black culture.

The third movement, "A Hymn of Sorrow," draws on the spiritual. The scene is set in a church, where an elderly preacher stands before a mourning congregation, a small coffin at his feet. As Ellington later explained, the use of a child's coffin was intentional. An adult coffin might have led to speculation about the man's death. A child's coffin would garner universal sympathy.

Symphony in Black concludes with "Harlem Rhythm," a modernistic view of Harlem's contemporary nightlife with its heady mix of alcohol, music, and dance. This is the scene most viewers associated with Harlem, and it arrives only after the other aspects of African American culture have been explored.

Gershwin described his *Rhapsody in Blue* as "a musical kaleidoscope of America—of our vast melting pot," born from "the soul of this great America of ours." With *Symphony in Black*, Ellington reminded listeners that the American soul, indeed the American sound, was strongly rooted in what he called "a rhapsody of Negro life."

Symphony in Black premiered in 1935—the same year as Gershwin's second opera, *Porgy and Bess*. Audiences couldn't help but note the differences. In all fairness, *Porgy and Bess* is worlds apart from *Blue Monday*. Gershwin spent several months along the South Carolina coast immersing himself in the music and culture of the Gullah community—descendants of enslaved African Americans living on the barrier islands near Charleston. In letters home, he expressed a deep appreciation for the culture he encountered, though he acknowledged that he never truly felt part of it. As a result, the music he composed for *Porgy and Bess* was not a direct transcription of what he heard but rather a creative interpretation—a musical evocation of the cultural encounter.

By the time Gershwin composed *Porgy and Bess*, he had embraced the idea that his primary task as a composer was to serve as an interpreter between disparate cultures, a goal that Ellington viewed as admirable but in many ways impossible. In an unguarded moment, Ellington confessed this opinion to a reporter, noting that although Gershwin's music was grand, it didn't capture the real spirit of the characters it portrayed. "[My *Symphony in Black*] was true to . . . the life of the people it depicted," he said. "The same thing cannot be said for *Porgy and Bess*." Almost immediately, Ellington regretted sharing this opinion. He contacted the reporter to request that his comment not be published, but it was too late. The article went to press. It is one of the few examples we have of Ellington speaking out in public against a fellow composer. "You can say anything you want on the trombone," he later noted, "but you gotta be careful with words." Throughout his career, this was one of Ellington's guiding principles.

Gershwin died young, in 1937, and for a decade his *Rhapsody in Blue* was memorialized in concerts, books, and on screen. Ellington continued his pursuit of an American sound, composing extended works like *Black, Brown, and Beige* for Carnegie Hall and thrilling audiences at the Newport Jazz Festival. He even had his portrait on the cover of *Time* in 1957. As Ellington's notoriety grew, Gershwin's began to fade. Although some might find it hard to believe, after World War II Gershwin's *Rhapsody in Blue* became a musical relic, a sonic symbol of a prewar America that no longer existed. So, what happened, you ask? When did *Rhapsody in Blue* make its comeback? For that, you can thank Leonard Bernstein.

Bernstein single-handedly revived the status of *Rhapsody in Blue* as a great example of the American sound. As Ryan Bañagale explains in his marvelous book, *Arranging Gershwin*, Bernstein "engaged with the work continually over the course of his multifaceted career, leaving his interpretive mark through copious concerts, broadcasts, recordings and writings." His first documented performance of the piece took place in 1937, but it was two decades later, during his inaugural season as the principal conductor of the New York Philharmonic, when he turned *Rhapsody in Blue* into a sonic symbol of America. Bernstein's appointment to the post in 1958 was a momentous occasion—the first time an American-born musician had taken the helm of such an important ensemble. Up to this point, European conductors had dominated American concert halls. So, to commemorate the milestone, Bernstein touted the greatness of homegrown talent with a year-long "root and branch exploration of American music." *Rhapsody in Blue* played a pivotal role in this programming.

Gershwin held a special place in Bernstein's identity as an American conductor. "The great tragedy for me, the musical tragedy of my life," he once admitted, "was I never met him." Bernstein remembered with great clarity the day he learned of Gershwin's death. He was eighteen, working in the Berkshires as a counselor at Camp Onota. In honor of the great man's passing, he arranged a performance of *Rhapsody in Blue* using the musical forces at hand, namely the camp's Rhythm Band supplemented with accordion, ukelele, and kazoos. Naturally, this wasn't the orchestration Bernstein used for his concerts with the New York Philharmonic, but the spirit was the same. As Bernstein often explained, he saw *Rhapsody in Blue* as a shape-shifting invention, a series of marvelous melodies strung together by improvisatory passages on the piano.

> You can cut out parts of it without affecting the whole in any way except to make it shorter. You can remove any of these stuck-together sections, and the piece still goes on as bravely as before. You can even interchange these sections with one another, and no harm done . . . or add new cadenzas, or play it with any combinations of instruments or on the piano alone . . . It's still the *Rhapsody in Blue*.

It should be noted that, for all his performances of *Rhapsody in Blue* during the 1958–59 season, Bernstein shunned the original "jazz band" orchestration created by Ferde Grofé in 1924. It was unsophisticated, in Bernstein's opinion, too "wrong side of the tracks." Instead, he created a version he believed might stand up better to European standards, a version that drew heavily from an orchestration Ferde Grofé had created in 1942 for "Grand Orchestra." In Bernstein's hands (he always conducted the work from piano, playing the solo passages himself), Gershwin's themes expanded, the tempos slowed, the syncopated rhythms softened. Gone were the banjo, the saxophones, and the klezmer smear of the opening clarinet line. In their place appeared French horns, timpani, and strings—grand orchestral music, Mahlerian in scope. Gershwin's multiethnic image of urban America disappeared, and in its place arose Bernstein's confident, assimilated "melting pot" version of the American sound, a sound that was preserved for eternity in the recording Bernstein created with the Columbia Orchestra in 1959. It is this recording that, over a half century later, still ranks as the most recognizable version of the piece.

Bernstein's embrace of *Rhapsody in Blue* accelerated the rejection of the piece in jazz circles. Eric Larrabe, in *Harper's Magazine*, called it a "pseudo-Lisztian pastiche, with a Tchaikovsky-like major theme, which borrows from jazz only those few blue notes and dance rhythms necessary to make it seem fresh and keep it moving." Similarly, in 1962, jazz historian Neil Leonard called *Rhapsody in Blue* "traditional music dressed in jazz costume and coloring—Liszt, as it were, in blackface, a rented tuxedo, and battered top hat."

Ellington responded in 1963 with his own orchestration of *Rhapsody in Blue*, one that paid tribute to Gershwin's original endeavor and the centrality of jazz. The performance opens with the famous ascending glissando, but instead of a clarinet, Harry Carney's baritone saxophone slows the climb with improvisatory flourishes before launching listeners into a harmonically lush and languid atmosphere. Gershwin's themes are all there, each recognizable, but colored differently, in smoky hues of blue and mauve. The harmonies are extended; gone are all traces of ragtime and Rachmaninoff. This is pure jazz, virtuosic jazz, a mix of swing, bebop, and cool. Ellington's take is truncated—the thematic presentation is tight and economical. Nonetheless, the distinctive sound of each instrument shines through, from Paul Gonsalves's tenor saxophone and Lawrence Brown's trombone to Ray Nance's shimmering trumpet. Conspicuously quiet until the very end is Ellington's piano, which offers an introduction of sorts to the cameo appearance of the clarinet (Jimmy Hamilton), playing the signifying glissando from Gershwin's original. Gonsalves's tenor saxophone responds in minor. The band then builds to the end, where a flourish in the piano followed by an unresolved cadence leaves listeners hanging, waiting for something new. It's Ellington's way of telling us that there is no definitive American sound. Like the nation itself, the American sound is always in flux, always changing, always in search of its best self. It's an important message: one worth listening to, but unfortunately not taken to heart often enough.

On New Year's Day 2020, *Rhapsody in Blue* entered the public domain, which means that anyone can perform and record it without permission and at no cost. Five years later, the original recording of *Rhapsody in Blue* also became free and clear for use. It will be interesting to see what musicians do with the work in the years to come, and how the composition will continue to lend its voice to the great American soundscape.

SAVING THE AMERICAN LANDSCAPE

·····

On August 18, 1928, George Gershwin penned a fiery letter to J. C. Rosenthal, the general manager of the American Society of Composers, Authors, and Publishers (ASCAP), complaining about the orchestrator of *Rhapsody in Blue*, Ferde Grofé:

> Mr. [Jerome] Kern at lunch the other day brought to my attention that Ferdie Grofe [sic] had listed among his compositions "The Rhapsody in Blue." Mr. Kern said he objected to this at the last meeting and he advised me to write to you about it. Mr. Grofe made a very fine orchestration from my completed sketch but certainly had no hand in the composing.... Hoping you will straighten this out.

One of the most intriguing qualities of *Rhapsody in Blue* is how it captured the invigorating soundscape of New York in the 1920s, with its crowded thoroughfares, bright lights, and soaring skyscrapers. As reviewers rightly noted after the premiere, although Gershwin was responsible for the catchy rhythms and melodies, the music's atmospheric effects were due to the orchestration by Grofé. Over the course of his career, Grofé made at least six separate orchestrations of *Rhapsody in Blue*: the original

1924 version for piano and jazz band, a version for theater orchestra in 1926, a concert band version in 1937, and three separate arrangements for symphony orchestra in 1937, 1939, and 1942.

The motivation behind the various orchestrations was cultural survival. Grofé—and, for that matter, Gershwin—wanted the work to have a life after Whiteman's famous Experiment in Modern Music. Re-orchestrating *Rhapsody in Blue* time and again was an act of cultural conservation. Grofé facilitated the continued popularity of Gershwin's composition by adapting it to changing tastes and artistic needs. Conservation—the act of protecting a resource for current and future generations—was an important concept to Grofé, one that reflected his interest in America's landscapes, influenced his approach to composing his own works for orchestra, and, eventually, informed a series of political debates concerning the nation's management of the Grand Canyon.

This chapter tells the story of Grofé's *Grand Canyon Suite*, a programmatic symphony that invites listeners to experience the rugged beauty of the nation's most famous natural wonder. Like *Rhapsody in Blue*, the *Grand Canyon Suite* is habitually described as quintessentially American. But in spirit and style, the two works are sonic opposites: cultured urban East versus wild rural West. Grofé composed *Grand Canyon Suite* in response to his own exploration of the land and its people. But in translating these experiences into art, he fused personal memory with collective myth for the sake of an engaging narrative. As a composer of popular music, Grofé never lost sight of what audiences wanted. Consequently, the lessons to be learned from his *Grand Canyon Suite* concern not only what he included in his vision of the American landscape, but what he left out.

Born on New York's East Side on March 27, 1892, Grofé came from a long line of professional musicians: his father was an opera singer, both his mother and maternal grandfather were professional cellists (the latter with the Metropolitan Opera orchestra), and his uncle served as concertmaster of the Los Angeles Symphony Orchestra. When Grofé was still an infant, his parents divorced, and his mother and grandfather took him to Southern California. In Los Angeles, Grofé began piano and violin lessons, and when he was seven, his mother separated from her second husband and moved with Grofé to Leipzig, Germany, where they remained for three years. There, his musical training continued with cello and viola lessons. Once back in Los Angeles, Grofé's relationship with his mother grew strained (he did not get along with his mother's third husband), and at age fourteen he moved in with his grandparents, who let him do as he pleased. Grofé dropped out of school at age fourteen and spent the next two years working odd jobs and expanding his proficiency in music. In addition to intensive study of the violin, viola, and piano, he took up the cornet and baritone horn.

It was around this time that he began to hire himself out as a freelance musician. In 1908, at age sixteen, he left home and for the next decade led a nomadic life, traveling from one small town to the next in search of work. As Grofé explained it, he had "itchy feet" and "never stayed in one place more than six months." Much of this time was spent in various parts of California, but in 1917 he made his way to Arizona, where he visited the Grand Canyon for the first time.

> I first saw it at dawn, because we got there the night before and camped. I was spellbound by the silence. Of course, then it got lighter. You could hear the birds chirping and nature coming to life. But when I first got there, it was just before dawn. It was getting lighter and lighter, and all of a sudden—bingo! There it was—the sun. . . . I get chills right now just thinking about it. I don't know—you feel awfully close to God there. It was overwhelming. . . . I couldn't hardly describe it in words, because words would be inadequate.

After this encounter, Grofé returned to Los Angeles, where he divided his time between playing viola with the Los Angeles Symphony Orchestra and piano in various dance bands. Between seasons, he toured the West, and as he put it "made frequent visits to the Grand Canyon, camped everywhere from the border to Mohave County . . . hobnobbed with Indians, did some gold prospecting with an old friend . . . [and] often heard the redskins' drums beating all night during their powwows." Grofé's use of the word "powwow" represents an Anglicized version of a Native American term. "Pau-wau" or "pauau" referred to a gathering of spiritual leaders or medicine men. And the term "pa wa," meaning "to eat," could be used to refer to a celebratory gathering. As

Grofé notes, he did not attend the powwows but rather heard them from afar. His use of the term "redskins" was not as racially loaded as it is today; nonetheless, it reveals that he viewed the powwow participants as distant and exotic.

Grofé looked back fondly on the "wonderful nights" he spent "on the desert." This was before the crowds of tourists and the easy-access highways. Determined to experience as much as possible, Grofé "rode all over the state in a cut-down Ford roadster," exploring the region's natural wonders in solitude.

> In those days one traveled Arizona with a so-called "strip-map," which meant that the only guides were landmarks like a certain farm, tree, fork of some stream, water-mill, giant cactus or ranch house. There were few signposts, and the roads were of the dirt and unimproved variety.

In 1920, while playing a gig in San Francisco, Grofé met Paul Whiteman. Excited by Whiteman's approach to music, Grofé agreed to join the Whiteman Orchestra as a pianist and arranger. When Whiteman returned to New York in 1921, Grofé followed, and for the next decade he brought to life, through his signature orchestrations, the Whiteman Orchestra's greatest successes, from "Whispering" and Gershwin's *Rhapsody in Blue* to Grofé's own *Broadway at Night* (1924), *Mississippi Suite* (1925), and *Metropolis* (1928).

Grofé adapted to the fast-paced life of a dance band musician and the syncopated rhythms of the local jazz scene. Still, invigorated though he was by life in Manhattan, memories of the Western landscape stuck with him. He returned to the Grand Canyon at least once a year. "It became an obsession," he later explained. "The richness of the land and the rugged optimism of its people had fired my imagination. I was determined to put it all to music someday."

That day came in 1926, when Grofé returned to Arizona with his family in tow—he was now married with a young son. "On that occasion," he later explained, "came to me the irresistible urge to put into music what I felt about the state and its wonders of nature. To me, they were epitomized, before all else, in the awe-inspiring magnificence and towering mystery of the Grand Canyon, which always had stimulated my imagination and tonal impressions. I saw color, but I 'heard' it too."

Grofé's musical turn toward the western frontier coincided with a move away from the jazz-infused style that characterized much of his work with the Whiteman band. He originally envisioned his soundscape of the Grand Canyon as a symphony in four movements: "Sunrise," "Painted Desert," "Hopi Indian," and "Sunset." Grofé later explained to reporters that he planned each movement as a living "picture"—a sonic visualization of the landscape. Grofé completed the first full draft of "Sunrise" in 1929. Here, he put to music the memories of his first impression of the Grand Canyon. "I was thinking of giving a musical portrait of the sun coming up in the early morning at dawn," he later explained.

> So, I have a timpani roll—a very soft roll—and I have the cricket effect. The crickets are still chirping away—muted trumpets—and then I have the first bird trills, singing in the trees, and later on the four-legged critters get moving around, and the two-legged feathery tribe, and it increases.... But the chord structure is the important thing. It moves up gradually... The intervals move higher—it gets brighter all the time, and there's more activity among the wild animals. There's no human element at all in it—it's all just nature... Then finally, the sun breaks over the rim of the canyon. That's the big chord at the end—the sunlight chord... and everything is just showered in light.

Content with the effect, Grofé began composing "Sunset," which he envisioned as a logical companion piece. He was on the ninth hole at the Saddle River Country Club in Hackensack, New Jersey, when the movement's main theme came to him.

> I was thinking of evening—a sort of meditation.... I thought of the end of the day, and the shadows falling, and quietude, like a meditation. And I wrote the melody in that vein. The melody suggested meditation.

"Sunset" captures the expansive calm of the desert as night approaches. Horn calls echo through the canyon, answered by the rushing tide of the river below as the final rays of sunlight glimmer across its surface. Listeners are lulled by the lengthening shadows as they sweep over the golden hues of sun-warmed sands. The sun slips silently behind the canyon rim as evening envelops the desert in a cloak of darkness.

Grofé completed the orchestrations for "Sunrise" and "Sunset" in August 1930. One month later, Whiteman premiered them at a concert in Cincinnati. Excited by the public's enthusiastic response, Whiteman asked Grofé if he had any additional "pictures" of the Grand Canyon. Encouraged, Grofé set to work right away on "Painted Desert."

> I went again to memories and envisioned a scene at Holbrook [Arizona], where I had been on the rim of the desert at early morn and gazed in rapt amazement at the changing colors and shadows.

Grofé later reflected on the sights and sounds that inspired him:

> I thought a lot of colors . . . different shades of browns and yellows . . . I thought in terms of all those colored rocks. And the silence—everything is so silent and desolate. It's a desolation and wasteland except for these brightly colored rocks.

In his original plan for the composition, Grofé had imagined the next movement as an evocation of Arizona's indigenous residents. During his earliest visits to Arizona, he had interacted regularly with members of the Hopi and Havasupai tribes. The Hopi were the most visible of the two. They lived in permanent homes and, as early as 1900, they participated in the ecosystem of the growing mining and tourist industries by working in local shops and creating art: kachina dolls, earthenware ceramics, and silver and turquoise jewelry. The Hopi give special meaning to various locations within the Grand Canyon. According to legend, the ancient warrior gods Pokanghoya and Polongahoya created the canyon and the river that runs through it by cracking open the earth with giant lightning bolts. At the river's edge, one finds the geologic dome called Sipapuni, which translates roughly to "Place of Emergence." Here is the point of origin for the Hopi people, similar in religious importance to Christianity's concept of the Garden of Eden.

For the Havasupai, the canyon is equally significant. Unlike the Hopi, the Havasupai did not participate as readily in the financial ecosystem that began to develop around the canyon at the turn of the century. They lived a more nomadic existence, moving in and out of the canyon along a series of winding footpaths, known today as the Bright Angel and Kaibab trails. In fall and winter they camped along the canyon rim, where they hunted and gathered food. In spring they ventured to the canyon floor, where they planted corn, beans, squash, melons, and pumpkins in cultivated fields. This area, now referred to as Indian Garden, is of vital importance to the Havasupai and their ancestors. Here are found some of the region's most important religious and archeological sites.

Grofé encountered the Hopi and Havasupai at the Grand Canyon largely thanks to President Theodore Roosevelt's interest in the region a generation earlier. In 1903, Roosevelt visited the Grand Canyon, where he met with Havasupai leaders at Indian Garden. Roosevelt described the canyon as "a natural wonder . . . absolutely unparalleled throughout the rest of the world." Five years later, he declared the region a National Monument under the Antiquities Act, a recent piece of legislation that gave him the authority to preserve areas of natural or historic interest on public lands. With regard to the Grand Canyon, Roosevelt's goal was to ensure that the region would not be tainted by commercial development.

> I have come here to see the Grand Canyon of Arizona. . . I shall not attempt to describe it, because I cannot. I could not choose words that would convey or that could convey to any outsider what that canyon is. I want to ask you to do one thing in connection with it in your own interest and in the interest of the country: to keep this great wonder of nature as it now is . . . I hope you will not have a building of any kind, not a summer cottage, a hotel, or anything else to mar the wonderful grandeur, the sublimity, the loneliness and beauty of the canyon. Leave it as it is. Man cannot improve on it, not a bit.

One of the primary purposes of the Antiquities Act of 1906 was to protect important archeological artifacts by enclosing them in regions specified as federally controlled areas. In the case of the Grand Canyon, this meant the protection of lands occupied by the Hopi and Havasupai. Roosevelt addressed this issue in his speech with "a word of welcome to the Indians here." He highlighted their contributions to the United States, how "they were good enough to fight and to die . . . and are good enough to have me treat them exactly as square as any white man." Roosevelt noted the "good many problems" faced by Native Americans, including "the unregulated Eastern philanthropist . . . All I ask is a square deal for every man," he claimed. "Give him a fair chance . . . and do not let him be wronged." Although no one asked the Hopi or Havasupai what they thought of Roosevelt's new legislation, his creation of the Grand Canyon as a National Monument preserved, at least briefly, their traditional culture and use of the land.

This was the Grand Canyon as Grofé first experienced it—when the Hopi and Havasupai were still of central importance to one's experience of the Grand Canyon. But in the intervening years, new political administrations brought new ideas about the government's role in managing the Grand Canyon.

In 1916, President Woodrow Wilson signed the National Park Service Organic Act, which formally established the National Park Service. The central mission of the new agency was to conserve the scenery and wildlife within the parks so that they could be enjoyed by all Americans in perpetuity. This and other Wilsonian legislation resulted in the displacement of native peoples in service of an ideology of purity—a purity that did not include the land's original inhabitants.

Wilson perpetuated the myth of the vanishing Indian to justify the seizure of native land. Using rhetoric that echoed that of President Andrew Jackson, he painted a picture of precolonial North America as an untamed wilderness, sparsely inhabited by "a few savage hunters," who "were annihilated or have melted away to make room for the whites."

Three years later, Wilson reclassified the Grand Canyon as a national park and put in motion a series of "improvements" that prioritized the recreational use of the region by tourists over its use by the Hopi and Havasupai. Additional changes came in 1921, when congressional legislation labeled the powwows Grofé had witnessed "Indian Offences" and effectively banned them in an effort to improve "the moral welfare of the Indians." In 1924 the Interior Department Appropriation Act was introduced, giving the National Park Service the authority to take control of Bright Angel Trail. By 1928, the Havasupai were removed indefinitely from their lands at Indian Garden.

These changes to the canyon landscape impacted Grofé's thinking about the content of his composition. As he later explained, in 1929 he shared his idea for a "Hopi Indian" movement with a recording supervisor at Victor named Eddie King. Wouldn't a cowboy riding into the canyon be more popular? King asked. "It seems to me that you're overlooking a good bet. You know every tourist goes down the Bright Angel Trail." Although Grofé had never ridden along the trail himself, he recognized the appeal of descending into the canyon and took King's suggestion to heart. "Oh, I grabbed onto it!" he later explained, "And I dropped 'Hopi Indian'—forgot about it, discarded it."

The new movement, titled "On the Trail," took listeners on an excursion. In Grofé's imagined journey down the Bright Angel trail, the cowboy rides a burro, who is featured prominently in the music. The movement begins with a dizzying descent in the strings (the opposite of *Rhapsody in Blue*'s ascending run in the clarinet). "I thought of the 'hee-haw' right away for the beginning. And then I thought of having a violin cadenza, to work on that 'hee-haw' business. *Daaa-um*—that interval, which I employed three or four times throughout the movement." A few minutes into the piece, the burro's rider adds his own voice to the soundscape with a lulling brass melody Grofé called a cowboy song. In its style and structure, it captures many of the melodic characteristics identified as Western by regionalist folklorists like B. A. Botkin (George Gershwin's cousin). Grofé claimed that the tune came to him while rocking his infant son to sleep. "It worked out fine as the cowboy's chant, as he's riding down the trail . . . following a pack train."

The cowboy and burro encounter various sights on their way through the canyon. "They come around a bend," Grofé noted. "And that's where you hear the waterfall." A bit further along, they encounter other people. Not the Havasupai who originally populated the canyon, but newcomers who have set up camp at Indian Garden and brought with them a bit of the outside world. "I imagined a halfway house, where they serve refreshments," explained Grofé. "There was a music box up on the mantelpiece above the fireplace. That's where the celeste comes in—that's the music box." As the movement concludes, and they "near the end of their trip, they're approaching the . . . floor of the canyon where Phantom Ranch is— and that's where it becomes very animated, very fast, because the nature of animals are, the closer they get to the stable, the faster they walk."

After the lengthy burro ride, listeners end their day in the canyon depths. Originally, "Sunset" was devised as the suite's final movement, but two weeks before the premiere, Grofé was inspired to add a fifth movement, titled "Cloudburst," during a trip to Chippewa Lake in northern Wisconsin. It was unseasonably warm for October, and the evening after Grofé's arrival a powerful thunderstorm arose.

> It reminded me of the cloudbursts I used to witness in Douglas, Arizona . . . It would terrify you. And this was almost like that. It shook the cabin . . . but it didn't last very long . . . I went out, and the moon was just coming out from behind a cloud . . . it was beautiful then. You could see the moon's reflection on the undergrowth and the bushes just glistening . . . That's all I needed. I sat down the next day and I thought out "Cloudburst."

Grofé finished the movement with little time to spare. According to a notation on the last page of the score, he penned the final notes on "Nov. 15, 1931 at 2:55am"—a mere week before the scheduled premiere.

In its final form, Grofé's music enabled listeners to experience a full day at the Grand Canyon, from sunrise to a late-night thunderstorm. Grofé captured in tones a picture-perfect image of the natural wonder, from the beauty of its vistas and trails to the terror of its thunderstorms. As he explained it, even those who had never experienced the Grand Canyon in person could, through his music, "almost see it without having seen it." By representing a day in the life of the Grand Canyon, Grofé "invited listeners to imagine themselves as part of the frontier environment."

Grofé's *Five Pictures of the Grand Canyon* (the work's original title) was premiered by Paul Whiteman and His Orchestra on November 22, 1931 at the Studebaker Theater in Chicago. The program wasn't limited to music by Grofé. Gershwin's *An American in Paris* was expected to be the concert highlight, but it was *Five Pictures of the Grand Canyon* that stole the show. As the *New York Times* noted, Grofé's "portrayal of nature's moods" was met with "recurring waves of enthusiastic approbation and cries of 'composer!'" In response, Whiteman repeated "On the Trail" as an encore, but "they kept applauding." Eventually, Grofé left his seat in the audience and came onstage, where, according to *Variety*, the audience "kept Grofé taking bends afterward for a couple of minutes." He had spent the last twelve years working behind the scenes, and now, with the enormous success of *Grand Canyon*, he finally found himself in the spotlight. On November 30, *Time* magazine revealed the real talent behind the Whiteman Orchestra: "Ferde Grofé has been Paul Whiteman's Man Friday, anonymously scoring tunes, embroidering them until even some of the sleaziest have taken on symphonic richness." A week later, *Scribner's* published a seven-page feature on Grofé, describing him as the "Ghost Writer of Jazz." Whiteman wasn't happy about his own characterization in the press and, to add insult to injury, Grofé resigned from the Whiteman Orchestra in December and took over as conductor of the Capital Theater Orchestra in New York.

With a larger ensemble at his disposal (sixty musicians), Grofé re-envisioned his *Five Pictures of the Grand Canyon*. His original orchestration had been for the twenty members of Whiteman's ensemble, and he was not fully satisfied with the effect. As he had done with Gershwin's *Rhapsody in Blue*, he created a new orchestration that took advantage of the sonic possibilities of a larger ensemble, and he renamed the piece *Grand Canyon Suite*. As he later explained, "I was able at last to draw upon the full resources of a modern symphony orchestra and make use of all the orchestral colors I needed to describe my tremendous subject in musical terms."

Grofé's revised orchestration only deepened the rift with Whiteman. Soon, the two were locked in a public tug-of-war over who would conduct the New York premiere. In the December 22, 1931 issue of *Variety*, Whiteman announced that he would debut the piece for NBC at the Metropolitan Opera House on February 28. Two weeks later, Grofé fired back in the same publication that, in fact, the actual premiere would happen under his baton on February 7, at a CBS-sponsored benefit concert for unemployed musicians at the Manhattan Theatre. With rival conductors backed by rival networks, the dueling announcements made headlines and stirred plenty of buzz in the press.

Tickets to Grofé's concert sold out quickly, and when the revised orchestration aired nationwide on CBS radio, the *Grand Canyon Suite* became an instant hit. In response, Whiteman scrapped his own concert plans and instead scheduled a three-day recording session at the RCA Victor studio, where he and his orchestra produced the first full-length recording of the piece in April 1932.

At around the same time, Robbins Music Corporation published an arrangement of the work for solo piano. The foreword, written by the publishers, focused on the descriptive elements related to the Grand Canyon's topography, the "relentless upheavals" and "magnitude" forged by the Colorado River. For "On the Trail," lyrics (by Gus Kahn) were added to the cowboy's song:

> *We'll ride away*
> *Along the trail*
> *That follows the sun*
> *And hope someday*
> *We'll meet some wonderful one*
> *I'll sleep tonight*
> *And dream of her*
> *My wonderful one.*

Insipid as the lyrics may seem today, they proved popular at the time, and many a young singer donned a cowboy hat and sang along.

"On the Trail" is the most famous movement of *Grand Canyon Suite*. Since its premiere, the jaunty rhythm of the burro's hooves, clopping along the trail, has been used in countless films and cartoons. In the 1930s, the music was ubiquitous in radio programming. For example, Philip Morris Cigarettes adopted "On the Trail" as its musical signature for all radio and TV programming, from the popular *Ferde Grofé Show* in 1933 to *I Love Lucy* in 1951. Orchestras across the country added the work to their repertoires. Arturo Toscanini greatly admired the suite. He made two recordings of the piece, in 1943 and 1949, calling it one of the finest orchestral masterworks by an American composer.

When Grofé was asked why he thought his *Grand Canyon Suite* had proven so popular with listeners, he reflected on the region's symbolic importance:

> I treasure my recollections of the place I am writing about; recollections sentimental, pictorial, romantic; recollections of grandiose Nature, of vast areas of eloquent solitudes, towering heights, silent deserts, rushing rivers, wild animal life; of health-giving ozone, magic dawns and resplendent sunsets, silvery moonshine, iridescent colorings of skies and rocks; and before all else, of a stock of men and women who breathe deeply and freely, live bravely and picturesquely, speak their minds in simplicity and truth, and altogether represent as typical and fine a human flowering as this land of ours has inherited from its pioneer days.

What Grofé failed to mention was his recollections of the Hopi and Havasupai people—their cultural practices and connection to the land. His *Grand Canyon Suite* does not fully reflect the region as he experienced it. Instead, it captures in sound the grandiose, "Indian-free" wilderness that most Americans imagined it to be. It offers a narrative of American progress—a progress built on exclusion.

Grofé was ever cognizant of what his audience desired. In its final form, *Grand Canyon Suite* instilled in listeners a sense of pride during the height of the Depression. It also provided politicians with a symbol of the nation's natural treasures and pioneering spirit—its ability to overcome hardship during times of adversity. As Grofé himself later explained:

> This composition was born of sight, sound, and sensations common to all of us. I think I have spoken of America in this music simply because America spoke to me, just as it has spoken to you and to every one of us. If I have succeeded in capturing some part of the American musical spirit, I am grateful that I was trained to do so. But this music is your music, and mine only in the highly technical sense that a copyright has been filed away with my name on it. Always we must realize

that there is much more to hear. Our land is rich in music, and if you listen you can hear it right now. This is our music you hear, surging forth, singing up to every one of us.

The early success of Grofé's *Grand Canyon Suite* led to additional legislation concerning the conservation of the Grand Canyon. At the peak of the composition's early popularity, when orchestras around the country were adding it to their repertoire, President Franklin Delano Roosevelt saw to it that the music's message of conservation was made a reality at the park itself. In 1933, his newly established Civilian Conservation Corps (CCC) set to work in the Grand Canyon, ensuring that the beauty of the natural wonder would be made accessible to future generations. The CCC became Roosevelt's most popular Depression-era program, and four federal agencies collaborated to make it a success. The Department of Labor worked with local welfare agencies to recruit men who had recently lost their jobs. Once selected, the Department of War handled their transportation to project sites, oversaw their housing in barracks, and managed their wages, meals, and medical care. Meanwhile, the departments of Agriculture and the Interior were responsible for designing and overseeing the projects carried out by CCC workers.

Over its nine-year run, the CCC completed a wide range of projects nationwide. The need for the program in the Grand Canyon was particularly urgent. Throughout the 1920s and early 1930s, the National Park Service had struggled to provide infrastructure for the increasing numbers of visitors. A federal review of park facilities revealed a high probability of visitor injuries due to deteriorating trails and inadequate facilities. Consequently, a total of six CCC companies were assigned to the Grand Canyon, with the first arriving in May 1933. Over the next few years, these men constructed roads, improved trails, expanded tourist lodging, landscaped the Grand Canyon Village area, and installed transcanyon telephone lines. Tourism numbers skyrocketed in the 1940s and 1950s, with most visitors arriving by car.

Grofé's *Grand Canyon Suite*, with its burro-riding cowboy, promoted the idea of conservation—enjoying the beauty of America's landscapes, but in moderation. As the century progressed, however, ideas about the best way to protect America's natural landscapes began to change. As tourism increased, advocacy groups like the Sierra Club and the Audubon Society highlighted the ecological damage that was occurring at the Grand Canyon because of human use. The focus shifted from conserving the landscape for future generations to preserving the region's indigenous flora and fauna by eliminating, or at the very least strictly limiting, the presence of humans in protected areas.

Of course, eliminating tourists from the Grand Canyon was unrealistic. That said, the push for preservation over conservation among environmental advocacy groups did influence the way the National Park Service and its associates in the tourism industry began to promote the Grand Canyon. Not surprisingly, Grofé's *Grand Canyon Suite* played a decisive role in this transformation.

In 1955, Walt Disney opened his much anticipated amusement park, Disneyland, in Anaheim, California. Encircling the park was a train line, built by Disney's corporate sponsor in the venture, the Santa Fe Railway. The Santa Fe line was the first to take tourists to the Grand Canyon, in the early twentieth century. At Disneyland, the Santa Fe Railroad also became the first to transport visitors to a new scenic attraction: the Grand Canyon Diorama, a 306-foot-long scenic rendering of the vast valley from the South Rim. At the opening ceremony in 1958, riders were greeted by Walt Disney himself, dressed as a train engineer, and a young "Indian boy" in traditional costume. Once aboard the train, visitors were transported into a long tunnel, where they experienced three-dimensional vistas of the Grand Canyon and its native wildlife while listening to excerpts from Grofé's *Grand Canyon Suite*.

For Americans unable to travel to Arizona, Disney offered a second option for experiencing the grandeur of the nation's most famous national park: a twenty-nine-minute live-action documentary titled *Walt Disney's Grand Canyon*, made in cooperation with the National Park Service, Grand Canyon National Park, and the Arizona Sonora Desert Museum. Directed by James Algar, the film presents "a pictorial interpretation of Ferde Grofé's *Grand Canyon Suite*." "Interpretation" is the key word here. Unlike Grofé's original program for the composition, which illustrates a single day at the Grand Canyon, Disney's film spans a full year, and, to accommodate the new narrative, Disney condensed Grofé's music and changed the order of the movements. There are no live actors or animated characters, no dialogue or narration. Instead, viewers are treated to an array of majestic nature scenes that highlight the region's wildlife and the stunning transformations of the landscape wrought by the changing seasons.

The film opens with the sounds of an orchestra warming up. A leatherbound book, decorated with Native American symbols, sits on a music stand. The instruments fall silent as the book opens. It is a musical score. The title above the music reads "Painted Desert and Sunrise." As the music begins, listeners familiar with Grofé's *Grand Canyon Suite* realize right away that the music's original narrative has been changed. The visuals cut to a bird's-eye view of the canyon at high noon. As the music to "Painted Desert" continues, viewers drift across the expansive landscape, like a bird in flight. There is no sunrise shown on screen. And when the music from Grofé's "Sunrise" finally sounds, the viewer has descended to the canyon depths, where the Colorado River rushes through the canyon, surging with the spring waters of newly melted snow.

The scene briefly shifts back to the musical score. The film's second movement, "On the Trail," begins. Now the focus is on the canyon's wildlife during the heat of summer. Gone are the burro and cowboy, replaced by a series of animals on the hunt for food: cougar, tarantula, roadrunner, and snake. An eagle hunts a young rabbit. The cougar tracks a deer. It is a visual medley of survival of the fittest in the canyon's harsh environment. There is no hint of human presence, only a display of the park's flora and fauna in all its rugged glory.

"Cloudburst" comes next, visualized through time-lapse scenes of clouds at dusk, rushing across the canyon skies. The light is muted; fall has arrived. The chill of autumn winds is evoked by the long shadows and roiling clouds that soon bring the violence of a lightning storm followed by winter's first snow.

The film concludes with the fourth movement, "Sunset and Finale." Here viewers witness the full onset of an icy winter in the canyon. Sunlight glistens off the snowy expanse and ice-coated branches. Instead of setting, the sun rises higher, melting away the vestiges of winter as cacti bloom and the canyon grasses sprout forth once again. An eagle soars high above the canyon and viewers fly with it, reliving the spectacular shots of the canyon in spring encountered at the beginning of the film.

Disney's *Grand Canyon* introduced a new generation of children to Grofé's *Grand Canyon Suite*. But it also shifted the music's message—from conservation to a kind of virtual preservation. Shown alongside *Sleeping Beauty* during its original theatrical run, the short film was seen by millions of children and their parents. It went on to win the 1959 Academy Award for Best Live Action Short. Unsurprisingly, the film's popularity helped fuel another wave of tourism to the park in the 1960s.

In 1966, as part of the National Park Service's fiftieth anniversary, Cornelius W. Heine, Special Assistant to the Director, delivered a speech at the Grand Canyon to visiting lawmakers. He reminded them of the Park Service's original mission: "to conserve the irreplaceable" and make it "available for the enjoyment of the people." These two goals—conservation and access—had often been in tension, Heine acknowledged. And yet, over the past fifty years, Americans had built "a noble conservation edifice." But the challenges were far from over. America had shifted from a rural to an urban society, he said, bringing both "benefits and problems" to the parks. He spoke of the need to foster national unity and pointed to Grofé's *Grand Canyon Suite* as a symbol of that shared identity—a work "born of the sight, sound, and sensations" of all Americans. "We Americans cannot look only to the past," Heine said. We "must have time and the quiet to listen, each in our own way, to the music of America," to "that human warmth and friendship and brotherly love which makes us One America in spirit and human relations."

To Heine, Grofé's suite wasn't just a celebration of nature. It was a path toward civil renewal. He urged the assembled politicians to support the National Park mission "by bringing more people to this land," where, he promised, "they will be genuinely uplifted and refreshed."

Both Disney and Heine turned to Grofé's suite as a way to highlight the Grand Canyon's importance to American identity. And yet, despite their success in drawing people in, neither addressed how the rise in tourism and the aging infrastructure were contributing to a widening gap between everyday life and the natural world. That disconnect soon found its way into congressional debates. If Americans were going to protect their natural resources, some lawmakers argued, they needed to understand them. And that understanding had to begin in the classroom.

The result was the Environmental Quality Education Act of 1970

(H.R. 14753), which created new programs to help schools teach environmental awareness and ecological responsibility. During congressional hearings, Carl J. Megel, Legislative Director of the American Federation of Teachers, spoke on behalf of 200,000 union members, voicing strong support for the bill. Only through education, Megel argued, can our nation's natural resources be preserved. Megel reminded lawmakers that America's early settlers had treated the land as if its resources were limitless. "In sanctifying the free enterprise system," he said, "we erred greatly in giving free rein to its polluting proliferation." Megel then quoted the environmentalist Barry Commoner, who warned of a dangerous modern myth:

> We who call ourselves advanced claim to have escaped from [primitive man's] dependence on the environment . . .We get [our water] by the turn of a tap . . .; we warm ourselves and cool ourselves with man-made machines. All this tends to foster the idea that we have made our own environment and no longer depend on the one provided by nature. In the eager search for the benefits of modern science and technology, we have been enticed into a nearly fatal illusion: that we have at last escaped from the dependence of man on the balance of nature.

To show how K–12 education might counter that illusion, Megel submitted a sample "ecology lesson plan," titled "Will We Survive?," designed for use across disciplines—from English and social studies to mathematics and biology. For the fine arts section, students were asked to listen to Grofé's *Grand Canyon Suite* and imagine how the composition "would have turned out if the environment had been polluted—obliterated." The exercise asked them to "analyze the environment" and "the impact of man since he became 'civilized' in that land."

The broader urgency behind this curriculum tied into a specific environmental crisis unfolding at the Grand Canyon: the fate of the region's wild horses and burros. Since the 1950s, the Park Service had viewed the animals as an ecological threat. Burros, in particular, were considered a "veritable pest," and rangers began culling them—sometimes by shooting them from helicopters. When these brutal tactics were reported in the press, public backlash was swift. In 1959, Congress passed the Hunting Wild Horses and Burros on Public Lands Act, which banned the use of motorized vehicles when hunting the animals. A second law, the Wild Free-Roaming Horse and Burro Act of 1971, called for the animals' protection on public lands, but left open a loophole: park officials could still remove them when necessary. In 1976, the National Park Service invoked that clause and began removing burros by "shooting, herding, or any means possible." The move sparked public outrage and led to another round of congressional hearings.

Leading the charge to protect the burros was Senator Charles Mathias Jr. of Maryland. In an emotional appeal on the floor of the senate, he cited Grofé's *Grand Canyon Suite* as proof of the animals' symbolic value:

> ... burros came to the Grand Canyon with the Spanish conquerors. Today, visitors ... have the opportunity to see the Grand Canyon burros making their way through that magnificent setting. And who can fail to imagine the scene as we hear the rhythm of the hoofbeat in "On the Trail," the most popular movement in Ferde Grofé's "Grand Canyon Suite?"

Thanks in part to this invocation of cultural memory—and Grofé's music—the burros were saved again, this time by legislation passed in 1977. Mathias warned that without action, these "symbols of our national heritage" would be "massacred by shooting," and that the "product of three centuries of struggles against adversity" would be "wiped out in five years."

Grofé made a deliberate choice to replace the "Hopi Indian" movement of the *Grand Canyon Suite* with "On the Trail"—a move clearly intended to help his music reach the widest possible audience. And it worked. Nearly fifty years after its premiere, "On the Trail" still echoed in the American imagination, even influencing the way lawmakers envisioned the Grand Canyon itself. But looking back on the history of Grofé's composition, it's hard not to wonder: What if he had stayed with his original plan? What if the heart of the composition had focused on the Hopi and Havasupai—the people he encountered when he first visited the canyon in 1917? Might they have become the cultural guides for generations of listeners? Would our national debates have focused on preserving Indigenous traditions rather than celebrating cowboys riding in on borrowed burros?

The power of music must not be underestimated. The sonic landscape Grofé created with the *Grand Canyon Suite* encouraged listeners to contemplate the importance of America's natural environment and humanity's place within it. As Disney revealed in its pictorial interpretation of the composition, the message behind the music has transformed over time, from ideas connected with conservation, to preservation, and back again. No matter the message, there is a power to the music that reaches beyond everyday experience. As Ferde Grofé Jr. noted, many years after his father's death, the work can be read as a metaphor of humanity's spiritual development:

> "Sunrise"—birth; "Painted Desert"—the mystique, the unknown, the divine unknown, if you like; "On the Trail"—the human comedy; "Sunset"—death. And then "Cloudburst" is death and resurrection, the battle of good and evil.

Many listeners find the music alluring, the younger Grofé concluded, "because they can identify some emotion in themselves in his work."

The *Grand Canyon Suite* reminds us that saving the American landscape means more than conserving natural resources and preserving flora and fauna. As the author, educator, and philosopher Luther Standing Bear observed in the early 1930s: "Only to the white man was nature a wilderness," a land populated "with wild animals and savage people." Grofé experienced the canyon before it became a national park. And what he left out of his music can be just as revealing as what he chose to include. As journalist David Treuer has pointed out, national parks don't just preserve places—they shape how we're taught to see and interact with the land.

Music has a way of lodging in our memories and quietly reshaping how we see the world. Grofé may not have set out to influence environmental policy, but that's exactly what his music did. His *Grand Canyon Suite* transformed the canyon into a symbol of pioneer spirit and national pride, even as it swept aside the deeper, more difficult truths about who once lived there and what was lost when they were forced out. In that sense, the suite offers a powerful lesson about saving the American landscape: The stories we tell don't just determine what we choose to protect, but also what we're willing to forget.

WITNESS FOR THE PROSECUTION

. . . . .

On a sunny afternoon in March 2022, President Joseph Biden announced to a group of civil rights advocates and politicians assembled in the Rose Garden that he had just signed into law H.R. 55, the Emmett Till Anti-Lynching Act. The legislation was a long time coming. As Biden explained, "it was over 100 years ago, in 1900, when a North Carolina Representative named George Henry White—the son of a slave, the only Black lawmaker in Congress at the time—first introduced legislation to make lynching a federal crime." That bill, along with "hundreds of similar bills," failed to pass, Biden added, "until today."

The signing of H.R. 55 was broadcast live by all the major news outlets and social media sites. Many of those witnessing the signing, in person and online, responded to the event by referencing the lyrics to "Strange Fruit," a protest song penned in the 1930s by a high school English teacher named Abel Meeropol, under the pen name Lewis Allan. In recent years, much has been written about this song and the performer who first made it famous, Billie Holiday. What hasn't been given as much attention is the full story behind the lyrics—the three concise stanzas, filled with horror and indignation, that took root in Meeropol's mind as a series of calamitous events in the 1930s exposed the nation's indifference to racial injustice.

When Meeropol composed his lyrics, lynchings were nothing new in the United States. Mob killings of black men—for they were almost always black men who were strung up, mutilated, and burned—had been occurring for decades. Although serious attempts had been made after the Red Summer of 1919 to push anti-lynching legislation through Congress, every effort had failed, and W. E. B. Du Bois continued to acknowledge each death by flying a flag outside his Fifth Avenue office that read "A Man was Lynched Yesterday."

The crash of the nation's stock market in 1929, and the economic hardships that followed, sparked an escalation of the violence. The new decade opened with a string of what came to be called "lynch carnivals"—horrific public events that were often organized in advance and drew crowds in the thousands. Meeropol read of these crimes in the press. There was no escaping the shocking details and horrifying photographs.

Two of the most widely reported lynchings occurred in 1930, while the victims were in police custody. On May 9, a black sharecropper from Sherman, Texas, named George Hughes was put on trial for supposedly raping the wife of his employer. When jury selection began, a mob gathered outside the courthouse. As the numbers grew, the protest turned violent. Stones smashed through the courtroom windows as an angry crowd burst through the front doors. The jury was evacuated, and Hughes was led downstairs and locked in a vault for protection until the trial could continue. It was at this point that the mob set fire to the courthouse and sabotaged the firehoses, ensuring that the flames would rage unchecked. When the smoke finally cleared, the vault containing Hughes was the only thing left standing. Using dynamite, the attackers opened the vault and retrieved Hughes's body. He had been asphyxiated by the smoke, but his death did not satisfy the mob. They dragged his corpse to the black business district, where they hung him from a tree and set him on fire. As the flames licked up around his flesh, the tendons in his arms and legs contracted, giving his body the appearance of a charred marionette. A vengeful crowd of several thousand stood and cheered at the gruesome sight. They then set to work burning the homes and businesses of Sherman's black residents.

Several months later, on August 7, a mob gathered in front of the local jail in Marion, Indiana. Three young black men—Tom Shipp, Abe Smith, and James Cameron—had been taken into custody, accused of rape and murder. When the sheriff refused to turn over his prisoners, the mob beat down the jail doors, pulled two of the prisoners, Smith and Shipp, from their cells, and brutally beat them. Shipp was then hung from the window bars of his cell while Smith was dragged outside to the courthouse square, where a large crowd of spectators had gathered. A noose was placed around his neck, and his arms were broken to prevent him from trying to get free. He was then hoisted high in the tree, where he suffered a slow and painful death. Shortly thereafter, some men retrieved Shipp's body from the jail and strung him up next to Smith. The corpses hung in the square for hours, while a celebratory crowd gathered below and gawked at the dreadful handiwork of the lynch mob. It was early morning when the sheriff finally removed the mutilated bodies from the town square.

The horror of these lynchings didn't end with the acts themselves. Attendees collected "trophies," which included everything from locks of the victims' hair and swatches of their singed clothes to amputated body parts. Professional photographers were on the scene as well, eager to document the ghastly event for profit. They printed the images on card stock and sold them as souvenirs. Today, these photos are easily found online. The image of George Hughes's lynching focuses on his charred corpse, with limbs akimbo. In the most famous photo of the Shipp and Smith lynching, the upper half of the image shows the men's mutilated bodies hanging from a tree. Below, a crowd of white spectators smile and socialize, as if the event were nothing more than a late-summer garden party.

In the days following each lynching, photographs documenting these events continued to be sold locally in drugstores and at newsstands. And as news of the horrific crimes spread, the images eventually appeared in nationally syndicated newspapers and magazines. As the Shipp and Smith lynching in Indiana revealed, these crimes against black Americans were not limited to the South. Lynchings were a national problem, and by the mid-1930s, they had occurred in every state of the union but four (all in New England). But it was this press coverage that exposed people across the nation to the horror and prevalence of the practice.

In 1930, Meeropol had just completed his second year teaching at Dewitt-Clinton High School, his alma mater. When he attended DeWitt-Clinton a decade earlier, it was an integrated public school on West 59th

Street (between Hell's Kitchen and San Juan Hill) that catered to the children of recently arrived immigrants and African Americans who had migrated from the South. Meeropol's parents had arrived as refugees, fleeing the anti-Semitic pogroms of what is now western Ukraine. At Dewitt–Clinton, Meeropol proved to be an engaged student, and even wrote the school's anthem—impressive, considering that his classmates included the musicians Thomas "Fats" Waller and Richard Rogers, and writers Lionel Trilling and Countee Cullen. Cullen and Meeropol were especially close. Both wrote for the school's publications, the *Clinton News* and *Magpie*, and both took an interest in social justice issues. In 1920, Cullen published "I Have a Rendezvous with Life" in *Magpie*. The poem is an early expression of racial uplift through art, and within weeks, it was reproduced in newspapers across the city. Meeropol witnessed his friend's success and took note of the power poetry could wield.

Upon graduating in 1921, Meeropol attended City College, where he earned a degree in English. Cullen attended NYU. The two became classmates again in 1925, when they enrolled in the same master's degree program at Harvard. In 1927, Meeropol returned to New York, where he accepted a job teaching English at Dewitt–Clinton. Cullen accepted a position at Frederick Douglass Middle School. The pair kept in touch and even shared some of the same students, the most notable being James Baldwin, who graduated from Frederick Douglass in 1938 and Dewitt–Clinton in 1941. With Cullen's encouragement, Meeropol published his first book, *The Dynasty of Dust and Other Poems*, in 1929. He married Anne Shaffer, whom he had met while serving as the artistic director at Camp Unity, an interracial summer resort in the Berkshire Mountains founded by the Communist Party. Like Meeropol, Shaffer taught in the public school system and was committed to a wide range of social justice issues.

The Meeropols moved to the Bronx when Dewitt–Clinton transferred to a sprawling new campus on Mosholu Parkway in 1929. The official opening day of the new facility—October 29—coincided with the crash of the stock market. In the years that followed, life at Dewitt–Clinton changed dramatically. The school went from a population of 6,275 students in 1926 to over 12,000 students in 1934. In these years, the school's demographics changed as well. The dropout rate rose exponentially as students' families suffered from unemployment, and disciplinary problems multiplied. The percentage of black students increased, from roughly 3 percent to well over 10 percent. In the 1930s, the central identity of Dewitt–Clinton shifted from a "school as academy" model to a "school as solver of all social concerns." This change affected Meeropol, politically and artistically. There was no avoiding the poverty and racial injustice affecting the lives of his students. Meeropol and his wife became more actively involved in the fight for civil rights and economic equality. They joined the teachers' union, became card-carrying members of the Communist Party of the United States of America (CPUSA), and participated in the civil rights–oriented Theatre Arts Committee (TAC). Meeropol also read and contributed regularly to left-wing publications including the NAACP's *The Crisis*, the CPUSA's *New Masses*, and the National Urban League's *Opportunity: Journal of Negro Life*, where Cullen served as an assistant editor.

Like many politically active members of his generation, Meeropol recognized the links between economic inequality and racism, and he supported a new political action organization called the League of Struggle for Negro Rights (LSNR), founded in 1930. The LSNR was closely aligned with the CPUSA. In addition to campaigning against Jim Crow laws and police brutality, the organization opposed fascism abroad and advocated for workers' rights in the United States. From its founding, the LSNR presented itself as an alternative to the NAACP, which it claimed was too closely tied to American capitalism. The conflict between the two groups came to a head in 1932, when the LSNR took the lead in offering legal aid to the Scottsboro Nine, a group of black youths aged thirteen to twenty, who had been falsely accused of raping two white women and given the death penalty in Scottsboro, Alabama. Condemned by the LSNR as a "legal lynching," the Scottsboro case cast a spotlight on the systemic racism plaguing the US justice system. It also led to the drafting of a "Bill of Rights for the Negro People," which demanded that the Roosevelt administration ensure that *all* Americans receive the rights outlined in the nation's constitution.

Meeropol's close friend Cullen responded to the LSNR's efforts. In 1934 he published his poem "Scottsboro, Too, Is Worth Its Song," an emotionally wrought appeal "to [white] American Poets" that criticized their indifference to racial injustice. But it wasn't just poets who seemed to look the other way. On January 9, 1934, an editorial in *New Masses* asked:

> What is the reason for the appalling apathy of the American intellectuals and liberals toward the atrocities perpetrated right here at home? Where is their sensitive liberal conscience? Their fine humanitarian instincts? Their vaunted sense of justice? How can they look a Negro in the face without feeling the burden of the lynchers' guilt upon their own shoulders? ... Is the almost daily shooting, hanging, burning of Negroes a matter simply for anemic commiseration over the dinner table? What will awaken them?

According to the Tuskegee Institute, roughly 3,800 lynchings occurred in the US between 1889 and 1935. The years 1933 to 1936 were especially brutal. As *New Masses* announced in its annual report on racially motivated violence, "Lynch law took the lives of forty-seven Americans in 1933, ten more than in 1932." And these numbers were far from complete. As the report explained, the list did not include "the murder of Negroes by police on slight or no provocation—almost a daily occurrence in Southern and even Northern cities." Accompanying the report was a gruesome illustration by Hyman Warsager of a half-naked black man hanging from a tree, its roots and his limbs extending from a US courthouse. The time had come for another attempt at passing anti-lynching legislation.

On January 5, 1934, two Democratic senators, Edward Costigan of Colorado and Robert F. Wagner of New York, introduced an anti-lynching bill drafted by Walter White, president of the NAACP. Securing anti-lynching legislation had been a priority for the NAACP since its founding in 1909. In fact, when the NAACP adopted "Lift Every Voice and Sing" in 1919 as the "Negro national anthem," Congress was debating a bill, proposed by Representative Leonidas Dyer of Missouri, which would have made lynching a federal crime. The Dyer bill passed in the House in 1922 but was filibustered in the Senate by a group of Southern Democrats who declared the bill an unnecessary incursion on states' sovereignty. Hoping to avoid a similar outcome, Costigan and Wagner approached the problem from a different angle. Instead of focusing on the act of lynching itself as a federal hate crime, their bill encouraged the prosecution of state officials and law enforcement officers who failed to protect prisoners in their custody from vigilante justice. It also proposed charging local municipalities a hefty fine when a lynching occurred within their boundaries. Supporters of the bill described the legislation as a first step towards the abolishment of lynching. Critics, which included the CPUSA and the LSNR, considered it a weak compromise.

Debate over the Costigan–Wagner bill occupied the press for well over a year. This was largely due to the efforts of Walter White, who organized a major art exhibition, co-sponsored by the NAACP and the College Art Association, titled *Art Commentary on Lynching*. He envisioned it as "a union of art and propaganda," and invited artists from across the country to participate, including Isamu Noguchi, Thomas Hart Benton, and José Clemente Orozco. The exhibition was on display from February 15 to March 2 and drew financial support from a notable group of patrons, including George Gershwin. Banned from the exhibition were artists with Communist affiliations, most notably those in the John Reed Club, an artists' alliance associated with the CPUSA. In retaliation, an alliance of Communist-leaning organizations (the John Reed Club, the Artists' Union, the Artists Committee of Action, LSNR, International Labor Defense, and the Vanguard) sponsored a competing exhibition titled *Struggle for Negro Rights*, which opened the day after *Art Commentary on Lynching* closed.

Together, these rival exhibitions drew thousands of attendees. Newspapers and magazines across the nation covered the exhibitions. *Time* magazine described the exhibitions in detail, and discussions of the politics behind the art appeared in *The Crisis*, *Opportunity*, and *New Masses*. One of the most striking works was Noguchi's *Death (Lynched Figure)*, a "pendant mass of silvered realism," slightly smaller than life size, which hung, inert, from an actual rope, its limbs twisting upward. Noguchi based his sculpture on the 1930 photograph of George Hughes's lynching in Sherman, Texas. It was one of the few works to appear in both exhibitions. A haunting photo and detailed description of the sculpture appeared in the March 1935 issue of *New Masses*.

Neither exhibition displayed photographs of lynchings, but in the weeks that followed, newspapers published an array of historic lynching photos that were believed to have inspired the artists. The most widely disseminated images were those of George Hughes in Texas and the Shipp and Smith lynching in Indiana. Added to these was a third, more recent image: the lynching of Rubin Stacy in Fort Lauderdale, Florida, on July 19, 1935. Accused of "threatening and frightening a white woman," Stacy was hung from a pine tree using a wire clothesline and then shot multiple times. As the photograph reveals, a large crowd of spectators gathered to gawk at Stacy's body, among them several young white girls, dressed in pinafores with bows in their hair. The NAACP produced a leaflet condemning the crime. Accompanying the photograph of Stacy's lynching was a damning commentary:

> Do not look at the Negro. His earthly problems have ended. Instead, look at the seven WHITE children who gaze at this gruesome spectacle. Is it horror or gloating on the face of the neatly dressed seven-year-old girl on the right?
>
> Is the tiny four-year-old on the left old enough, one wonders, to comprehend the barbarism her elders have perpetuated?

Intended for a white audience, the leaflet implored readers to "write to your Congressmen and the ... Senators from your state" in support of anti-lynching legislation. It asked readers to think about the future, of the "psychological havoc ... being wrought in the minds of the white children" who witness these crimes. "Into what kinds of citizens will they grow up? What kind of America will they help to make after being familiarized with such an inhuman, law-destroying practice as lynching?"

Questions such as these struck at the heart of Meeropol, the educator and social justice advocate who spent his days mentoring the young men at Dewitt–Clinton High School. During the final months of 1935, while debates over anti-lynching legislation continued to dominate the news, Meeropol set pen to paper and composed the three-stanza poem that changed America:

> *Southern trees bear a strange fruit,*
> *(Blood on the leaves and blood at the root,)*

Black body swinging in the southern breeze,
Strange fruit hanging from the poplar trees.

Pastoral scene of the gallant South
(The bulging eyes and the twisted mouth,)
Scent of magnolia, sweet and fresh,
(And the sudden smell of burning flesh.)

Here is a fruit for the crows to pluck,
For the rain to gather, for the wind to suck,
For the sun to rot, for a tree to drop.
Here is a strange and bitter crop.

Meeropol's poem is arguably one of the most gripping examples of protest literature ever created. It is an emotionally wrought work, fueled by horror and outrage. The poem's power comes from Meeropol's mix of figurative language, evocative imagery, and graphic description. The fruit metaphor of the first verse suggests a sense of normalcy, as if lynched bodies are a regular occurrence in nature. The second verse relies on sensory descriptions. Meeropol interjects evocations of "the gallant South"—its pastoral landscapes and fragrant magnolia blossoms—with graphic images of brutal torture. Even Meeropol's choice of punctuation, the use of parentheses to separate the graphic imagery from the rest of the poem, accentuates the poem's disparate visions of the South; it might even be read as a reflection of white society's desire to unsee or ignore the horrors of lynching. In the final verse, Meeropol uses the fruit metaphor again, this time as a means of highlighting society's indifference to black lives, the "strange and bitter crop" that America has ignored and left "to rot."

Meeropol was once asked what inspired him to write "Strange Fruit." It was "in the early thirties," he responded. "I saw a photograph of a lynching published in a magazine devoted to the exposure and elimination of racial injustice. It was a shocking photograph and haunted me for days. As a result, I wrote 'Strange Fruit' as a poem."

There has been much speculation over which photograph Meeropol was referring to. Many have conjectured that it was the image of Shipp and Smith in Indiana. Certainly, this is the most famous lynching photograph dating from the 1930s, and the stark difference between the lynched bodies above and the reveling spectators below resembles the disparate visions in Meeropol's second verse. That said, many details in the photograph don't match Meeropol's text, and the image of Shipp and Smith never appeared in the magazines "devoted to the exposure and elimination of racial justice" that Meeropol habitually read, namely *New Masses*, *The Crisis*, and *Opportunity*. Perhaps Meeropol got his inspiration from the photo of George White, published in *New Masses* in 1934, or that of Rubin Stacy, which appeared in *The Crisis* in 1935. It hardly matters which photograph haunted Meeropol; what matters is how he responded—by turning art into political protest. "Strange Fruit" was not born from a single image but from years of witnessing the nation's indifference to racial violence. It stands as a fierce outcry, a testament to poetry's power to confront injustice.

Meeropol submitted his poem to *New Masses*, and in February 1936 the magazine offered to publish the poem, but it never appeared. It is not known whether Meeropol withdrew his submission or *New Masses* rescinded its offer due to a change in the political climate; in March, another anti-lynching bill had died in the Senate. Whatever the case, Meeropol resubmitted his poem, this time to the union magazine *New York Teacher*, where it finally appeared in January 1937 under the title "Bitter Fruit."

Meeropol set "Bitter Fruit" to music, changing the title to "Strange Fruit" as a means of separating the two. "My wife, Anne Allan, sang it around at small gatherings," he explained. These included union meetings and cabaret performances hosted by the Theatre Arts Committee. "Laura Duncan, a young black woman with a fine voice," also began singing it "at various places," including "summer camps." In July 1938, Duncan performed the song "at a mass meeting at Madison Square Garden" protesting fascism. In the months that followed, "Strange Fruit" continued to garner attention. "The Teacher's Union chorus presented it at one of their meetings," Meeropol explained. For this performance, Earl Robinson prepared a new arrangement, which was performed again as part of the TAC Cabaret "by four young Black men"—Traverse Crawford, Otho Lee Gaines, Harry Lewis, and Elmaurice Miller—"from the Broadway show *Sing Out the News*." Max Gordon was the producer of *Sing Out the*

News, and it was his brother, Robert H. Gordon, who directed the TAC Cabaret. Like Meeropol, Bob Gordon and the other members of TAC sought "to serve as the voice for all progressive and anti-fascist theatre artists" and to use their art "for the highest purpose it can have—to make this a better world in which to live." In keeping with TAC's commitment to civil rights legislation, their cabaret performances were integrated. In addition to Meeropol's "Strange Fruit," the TAC Cabaret featured readings of James Weldon Johnson's poetry, musical sketches promoting desegregation, and a dramatic reading by Canada Lee about the lynching of a black soldier in uniform upon his return from World War I. Of all these performances, however, Bob Gordon was most taken with "Strange Fruit." Gordon had recently signed on as the talent scout for Café Society, a new Popular Front establishment in Greenwich Village advertised as "The right place for the wrong people." When he heard Meeropol's anti-lynching song, he thought it would be perfect for the club's house singer, Billie Holiday.

Meeropol was familiar with Holiday's style. In 1935, she appeared in Duke Ellington's *Symphony in Black*. One year later, her recording of "Summertime," from Gershwin's *Porgy and Bess*, was declared "a record that has no equals" in the pages of *New Masses*, where Holiday was named "the most original and sincere of the Negro blues singers." The review was written by John Henry, the pen name of Holiday's agent at the time, John Hammond. Hammond had secured Holiday the position of house singer at Café Society.

Located in what had previously been a basement speakeasy on Sheridan Square, Café Society was founded by a former shoe salesman named Barney Josephson, who was frustrated by the racial segregation that defined New York's nightlife. "I wanted a club where blacks and whites worked together behind the footlights and sat together out front." He also wanted to transform entertainment into a tool for social commentary. As he explained to a reporter for the *New Yorker*: "I had been to Europe in the early thirties, and had visited the political cabarets," so "I conceived the idea of presenting some sort of satire" at Café Society, "and alternating it with jazz music." A typical evening included performances from a featured vocalist or dancer, accompanied by a small jazz band. A comedian served as emcee. Like Meeropol, Josephson had strong ties to the

CPUSA. His brother, Leon Josephson, worked as a lawyer for the International Labor Defense and had been one of the leading sponsors of the *Struggle for Negro Rights* art exhibition.

Meeropol liked the idea of Holiday singing "Strange Fruit." He knew she would imbue it with meaning in a way that he and Anne (an amateur singer) never could. So, on a cold evening in January 1939, he made his way to Café Society with a copy of "Strange Fruit" under his arm. Gordon and Josephson had set up the meeting, apparently without Holiday's knowledge. They told Meeropol to wait until after her last set. Once the club closed and the bartenders were sweeping up, Josephson fetched Holiday from the dressing room backstage. She stood by the piano and listened silently as Meeropol played his song. As Meeropol later explained, she didn't take to it at first. "To be perfectly frank, I didn't think she felt comfortable with the song," he said. "Strange Fruit" was markedly "different from the usual genre of songs" she sang, and she was "not communicative at all." But at the urging of Josephson and Gordon, Holiday agreed to add "Strange Fruit" to her set list, and from that day forward, the song became a hallmark of Café Society. As Josephson explained, "I was doing agitprop . . . to me ["Strange Fruit"] was a piece of propaganda."

From the beginning, Holiday's performances of "Strange Fruit" adhered to a choreographed ritual designed for dramatic effect. She reserved the song for the end of her set, and Josephson made sure that all food and drink service stopped ahead of time to avoid the distraction of clinking glasses and plates. As the first chords of the piano accompaniment sounded, all lights in the club went dark except for a single spotlight illuminating Holiday's face. She sang with great emotion—the pain of each line reflected in her voice and expression. At the song's conclusion, Holiday left the stage. "There were no encores after it," Josephson later explained. "People had to remember 'Strange Fruit,' get their insides burned with it."

In her autobiography, Holiday described the first time she sang the song in public. For a moment, she wondered if she had made a mistake. "There wasn't even a patter of applause when I finished. Then a lone person began to clap nervously. Then suddenly everyone was clapping." Meeropol witnessed this performance. "She gave a startling, most dramatic and effective interpretation," he later explained. She "could jolt an audience out of its complacency anywhere. This was exactly what I wanted the song to do and why I wrote it. Billie Holiday's styling of the song was incomparable and fulfilled the bitterness and the shocking quality I had hoped the song would have."

The song's perspective and meaning changed dramatically once Holiday began singing it. No longer a metaphorical tale about the horrors wrought in the "gallant South," the song took on a visceral quality at Café Society. White listeners witnessed the consequences of lynching, the heart-wrenching anger and sorrow. They heard directly the voice of the oppressed and, to a certain extent, became associated with the accused. Black listeners often noted how empowering it felt to witness Holiday's performance in person. "It was incredible, man," noted journalist Vernon Jarret. "She was standing there singing this song as though this was for real, as if she had just witnessed a lynching. That's what knocked me out. I thought she was about to cry." The singer Lena Horne also remembers the first time she heard Holiday perform "Strange Fruit": "[she] was putting into words what so many people had seen and lived through. She seemed to be performing in melody and words the same thing I was feeling in my heart."

Holiday made "Strange Fruit" her own at Café Society, and in doing so changed the meaning and social impact of the song forever. Although she later confessed that singing the song could be emotionally draining, she knew she had no choice. "I have to sing it," she said. "'Fruit' goes a long way in telling how they mistreat Negroes down South."

Throughout the dark winter months of 1939, Holiday's performances of "Strange Fruit" became a must-see attraction for locals and tourists alike. As another attempt at anti-lynching legislation made its way through Congress, Josephson launched an ad campaign in the *New Yorker* that asked readers: "Have you heard 'Strange fruit growing on Southern trees' sung by Billie Holiday at Café Society?" Labor organizers also drew attention to the song. In March 1939, Emanuel Levin quoted the lyrics to "Strange Fruit" in *Fraternal Outlook* (the official magazine of the International Workers Organization) and noted: "This strange fruit is a gruesome warning of the poison that is eating at the very root of American democracy itself." Levin urged his readers to send a copy of Meeropol's text to their congressmen and senators and demand passage of the latest anti-lynching bill "so that we will in some measure be free from the constant dread of a noose, a burnt tree, a dangling body filled with the bullets of a raging mob."

Aware of the mounting popularity of "Strange Fruit," Holiday set her mind to recording the song. She was under contract with Vocalion Records, a subsidiary of Columbia committed to recording black artists, but Columbia argued that the song's controversial subject matter and link to current politics would cause problems for the label in the South. So Holiday reached out to Milt Gabler, a left-leaning fan who ran the independent label Commodore Records out of his music store on West 52nd Street. Gabler jumped at the opportunity to add Holiday to his roster of artists, and on April 20, 1939, Billie Holiday and Her Orchestra (i.e., the eight musicians who played in the house band at Café Society), cut four sides under his guidance. Two months later, "Strange Fruit" was released as the B side to "Fine and Mellow," a seductive blues penned by Holiday herself. The record sold well, reaching number sixteen on the charts in July 1939.

Many have claimed that Meeropol was not credited on Holiday's first recording. This is false. His pen name "Lewis Allan" was listed on the Commodore label as the song's sole composer, and within weeks of the recording's release the New Theatre League, a left-wing federation of small theaters founded in 1935, "printed the song in sheet music form for distribution," which led to additional performances and royalties for Meeropol. As the song's popularity spread, journalists documented its cultural and political impact. In October 1939, Samuel Grafton wrote in the *New York Post*:

> This is about a phonograph record which has obsessed me for two days. It is called "Strange Fruit" and it will, even after the tenth hearing, make you blink and hold on to your chair. Even now, as I think of it, the short hair on the back of my neck tightens and I want to hit somebody. I know who, too . . . If the anger of the exploited ever mounts high enough in the South, it now has its "Marseillaise."

In an article titled "Strange Record," *Time* printed the first verse of "Allan's grim and gripping lyrics" and described it as "a prime piece of musical propaganda" for the NAACP. Shortly thereafter, the editors of *Record Book* praised Holiday's activist contribution: "Billie's sympathetic and faithful interpretation of the realistic lyrics of 'Strange Fruit' makes this one of the most effective of the 'socially conscious' songs." In an open letter to Holiday, a columnist for the *Los Angeles Daily News* claimed that "no expert record collector is without" her recording of "Strange Fruit." He then speculated that Columbia must have "sure kicked themselves" for passing on the recording, since "Strange Fruit" was "one of the greatest of all sellers."

The song drew mixed reviews from the black community. Some, like Walter White, president of the NAACP, praised its powerful visual imagery. Others, most notably Paul Robeson, objected to its portrayal of black people as victims. In June, the *Atlanta Daily World* applauded the "buxom blues singer" for her willingness to stand up against "lynching evils," explaining that she "was moved to have the recording made because of the full significance of the song's value in the fight to wipe out lynching in the United States." The *New York Age* declared it "the first phonograph recording in America of a popular song that has lynching as a theme." And the *Amsterdam News* encouraged its readers to purchase the record: "By all means get a load of the recording of 'Strange Fruit' . . . although you'd never guess from the title, it is a swell bit of propaganda against lynching." In contrast, a reporter for the *Baltimore Afro-American* wondered if Holiday's performance of "Strange Fruit" would "incite or condemn mob action." And Evelyn Cunningham, who worked for the *Pittsburgh Courier*, called the song "a marketing device for [Holiday]."

Many black musicians felt the importance of "Strange Fruit" right away. "When [Holiday] recorded it, it was more than revolutionary," said Max Roach. "She made a statement that we all felt as black folks. No one was speaking out. She became one of the fighters, this beautiful lady who could sing and make you feel things. She became a voice of black people, and they loved this woman."

It helps to put Holiday's recording in perspective. In 1939, Hattie McDaniel, who played Mammy in *Gone with the Wind*, became the first African American woman to win an Oscar—for a role that perpetuated pejorative stereotypes. 1939 also witnessed opera singer Marian Anderson's performance in front of 75,000 people at the Lincoln Memorial, where she was praised for her mastery of classical music. Billie Holiday accomplished something markedly different with her performance of "Strange Fruit." Instead of adhering to a stereotype or performing in a style associated with white European culture, Holiday embodied the reality of racial oppression in America. Her performances of "Strange Fruit," both live and recorded, made her a witness for the prosecution in the nation's legal battles over lynching. In the years that followed, "Strange Fruit" continued to serve as an important tool in the fight against racial violence.

On February 14, 1940, the executive secretary of the Theatre Arts Committee, Sheelagh Kennedy, mailed each member of the US Senate the sheet music to "Strange Fruit." The House had recently voted, 252–131, to pass the Gavagan Anti-Lynching Bill, and, as Kennedy explained in his accompanying letter, he was hoping that Meeropol's song would convince the Senate to follow suit. "America is a nation which has in the past and will increasingly in the future, be called upon to exercise its influence on behalf of persecuted minorities in other parts of the world," he wrote. "It is not beyond the realm of possibility that the good faith of this nation may be questioned if we continue to allow a minority in our own country to be persecuted—murdered by mob violence, which is condemned by the federal government." Kennedy asked senators to study Meeropol's lyrics carefully and to remember that "literally millions of Americans . . . have found the words of 'Strange Fruit' terribly and strangely moving."

The Gavagan Anti-Lynching Bill failed in the Senate, but musicians refused to be silent. Holiday sang "Strange Fruit" at every opportunity. Laura Duncan also continued to perform the song. She sang it at the Golden Gate Ballroom in Harlem as part of Paul Robeson's CPUSA-sponsored pageant *The Negro in American Life*, in March 1940, and throughout the war years she traveled up and down the East Coast, singing "Strange Fruit" at anti-fascist rallies and meetings of the National Negro Congress and the CPUSA. Jazz musician Sidney Bechet added "Strange Fruit" to his nightclub set, and in 1941 he and Willie "The Lion" Smith recorded a haunting instrumental version for Victor Records. Black folk singer Josh White began singing the song, too, and by 1943, it had become a staple of his set list. He first recorded the tune in 1949. White's take on "Strange Fruit" is melancholy in tone yet emotionally charged. His guitar playing is sparse, his voice deep and somber. As the song progresses, the intensity of White's singing increases, building to an emotional release. He holds the final note for several seconds, allowing the full weight of the song's message to sink in.

Musicians were not the only ones to embrace Meeropol's message. In 1943, dancer Pearl Primus premiered a performance of "Strange Fruit" that did not use music. Instead, she interpreted through movement a recitation of Meeropol's lyrics, read by actor Gordon Heath. Primus's work is an evocation of a witness's response to racial violence. "The dance begins," she explained, "as the last person" starts "to leave the lynching ground, and the horror of what she has seen grips her, and she has to do a smooth, fast roll away from that burning flesh." As Heath later explained, the continuation of racial violence charged each performance, and by 1945, they were regularly performing the dance piece at Josephson's Café Society. Primus did not shy away from promoting her version of "Strange Fruit" as a critique of American society. "In America's bosom we have the roots of democracy, but the roots don't mean there are leaves," she explained. "The tree could easily grow bare. We will never relax our war efforts abroad, but we must fight at home with equal fierceness. This is an all-out war; we will not stop fighting until everyone is free from inequality."

The politicization of "Strange Fruit" by left-wing activists eventually led to problems for Meeropol and his associates. On September 8, 1941, Meeropol appeared before the Rapp–Couderet Commission, which had been tasked with identifying Communist infiltration into the New York public school system. Meeropol was questioned about his role in the Teachers' Union, his performances with TAC, and his use of the pseudonym Lewis Allan. He was peppered with questions about his political beliefs and his affiliation with various Communist organizations. Had he ever been a member of CPUSA? No, lied Meeropol. Did the Communists pay him to write "Strange Fruit"? Again, Meeropol answered no. "I wrote 'Strange Fruit' because I hate lynching, and I hate injustice, and I hate the people that perpetuate it."

Shortly after the hearing, Meeropol resigned from his position at Dewitt–Clinton High School and moved to Los Angeles, where his friends from TAC helped him secure freelance work as a songwriter in the film industry. His biggest hit in Hollywood was "The House I Live In," made famous by Frank Sinatra in 1945.

In 1946, the House Un-American Activities Committee (HUAC) began investigating alleged Communist sympathizers, which caused problems for Meeropol once again. The effects of the HUAC investigations, and the public hearings that followed, were devastating for the entertainment industry. Among the hundreds of performers who suffered during what came to be known as the Red Scare were many who had been associated with the promotion of "Strange Fruit."

Barney Josephson and his brother were both targeted by HUAC. Leon went to jail for refusing to name his associates. Barney was forced to close Café Society when the right-wing media tagged it a hotbed of Communist activity. Laura Duncan, Pearl Primus, and Josh White were questioned by HUAC and consequently blacklisted in the 1950s. The government confiscated their passports, which effectively put an end to their careers. To avoid similar persecution, the Meeropols cut all ties with the CPUSA in 1947. But this was to little avail. In 1948, the FBI opened a file on the couple and fervently tracked their activities for the next two decades. As Meeropol later explained, the Red Scare was "an era of repression ... Many writers and others were cruelly blacklisted and hounded. Many of us felt the hot breath of fascism. It was a troublesome period for me."

Curiously, Holiday was never officially accused of being a Communist. Instead, her legal troubles centered around her heroin addiction. In 1947, she was convicted on a federal narcotics charge, for which she spent a year in prison. Shortly after her release in May 1948, she relaunched her career with a concert at Carnegie Hall. The experience of prison changed Holiday, and this change affected her performances of "Strange Fruit." Lynching was now a metaphor for her own tragic struggles. It was "like she was singing to herself" and saying "This is for me. Fuck all of you!'" one observer noted.

> She impressed me as someone who had also been wronged, as if she'd been lynched herself in some fashion or another. There was a sense of resignation as if "these people are going to have power for a long time, and I can't do a damn thing about it

except put it in a song... We're all taking a screwing, someone is messing with us, this is a fucked-up situation"—like she was psychoanalyzing herself and the black condition, telling us there were "no escape" signs up, regardless of how great you were. I don't think it was just that she was high. She was making her peace with her own lynched existence.

Throughout the 1950s, Holiday was the only one still performing "Strange Fruit." The song's Communist affiliations had scared everyone else away. In her final years, Holiday noticed that audiences had become less responsive to the song, too. In 1956, she performed it at a Miami nightclub, and most of the audience stood up and walked out.

Billie Holiday died in 1959, and many people, including Meeropol, believed that the song had died with her. But such was not the case. Carmen McRae and Nina Simone revived the song in the 1960s in response to the violence against African Americans during the height of the civil rights movement. In the decades that followed, a variety of performers recorded the song as an act of artistic activism. In 1999, *Time* magazine named "Strange Fruit" the "song of the century." Three years later, the Library of Congress added Holiday's 1939 performance to the National Recording Registry. Over the last two decades, "Strange Fruit" has continued to grow in popularity.

The election of Donald Trump and the rise of the Black Lives Matter movement led to renewed interest in "Strange Fruit." In 2017, Rebecca Ferguson, a British singer of Jamaican descent, was asked to perform at Trump's first inauguration. Ferguson, who made her mark in 2010 singing Sam Cooke's civil-rights anthem "A Change is Gonna Come" as a contestant on *The X-Factor UK*, said she would consider the invitation on one condition: "You allow me to sing 'Strange Fruit,' a song that has huge historical importance." Needless to say, her request was denied.

Writer Kenya Barris also noted the rising importance of "Strange Fruit" after Trump's election. Barris used Nina Simone's version of the song in a 2017 episode of his award-winning television series *black-ish*, noting that the music represented those who "felt like they were not part of this election or their voice wasn't counted."

During Trump's first term as president, the nation's awareness of violence against people of color grew exponentially. Black Lives Matter took the nation by storm, and politicians responded. In 2018, Senator Kamala Harris proposed the Justice for Victims of Lynching Act, which passed in the Senate but was denied a vote in the House of Representatives by the Republican Speaker of the House, Paul Ryan. Two years later, on February 26, 2020, the House passed a revised version of Harris's bill, now titled the Emmett Till Anti-Lynching Act. This time, passage in the Senate was blocked by Republican Rand Paul. But that was not the end of the fight for justice. On May 21, 2020, the murder of George Floyd by white policemen rocked the national consciousness. Like the photos that had circulated a century earlier, the video of the graphic violence and inhumanity of Floyd's murder forced America's citizens to pay attention. Once again, Meeropol's "Strange Fruit," as performed by Billie Holiday, served as an historic witness for the prosecution. As Representative Eddie Bernice Johnson of Texas explained when she addressed her congressional colleagues on February 23, 2021:

> I rise today to recognize the extraordinary achievements in the life of Billie Holiday—a gifted vocalist, a dedicated activist, and a cultural icon.... Amid heightened racial tensions in the 1930s, Billie Holiday introduced a new genre of protest-melody. In her hit rendition of "Strange Fruit," she posed an unapologetic and uncensored challenge to the injustice of lynching Black Americans at one of the darkest moments of history in our nation. Burdened by the weight of the song's message and facing public backlash, she continued to perform and record it to reach a greater audience. Despite the vitriolic backlash, "Strange Fruit" quickly became the unofficial anthem of the anti-lynching movement and was an early mantra towards the success of the larger civil rights movement.

Representative Kweisi Mfume expressed a similar message:

> "Strange Fruit," written by Abel Meeropol and recorded by Billie Holiday in 1939, captures the sadness and sadistic nature of lynchings in America.... The Emmett Till Anti-Lynching

Act will serve as a prosecutorial weapon to put an end to the vile practice of lynching that has contributed to racial violence in the United States for far too long. It is a bill that provides some degree of healing for a nation that still hasn't fully come to grips with the violent racism of its past and will serve as a way forward to deal with "the strange fruits hanging from its (sick) poplar tree."

More than any other song, "Strange Fruit" has changed America. It has become a part of the nation's past and present. Meeropol planted a seed when he wrote "Strange Fruit," and performers like Billie Holiday, Pearl Primus, and Josh White gave it the required nourishment. Now, nearly a century later, the successful passage of the Emmett Till Anti-Lynching Act reveals that the song has finally germinated and taken root.

A NEW VISION FOR AMERICA

•••••

Not every important intersection between Congress and music revolves around legislation. On May 23, 1953, composer Aaron Copland received a telegram that made his blood run cold:

> YOU ARE HEREBY DIRECTED TO APPEAR BEFORE THIS COMMITTEE ON MONDAY MAY TWENTYFIFTH AT TWO THIRTY PM ROOM 357 SENATE OFFICE BUILDING WASHINGTON DC –
>
> JOE MCCARTHY CHAIRMAN SENATE PERMANENT SUBCOMMITTEE ON INVESTIGATIONS

As disturbing as the missive was, it did not come as a surprise. The FBI had been tracking Copland's activities for several years, and his name had appeared countless times on lists of suspected Communists compiled by the House Un-American Activities Committee. Its interest in Copland was the result of Senate Republicans' obsession with rooting out supposed Communist infiltration of the US government. For Copland, it all began in 1949, when *Life* magazine published photographs of fifty "hardworking fellow-travelers" and "soft-headed do-gooders" who had reportedly been duped into supporting Communist causes. These "subversives" were not "the most notorious" Communists, the article explained, but rather the most influential. Alongside Copland were photos of composers Leonard Bernstein and Dean Dixon, actor Charles Chaplin, scientist Albert Einstein, writers Langston Hughes, Thomas Mann, and Norman Mailer, and Congressman Adam Clayton Powell Jr.

One year later, Copland's name appeared on a more expansive list, the notorious *Red Channels* report, published by the right-wing journal *Counterattack*, which led to the blacklisting of the musician and activist Josh White, among others. *Red Channels* fueled a series of political investigations into the entertainment industry over the next few years, and in 1953 Copland became a target. For several months, Senator McCarthy's Permanent Sub-Committee on Investigations into Communist Activities pursued Copland relentlessly, causing the cancellation of commissions and performances of his music and the severing of ties to several universities.

One of the most puzzling things about McCarthy's attack was the fact that during the years Copland was supposedly participating in un-American activities, he was composing music that was generally heralded, by audiences and politicians alike, as patriotic Americana. In history books and documentaries, Copland is regularly referred to as the "Dean of American Music"—a composer whose most famous works, with their slow-changing harmonies and expansive lyricism, evoke the pioneer spirit and vast plains of rural America. Copland is best known for the pieces he composed in the early 1940s: *Lincoln Portrait* (1942), *Rodeo* (1942), *Fanfare for the Common Man* (1942), and *Appalachian Spring* (1944). What few listeners realize, however, is that Copland's commitment to writing music for the people was fed in many ways by his early interest in the cultural and political goals of the Popular Front, a loose alliance of progressive political organizations that emerged in the 1930s.

Copland was born in Brooklyn, New York, on November 14, 1900, the youngest of five children. Like Gershwin, he was the son of Jewish Russian immigrants. Unlike Gershwin, his musical training was firmly grounded in the traditions of European classical music. In his youth, Copland studied classical piano, music theory, and composition with private tutors. These pursuits were funded by the profits from his father's successful department store. At age twenty, Copland left for Paris, where he began studies at the Conservatoire américain de Fontainebleau with the renowned pedagogue Nadia Boulanger. Copland had reservations, at first, about studying with Boulanger. "No one to my knowledge had ever before thought of studying with a woman," he confessed. But three years under her tutelage proved transformative. "It was wonderful for me to find a teacher with such openness of mind... The confidence she had in my talents and her belief in me were at the very least flattering and more—they were crucial to my development at this time of my career."

Copland returned to New York in 1924, just in time to witness the public's excitement over the premiere of Gershwin's *Rhapsody in Blue*. He didn't get what all the fuss was about. In the years that followed, Copland offered his own take on jazz-infused music with his *Music for Theatre* (1925), Piano Concerto (1926), and Piano Variations (1930). He didn't reference Gershwin the way Ellington had in *Creole Rhapsody* and *Symphony in Black*. Instead, he opted to ignore Gershwin completely. In these early works, Copland challenged audiences with his use of extended dissonances and clashing rhythms. Nonetheless, comparisons to Gershwin were made. After the premiere of Copland's Piano Concerto, a reporter asked him what he thought of "Mr. Gershwin's jazz." Copland replied: "Gershwin is serious up to a point. My idea was to intensify it. Not what you get in the dance hall but to use it cubistically—to make it more exciting than ordinary jazz."

Copland's disdain for Gershwin's success was rooted in more than the music. Simply put, Gershwin's embrace of capitalism offended Copland, who began taking an interest in left-wing politics in the late 1920s. While Gershwin was playing his *Variations on "I Got Rhythm"* to sold-out audiences across the country in 1934, Copland was giving speeches at Communist political rallies and publishing the pro-labor protest song "Into the Streets, May 1st" for the Workers' Music League.

Like Abel Meeropol, the left-wing composer of "Strange Fruit," Copland viewed Communism as an anecdote to the inequalities created by American capitalism. Although Copland never became a card-carrying member of the Communist Party of the United States of America, he toyed with joining the Socialist Party, and in collaboration with the CPUSA he fought for workers' rights and social justice issues. Copland's interest in music and politics came together during his early involvement with the Pierre Degeyter Club, a workers' music alliance named after the composer of the Communist anthem "The Internationale." Copland became a founding member of the Composers' Collective, a subgroup within the Degeyter Club committed to creating proletarian music as a tool on the cultural front. His close colleague in the Collective was Charles Seeger, father of Pete Seeger, who would later play a prominent role in the folk music revival of the 1960s. In the 1930s, Pete attended meetings of the Collective with his father, and he remembered hearing Copland talk about the power of music to effect political change. "I got the feeling that here were people out to change the world. The world might be corrupt, but they were confident they could change it."

Copland's engagement with the Composers' Collective led to a transition in his musical style, from the abstract, modernist compositions of the 1920s to a more accessible, populist style in the 1930s and 1940s. He grew interested in the idea of creating distinctly American music that featured simple, memorable melodies and rhythmic patterns drawn from American folk traditions. He also began to use more conventional harmonic structures and tonalities, which made his music more accessible.

Three of the earliest works to reflect Copland's interest in a new, approachable style were the tone poem *El Salón México* (1936), with its sonic references to various social classes; his first ballet, *Billy the Kid* (1938), which evoked an idyllic frontier threatened by industrialization; and his film score for *The City*, a documentary produced for the 1939 World's Fair as part of the exhibit "City of Tomorrow." *The City* presented a damning image of the destruction and inequality wrought by capitalism during the industrial age, and Copland's music played a decisive role in drawing a distinction between "the wasteland of dehumanizing machines, environmental pollution, and anonymous masses" of the city and the "good life" that arises when communities are designed with nature, clean air, and fresh water in mind. Copland's soundtrack, with its contrast of abstract dissonance (industrialization) and slow-changing harmonies and expansive lyricism (nature-centered suburbs), promoted an idyllic American future, free of industrial waste and economic suffering.

Throughout the 1940s, Copland continued to compose one populist work after another, expanding, with each success, his new vision for America. For example, in *Lincoln Portrait*, for orchestra and narrator, Copland pieced together a subtly socialist message using quotes from the president's most famous speeches. And in *Rodeo*, Copland's second ballet set in the Southwest, he promoted progress and social change through a celebratory portrayal of working-class cowboys. Copland's *Fanfare for the Common Man*, a work for brass and percussion composed in response to the United States's entry into World War II, took its title from "The Century of the Common Man," a speech delivered by the pro-Soviet vice president Henry Wallace in 1942 that defined the war as a struggle for social justice: "This is a fight between a slave world and a free world," declared Wallace. "Just as the United States in 1862 could not remain half slave and half free, so in 1942 the world must make its decision for a complete victory one way or another." Although rarely discussed, a similar sentiment served as the foundation for Copland's most enduring work, the music he composed for Martha Graham's ballet *Appalachian Spring*.

The story of *Appalachian Spring* begins in July 1942, when Elizabeth Sprague Coolidge, a wealthy patron of the arts, commissioned the choreographer Martha Graham to produce two ballets to be performed in October 1943 at the Library of Congress in Washington, DC. Coolidge is important in the history of American concert music. In an effort to encourage a new generation of serious music-makers, she offered financial support to young composers and, in the 1920s, financed two prominent initiatives: the establishment of a foundation committed to the promotion of contemporary chamber music in the United States and abroad, and construction of a concert hall at the Library of Congress that still bears her name. Coolidge's linking of her philanthropy to the Library of Congress was not by chance. A central goal of her patronage was to associate the nation's political interests to its musical activities. To this day, the Coolidge Auditorium hosts numerous music events each year, many of which relate to important cultural and political issues.

Coolidge left it to Graham to find the composers for her ballets, and Graham thought of Copland right away. She had choreographed to his music before—in 1931 she had used his Piano Variations as the score for her ballet *Dithyrambic*—and the prospect of collaborating with Copland on a newly-conceived work excited her.

Copland agreed to work with Graham on one condition: that he have some say in the ballet's narrative, length, and instrumentation. Graham agreed and immediately sent him the script for a Medea-themed narrative called "Daughter of Colchis." Copland rejected this proposal outright and requested that Graham come up with something more firmly tied to American history. To give her a sense of what he had in mind, he suggested something similar in tone to the film *Our Town*, for which he had supplied the soundtrack two years earlier. Based on the play by Thornton Wilder, *Our Town* portrays everyday life in the small town of Grover's Corners, New Hampshire. Copland was proud of his score, which had been nominated for an Oscar, and he was interested in writing something like it again. Graham took the suggestion to heart, and several months later, in May 1943, she sent Copland a new scenario: a Civil War drama titled "House of Victory," which Copland found markedly more appealing. In her outline of the narrative, Graham described it as "a legend of living in the AMERICAN PLACE... the kind of living that makes the village and the small town." She described a work ripe with emotion: "There will be moments of great dramatic urgency, of conflict and anguish, side by side with moments of lyric awareness of the most simple things of living—a sense of countryside, fields and the usual in a people's life." Regarding the scenery, she envisioned a minimalist set: "There will be no heavy constructions; only the frame of a doorway, a platform of the porch, a Shaker rocking chair with a bone-like simplicity of line, and an old-fashioned rope swing." The sole cultural reference—Shaker—sparked Copland's imagination. On June 8, 1943, he wrote to Harold Spivake, head librarian at the Library of Congress: "I think I have my first theme!" That theme was "Simple Gifts," a hymn composed by the Shaker elder Joseph Brackett in 1848.

Copland's interest in the Shakers is not surprising. In mid-century scholarship, the Shakers' commitment to rural life, egalitarianism, and communal living was presented as a progressive alternative to the rise of capitalism, a form of "religious communism." Also appealing to Copland was the high value the Shakers placed on music and dance. In his search for a Shaker tune, Copland consulted Edward Andrews Deming's *The Gift to Be Simple: Songs, Dances and Rituals of the American Shakers*. Published in 1940, the book offered a mix of historical information and transcribed songs. As Copland later explained, "Simple Gifts" was "unknown to the general public" when he first came upon it, but there was something in its lilting melody that spoke to him right away. It seemed "ideal for Martha's scenario and for the kind of austere movements associated with her choreography."

In her "House of Victory" script, Graham outlined a series of events that defined small-town life in early America. Set in a fictional locale called Eden Valley, the narrative featured four principal characters: the Mother, who serves as "the matriarch, the constant figure that exists regardless of time and period;" the Daughter, who embodies "what one thinks of as the Pioneer Woman"; the Citizen, her future husband, who represents "the kind of man that became the abolitionist, the John Brown"; and the Fugitive, "the man who is hunted, persecuted," and marked by his "unconscious agony for freedom." As Graham described in a note to Copland, the presence of the Fugitive was vital to the ballet's message, and she was depending on him to define the character through music: "He is really the slave figure of the Civil War, but should have a broader meaning as well. He will be seen in the half-light and shadows. There will be a real sense of dance about him. Whether you want to use a negro melody, a sense of frantic simple prayer or not, is up to you." The other characters in the ballet (a Younger Sister, Two Children, and Neighbors), would play less prominent roles. Their primary purpose, as Graham explained it, was to flesh out the community and offer a contrast to the principals.

As Copland began work on the score, he wrote to Graham requesting edits to the script. Although "House of Victory" showed promise, and he embraced the Civil War narrative, changes would need to be made before he could complete a full score. To begin, he was wary of Graham's plan to include recitations of Bible passages throughout the ballet. He also rejected her desire to include scenes from Harriet Beecher Stowe's *Uncle Tom's Cabin* in the ballet's narrative. The appearance of the Fugitive, and his interactions with the Citizen, would be enough, Copland believed, to communicate the ballet's central message of America's fight for justice.

Graham acquiesced, and in July she sent Copland a revised scenario. No longer titled "House of Victory," the document was simply labeled "Name?" Gone were the scenes of *Uncle Tom's Cabin* and many of the biblical passages. In their place was a new symbol of identity and unity, a character identified as "an Indian Girl," whom Graham envisioned as the spiritual anchor of the ballet. Graham got her idea for this character from "The Dance," an idyllic verse in Hart Crane's epic poem *The Bridge* (1930), which attempts to "revitalize the native past" and "link it to national lore" and the beauty of nature. In her revised script, Graham acknowledged that Copland might not like her addition of the Indian Girl. Nonetheless, she believed the character's inclusion was important.

> There is no reason in one sense for her to be there, that is the purely realistic sense. And yet she is always with us ... in the names of our cities, rivers, states, and in the play of all of us as children. We can never escape the sense of her having been here and of her continual existence as the supreme spectator to all our happenings. She is the symbolic figure of the land, the Eve of our Genesis.

In her efforts to convince Copland to embrace the Indian Girl, Graham assured him that he would not be expected to "write Indian music as we call it," and she noted that the character "will in no sense do Indian dancing." Instead, she would "add to a sense of place" since "she is deep in our nostalgia." Graham envisioned the Indian Girl as a symbol of the nation's forgotten past: "There is nothing exactly native about [her]," Graham noted. "She is not an Indian's Indian but a white person's Indian." This last line, no doubt, troubled Copland.

Copland had witnessed the chaos that could ensue when "the Indian" was venerated as a symbol of America by non-Natives. In 1913, then President Taft signed a bill into law allotting federal lands near the Statue of Liberty for the construction of a National American Indian Memorial. The plan received broad coverage in the press and healthy support among local politicians and residents, but it was never realized. The essential problem was a disagreement over the monument's message. Was it a tribute to the indigenous people who had lost their lives and been pushed from their lands, a monument of victory over the Indians by white settlers, or a memorial to a vanishing race? Copland had no interest in confronting such questions in his ballet music. So, instead, he began working from the new script, but without reference to the Indian Girl. Over the next eleven months, he composed music around eight central scenes described in Graham's script.

The first three scenes (Prologue, Eden Valley, and Wedding Day) reflected what Graham had defined as "the lyric awareness of simple things," of creating a new community in a new land. These were followed by an Interlude, for which Graham had suggested that Copland compose "a theme and variations rondo" as a way of capturing "the simplicities of a telescoped day in which people behave as though working and playing together in a common bond of time and place." For this scene, Copland implemented "Simple Gifts" as the unifying theme. Scenes five through seven (Fear in the Night, Day of Wrath, and Moment of Crisis) evoked the racial conflict of the Civil War. The Fugitive appears, distraught and fearful. The Citizen rushes to protect him, then departs to fight for justice. The final scene, The Lord's Prayer, expressed the peace that returns once the conflict is resolved. As Graham explained in a later draft of the script: "This could have the feeling of either a Shaker meeting where the movement is strange and ordered ... or it could have a feeling of a negro church with the lyric ecstasy of the spiritual about it.... It is the sort of thing felt on Sunday in a small town."

Copland worked on the music in fits and starts. Although the opening scene "was almost done" by mid-July 1943, completing the ballet in time for the scheduled premiere in October was out of the question. Copland was in Hollywood, entrenched in a pro-Russian film project, *The North Star*, about Germany's invasion of Ukraine, and Graham was encountering delays in the other ballet she had commissioned for the event. Consequently, both performances were postponed, and Copland continued to work on the score between other obligations, sharing excerpts with Graham whenever possible.

In January 1944, Graham started mapping out the choreography. Copland had completed roughly half of the score at this point, and Graham hounded him for more. Five months later, in June 1944, he sent her the complete piano score and a homemade piano recording she could use in rehearsals. Graham was thrilled. On August 5, she wrote to Copland: "The music is so knit and of a completeness that it takes you in very strong hands and leads you into its own world"—so much so that "I have been ... cursing over that not-so-good script," she confessed. "But what you did from that has made me change [my ballet] in many places.... I will not stop to tell you all about it," she continued, "but I am excited." Graham concluded by praising Copland's choice for the central musical theme: "I also know that the gift to be simple will stay with people and give them great joy."

While Copland spent the summer in Mexico orchestrating the work (originally scored for thirteen instruments: flute, clarinet, bassoon, piano, four violins, two violas, two cellos, and bass), Graham worked in her New York studio finalizing the ballet's visual elements, namely the set and choreography.

The set was created by the Japanese American sculptor Isamu Noguchi, the artist whose "Death" sculpture had caused such controversy in the lynching exhibitions sponsored by the NAACP and the CPUSA in 1935. Noguchi's career was just taking off when the Japanese bombed Pearl Harbor in 1941. In response to the backlash against Japanese Americans, he voluntarily traveled to Arizona and entered the Poston Internment Camp, the largest of ten concentration camps set up by the US government during World War II. Noguchi spent six months at the camp, and shortly after his release Graham hired him to create the sets for *Appalachian Spring*. Using spare lines and open spaces, Noguchi's minimalist set faithfully brought to life the vision Graham had described in the first "House of Victory" script: "a new town, someplace where the first fence has just gone up." As Copland later explained, the "farmyard was suggested by a simple fence rail and the house a peaked entrance and one wall.... The rocking chair for the Pioneer Woman was only the suggestion of a chair." Commissioning Noguchi for the set was "a real breakthrough," claimed Erick Hawkins, one of the original dancers. "Dancing in Noguchi's sets, you felt you were in a world that the great sculptor had created, a whole new world, one that was not on a stage."

The premiere of *Appalachian Spring* finally took place on October 30, 1944, a year later than originally planned. The occasion was nonetheless festive. Elizabeth Sprague Coolidge was celebrating her eightieth birthday, and the auditorium bearing her name was filled with foreign dignitaries, members of Congress, and their staff. Copland had not attended any of the rehearsals, but he made an effort to be there for the first performance. As he took his seat between Coolidge and Graham and looked at the playbill, one of the first things he noted was the ballet's title: *Appalachian Spring*. Where had that come from? Copland and Graham had never settled on a title, and when Copland had submitted his final score several months earlier, it was simply labeled "Ballet for Martha." As Graham explained, *Appalachian Spring* was a last-minute decision.

It came from a line in Hart Crane's *The Bridge*, and she chose it because she liked the way it sounded. Although Copland had nixed her idea of an Indian Girl, a reference to her origins was embedded in Graham's title for the ballet.

As Copland continued to peruse the playbill, he noted yet another change. Much to his surprise, Graham had drastically changed the narrative and cast of their ballet. A brief synopsis described the new narrative:

> Part and parcel of our lives is that moment of Pennsylvania spring when there was "a garden eastward of Eden." Spring was celebrated by a man and woman building a house with joy and love and prayer; by a revivalist and his followers in their shouts of exaltation; by a pioneering woman with her dreams of the Promised Land.

Like the *Grand Canyon Suite*, one of the most fascinating aspects of *Appalachian Spring* is not the story it tells in its final version, but rather the story that was abandoned over the course of the work's evolution. As Graham's brief synopsis reveals, she condensed the cast and transformed the plot after receiving the final score from Copland. In addition to changing the identities of the principal characters, she removed all references to the Civil War and the horrors of enslavement. In its new iteration, The Mother, Daughter, and Citizen were now identified as a Pioneering Woman, Bride, and Husbandman. Instead of the Fugitive, audiences encountered a revivalist preacher and his four female followers. The dark music that Copland had composed as a representation of the fear and violence associated with the enslaved man's attempted escape now stood for the fire and brimstone of evangelical fury. As Copland put it, the "music composed for one kind of action, had been used to accompany something else."

With her revisions to the ballet's cast and narrative, Graham imbued Copland's music with a meaning that departed greatly from his original intention. As Annegret Fauser has noted in her excellent exploration of the ballet, "*Appalachian Spring* became a work about white America for white audiences." It presented a mythical narrative of the nation's founding and pioneering spirit, rather than a sobering tale of racial conflict.

Copland took the changes in stride, considering them part and parcel of artistic collaboration. *Appalachian Spring* wasn't the first time the "meaning" of his music had been altered by others. In 1936, Copland had composed "Ballad of Ozie Powell," a musical setting of Langston Hughes's poem memorializing the unjust imprisonment of one of the Scottsboro Boys. The following year, Copland submitted the score to CBS for national broadcast. CBS aired the premiere under the generic title "Music for Radio" and asked listeners to send in their suggested titles for the work. *Saga of the Prairie* was deemed the winning submission. Thus, Copland's tribute to a wrongfully convicted black man was recast by his sponsors into an homage to the pioneer spirit of westward expansion. Similarly, Copland's musical depiction of a black man escaping enslavement in "Ballet for Martha" became the soundtrack for a white, revivalist preacher in *Appalachian Spring*.

The question arises: Why did Graham make these changes? She never discussed her revision in any detail, and for several decades the content of the original scripts was not public knowledge. As Graham expressed in her correspondence with Copland, by the time she received his final score in July 1944 she had become disenchanted with her original "not so good script." The mood of the nation had changed considerably since they had embarked on their project. Vice President Wallace, who had described World War II as "a fight between a slave world and a free world," had recently fallen from favor, and Roosevelt had dropped him from the national ticket. Also different was the nation's attitude toward the war. With each passing month, the promise of an Allied victory seemed more certain. Graham picked up on the growing optimism and, in an effort to respond to the new political climate, she changed the focus of her ballet from a contemplation of America's struggle against injustice to a celebration of its pioneering spirit and future possibilities. As Erick Hawkins explained, "We all had such wonderful hope." *Appalachian Spring* promised a bright future for the nation. "It was a time when we all thought that American art was going to blossom and continue to blossom."

Appalachian Spring was hailed by critics and audiences alike. In the months that followed, Graham took the ballet on a national tour and Copland created an orchestral suite, also titled *Appalachian Spring*, which was performed by leading orchestras across the country. Although Copland described the suite as "a condensed version of the ballet" that contained "all essential features" of the original, this was not entirely true. In his version for the concert stage, Copland eliminated completely the eight minutes of dark, discordant music he had originally composed to accompany the struggles and fear of the fugitive slave. The result—the *Appalachian Spring* with which most of us are more likely to be familiar—is a musical work free of conflict and self-doubt: an upbeat celebration of small-town life in rural America.

Looking back on the reception history of *Appalachian Spring*, one thing becomes clear: the composition's early success had much to do with a change in political mood. On May 8, 1945, the front page of the *New York Times* featured two stories that struck Copland as monumental: Allied forces had won the war over fascism in Europe, and *Appalachian Spring* had been awarded the Pulitzer Prize in Music.

The Pulitzer Prize is one of the most prestigious awards in American arts and letters. Created in 1917 as "an incentive to excellence" in the fields of journalism, literature, drama, and education, the prize was awarded to those who displayed a "clearness of style, moral purpose," and the "power to influence public opinion in the right direction" in their respective fields. The Pulitzer Prize in Music was introduced twenty-six years later, during the height of World War II. According to the guidelines, it was awarded for a "distinguished musical composition in the larger forms of chamber, orchestral or choral music, or for an operatic work (including ballet), performed or published during the year by a composer of established residence in the United States."

Like the prizes in other fields, the Pulitzer Prize in Music acknowledged a work that reportedly opened America's eyes to the truth and promoted public good. William Schuman's Secular Cantata No. 2: *A Free Song* received the first prize in 1943. Using texts by Walt Whitman, this two-movement work for orchestra and chorus captured the mood of a nation at war. As Schuman explained: "The first movement is a kind of requiem but more than just a prayer for the dead—it points a lesson. The second movement is in complete contrast and is in the nature of a very militant 'pep talk.'" Schuman composed the cantata as an act of public service. "Since I cannot serve in the Specialist Corps, I am trying to do what I can with my pen," he explained. "If I've done my job well it can't help but be a moving patriotic affair." The second Pulitzer Prize in Music went to Howard Hanson for his Symphony No. 4, Opus 34 ("Requiem"). Hanson composed the piece in memory of his father, but the grandeur of the music struck listeners as more universal in scope. Each of the work's movements takes its title from a section of the Requiem mass, and in 1944, as the number of US military fatalities increased, Hanson's symphony resonated with a nation at war.

Copland was the third American composer to be awarded the Pulitzer Prize in Music, and by the time *Appalachian Spring* premiered, the nation was ready for an uplifting message. A "real triumph" was how John Martin, a critic for the *New York Times*, described *Appalachian Spring*. "Aaron Copland has written a score of fresh and singing beauty," he claimed. "It is, on its surface, a piece of early Americana, but in reality it is a celebration of the human spirit.... There is throughout the work a very moving sense of the future, of the fine and simple idealism which animates the highest human motives."

The success of *Appalachian Spring* was built on Copland's ability to create in musical tones what many listeners interpreted as a sonic symbol of the nation's pioneering spirit. In many ways, the work served as the apex of the "music for the people" that Copland had been creating since the 1930s, when the adoption of hymns and folk tunes played an important role in the creation of an American sound. But once the war ended and fears about the Soviet Union and Communism began to increase, accessible, proletarian music began to be seen in conservative circles as an indication of anti-American activities.

An early sign of the trouble to come involved the Motion Picture Alliance for the Preservation of American Ideals (MPA), a political action group cofounded by Walt Disney. In 1947, the MPA published a pamphlet for filmmakers advising avoidance of "subtle communistic touches" in their films. The pamphlet included a list of ideological prohibitions: "Don't smear the free-enterprise system... Don't smear industrialists... Don't smear wealth... Don't smear the profit motive... Don't deify the 'common man'... Don't glorify the collective." The checklist read like a prohibition of Copland's populist style and the compositions that had brought him national fame. Right-wing politicians paid attention to the prohibitions and soon set their sights on actors and musicians whose work reflected "un-American" ideas.

Copland's public support of the Progressive Party candidate, Henry Wallace, in the 1948 presidential election did little to dissuade his critics. They also found his public declarations in favor of stronger US–Soviet relations troubling. In March 1949, Copland attended the Cultural and Scientific Conference for World Peace at the Waldorf-Astoria Hotel in New York. Here, left-leaning American artists and scholars from all disciplines interacted with their Soviet counterparts in an event *Time* magazine called "a comic opera" with "tragic implications." Copland delivered a speech as part of the conference's Fine Arts Panel. In his address, he criticized the US government and its promotion of Cold War policies. "I am here this morning as a democratic American artist... not at all interested in doctrinaire Communism, but very much interested... in the policies of the United States, and in how those policies will affect artists in the United States." Copland criticized the polarization of US politics since the end of the war: "There is a concerted effort on the part of the press and radio to convince the American people that nothing remains for us but to make a choice between two diametrically opposed systems of thought... blacks and whites, East and West, Communism and the Profit System." Most importantly, he described what he saw as the negative effects of current political policies on artists in the United States:

> Lately I've been thinking that the Cold War is almost worse for art than the real thing—for it permeates the atmosphere with fear and anxiety. An artist can function at his best only in a vital and healthy environment for the simple reason that the very act of creation is an affirmative gesture. An artist fighting in a war for a cause he holds just has something affirmative he can believe in. The artist, if he can stay alive, can create art. But throw him into a mood of suspicion, ill-will and dread that typifies the Cold War attitude and he'll create nothing.

Copland described the arbiters of the Cold War as "men who have lost faith—men who are intent upon stirring up fears and hatreds that can only breed destruction." He warned: "No art can thrive for long in that kind of world." Cultural barriers between nations only worsen the problem. "How unfortunate," he concluded, "that our lawmakers have so little conception of the way... our composers, painters, and writers might be used... to draw closer bonds between our people and those of other nations."

Copland's speech caught the attention of journalists, who distorted his message. Instead of reporting the composer's call for greater understanding among nations, he was pegged as a "soft-headed do-gooder" with Communist inclinations. In the months that followed, his leftist views led to increased scrutiny. In 1950, his name was added to an FBI list of politically suspicious artists, and in 1953, a performance of *Lincoln Portrait* planned for President Eisenhower's inauguration was withdrawn from the program. The cancellation caused an uproar in the press, and the congressman who had instigated it—Fred E. Busbey, a Republican from Illinois—defended his actions in a speech in the House of Representatives. Busbey began by explaining that the cancellation of *Lincoln Portrait* had nothing to do with Copland's talent as a composer, and everything to do with his political affiliations:

> As I have but a passing knowledge of music, I cannot and do not offer any comments on the quality of Mr. Copland's work. However, when I learned that this piece of music was to be played at the inaugural concert, I voiced my objections with all the vigor at my command. My objections were based on but one thing—the known record of Aaron Copland for activities, affiliations, and sympathies with and for causes that seemed to me to be more in the interest of an alien ideology than the things representative of Abraham Lincoln...

Busbey portrayed the potential inclusion of Copland's music in the inaugural festivities as a continuation of Communism's threat to democracy:

> For nearly 20 years, the Communist Party devoted time and effort to infiltrating the various departments of our Federal Government while the Democrats were in control of the

executive branch.... I fought this infiltration of government under the Democratic Party, and I assure you I will continue to fight this infiltration under the Republican Party.

For several minutes, Busbey railed against the many "Communist fronts" that had "mushroomed over the years" in the United States. He then doubled down on his decision to cancel Copland's music:

> With all the music of fine, patriotic, and thoroughly American composers available to the concert committee of the Inauguration Committee, 1953, I not only questioned the advisability of using music by a composer with the long record of questionable affiliations of Mr. Copland, as reported by the House Committee on Un-American Activities, but protested the use of his music.
>
> I sincerely believe the Republican Party would have been ridiculed from one end of the United States to the other by the press, columnists, and radio commentators if any of Copland's music was played at the inauguration. Whether or not I was justified in the stand I took, I will leave to you, after you have carefully read the record of Aaron Copland, as furnished to me by the House Committee on Un-American Activities.

At this point, Busbey named thirty-four events and organizations that HUAC had deemed to be closely aligned with Communism, noting that each could be found on government watch lists and each could be linked to Aaron Copland. He then concluded:

> The real issue involved is whether the Republican Party should lay itself wide open at the beginning of its administration by permitting music to be played by a composer who has been cited as having been associated in various ways with numerous Communist and Communist-front organizations, each of these organizations having been so designated by either the Attorney General of the United States or the House Committee on Un-American Activities.

Three months later, Copland received the subpoena to appear before the Senate Permanent Subcommittee on Investigations into Communist Activities. Copland and his attorney arrived at the Capitol at 2:30 p.m. on May 25. There, he was questioned for roughly two hours in a private hearing led by Senator Joe McCarthy, chief counsel Roy Cohn, and several members of the Senate Subcommittee. McCarthy had risen to national fame in 1950 when he asserted that he had a list of 250 Communist Party members who had infiltrated the State Department. When McCarthy subpoenaed Copland to testify he had three objectives in mind: first, he wanted Copland to admit to being a Communist; second, he hoped to "discredit . . . the formerly Democratic-controlled State Department" by exposing their sponsorship and promotion of Communist artists like Copland; and finally, he planned to extract from Copland the names of other artists and intellectuals with Communist affiliations. As the transcript of the hearing reveals, he failed in all three objectives. Copland remained calm throughout the proceeding, denying all allegations that he had ever knowingly supported the Communist Party. And he refused to name names. Below is a typical exchange:

MCCARTHY: Mr. Copland, have you ever been a Communist?
COPLAND: No, I have not been a Communist in the past and I am not now a Communist.
MCCARTHY: Have you ever been a Communist sympathizer?
COPLAND: I am not sure that I would be able to say what you mean by the word "sympathizer." From my impression of it I have never thought of myself as a Communist sympathizer.
MCCARTHY: You did not.
COPLAND: I did not.
MCCARTHY: Did you ever attend any Communist meetings?
COPLAND: I never attended any specific Communist party function of any kind.
MCCARTHY: Did you ever attend a Communist meeting?
COPLAND: I am afraid I don't know how you define a Communist meeting.
MCCARTHY: A meeting you knew then or now had been called

by the Communist Party and sponsored by the Communist Party.

COPLAND: Not that I would know of. No.

MCCARTHY: Did you ever attend a meeting of which a major or sizable number of those in attendance were Communists?

COPLAND: Not to my knowledge.

MCCARTHY: Were you ever solicited to join the Communist Party?

COPLAND: No.

MCCARTHY: Did anyone ever discuss with you the possibility of your joining the Communist Party?

COPLAND: Not that I recall.

MCCARTHY: So, your answer at this time is that you can't say definitely whether you have been asked to join the Communist Party or not?

COPLAND: No.

As the questioning progressed, McCarthy grew markedly more frustrated with Copland's elusive answers. Eventually, he offered the composer a firm warning.

> One of the reasons you are here today is because of the part you played in the [State Department's] exchange program... and you have a public record of association with organizations officially listed by the Attorney General... May I give you some advice. You have a lawyer here. There are witnesses who come before this committee and often indulge in the assumption that they can avoid giving us facts. Those who underestimate the work the staff has done in the past end up occasionally before a grand jury for perjury, so I suggest when counsel questions you about these matters that you tell the truth or take advantage of the Fifth Amendment.

Copland responded: "I came here with the intention of answering honestly all questions put to me. If I am unable to do that, it is the fact that memory slips in different ways over a long period of time."

McCarthy and Cohn continued pummeling Copland with questions for another hour and a half. With each query, Copland responded evasively: "I do not recall. . . . Not to my knowledge. . . . I wouldn't know." Following the hearing, Copland issued a public statement:

> On late Friday afternoon, I received a telegram from the Senate Permanent Subcommittee on Investigations to appear as a witness. I did. I answered to the best of my ability all of the questions which were asked me. I testified under oath that I have never supported, and am now opposed to, the limitations put on freedom by the Soviet Union . . . My relationships with the United States Government were originally with the Music Advisory Committee to the Coordinator of Inter-American Affairs and later as a lecturer in music in South America and as a Fulbright Professor. In these capacities my work was limited to the technical aspects of music.

Copland had been told by Cohn that he was still under subpoena and would likely be called to testify soon again. Consequently, he spent the following two weeks working with his lawyer to strengthen his defense. Luckily for Copland, McCarthy and Cohn had made no mention of his Communist anthem, "Into the Streets, May 1st." In fact, they had made no mention of any of his music. As Copland noted in his diary the day after testifying, "My impression is that McCarthy had no idea who I was or what I did." There was a different passion at work in the senator. "When he touches on his magic theme, the 'Commies' or 'communism,' his voice darkens like that of a minister," Copland noted. "He is like a plebeian Faustus who has been given a magic wand by an invisible Mephisto—as long as the menace is there, the wand will work. The question is at what point his power grab will collide with the power drive of his own party."

Copland's question proved prescient. Within a year, McCarthy and Cohn were accused of using improper pressure to influence the army in their anti-Communist crusade. The Army–McCarthy hearings were broadcast live on television, and the media coverage contributed to McCarthy's decline in popularity. On December 2, 1954, the Senate voted 67–22 to censure McCarthy, which effectively put an end to his political career.

As McCarthy faded from view, Copland worked to escape the shadow of his left-leaning political past. The FBI opened an investigation into his testimony, and for several months it looked as though he might be charged with perjury and/or fraud. Copland was also banned from leaving the country as he struggled, for over a year, to have his passport reissued. The entire experience was stressful and time-consuming, not to mention expensive. But Copland held strong, and in November 1955 he finally received news from the State Department that there was "insufficient evidence to warrant prosecution."

Despite Copland's legal troubles with the government, his work as a composer of American music continued to be acknowledged by various arts organizations. In 1954 he was named a member of the American Academy of Arts and Letters, which went on to award him their Gold Medal in 1956. Prestigious universities, including Princeton and Brandeis, honored Copland with honorary degrees. And the nation's leading orchestras continued to program his works regularly and "firmly defended him against the occasional threats and crank protests" from right-wing groups like "the John Birch Society and American Legion."

Copland emerged from the political persecution of the 1950s with his reputation intact and, as the years progressed, America's politicians embraced his music once again. President Kennedy was the first to invite him to the White House, in 1961. In 1964, Lyndon B. Johnson awarded Copland the Presidential Medal of Freedom. And in 1973 Richard Nixon requested that Copland's *Lincoln Portrait* be performed at his second inauguration. Rosalynn Carter served as the narrator of the same work in 1976 at a fundraiser for her husband's presidential campaign. Four years later, President Jimmy Carter hosted an eightieth birthday celebration for Copland at the Kennedy Center, with *Appalachian Spring* its centerpiece. Pearl Lang, one of the original dancers in the ballet, praised Copland's contribution to America's self-image:

> We thank Aaron ... for the energy his music ignites in us, and for the limitless space that we hear in his sound. With Aaron's music, one leaps not across the stage, but across the land. And

above all, we thank him for the wonder of that defiant innocence and affirmation that sings in his music about America.

Ronald Reagan selected Copland works for both his inaugurations: *Fanfare for the Common Man* in 1981 and "Simple Gifts," sung by Jessye Norman, in 1985. In 1993, Marilyn Horne performed "Simple Gifts" for Bill Clinton's inauguration. But true vindication finally arrived on September 23, 1986, when the House of Representatives voted unanimously to honor "the incomparable contributions of Aaron Copland to American musical composition" by awarding him its highest civilian honor, "a special congressional gold medal."

Copland's music had become so firmly embedded in American identity by the 1980s that even a performance by Soviet defectors could not raise the specter of "un-American activities." In 1987, Rudolf Nureyev and Mikhail Baryshnikov danced the lead male roles in *Appalachian Spring* to a sold-out house in New York. The reviews were glowing. As a reporter for the *New York Times* noted:

> The idea of two fellows from Leningrad being able to portray quintessential American Yankees might stretch the imagination. But that is what Mikhail Baryshnikov and Rudolf Nureyev actually pulled off last night through their first-ever joint performance in "Appalachian Spring"... The Shaker woodwork that inspired Isamu Noguchi's set and the Shaker hymn, "'Tis the Gift to Be Simple," that Aaron Copland incorporated into his celebrated score, blow in a breeze of open-frontier optimism.

AMERICA'S SECRET SONIC WEAPON

When President Dwight D. Eisenhower came into office in 1953, America was suffering an identity crisis. US soldiers were dying in Korea. The nuclear arms race with the Soviet Union had reached a dangerous impasse. Racial segregation and discrimination persisted unabated, and the Red Scare continued to fuel Senator McCarthy's witch hunts. The nation was torn between promoting democracy and containing Communism. Consequently, its role as a global superpower was being questioned on various fronts, both foreign and domestic. As Eisenhower explained in his first State of the Union address in February 1953, there was still much work to be done. "Our country has come through a painful period of trial and disillusionment since the victory of 1945," he noted. "We anticipated a world of peace and cooperation. The calculated pressures of aggressive communism have forced us, instead, to live in a world of turmoil."

Eisenhower confirmed that the Soviet Union possessed atomic weapons, marking a fundamental shift in the balance of power. He also revealed that the government's domestic failures had become fodder for negative propaganda abroad. "From this costly experience we have learned one clear lesson, that the free world cannot indefinitely remain in a posture of paralyzed tension." Eisenhower promoted the embrace of a coherent global policy. "The freedom we cherish and defend in Europe and the Americas is no different from the freedom that is in peril in Asia," he noted. "There is but one sure way to avoid global war, and that is to win the Cold War." Congress cheered.

In the months that followed, the plans laid out in Eisenhower's speech began to take shape. Frustrated by the persistent stereotype of Americans as "a race of materialists" lacking "worthwhile culture of any kind," and eager to counter Soviet criticism of racial injustice in the United States, Eisenhower established a new government agency: the United States Information Agency (USIA), known internationally as the United States Information Service (USIS).

The USIA's mission was to shape global public opinion by promoting a positive image of the United States as a beacon of freedom and democratic values. In a speech to members of the State Department, the agency's first director, Theodore Streibert, outlined the urgent need for this new initiative.

> Throughout the world, there is widespread misunderstanding of the United States.... The Communists are quick to take advantage of this in the lies they are spreading about us.... We must make known to the people throughout the world what we are, what we believe, what we seek as a nation. And we must combat Soviet propaganda. This is the job of the United States Information Agency.

The USIA pursued a range of propaganda projects, from establishing English-language American libraries abroad to publishing popular magazines and producing radio programs and films aimed at foreign audiences. But Eisenhower wanted more, and in July 1954, he wrote to the Senate requesting funds to cover the costs of foreign tours by American musicians, dancers, and theater groups. "The contribution which such presentations make toward a better understanding of America can scarcely be exaggerated," he wrote. "I consider it essential that we take immediate and vigorous action to demonstrate the superiority of the products and cultural values of our system of free enterprise." Within a few weeks, a proposal was written, and Congress appropriated the needed funds through an emergency measure called the Cultural Presentations

Program. The American National Theatre and Academy (ANTA) was charged with establishing advisory panels of experts in the various arts. The first Music Advisory Panel comprised leading figures in the realm of classical music, including the composers Howard Hanson, William Schuman, and Virgil Thomson, the conductor Milton Katims, and the music critic Alfred Frankenstein. When the Music Panel met for the first time, in October 1954, a representative from the State Department briefed them on their mission: to select individuals and ensembles who could "counteract Russian propaganda" through the superiority of their performances.

Given the musical interests represented by the original Music Advisory Panel, it is no surprise that the first performers sent abroad were classical musicians. These included soloists from the Metropolitan Opera, noted chamber music groups, and large ensembles, including the New York Philharmonic and the Boston Symphony Orchestra. The goal of these tours was to demonstrate that the performing arts in America had reached a level of accomplishment and sophistication equal to that of Europe.

Popular music was excluded from these early tours. As one Advisory Panel member noted in 1955, "show tunes and folk music should be discouraged, as there are no standards to judge 'light music' except 'charm,' and charm is hard to judge." Nonetheless, popular music reached foreign audiences through targeted radio broadcasts. In January 1955, the admired radio host Willis Conover launched a new program titled *Music USA* on Voice of America radio. VOA was founded in 1941, when the United States entered World War II, and from the beginning it broadcast pro-American propaganda programming, in multiple languages, via shortwave radio to listeners around the world. Since VOA was officially recognized as government propaganda, its programs were not broadcast in the United States, and during the McCarthy era VOA was gutted, due to false accusations of Communist infiltration. The launching of Conover's *Music USA* was an effort by USIA to revive VOA, and it succeeded beyond everyone's expectations.

The first hour of *Music USA* was dedicated to popular music (rock, folk music, and popular ballads); the second hour focused solely on jazz. *Music USA* was not the first jazz program on VOA, but it was the most successful and enduring. Not even Leonard Feather's *Jazz Club USA* (1950–52) came close to the success of Conover's *Music USA*, which soon attracted 100 million listeners around the globe, many of them behind the Iron Curtain. To accelerate the impact of jazz, thousands of transistor radios were distributed throughout Asia, Africa, and the Middle East by USIA, ensuring that foreign audiences would listen to "defenses of U.S. foreign policy along with Conover's *Music USA* show."

For Conover, jazz served as the perfect metaphor for American democracy: "Jazz is a classical parallel to our American political and social system." In a democracy, he often explained, "we agree in advance on the laws and customs we abide by, and having reached agreement, we are free to do whatever we wish within those constraints. It's the same with jazz. The musicians agree on a key, the harmonic changes, the tempo and duration of the piece. Within those guidelines, they are free to play what they want."

Despite Conover's beliefs and the popularity of VOA programming, which featured many African American performers, the Soviet Union's anti-American propaganda continued unabated as racial conflict in the United States continued to make international headlines. Especially detrimental to America's image abroad were reports surrounding the brutal lynching of fourteen-year-old Emmett Till in Mississippi in August 1955, the hostility faced by Rosa Parks four months later when she refused to give up her seat to a white man on a bus in Montgomery, Alabama, and the continued conflicts over the desegregation of public schools despite the passage of the Supreme Court's 1954 ruling in *Brown v. Board of Education*, which declared the "separate but equal" practice of racial segregation in US public schools unconstitutional. As the State Department reported, "no American problem receives more wide-spread attention . . . than our treatment of racial minorities, particularly the Negro." It has become "our Achilles' Heel."

To address this issue, a former member of the American National Theatre and Academy, Robert Breen, suggested sending a touring production of George Gershwin's *Porgy and Bess* to Europe and Latin America. Breen's self-interest was not lost on government officials; the production was one that Breen had co-produced on Broadway in 1953 and had toured nationally in 1954. Breen argued that, by demonstrating both the genius of a great American composer and the musical talents of literally dozens of black performers, *Porgy and Bess* would quell anti-American propaganda abroad. If only this had been true. Although the singers and dancers in *Porgy and Bess* enthralled foreign audiences, the opera itself did little to mitigate negative perceptions of race relations in the United States. Instead, the opera's storyline, degrading stereotypes, and use of black dialect perpetuated the images of racial oppression promulgated by the Soviets. Breen requested that his production of *Porgy and Bess* be sent "to Moscow and satellite capitals," but Herbert Hoover Jr., Under Secretary of State, and Theodore Streibert, the director of USIA, "felt that such a tour was 'politically premature.'" When the State Department refused to provide funding, Breen reached out to the Soviet Ministry of Culture, which agreed to sponsor a three-week appearance in Moscow. This was followed by performances in Bucharest, Budapest, Warsaw, Prague, and Berlin. Breen put his own ego ahead of US foreign relations, and "in each of these countries, all [of the production's expenses were] paid by the respective Communist governments."

As the fallout from Breen's Eastern Bloc tour made its way into State Department reports, USIA officials came to the realization that classical music alone, even when performed by black Americans, could not effectively put to rest claims about racial strife in America. A new cultural offensive was needed in the Cold War, and Congressman Adam Clayton Powell Jr., representing the New York district of Harlem, had a plan.

In April 1955, Powell had attended the inaugural Afro-Asiatic Conference in Badung, Indonesia. Eisenhower had refused to send an official representative to the gathering since most of the twenty-nine nations involved had not aligned themselves with the United States. Powell attended not as a US congressman but as a freelance journalist. When a reporter at the conference asked Powell if he hoped "to represent the American viewpoint" in Badung, his response was direct:

> I not only hope to represent the American viewpoint as we commonly think of it, but as a Negro member of the United States Congress, I hope to prove to the peoples of Asia and Africa that this country has a very large minority of colored peoples from Puerto Rico, Mexico, and Negro people. And by

that racial link, I think that we can establish a bond between our country and their countries, which will guarantee world peace, because no one would dare defy the peoples of Asia, Africa, *and* North America.

When Powell returned from Indonesia, Congress gave him a standing ovation, and his colleagues began to take more seriously his recommendations for improving America's race relations at home and its reputation abroad. Powell made the most of the moment. He lobbied for voting rights and improvements in public school education. He also called for a change in Eisenhower's Cultural Presentations Program.

Powell was married to Hazel Scott, a noted jazz pianist whose career had been thwarted by McCarthy's anti-Communist attacks. Powell saw black culture, in particular jazz, as the best way to intervene in the Cold War cultural conflict. Jazz was America's greatest indigenous art form, he argued. Born of black culture, it had the power to win over the hearts and minds of the people and, by extension, the governments of Africa and Asia. On November 6, 1955, Powell's point of view was corroborated by a headline in the *New York Times*: "United States Has a Secret Sonic Weapon—Jazz."

The article, penned by Felix Belair Jr., a political correspondent sent to cover the postwar recovery of Europe, described the overwhelming success of Louis Armstrong's most recent tour abroad. Belair labeled Armstrong America's "most effective ambassador" and defined jazz as an essential export. "All Europe now seems to find American jazz as necessary as the seasons," Belair noted. Puzzled by the choice of classical music over jazz, he wondered why "the United States Government, with all the money it spends for so-called propaganda to promote democracy," was not using "more of it to subsidize the continental travels of jazz bands and the best exponents of the music?" For it wasn't just Europeans who had fallen "captive" to jazz. The music was so popular in the Soviet Union and "the satellite countries" that "men have actually risked their lives to smuggle recordings of it behind the iron curtain, and by methods that profit motives cannot explain."

"American jazz has now become a universal language," continued Belair. It was an effective "sonic weapon" because "everyone knows where it comes from and where to look for more." When it came to cultural diplomacy, Belair concluded, jazz was a logical choice. "There is not a wide difference between the best symphony orchestras of the United States and Europe . . . but nobody plays jazz like an American."

Belair's article made waves in the United States. Shortly after its appearance, a reporter for *U.S. News and World Report* asked Louis Armstrong if he thought sending jazz musicians abroad would improve America's image. Armstrong responded: "It's the first thing I said when I read that [the black track star] Jesse Owens is going all over Europe. We oughta do the same thing. . . . Just think, if they sent this combo around to a big stadium where thousands of people could hear it—I think it would do a lot of good." The State Department agreed. Its end-of-the-year report to Congress noted the "tremendous popularity" of recent jazz performances abroad and the attention jazz had been receiving in the press. Perhaps the time had come to expand the musical offerings supported by the president's Cultural Presentations Program. "Jazz has come to represent a kind of international brotherhood and . . . jazz, truly an American product, has high propaganda value—for to be interested in jazz is to be interested in things American," stated the report.

Powell embraced the State Department's change of heart. Let the world experience "real Americana," he told the president. Acknowledging the symbolic power of an American genre deeply rooted in black culture, Eisenhower supported its addition to the nation's arsenal of Cold War weapons and, for the first time in US history, "congressional leaders entered into conversations about the legislation of jazz."

The initial outcome of these discussions was the establishment of the State Department's Jazz Ambassadors program. A jazz specialist, Marshall Stearns, was invited to join the Music Advisory Panel, and he quickly proposed a range of possible performers: Louis Armstrong, Count Basie, Duke Ellington, Dizzy Gillespie, and Stan Kenton, to name just a few. Powell became the congressional spokesperson for the program, and in January 1956 he appeared on *CBS News Report* to announce that the US would soon be sending the nation's finest jazz musicians around the globe. "We've just decided that we're going to shift the emphasis [of our State Department tours] to jazz . . . and send these artists over where they can reach the masses of the people of Asia and Africa." Powell had played a role in choosing who the first Jazz Ambassador would be, and he took great pride in announcing, "One of the people who we're planning to use, is my friend Dizzy Gillespie—the father of modern jazz." As Gillespie later explained, "I took it as an honor, really, because they had many people they could've chosen as the first one to represent the State Department on that tour. I felt highly honored ... and I sort've liked the idea of representing America."

The State Department's choice of Gillespie might seem surprising given Louis Armstrong's popularity abroad. But there were several important factors that influenced the choice. Most importantly, Gillespie was an incredibly talented musician with great stage presence and a genial personality. Like Armstrong, he enjoyed an international following. Unlike Armstrong, he was relatively young, just thirty-eight years old. And as Powell had explained to his colleagues in Congress, Gillespie was an innovator of the energetic modern jazz sound known as bebop. Gillespie also had a history of political activism, and he insisted on speaking his mind. This was especially important to Powell.

Gillespie believed that understanding the past was an effective way to promote justice and equity in the future. When the State Department requested that he attend a pre-tour briefing on the hot-button issue of race relations in the United States, Gillespie responded: "I've got three hundred years of briefing. I know what they've done to us, and I'm not gonna make any excuses. If they ask me any questions, I'm gonna answer them as honestly as I can." As he explained, "I wasn't going over to apologize for the racist policies of America." Instead, Gillespie was free to talk about life in America as he had experienced it. Displaying American freedom was the central goal of his first tour. And as Gillespie demonstrated to the audiences he encountered, an American, even a black American, could criticize his government without fear of punishment.

Gillespie left for the Middle East in March 1956 and performed in Iran, Syria, Pakistan, and Lebanon—all nations that had been represented at the Afro-Asiatic Conference—before traveling on to Turkey, Yugoslavia, and Greece. As historian Penny Von Eschen has noted, careful calculations went into planning the tour's itinerary, which moved along "the Eisenhower administration's conception of a 'perimeter defense' against the Soviet Union."

Accompanying Gillespie were nineteen bandmates, including twenty-two-year-old Quincy Jones, who served as the ensemble's primary arranger and music director, and Melba Liston, who also arranged and played trombone. As Gillespie explained: "We had a complete 'American assortment' of blacks, whites, males, females, Jews and Gentiles in the band." Such a diversity was not lost on the audiences that attended their performances.

Marshall Stearns, the jazz specialist who had been added to the Music Advisory Panel, traveled with Gillespie and served as an MC of sorts, offering commentary before or after concerts on the history of jazz and its importance in American culture. Stearns described jazz as a music of the people. The importance of this message wasn't lost on Gillespie, who insisted that people from all ranks of society be given the opportunity to hear his music. "They priced the tickets so high that the little people we were trying to gain friendship with couldn't make it," explained Gillespie. At their first performance in Karachi, Pakistan, Gillespie noticed numerous empty seats. "So, I asked the impresario, I say, 'How many [unsold tickets] you got?' . . . I took a whole batch of tickets, went out in the park, and gave them away." At the next concert, "we had a full house, a beautiful audience."

Between performances, Gillespie made a point of connecting with local musicians. There is a famous photograph from the tour showing Gillespie playing his trumpet in front of a cobra as it rises from a basket. What is not widely known is that literally seconds after the photo was snapped, the cobra lunged forward and struck the bell of Gillespie's horn. "Dizzy almost turned white," drummer Charlie Persip recollected. "That was really frightening!" Gillespie gained some insight that day, not just about the dangers of snake charming but about what the cultures he encountered could teach him. "The musicians treated us great. They played concerts for us in the studios when we went different places and they showed us things," explained Gillespie. "You know, I'm always interested in the ethnic background of the music, the soulful music of a people. I learned a lot over there. I learned some scales and [later] made some recordings with Stuff Smith using some of those scales . . . that came out of Pakistan." The tune "Rio Pakistan" shows the influence of his global contacts. While the underlying rhythmic ostinato has echoes of Brazilian samba, the opening theme, a take on "Joy to the World," evokes the raag scaler patterns of traditional Pakistani music. "It was very exciting and very gratifying to listen to another type of music than what I played," Gillespie recalled. When he returned to the US, he released a range of albums connected to his work as a jazz ambassador: *World Statesman* (1956), *Dizzy in Greece* (1957), and the posthumously released *Dizzy in South America* (1999).

State Department reports of the Gillespie tour were overwhelmingly positive. With Gillespie at the helm, the US government had successfully used jazz as a "secret sonic weapon" in the Cold War. But not everyone in Congress was pleased. As plans for a second Gillespie tour were being made, Representative John Rooney, a New York Democrat, lobbied to shut the program down. In the Senate, the Southern segregationist Allen J. Ellender of Louisiana complained: "I have never heard so much noise in all my life. . . . To send such jazz as Mr. Gillespie, I can assure you that instead of doing good it will do harm, and the people will really believe we are barbarians." At Ellender's urging, the Senate Appropriations Committee added a stipulation to its appropriations bill banning the use of funds for future foreign tours by "jazz bands." Although the stipulation was later excised from the final version of the bill, continued resistance to the Jazz Ambassadors program by some members of Congress affected the content of the program and its reception by the American public. For example, a group called the White Citizens Council of Alabama denounced jazz, claiming it was part of a "plot to mongrelize America." Nonetheless, on August 1, 1956, the Eighty-Fourth Congress agreed to extend the special appropriations that had been designated for the President's Emergency Fund and formalize them into the President's Special International Program. These new funds paid for an additional Gillespie tour, this time to South America, and a tour by Benny Goodman to East and Southeast Asia.

Benny Goodman and His Orchestra began their tour for the State Department in December 1956 and spent seven weeks performing in Burma, Cambodia, Japan, Hong Kong, Malaya, Singapore, South Korea, and Thailand. At the urging of his agent, John Hammond, Goodman had crossed the color line in 1936 and formed a quartet with pianist Teddy Wilson and vibraphonist Lionel Hampton, both black, and the drummer

Gene Krupa. When Goodman played Carnegie Hall in 1938, he was the first to do so with black and white musicians. By 1956, his big band was fully integrated.

State Department officials reported that Goodman's Jazz Ambassador tour "strengthened the impression that America is not only great in modern plumbing and fancy cars, but in things of the spirit and the Arts." Goodman relished his time as a jazz ambassador and lobbied hard to be sent to the Soviet Union. But he would have to wait. The State Department had set their sights on someone else for that inaugural mission: Louis Armstrong.

Armstrong's ambassadorial abilities had become an important aspect of his brand as a performer. In May 1956, shortly after Gillespie returned from his first tour, Armstrong (nicknamed Satchmo) released *Ambassador Satch* with Columbia Records. The album was the brainchild of producer George Avakian, who wanted to draw attention to Armstrong's international fame. Although the record was advertised as a compilation of live recordings from the 1955 tour, in truth it was a heavily produced and edited album that contained studio-recorded tracks and canned applause.

In October 1957, United Artists released *Satchmo the Great*, a feature documentary film written and produced by newsman Edward R. Murrow, host of the popular CBS television show *See It Now*. *Satchmo the Great* promoted Armstrong as "an ambassador with a horn" and featured extensive footage of his 1955 European tour. During the filming of the documentary, Murrow got the idea of taking Armstrong to Africa, and a visit was planned to the British West African colony of the Gold Coast. Murrow reasoned that capturing footage of Armstrong's first encounter with Africa would make for powerful cinema, and he was right. His two-day visit in May 1956 proved to be a life-changing event, not only for himself but also for the Gold Coast, which was in the final stage of becoming the independent nation of Ghana. When Armstrong and His All Stars arrived at the airport in Accra, over 10,000 fans greeted them on the tarmac, waving signs and yelling "Armstrong Akwaba!" (Welcome Armstrong!). As Armstrong descended the steps from the plane, thirteen African bands perched atop trucks began playing and singing "All For You, Louis, All For You!" Armstrong was so moved that he pulled out his trumpet and began to play along. As the journalist Robert Raymond noted: "The noise and the clamor rose to the skies in the greatest paean of welcome Accra had ever known."

Armstrong offered a series of performances for a wide range of audiences during his two days in Accra, where he met with the region's tribal leaders. He also interacted with Kwame Nkrumah, prime minister of the Gold Coast and future president of Ghana. At one his concerts, Armstrong performed a tune titled "Black and Blue," which he dedicated to Nkrumah. Composed in 1929 by Fats Waller, with lyrics by Harry Brooks and Andy Razaf, the song expressed a universal message about the internal pain felt by black victims of racial prejudice and colonialism:

> *They laugh at you, and scorn you too.*
> *What did I do to be so black and blue?*
> *I'm white inside, but that don't help my case,*
> *'Cause I can't hide what is in my face.*
> *How will it end? Ain't got a friend.*
> *My only sin is in my skin.*
> *What did I do to be so black and blue?*

After the release of *Satchmo the Great*, rumors began to circulate that "Ambassador Satch" would soon be traveling to the Soviet Union for the State Department. But contract negotiations between USIA and Armstrong's management broke down in September 1957, when President Eisenhower refused to intervene in the racial crisis developing in Little Rock, Arkansas.

The crisis began when nine black students attempted to integrate Central High School. On September 2, the night before the first day of classes, Arkansas governor Orval Faubus ordered the state's National Guard to block their entrance, saying: "I must state here in all sincerity, that it is my opinion, yes, even a conviction, that it will not be possible to restore or to maintain order and protect the lives and property of the citizens if forcible integration is carried out tomorrow in the schools of this community." When the nine students arrived, they were met by an angry white mob. Over the next three weeks, televised newscasts broadcast the escalating conflict as the whole world watched. Nonetheless, Eisenhower refused to send federal troops to protect the students. This inaction enraged Armstrong, and in a published interview he called Eisenhower "gutless" and Governor Faubus an "uneducated plow boy." Armstrong called off the negotiations for a State Department tour and voiced his dissatisfaction to the press: "The way they are treating my people in the South, the government can go to hell.... It's getting almost so bad a colored man hasn't got any country."

Worried that "Ambassador Satch" might spark a diplomatic crisis, Secretary of State John Foster Dulles warned Attorney General Herbert Brownell that the events unfolding in Arkansas were "ruining our foreign policy." Two weeks later, under mounting pressure, Eisenhower deployed the National Guard to the state, but the delayed response wasn't enough to make Armstrong change his mind.

The continued racism in America, and its effect on the nation's reception of jazz, became an increasingly hot topic in 1957. Angered by the continued battles in Congress over the Jazz Ambassador program, Gillespie co-authored an article for *Esquire* in June titled "Jazz Is Too Good for Americans," in which he highlighted the sharp contrast between the attitudes of politicians like Ellender and Rooney and the enthusiastic crowds he encountered abroad:

> Jazz, the music I play most often, has never really been accepted as an art form by the people of my own country.... To them, jazz is music for kids and dope addicts.... As an American, I'm deeply sorry that they [foreign countries] have beat us to the punch in exploiting so fully a music we originally created. Most of all—and this is the really great irony—I'm disappointed that the enormous upswing in jazz enthusiasm abroad has been accompanied by a decline in several major areas of jazz interest here at home.

Toward the end of the article, Gillespie made a case for continuing the Jazz Ambassador program, explaining that "this lionizing of American jazzmen overseas has had a great effect on our morale." He also suggested that Congress should advocate for stronger jazz appreciation programs in the United States, "taught to school children at all levels of their education." Although Congress would not embrace such an education program for many years to come, it continued to approve funds for additional tours.

In March 1958, Dave Brubeck set off on the first of several successful trips for the State Department. Accompanying Brubeck were the members of his racially integrated quartet (saxophonist Paul Desmond, drummer Joe Morello, and bassist Eugene Wright), his wife, Iola, and his young sons, Darius and Michael. The group began their trip by traveling through East Germany to Poland. This was the first time a Jazz Ambassador had ventured behind the Iron Curtain, and the experience inspired Brubeck to compose the tune "Brandenburg Gate."

In Poland, audiences were welcoming and passionate. A small group of young enthusiasts followed the ensemble across the country, attending all twelve concerts. Brubeck often spoke at his performances. "I see the audience as a co-creator, the fifth instrument in our quartet," he explained. "The way in which the musicians and listeners meet is shaped by how the audience chooses to play its part, always a new one. The first duty of a jazz musician is to unite the audience so that it is one," he continued. "That inspired moment of unity is the purpose of jazz." Brubeck deeply believed in the mission he was on, and he received shouts of adulation when he told his listeners in Poland: "No dictatorship can tolerate jazz. It is the first sign of a return to freedom."

Brubeck visited Chopin's birthplace just outside of Warsaw. Inspired by the experience, he composed a tune called "Dziekuje," Polish for "thank you," which features a Chopin-inspired introduction on the piano. Brubeck premiered "Dziekuje" in Poznan, at his final concert in Poland. As he later explained, the tune was his way of giving something back to the people who had welcomed him.

After Poland, the quartet traveled on to Turkey, India, Ceylon (now Sri Lanka), Pakistan, Afghanistan, Iran, and Iraq, where their fascination with non-Western music grew. In Ankara, Brubeck invited local musicians to join the quartet onstage. Together they performed fifteen choruses of "All the Things You Are," a 1939 tune by Jerome Kern. As he had done before, Brubeck composed a tune, "The Golden Horn," as a way of giving back. Named after the primary inlet of the Bosporus Strait, which divides Europe from Asia, the tune combines a Turkish theme based on "the rhythmic pattern of the Turkish phrase *çok teşekkür ederim*" (thank you very much) with Western harmony. Similarly, in India, Brubeck incorporated local rhythms into the tune "Calcutta Blues."

Shortly after their return to the United States, the Dave Brubeck Quartet recorded a new album for Columbia in New York. Titled *Expressions of Eurasia*, the album featured an array of newly-composed tunes inspired by their experiences as Jazz Ambassadors. As Brubeck explained in the liner notes:

> These sketches of Eurasia have been developed from random musical phrases I jotted down in my notebook as we chugged across the fields of Europe, or skimmed across the deserts of Asia, or walked in the alleyways of an ancient bazaar.... I tried to create an *impression* of a particular locale by using some of the elements of their folk music within the jazz idiom.

The album included the tunes mentioned above as well as "Nomad," which Brubeck co-wrote with his wife, Iola, and "Marble Arch." Brubeck composed a seventh tune for the album, "Blue Rondo à la Turk," but reserved it for the 1959 release *Time Out*, one of the greatest-selling jazz albums of all time.

In October 1960, Louis Armstrong finally made his ambassadorial status official when he and His All Stars embarked on a three-month tour across the African continent. They performed in twenty-seven cities, thrilling crowds in the Republic of the Congo, Egypt, Liberia, Mali, Senegal, Sierra Leone, Sudan, and the United Arab Republic. The tour was a huge success, despite the toll it took on performers. Singer Velma Middleton suffered a stroke and died, and Armstrong was ordered to take a break due to fatigue. Several times a week, reports and photos from the tour were featured in American newspapers. But as Dave and Iola Brubeck noted, there seemed to be a disconnect between the message promoted by the Jazz Ambassadors abroad and the reality of everyday life at home.

"The entire jazz community was elated with the official recognition of jazz and its international implications," noted Iola Brubeck, but too many government officials wanted to ignore the continued struggle for civil rights at home. To draw public attention to this issue, the Brubecks joined forces with Armstrong in 1961 and produced a musical titled *The Real Ambassadors*, which offered a satirical critique of the hypocrisy still inherent in the government program, while celebrating Armstrong's key role as a musical diplomat and defender of the civil rights movement. *The Real Ambassadors* was recorded in 1961 and performed live at the 1962 Monterey Jazz Festival. Received with great critical acclaim, the musical set the stage for the most active jazz ambassador in US history, namely Washington, DC native Duke Ellington.

Duke Ellington and His Orchestra toured for the State Department more than any other ensemble, and their participation marked a new chapter in the Jazz Ambassadors program. In 1962 the Kennedy administration laid down new guidelines for the State Department tours in a report that justified the payment of "high salaries to outstanding artists... on the basis of extraordinary artistic talent," and recommended that performers "interact with foreigners offstage so that young people, especially, could meet the performers and, when applicable, exchange skills and stories with them."

Ellington's first tour began in the fall of 1963 with a three-month journey that took him and his band to a range of nations, mostly in the Near and Middle East. Their itinerary started in Syria, then continued to Jordan, Afghanistan, India, Ceylon, Pakistan, the region now known as Bangladesh, Iran, Iraq, and Lebanon. As Harvey G. Cohen explains in *Duke Ellington's America*, the band was originally scheduled to perform in Turkey, Cyprus, the United Arab Republic, Greece, Egypt, and Yugoslavia, too, but the final leg of the tour was canceled due to the assassination of President Kennedy. The publicity put out by the State Department described Ellington as a symbol of the best in American culture. To borrow a phrase from cultural historian Reinhold Wagnleitner, Ellington's first State Department tour showed Congress and the State Department that jazz didn't need propaganda to succeed; "it was the propaganda that needed jazz." This is perhaps most clearly shown in the numerous articles about Ellington that appeared in local papers, side by side with reports of US government support for the civil rights movement.

Shortly after Ellington returned from his first tour as jazz ambassador, Gillespie set his sights on a new residence in Ellington's hometown—namely, the White House. Although Gillespie embarked on his presidential campaign in jest, his underlying message was completely serious: American politics needed new energy. The chorus to Gillespie's 1964 campaign song, a rewrite of the Jon Hendricks tune "Salt Peanuts," said it all:

> Your politics ought to be a groovier thing.
> Vote Dizzy! Vote Dizzy!
> So, get a good president who's willing to swing.
> Vote Dizzy! Vote Dizzy!

Gillespie promised that, if elected, he would rename the White House "the Blues House" and appoint a stellar cabinet: Duke Ellington as secretary of state, Max Roach as defense secretary, Peggy Lee as labor chief, and Miles Davis as director of the CIA. All joking aside, the impetus for Gillespie's campaign was to address the issues at stake in 1964 and raise money for civil rights organizations such as CORE (Congress of Racial Equality) and the Southern Christian Leadership Conference. Gillespie touted his experience as a Jazz Ambassador as proof of his foreign policy competence. Even after he pulled out of the race, talk show hosts and journalists continued to comment on the symbolic connections between jazz, American democracy, and the nation's foreign policy.

Gillespie didn't make it to the White House, but Ellington did, albeit not as president or secretary of state. On April 29, 1969—his seventieth birthday—he was invited to the White House and presented with the Presidential Medal of Freedom. He was the first jazz musician to receive such an honor. In his remarks, Richard Nixon referenced not only Ellington's talent but also his success as a cultural diplomat:

> When we think of freedom, we think of many things. But Duke Ellington is one who has carried the message of freedom to all the nations of the world through music, through understanding—understanding that reaches over all national boundaries and over all boundaries of prejudice and over all boundaries of language.

After receiving the Presidential Medal of Freedom, Ellington was sent on numerous diplomatic tours by the State Department. Between his trip to Burma in 1970 and his tour of Asia in 1972, he performed in over forty countries on four continents under State Department auspices. Yet, despite this success, change was in the air. The Vietnam War, Watergate, and the energy crisis caused many politicians in Washington to call into question the financial commitment required for the government's continued sponsorship of the tours. Consequently, the State Department sought new ways to offset the program's cost while simultaneously reaching out to new audiences. Beginning in the 1970s the tours were outsourced to a private entity, Festival Productions, under the directorship of George Wein, founder of the Newport Jazz Festival. Ellington's final tours were under Wein's management, as were those of other top performers: Lionel Hampton, Earl Hines, Rahsaan Roland Kirk, Charles Mingus, Oscar Peterson, and Sarah Vaughan. Although the tours were now shorter, they still proved effective, and State Department officials praised the participants for being "superb representatives of the United States in every way."

Despite the continued success of the Jazz Ambassadors program, some policymakers in Washington voiced concern over the changes privatization had brought to the program. Was the government's commitment to jazz growing less focused? Would the image of jazz as a specifically American genre be maintained by private investors? To preserve the importance of jazz as a symbol of American identity, Representative Robert C. Wilson of California introduced a joint resolution (H.J.Res. 395) on February 28, 1973, to declare "the national music of the United States to be jazz." The measure failed to pass, and Congress's support of jazz began to wane. In 1978 the Jazz Ambassadors program was downsized dramatically and transferred from the State Department to the newly formed US International Communications Agency. Although National Endowment for the Arts funding was earmarked specifically for jazz in 1982, discussions of the genre had all but disappeared from Congress.

Representative John Conyers Jr. of Michigan is largely responsible for reinvigorating jazz appreciation among Washington politicians. Conyers had been an active participant in the civil rights movement, and he wrote the legislation that made Martin Luther King Day a national holiday. In 1981 Conyers created the Parker-Coltrane Political Action Committee to raise funds for prospective black congressional candidates. When asked why he named the PAC after two saxophonists he replied, "Politics is everybody's business—including people who dig great jazz." These efforts reflect Conyers's belief in the cultural importance of the genre. On September 25, 1986, he proposed "A concurrent resolution designating jazz as an American national treasure" (H.Con.Res. 396). The goal of the bill was to ensure that jazz, "a rare and valuable American treasure," would be "preserved, understood and promulgated." As the title of this resolution indicated, it was concurrent with a Senate resolution (S.Con. Res. 170) introduced by Alan Cranston of California on October 15, 1986. Although neither resolution gathered enough support for passage, Conyers and Cranston refused to give up. In 1987 they introduced revised versions in the House and Senate (H.Con.Res. 57 and S.Con.Res. 23), both of which passed unanimously under the general title of the Jazz Preservation Act. For the first time in history, jazz was officially recognized as a national treasure, "an indigenous American music and art form, bringing to this country and the world a uniquely American musical synthesis and culture through the African-American experience."

But the legislation of jazz required more than simply stating its value as a national treasure. In a 1990 congressional bill sponsored by Senator J. Bennett Johnston of Louisiana, then chair of the Senate Appropriations Subcommittee for the Department of the Interior, the secretary of the interior was asked "to conduct a study of the feasibility of establishing a unit of the National Park System to interpret and commemorate the origins, development, and progression of Jazz in the United States" (S. 2846). Because New Orleans was seen as the ideal location for the proposed national park for jazz, Louisiana representative Lindy Boggs introduced a similar resolution in the House. After much debate, the House and Senate passed both bills, which called for the establishment of the Preservation of Jazz Commission. The commission was charged with overseeing the congressionally mandated study, which proved to be divisive in the greater New Orleans community. In general, some white New Orleans residents were troubled by the commission's definition of the origins of jazz as strictly African American. Local jazz historian Al Rose even went so far as to argue that the so-called "myth of jazz's African origins" was blocking recognition of the contributions made by other ethnic groups. Race became an inflammatory topic during public discussions of the study. Consequently, when the commission's report was submitted one year later, all ethnic categories were removed from the definition of jazz.

In 1993, Louisiana representative William J. Jefferson and senator J. Bennett Johnston introduced the New Orleans Jazz National Historic Park Act into the House and Senate (H.R. 3408, S. 1586). After much debate, it was voted into law as an amendment to the California Desert Protection Act of 1994 with no mention of the music's African American origins. References to the African American roots of jazz were also absent in a second legislative action that year, S.J.Res. 182, a "joint resolution to designate the year 1995 as 'Jazz Centennial Year.'"

In response to these changes in the legislature's definition of jazz, Representative Conyers reintroduced H.Con.Res. 57 in 1997, "expressing the sense of Congress respecting the designation of jazz as a rare and valuable national treasure." This resolution, which attempted to reinsert recognition of "the African-American experience" into the origins of jazz and describe the genre as "a unifying force, bridging cultural, religious, ethnic, and age differences in our diverse society," was passed on to committee and then abandoned.

The decision of the 105th Congress not to vote on this last resolution reveals how attitudes toward jazz began to change in Washington's political circles after the Cold War. Instead of defining jazz as an art form rooted in African American culture, Congress began to describe the genre as an art form "indigenous to the United States" that "incorporates and transcends differences of nationality, religion, language, culture, socioeconomic status, and race." Consequently, Representative Conyers and his colleagues Charles Rangel, Frank Pallone Jr., and Eleanor Holmes Norton began to seek new ways of recognizing the African American contribution to jazz. Since 2002, various concurrent resolutions in the House and Senate have noted the contributions of individual African American jazz musicians: Lionel Hampton, Dinah Washington, William "Count" Basie, Duke Ellington, Shirley Horn, Miles Davis, Jon Faddis, and Lena Horne. In the case of Duke Ellington, the bill not only honored his life and work but also recognized "the Duke Ellington School of the Arts in Washington, D.C., on the occasion of its 30th anniversary" and pledged support for "the annual Duke Ellington Jazz Festival to be held in Washington, D.C." The inaugural festival, which took place in September 2005 and was funded by private donors and corporate sponsors, included a congressional resolution in support of the festival and participation by one hundred members of Congress. Representative Eleanor Holmes Norton presented Dave Brubeck with the first Duke Ellington Festival Lifetime Achievement Award at an opening congressional reception on Capitol Hill, and most concerts featured at least one politician as honorary host or speaker. In 2010, due to a change in the festival's mission, the Duke Ellington Jazz Festival was renamed the DC Jazz Festival. Instead of merely "preserving" the rich history of jazz, festival organizers wanted to showcase the diverse jazz scene of the host city and promote contemporary jazz as an ever-expanding and inclusive art form.

Over the last seventy-five years, decisions made in Washington have facilitated the establishment of jazz as an important element in America's cultural identity. But as Congress's definition of jazz has changed, so too has the genre itself. What America needs is not a Jazz Preservation Act but a commitment to jazz conservation. Thanks to the commitment of countless musicians, jazz has continued to grow more inclusive both at home and abroad. The Jazz Ambassadors set the precedent for real change by reaching out to foreign audiences, sharing their culture and ideas, and learning from those they encountered. As a Polish fan once explained to Dave Brubeck: "What you brought [us] wasn't just jazz. It was the Grand Canyon. It was the Empire State Building. It was America."

THERE'S A PLACE FOR US... SOMEWHERE

■ ■ ■ ■ ■

On September 22, 1961, President John F. Kennedy welcomed a bipartisan group of congressmen and cabinet officials into the Oval Office when he signed the Juvenile Delinquency and Youth Offenses Control Act into law. Under this piece of legislation, Kennedy announced that the federal government had finally become "an active partner with States and local communities" in their efforts to "control the spread of delinquency... and stem the tide... of youthful offences."

Kennedy's signing of the law came as something of a surprise. He had paid little attention to juvenile delinquency during his presidential campaign, even though polls had shown that most Americans believed that as a Democrat he would handle the issue better than his Republican rival, Richard Nixon. Shortly after his inauguration, however, Kennedy's attitude changed. In May 1961, he established the President's Commission on Juvenile Delinquency and Youth Crime, placing his brother Robert, the new attorney general, at the helm. The commission drew up a report that declared juvenile delinquency a "national emergency" and linked its recent increase to a range of social and infrastructure problems, from substandard housing, family disintegration, and high unemployment to racial discrimination and poor education. In response to the report, Kennedy called on Congress to draw up new legislation, which was done in record time. Overseeing the whole process was Adam Yarmolinsky, a lawyer and behind-the-scenes aide to President Kennedy. When Yarmolinsky was asked several years later what had sparked his boss's interest in juvenile delinquency, he offered a curt, three-word response: "*West Side Story*."

West Side Story is a foundational work in American musical theater. A retelling of Shakespeare's *Romeo and Juliet* set in a poverty-stricken immigrant neighborhood in New York City, the work uses compulsive music and explosive dance to highlight troubling American social problems. The show premiered on Broadway in 1957 and transferred to the silver screen in 1961. Since then, audiences around the world have witnessed countless revivals and reimaginings, each a reflection of contemporary struggles and prejudices.

The creation of what would become *West Side Story* began in January 1949, when the dancer–choreographer Jerome Robbins reached out to composer Leonard Bernstein and playwright Arthur Laurents with a "noble idea: a modern version of *Romeo and Juliet* set in slums at the coincidence of Easter–Passover celebrations." In its initial form, the musical's action "was conceived as taking place on the East Side of New York" and "involving as the feuding parties Catholics and Jews." Characterized by "a certain amount of slugging and blood-letting," Robbins's idea "seemed to match the Romeo story very well," Bernstein explained, "except this was not a family feud but religion-oriented."

From the beginning, the focal point of this modern take on *Romeo and Juliet* was not the lovers themselves but the societal conflict that kept them apart. Robbins's conceptualization of the tragedy through the lens of religious conflict appealed to Bernstein and Laurents. Like Robbins, they were the sons of Jewish immigrants and had experienced firsthand the destructive power of anti-Semitism.

Work on the project began right away. During the first two weeks of January, the team met in person on several occasions and hammered out a series of brief outlines, now preserved in the Library of Congress. News of the work-in-progress spread quickly. On January 27, the *New York Times* ran a story announcing that Shakespeare's tragedy was about to "undergo local renovation by Bernstein, Robbins, and Laurents"—three rising stars in their respective fields. Bernstein, "the well-known pianist–composer–

conductor," had been in the headlines since 1943, when he made a surprise debut on the conductor's podium of the New York Philharmonic. The following year, he and Robbins joined forces, wowing audiences with their ballet *Fancy Free* and Broadway smash musical *On the Town*. Laurents, a serious playwright, was new to the team. As an army sergeant, he had spent the war years writing scripts for military training films before splashing onto the New York theater scene in December 1945 with *Home of the Brave*, a biting critique of anti-Semitism in the US military. As the *New York Times* explained, the trio's forthcoming musical was "as yet untitled" and "still in the preliminary stages." Nonetheless, it was expected to "arrive in New York next season"—a prediction that proved wildly optimistic.

As work on the show progressed, Robbins, Bernstein, and Laurents discovered that their individual visions for the project differed markedly. From the beginning, Robbins had been interested in creating a dance-heavy musical centered on a modern-day Romeo and his struggles in contemporary society. In contrast, Bernstein envisioned a "great American opera," tentatively called *Operation Capulet*, with a focus on "Juliet, who is Jewish" and her family, newly arrived from Eastern Europe. Laurents argued for a more sociological approach to the project. Using the title *East Side Story*, he crafted a dialogue-heavy narrative that pitted the lovers' naïve idealism against the squalid reality of their life in the tenements. The biggest disagreements involved Bernstein's vision for the music. "I want to make one thing clear before we go any further," declared Laurents, "and that is that I'm not writing any fucking libretto for any goddamned Bernstein opera!" Not surprisingly, the collaboration soon fractured.

As winter shifted to spring, the trio attempted to work long distance, with Laurents in California, Bernstein on a conducting tour in the Midwest, and Robbins at home in New York. In mid-April, Laurents sent his colleagues a draft of the first few scenes of Act I. A heated phone call between Bernstein and Laurents came next, followed by a letter from Laurents that tried to resolve the misunderstanding.

> *Dear Lenny,*
> *I'm sending a copy of this to Jerry [Robbins] so that there won't be any wheels within wheels and we'll all be abreast of what is what. Quite*

> *frankly, I was disturbed by our phone conversation Monday night. Unless I seriously misinterpreted you, this is what I understood you to say: You conceive of the show's script as being written in an almost purely poetic style; you have doubts (understandable) whether I can write in that style without forcing; and—most important—if my writing cannot be that poetic, then you would not have complete faith in the project and, therefore, would rather abandon it before spending any actual working time on it.*

Laurents continued by explaining that he had already "spent a good deal of time and money" working on the show, and "would not have worked on it . . . all these weeks . . . had I not, quite naturally, assumed . . . we were going to do it." He then pushed back on Bernstein's "conception" of the work, remarking that the production should have "less music," not more.

> *I am not adamant or absolute in my feelings; they can be modified. But a musical show (and I see this as a musical show or whatever you want to call it, but not as an opera or even a modified opera) is a collaboration. A collaboration calls for compromise. . . . We all know each other's work, we all can concede and adjust, and there can be a meeting point.*

Bernstein's response is not preserved, but a follow-up letter from Laurents reveals that by the end of April the composer had pulled out of the project:

> Dear Lenny,
>
> I'm sorry you've decided not to do the show, sorrier still because of the main reason which led you to drop out. . . . One thing I'd like to make clear—and I trust you will believe me. I did not start out with "a priori prejudices." Rather, I started out with admiration for your work and eagerness to be your friend. Along the line, hostility popped up. But since I felt it from you, just as you said you felt it from me, and made the exact same efforts you did, I can only conclude we were both projecting a little and, possibly, were further impaired by the occasional whispers ever present.

Laurents regretted that they "had such a short run" and hoped that now "that the tension is gone" they "can become friends." He closed the letter by wishing Bernstein the best: "Whatever show or venture you embark on next, please know I'll be rooting for you."

It is important to acknowledge the rift that developed between Bernstein and Laurents early on, especially since Bernstein offered a rosier version of events in the production diary he wrote in 1957 and published in the playbill distributed at performances of *West Side Story*. Here, Bernstein claimed that he thought Laurents's *East Side Story* script contained "much good stuff," and that the early dissolution of their collaboration was due to conflicting work schedules. In a letter to a friend, however, Bernstein offered a more candid description of why he quit the project: "I remember receiving about a dozen pages [from Laurents] and saying to myself that this is never going to work. . . . I had a strong feeling of staleness of the East Side situation, and I didn't like the too-angry, too-bitchy, too-vulgar tone of it." This animosity between Bernstein and Laurents never went away completely, even after they reconciled, and it eventually fueled some of the animosity expressed by the characters in *West Side Story*.

Six years passed before Robbins, Laurents, and Bernstein reunited. During that time, all three were ensnared in the fraught world of American Cold War politics. In 1949, *Life* magazine included Bernstein's photo alongside Aaron Copland's in an exposé on Communist "fellow travelers." A year later, the infamous *Red Channels* report named Bernstein, Robbins, and Laurents as Communist sympathizers. The FBI opened files on them, and each responded differently.

Bernstein quietly resigned from conducting jobs as political pressure mounted. In 1950, the Truman administration removed his music from overseas US libraries, and in 1953 Eisenhower's State Department labeled him a "security risk" and pulled his passport. Summoned to Washington, DC, Bernstein, with help from his lawyer James McInerney—"an old Commie-chaser" whom Bernstein admired, despite the $3,500 fee—filed an affidavit denying Communist ties. Bernstein claimed that he had been "improperly exploited by cleverly camouflaged organizations, which concealed their true objectives and Communist aims," and cited Paul Robeson as an example. When accusations resurfaced in 1956, this time from Representative John Rooney and the House Appropriations Committee, Bernstein turned to his new ally Senator John F. Kennedy, who discreetly shut down the inquiry.

Laurents and Robbins fared worse. Laurents, whose passport was also revoked in 1953, admitted to Communist political affiliations but refused to name others. Though he eventually regained his passport, Hollywood blacklisted him, and he lived abroad for over a year to evade direct entanglement with the House Un-American Activities Committee—a fate that Robbins, unfortunately, did not avoid.

In May 1953, Robbins publicly testified as a cooperating witness before HUAC. As he confessed in his diary, he was afraid that his homosexuality would be exposed if he did not testify. Hand in hand with the Red Scare over Communism, a homophobic panic known as the Lavender Scare swept the country after World War II. It began in 1950, when a Senate report declared homosexuals unfit for employment in the federal government. Two years later, the State Department fired 126 homosexuals as alleged "perverts." And in April 1953 Eisenhower issued Executive Order 10450, which described homosexuality as an "immoral" behavior and "sexual perversion." In his testimony, Robbins confessed to past membership in the CPUSA and named eight colleagues still active in the party. Robbins's career survived, but at a personal cost. "You were a shit [for testifying]," Laurents told him. Although the two would soon collaborate again, their friendship never fully recovered.

These political wounds left Bernstein, Laurents, and Robbins more cynical in their view of American society. When they finally agreed to work together again in the mid-1950s, it wasn't Shakespeare's love story that drew their interest but a darker story by James M. Cain, author of *The Postman Always Rings Twice* and *Double Indemnity*.

While in Italy in 1955, Bernstein was asked to score a musical based on Cain's *Serenade*, a project that Laurents had been contracted to work on, too. Set in Mexico and the US and loosely based on Bizet's *Carmen*, *Serenade* tells the story of an opera singer who discovers his homosexual tendencies through a series of sexual encounters. Bernstein had been a fan of the novel since its publication in 1938. Like Laurents, he was drawn to Cain's exploration of homosexuality in artistic circles. Laurents was open about his sexual preference for men. Bernstein, not so much. Since 1951, he had been married to actress Felicia Montealegre, who was aware of his sexual preferences. "You are a homosexual and may never change," she wrote to him shortly after their honeymoon.

When Bernstein returned to New York, he and Laurents approached Robbins about *Serenade*. Robbins declined. As Laurents recalled, "Jerry brushed us aside: if we were all going to do a musical, why not 'Romeo'? Bernstein agreed, and *Serenade* was abandoned. Days later, the *New York Times* announced that Bernstein, Laurents, and Robbins had taken "from their idea bank a notion they have been saving for some time." Still labeled *East Side Story*, the musical was back on track.

As work on the project started up again, Laurents grew less convinced that the Catholic–Jewish conflict should be at the heart of the story. "My reaction was it was *Abie's Irish Rose*"—a popular play from the 1920s that had just been revived on Broadway. In a letter to Bernstein dated July 19, Laurents enclosed a revised outline for their project, which he also sent to Robbins. Though he described it as "the barest of skeletons," Laurents wrote that he hoped it might "be some sort of basis for all of us to do some thinking on before we meet again." The outline replaced the Catholic–Jewish conflict with a narrative about feuding gangs. "I don't know whether you've been so busy that you've missed all the juvenile gang war news. Not only is it all over the papers every day, but it is going to be all over the movie screens," wrote Laurents. Indeed, 1955 saw the premieres of two major films highlighting juvenile delinquency: *Rebel Without a Cause*, starring James Dean and Natalie Wood, and *Blackboard Jungle*, featuring Sidney Poitier. "By accident, then, we have hit on an idea which is suddenly extremely topical, timely, and just plain hot," Laurents wrote. "For this reason, I hope we can get to serious work on it as early as we planned." Laurents concluded his letter by drawing Bernstein's attention to a revision in the work's setting: "Incidentally, I hope you noticed that I didn't say 'East Side Story.' This was because of our mutual feeling that the locale should not be specific or definitely placed in any specific city." Bernstein had been pushing for a universal story in an unnamed urban locale. Of course, this would eventually change, but it is worth noting that in July 1955 the idea of depicting warring gangs was not yet tied to a specific city or ethnic group. Instead, the focus was on juvenile delinquency more generally, a sociological problem that had been making waves in the halls of Congress.

In the spring of 1953, a subcommittee of the Senate Judiciary Committee hosted a series of televised public hearings committed to finding the cause of juvenile delinquency. "As a nation," said the committee chairman, Republican Senator Robert Hendrickson, "we must find out what is causing this increasingly serious problem and what can be done to prevent it." After three days of testimony, the Subcommittee on Juvenile Delinquency came to the consensus that the primary cause for the rise in gang violence was comic books, specifically the horror and crime comic books that had recently become popular among adolescent boys. The hearings generated widespread media attention, which led to a negative perception of comic books among parents and educators. In response, the comic book industry established the Comics Code Authority (CCA) in 1954, which significantly changed the content and nature of comic books for decades.

At the hearings, William Gains, president of Entertainment Comics, the primary publisher of American horror comics, argued that blaming his product for juvenile delinquency was preposterous. "The truth is, that delinquency is a product of the real environment in which a child lives—and not of the fiction he reads." The press generally agreed. Since 1950, investigative reporters across the country had been attributing the rise in youth violence to ethnic conflicts. In one of the earliest reports on the problem, the *New York Times* named the East Bronx as the "deadliest of teen war areas," due to "the influx of Negro and Puerto Rican families." The recent wave of migration had reportedly caused "the Irish and Italian street gangs" to wage "savage war on the newcomers." These "pitched battles in the streets and parks" involved "knives and guns," and "for every youth killed . . . at least five [were] seriously wounded." This was the type of reporting that Laurents was referring to in his letter to Bernstein. He believed that ethnic conflict was the sociological condition that could make their adaptation of *Romeo and Juliet* culturally relevant.

As the focus shifted from religious conflict to gang warfare, Laurents, Robbins, and Bernstein experimented with various ethnicities. Early on, they toyed with the idea of changing the musical's oppressed group from Jews to African Americans. Hollywood had effectively done the same with the film adaptation of Laurents's *Home of the Brave* in 1949, switching out the original Jewish protagonist for a black man. But Bernstein quickly nixed this idea. As one of his friends had pointed out to him in a letter, "there are historical connotations involved in *Romeo and Juliet*," and he couldn't help but wonder, "how fully could one accept a Negro as Romeo and a white girl as Juliet—even though the whole medium is, to begin with, artificial?"

The next conflict they considered was Mexicans versus Americans. This fell through, too. The eventual decision to pit a gang of Puerto Rican youths against a gang of Anglo-Americans appears to have been reached in late August. Bernstein was conducting the Hollywood Bowl orchestra in Los Angeles, where Laurents was working on a screenplay, his name having finally been removed from the film industry's blacklist. According to Bernstein's fictionalized production diary, he and Laurents were sitting by a swimming pool on August 25 (Bernstein's birthday) when the decision was made to focus "on two teen-age gangs as the warring factions, one of them newly arrived Puerto Ricans, the other self-styled 'Americans.'" As Laurents tells it, Bernstein saw an article in the *Los Angeles Times* about the rise in Latino gangs. "Lenny said: 'What about doing it about the Chicanos?'" Laurents admitted that he didn't know Los Angeles well enough to write a script based in the city. Could the same idea be transferred to New York? "In New York, we had the Puerto Ricans, and at that time the papers were full of stories about juvenile delinquents and gangs. We got really excited and phoned Jerry, and that started the whole thing."

Shifting the ethnic identity of the musical's newly arrived characters from East European Jews to Puerto Ricans set Bernstein, Laurents, and Robbins adrift in uncharted waters. New York's Puerto Rican population had tripled in the last decade, and newspaper headlines regularly highlighted the effects: "Little Puerto Rico, a Gigantic Sardine Can," "Puerto Rican Influx Overcrowds Schools," "Crime Festers in Bulging Tenements." In February 1955 the civil rights advocate Charles Abrams published an article titled "How to Remedy our 'Puerto Rican Problem'" that described "the slums of Harlem, where most Puerto Ricans have found shelter," as "among the worst in the world." Similar descriptions were given of San Juan Hill, where "many families packed into subdivided apartments that violated the city's housing code," and the majority of residents "lived in buildings that lacked central heating" and private toilets. These conditions were a world away from the New York Robbins, Laurents, and Bernstein knew. As Robbins later admitted, venturing into these Puerto Rican neighborhoods was like entering a foreign realm: "The streets are darker, the signs are in Spanish, and the people lead their lives on the sidewalks." The team never felt fully comfortable immersing themselves in the community they had committed to writing about. As Bernstein later explained: "We visited a gym in Brooklyn where there were different gangs that a social organization was trying to bring together," but "I don't know if too much eventually got into *West Side Story*." In the end, the decision to feature a Puerto Rican gang in the musical was more a matter of convenience than true cultural interest. "The Puerto Rican thing had just begun to explode," explained Bernstein. Like juvenile delinquency, it was a topic ripe for artistic development.

Bernstein and Laurents had originally planned to write all the lyrics themselves, but as work on the musical progressed they realized they needed help. In September, the seasoned lyricists Betty Comden and Adolph Green were approached, but their busy schedule kept them from signing on. Laurents recommended Stephen Sondheim, a twenty-five-year-old aspiring Broadway composer he had recently met at a party. Sondheim hesitated at first: "I can't do the show. I've never been that poor, and I've never even known a Puerto Rican." But Laurents and Bernstein assured him not to worry. Eventually, Sondheim's mentor, Oscar Hammerstein II, convinced him to take the job, noting that he would benefit from making his Broadway debut as part of a winning team.

With Sondheim on board, the foursome began to work in earnest. A primary concern for everyone involved was developing the ethnic conflict. Even the musical's central love song, "Somewhere," was designed to serve as a foil to the racial discord. In every aspect of the musical—dialogue, dance, music, and lyrics—attention was focused on creating distinct characteristics for each gang. Laurents began by developing contrasting speaking styles for the two groups. He had the Puerto Ricans speak with heavy accents and a smattering of Spanish words and phrases in a nod to their Hispanic origins. The "Americans" spoke in a more colloquial, streetwise manner filled with fictionalized slang, like "cracko jacko" and "frabbajabba," that presented an air of streetwise authenticity without the use of offensive words. Laurents also gave each gang a symbolic name.

He dubbed the Puerto Rican gang the Sharks, a label that evokes predatory, dangerous creatures. In contrast, he named the white "American" gang the Jets, a non-threatening name associated with speed, power, and modernity. In the opening scene of Laurents's script, the Jets appear "in possession of the area: owning, enjoying, loving their 'home.'" The instigating conflict occurs when the Sharks arrive. Throughout the musical, they are defined as an invasive force: "Them PRs are the reason my old man's gone bust," claims one of the Jets. "My old man says them Puerto Ricans is ruinin' free ennaprise," says another. "These PRs are different" from other immigrants, states a third. "They keep on coming like cockroaches."

In his choreography, Robbins devised distinctive dance styles for the two gangs. Movement served as a narrative tool for Robbins, and he drew on cultural stereotypes as a means of choreographing ethnic difference. For example, the Puerto Ricans are given fluid, hip-swaying motions and rhythmic footwork that evoke sensualism and passion, stereotypical references to their Latin American heritage. In contrast, the "Americans" are defined by sharp, angular, aggressive movements, which reference bebop jazz and modern dance. The staccato actions and strong lines suggest rebellious energy. Unlike the Sharks, whose polyrhythmic style is built on intricate and varied patterns, the Jets tend to move in a uniform, synchronized manner, suggesting their tight-knit solidarity and the strict hierarchy within their group. Their dance numbers, such as the iconic "Cool," emphasize disciplined, coordinated movements that convey a desire for dominance and control.

Of course, Robbins's distinctive choreography was heavily reliant on Bernstein's music. Like his colleagues, Bernstein mined cultural stereotypes when creating the sonic worlds of the Sharks and Jets. For the Sharks, he drew from an array of Latin-infused styles. His musical references did not come directly from contemporary Puerto Rican culture, but rather were an amalgamation of the commercialized "Latin Craze" music that had swept through the US in the 1930s and 1940s in films like *The Cuban Love Song* (1930) and *Down Argentine Way* (1940), musicals like *Too Many Girls* (1939) by Richard Rodgers and Lorenz Hart and Cole Porter's *Mexican Hayride* (1944), and concert works like George Gershwin's *Cuban Overture* (1932) and Aaron Copland's *El Salón México* (1936). For the Jets, he borrowed motifs from contemporary jazz and traditional musical comedy. By the time Sondheim joined the project in late October, Bernstein had already begun composing two of the tunes that defined the feuding ethnicities: "America" and "Cool."

Like many composers, Bernstein often recycled tunes. For "America," the primary dance number that defines the Puerto Ricans, he recycled music that he had composed many years earlier. "I had conceived an idea for a ballet when I was in Key West in 1941," Bernstein explained. "I was crazy about Cuban music. The ballet was to be called *Conch Town*. It never got finished. It was always lying around and part of it got used in *West Side*." The most striking feature of "America" is its metric pulse, which undulates between duple and triple beat patterns. This rhythmic interplay propels the song forward. In the original stage version of *West Side Story*, "America" is performed by the Sharks' Puerto Rican girlfriends, who debate the pros and cons of their move to New York. Sondheim did little research before writing the lyrics, and it shows. In addition to simplifying the complexity of the immigrant experience, he set up an ill-informed contrast between Puerto Rico and the United States. Puerto Rico is described as an "ugly island," a place of squalor and "tropical diseases" that one should be glad to leave behind. In contrast, America is presented as a land of material wealth and opportunity with modern conveniences like washing machines and shiny new cars. "America" is the only number that defines the Puerto Rican experience in *West Side Story*. The Sharks, specifically, do not have their own song. In contrast, three songs are dedicated to the backstory and character development of the Jets.

The musical's opening number, "Jets Song," serves as an anthem of the gang's identity. Borrowing text from Laurents's original script, Sondheim created lyrics that describe a close-knit group, bound by fidelity and toughness: "Here come the Jets like a bat out of hell— / Someone gets in our way, Someone don't feel so well!" The Jets see themselves as masters of their own turf. Their sense of superiority is fed by an aggressive disdain for outsiders: "We're drawin' the line, so keep your noses hidden! / We're hangin' a sign, says 'Visitors forbidden'— / And we ain't kiddin'." As this song demonstrates, the core of the Jets' identity is tied to keeping the Sharks, and by extension the Puerto Rican community, at bay.

The next Jets song, "Cool," occurs right before the first rumble. Like

"America," Bernstein had composed most of the song before Sondheim joined the project. The music is related to Bernstein's interest in contemporary jazz. In January 1955, Bernstein was appointed conductor of the NBC Symphony, then known as the Symphony of the Air Orchestra. On March 16, the orchestra premiered a new symphonic suite by Duke Ellington called *Night Creatures*. As a review in the *New York Times* explained, Ellington replaced Bernstein at the podium that evening, and his *Night Creatures* offered a new take on modern music: "an expansiveness and mood rarely encountered in the brief numbers one hears generally in jazz circles." The *Times* reviewer found the work's second movement, "Stalking Monster," especially impressive. This section "used figures in the high treble and low bass to develop an eerie atmosphere," he noted. "It was an effective idea." Bernstein clearly agreed; he used the opening passages of "Stalking Monster" several months later when composing his own "eerie atmosphere" in "Cool."

Melodically, "Cool" is built around fragmented bebop motifs that convey dissonance and tension. The sharp, staccato notes create a feeling of nervous energy, further underscored by sudden dynamic shifts that suggest the gang members' struggle to maintain control. The lyrics accomplish a similar objective. At this point in the musical, the Jets are on edge, simmering with anger and fear after a series of escalating confrontations with the Sharks. The lyrics express their desperate attempt to impose control over their emotions. They use the command to "stay cool" as a mantra to prevent them from spiraling into violence.

Throughout the creative process, Laurents pushed his collaborators to include content that reflected current views about the cause of juvenile delinquency. For example, in act one, scene six, as the Jets bide their time in a drugstore waiting for the Sharks to arrive for a "war council," the youngest Jet, Baby John, is shown reading a comic book. And later, after the deadly rumble, the Jets endear themselves to audiences in yet another song, "Officer Krupke," a slapstick comedy number that ticks through the long list of societal problems—broken family, inadequate education, an unfair judicial system, mental illness—that have left them "so disturbed" and "misunderstood."

With their portrayal of the Jets, the creators of *West Side Story* offered a subtle critique of contemporary political discourse around juvenile delinquency. At one point there were plans to reference other political issues, nuclear warfare and sexual fluidity, in two additional songs for the Jets: "Atom Bomb Mambo" and "Like Everybody Else." These numbers were cut before the premiere.

Rehearsals for *West Side Story* began in June 1957 and ran for eight weeks. Robbins took complete control of the process. From the first day, he insisted that the cast use method acting, "an experiential, quasi-psychoanalytical approach" developed in Russia by Konstantin Stanislavski. Popular since the 1930s, the goal was for each cast member to embody fully the identity of their character. Robbins wanted the actors to live the ethnic hatred of the story. Consequently, he divided the cast into rival groups, Puerto Ricans vs. "Americans," and demanded that they stay in character on stage and off. The realism of Robbins's approach heightened the animosity expressed on stage. As a reporter for the *Washington Post* noted, the actors appeared to have literally transformed into the delinquents they were meant to portray: "Policemen along the 52nd St. beat are having a spot of trouble trying to decide which passing youths are juvenile delinquents and which are merely singers and dancers on their way to rehearsals for 'The West Side Story' at the ANTA Theatre."

West Side Story opened for previews at the National Theatre in Washington DC on August 19, 1957. The choice of the nation's capital was no coincidence. The musical engaged directly with domestic politics, and what better place to get a read on how that message might land than a half mile from the White House. "Everyone's coming," Bernstein wrote to his wife four days before the premiere, "even Nixon and 35 admirals." There were many senators in the audience, including J. William Fulbright and Jacob K. Javits. Eisenhower's chief of staff, Sherman Adams, attended, as did Supreme Court Justice Felix Frankfurter, Mrs. Robert Kennedy, numerous State Department officials, and at least three ambassadors.

During intermission, Bernstein made his way to the foyer to judge firsthand the audience's reaction. As a local reporter noted, "He was a little disconcerted" when "a woman who identified herself as a one-time social worker in a tough neighborhood" proclaimed: "It's all so real, so true. It chills my blood to remember." "It isn't meant to be realistic," Bernstein responded. "Poetry—poetry set to music—that's what we were trying to do."

When the reviews came in, they were generally positive. Richard L. Coe, theater critic for the *Washington Post*, declared himself "tremendously moved" by the musical's "uniquely cohesive comment on life." Bernstein's "flowing music... makes us feel what we do not understand," noted Coe. "It is a musical comment with only implied blame." Paul Hume, music critic for the *Post*, was less impressed. Hume avoided the musical's sociological message, noting only that the plot concerned "immigrant Puerto Ricans and native New Yorkers separated into gangs that are so unhappily in the news today." A letter to the editor complained about the musical's adulation of violent criminals. Coe responded in a second review, published eleven days later: "In *West Side Story*, four men are taking a timeless view of one of our society's sorriest phenomena, the teen-age gangs of a great city." Consequently, "it is ridiculous to say that *West Side Story* glorifies young thugs," he noted. "What the music tells us is what, in our outrage, we easily forget: that within all of us beat the same emotions, primitive urges, lyrical dreams, cynical experiences, [and] questioning fears."

West Side Story was the first Broadway musical to question the inevitability of the American dream. Its tragic depiction of violence and juvenile delinquency made Robbins, Laurents, Bernstein, and Sondheim the talk of the town. At a public ceremony on August 30, the four men received a "gold key" to the city. As a report in the *New York Times* explained: "[DC] Commissioner [Robert E.] McLaughlin told the collaborators on *West Side Story* today that it was 'amazing you could make a musical out of the problem of juvenile delinquency,' and expressed hope that it might contribute to an understanding of the problem." In response to the commissioner's comments, Bernstein took it upon himself to explain again "that the theme was not really juvenile delinquency, but the racial and national frictions that provide the seed ground for juvenile delinquency and gang warfare."

References to *West Side Story* soon made their way into DC politics. On September 13, 1957, Judge Orman W. Ketcham urged city commissioners to restore the $44,000 they had recently trimmed from the juvenile court's budget. "I don't want to see the *West Side Story* happening here," he said. Federal politicians showed concern, too. After attending a performance of the musical, Democratic Senator Hubert Humphrey of Minnesota proposed a Youth Conservation Corps modeled on the Civilian Conservation Corps of the 1930s, arguing that physical labor would stem the violent reality of *West Side Story*. Humphrey's proposal languished in Congress; conservatives opposed the program's cost, and liberals worried that "the boot camps would become alternative detention facilities," and that "the structural causes of juvenile delinquency" would only worsen.

In general, politicians ignored the "Puerto Rican problem" outlined in *West Side Story*. But members of the Puerto Rican community did not. According to Bernstein, a reporter from *La Prensa* left a telephone message on opening night complaining about the song "America." They said that "the show would be picketed when we came to New York unless we omitted or changed the song." Sondheim fielded complaints as well. "I got a letter complaining about the one line 'Island of tropic diseases.'" The author was "outraged on behalf of Puerto Rico, claiming that we were making fun of Puerto Rico and being sarcastic about it. But I didn't change it," Bernstein interjected, "it wasn't just that line they objected to. We were insulting not only Puerto Rico but the Puerto Ricans and all immigrants.... We met that threat by doing nothing about it, not changing a syllable, and we were not picketed."

West Side Story opened on Broadway at the Winter Garden Theater on September 26, 1957. Reviews were good but not glowing, and in the *New York Times*, there was more pushback from scholars and community activists about inaccuracies in the musical's depiction of Puerto Rico. For example, in "The Facts Don't Rhyme," Howard A. Rusk MD presented scientific data that disproved the assertion that the island was rife with tropical diseases. And in "The Puerto Rican Adapts Remarkably," Rev. David W. Barry used firsthand knowledge to refute the stereotypical images of Puerto Ricans in songs like "America."

Spanish-language newspapers in New York and San Juan published the opinions of Puerto Rican politicians who had seen the show. As a reporter for *El Mundo* explained, *West Side Story* revealed the "tragic intolerance that Puerto Rican migrants face in New York." The negative perceptions became so dire that Puerto Rico's governor, Luis Muñoz Marín, "hired a public relations firm to convince mainland Americans that Puerto Ricans were not gangsters."

West Side Story laid bare the destructive force created when poverty, social indifference, and racism mix—and journalists in New York paid attention. Within a few weeks of the premiere, reporting about juvenile delinquency began to change in tone. Detailed descriptions of crime and violence gave way to sympathetic descriptions of underprivileged urban youth. For example, in September 1957, the *New Yorker* published "The Cherubs Are Rumbling," an in-depth account of a community dance in Brooklyn hosted by a teenage street gang, organized to promote greater socialization among gang members and steer them away from violent behavior. The article introduced readers to an array of juvenile delinquents, taking care to describe them as complex individuals with different backgrounds, behaviors, and attitudes. Special emphasis was placed on the sense of community found in gang culture. Although conflict and violence are described as regular features of gang life, the article also notes the potential for positive change when communication and mediation take the place of violence.

Several months later, the *New York Times* ran a seven-part investigation into the city's "shook-up generation." Penned by Harrison E. Salisbury, the series described the city's most troubled youth and the circumstances that led to their delinquency. "The gang is youth's last-ditch answer to adult pressures and conflicts," states Salisbury. "There is nothing romantic about the gang—*West Side Story* with its Romeo-and-Juliet legend to the contrary. The gang is pitiful, tragic, dangerous."

Similar in tone to "The Cherubs Are Rumbling," Salisbury's reporting offers a gritty yet sympathetic portrayal of New York's juvenile delinquents and the social infrastructure that has failed them: families, schools, public housing, the courts, and the health care system. Each installment describes real-life teens, some of whom resemble characters in *West Side Story*. For example, in the second installment readers meet Vincent, leader of the Silver Arrows, one of the roughly hundred "bopping (fighting) street gangs of New York City." Vincent "is a slender Puerto Rican youngster of 17 years of age who looks like an Aztec prince. He combs his black hair in a massive crest and carries his head high." Although "most gang members come from broken families," Vincent does not. He "is the only member of his family who is involved with gangs. 'I'm the only bad one,' he says shyly." Salisbury dedicates several paragraphs to explaining

Vincent's backstory and concludes that racism, more than anything else, is the source of Vincent's troubles. "Vincent learned street fighting in the Italian neighborhood" where his family first lived when they arrived in 1949. "He remembers being beaten up every day 'just because I was a Puerto Rican.'"

Salisbury concludes the series by describing the government's failed attempts to solve the problem of juvenile delinquency. After running through a litany of causes and responses similar to those outlined in "Officer Krupke," Salisbury notes that the biggest obstacle to eliminating youth violence is indifference: "For most New Yorkers the problem of delinquency does not seem to be immediate or personal." Most simply believe that it's not their problem to solve. "But for some citizens it is a problem of survival," not just "today and this week" but in perpetuity. Salisbury ends the article with a reference to *West Side Story*. When "Doc . . . tells the teenage Jets . . . 'You kids are making this a lousy world.'" The kids respond: "But that's the way we found it."

Despite all the attention it received in New York, *West Side Story* was not a blockbuster hit. As producer Hal Prince later explained, "The show did not . . . sell out for the year or so it ran on Broadway. It also had maybe a hundred walk-outs every single night—people totally confused by what it was, and rejecting it." For many, *West Side Story* exposed an aspect of American society that they did not want to see. This was especially true for some State Department officials.

In April 1958 Moscow's Moiseyev Dance Company arrived in New York as part of a carefully crafted cultural exchange between the Soviet Union and the United States. During their stay, the dancers attended a matinee performance of *West Side Story*, and Igor Moiseyev was so impressed that he urged the Soviet embassy to bring the production to Moscow. This request was repeated at least twice over the next year, once when a group of Soviet students visiting the United Nations attended a performance, and again in April 1959 when the Bolshoi Ballet visited New York. On each occasion, the State Department said no. As *Washington Post* critic George Dixon explained, *West Side Story* was seen as "playing straight man for Russian propagandists": if audiences in Iron Curtain countries saw the "young hoodlums knife each other on the streets of New York," they would interpret it "as typical young American behaviorism." Sending *West Side Story* behind the Iron Curtain would surely undermine all the progress being made by the State Department's Jazz Ambassadors tours. The Russians realized this, as did President Eisenhower. Under his watch, no production of *West Side Story* would be sent to Communist countries. Instead, Eisenhower focused his attention on a new, large-scale cultural initiative: the construction of Lincoln Center for the Performing Arts on New York's west side.

On May 14, 1959, Bernstein greeted President Eisenhower at the corner of 64th Street and Broadway to break ground for Lincoln Center. As Eisenhower lifted the first shovelful of dirt, he proclaimed that the new venue would be "a mighty influence for peace and understanding throughout the world." But before that, in August 1960, the demolition site, with its blocked-off thoroughfares and crumbling brownstones, became the primary set for the filming of a major motion picture: *West Side Story*.

It was the film version of *West Side Story* that had the greatest impact on US politics. Released in October 1961 and co-directed by Jerome Robbins and Robert Wise, the film increased awareness of juvenile delinquency and intensified the image of Puerto Ricans as "outsiders" in American society. As the filmmaker and scholar Frances Negrón-Muntaner has noted: "There is no single American cultural product that haunts Puerto Rican identity discourses in the United States more intensely than the 1961 film *West Side Story*." The film deepened the racial and cultural stereotypes already present in the stage version. For example, Rita Moreno was the only cast member of Puerto Rican heritage. She and all the other actors depicting Puerto Ricans were forced to darken their skin tone with makeup. Vibrant costumes further exoticized the Puerto Rican characters, emphasizing their "otherness" and distancing them from the white "Americans." Changes were made in the performance of "America," too. Instead of being sung by women only, as it had been in the stage version, the film version pits assimilated, hard-working female Puerto Ricans against the angry, unemployed Sharks. Changes such as these were noted by Puerto Rican advocates. As a disgruntled viewer named R. Domínguez expressed in a letter to Robbins and Wise shortly after the film's release, *West Side Story* "is the most powerful piece of anti-Puerto Rican propaganda to be released by any film studio in the United States of America and overseas." Domínguez describes the film's "portrayal of the Puerto Rican youth as a pack of hoodlums, their identification with switchblades, knifing, sexual looseness, delinquency, racism and murder" as "an unjustified and irresponsible defamation of a minority group." He then notes that the directors' "irresponsible smear under the name of entertainment will help to undermine everything that my people are striving for.... [You are] exposing my people to the insulting attitudes of the masses. You are stereotyping the Puerto Rican minority in the most sordid manner possible." Domínguez concludes by describing the film's effect on the Puerto Rican minority in the United States, which "has been struggling against discrimination and second-class citizenship for over two generations." Because of *West Side Story*, he claimed, Puerto Ricans have been pushed "one step backwards in our struggle for social and economic equality."

Few journalists commented on the negative portrayal of Puerto Ricans. Those who expressed disappointment in the film often did so in comparison to the original stage version. A reviewer for the *New York Times* described the film as "a Disneyfied version of gang warfare," wherein "the immediacy of the original ha[s] been softened" and "its impact blunted." Laurents agreed. Like Bernstein and Sondheim, he had not been involved in the production of the film, which he called "appalling":

> Film is either realistic or surreal. And a musical, to succeed, needs illusion. *West Side Story* begins, and you see all these boys, with dyed hair and color-coordinated sneakers, doing tour jetés down a New York street.... And then, when the so-called Puerto Ricans came on, made up to look like Day-Glo characters for some caricature of what they think Hispanics are—it was really disgraceful.

The State Department voiced its concerns, too. On November 22, Assistant Secretary of State Philip Coons warned Wise that the film could "lend itself to exploitation by the Communists." Coons requested that some sort of explanatory text be added at the beginning of the film—"a tribute or dedication to the people of all racial and nationality backgrounds in the United States who, working together, have made great strides toward overcoming the conflicts depicted, and who are still working hard on the unfinished business of our democratic society." Needless to say, no such explanation was ever attached to the film. As Wise noted in his response to Coons, such a supplement could be "singled out" as a "propaganda device."

Ironically, the State Department's fear that *West Side Story* would appeal to the Soviets was soon realized in a popular comic book. In the April 1963 issue of *Mad Magazine*, William Gaines ran a parody of the musical set outside the United Nations building in New York. Riffing on "the Jet Song," Nikitia Khrushchev and his Communist allies dance in unison as they sing:

When you're a Red
You're a Red all the way
From your first Party purge
To your last power play!

When you're a Red
You've got agents galore;
You give prizes for peace
While they stir up a war!

You set off a test,
And when you're halfway through it—
You point at the West
And say they drove you to it!
That's how you do it!

Despite the critiques and parodies, *West Side Story* won ten Academy Awards, including Best Picture, Best Director, Best Costume Design, Best Original Musical, and Best Supporting Actress for Rita Moreno. The film's commercial success played a huge role in its continued dissemination, especially among politicians. In 1962, President Kennedy hosted a screening of the film at the White House on at least three occasions. And his interest in its message contributed to his continued efforts to reduce crime among urban youth.

As the decades progressed and *West Side Story* became a staple in college, high school, and regional theater productions, attitudes toward the musical began to change for two basic reasons. First, prominent scholars like Frances Negrón-Muntaner, Arlene Dávila, Juan Flores, Manuel M. Martín-Rodríguez, Carmen Dolores Hernández, and Ramón Rivera-Servera began to publish insightful critiques that emphasized the problematic nature of *West Side Story*'s portrayal of Puerto Ricans. Second, its status as a "classic" American musical, representative of the 1950s, led to a general sense among audiences that the story was a slice of history, as opposed to a reflection of contemporary society. Consequently, references to *West Side Story* by politicians began to change.

Over the last three decades, nearly every congressional debate concerning gang violence has been punctuated with a reference to *West Side Story*. In each instance, however, the musical is presented as a reference point, a sociological snapshot of gang culture in its infancy, when the violence and links to drug culture seemed less malevolent. For example, Senator Dianne Feinstein of California noted in her presentation of the Federal Gang Violence Act of 1996 that "today's gangs are not the bands of loosely organized street kids glamorized in *West Side Story*." And in 1999, when a hearing on school violence took place in the House of Representatives, Gary L. Walker, vice president of the National District Attorneys Association, called for stricter juvenile sentencing, noting that "we must not excuse the behavior" of violent youth who claim "I am depraved on account of I am deprived" like the youth "from *West Side Story*." Similarly, in 2003, when Senator Jeff Sessions addressed the Judiciary Committee during an inquiry into gang violence, he declared: "Gangs in America are no longer the romanticized, movie-like characters depicted in *West Side Story*. In reality, gangs now resemble organized crime syndicates, who readily engage in gun violence, illegal gun trafficking, illegal drug trafficking, and other serious crimes." Today, the most abhorrent gang violence is too often unjustly blamed on Latino youth. Consequently, some of the most recent productions of *West Side Story* have sought to dilute the musical's negative portrayals of Puerto Ricans.

In 2009, Arthur Laurents directed a revival of *West Side Story* on Broadway. Determined to update the show for a twenty-first-century audience, he made several changes, the most notable being the casting of Latine actors to play the Puerto Rican characters and the inclusion of some Spanish dialogue and lyrics. "My biggest challenge," Laurents noted, was that "even in the age of Obama, there are people who don't want change, certainly not in a show that's considered a classic." But Laurents believed he had no choice. "We had to change it. I couldn't just do a replica of the original. We had to ask ourselves: Why are we doing it now?"

Laurents reached out to Lin-Manuel Miranda, creator of the Tony Award-winning musical *In the Heights*, to supply the Spanish text. Miranda had grown up loving *West Side Story*: "As a piece of art, I think it's just about as good as it gets." But he has also acknowledged that for Puerto Ricans the musical is both a blessing and a curse. It was the first musical to shine a spotlight on Puerto Ricans, but it did so in a superficial, stereotypical way. Consequently, Miranda's goal was to give the characters more depth. "It was a tall order, but a really fun challenge," he said. Miranda updated the Sharks' dialogue with Spanish slang and curse words. For example, when Chino tells Maria that Tony has killed her brother Bernardo, the original "He killed your brother!" is presented as "¡Ése cabrón mató a tu hermano!" [That bastard killed your brother!] Similar changes were made to the songs "A Boy Like That" and "I Feel Pretty." In the former, stronger language, such as "ese cabrón," is used to convey Anita's disdain for Tony, whom she calls a criminal and murderer. In "Siento Hermosa" (I Feel Pretty), Maria embraces a more sexualized persona, noting the beauty of her behind (*atras*) as she stares at herself in the mirror.

Laurents was thrilled with Miranda's Spanish content. "It gave the show a new life, a new edge," he said. "The Sharks are isolated, they face terrible bigotry, and we could illustrate this now by using Spanish in key songs and scenes. It was the kind of change the show needed." Until it wasn't. Several months into the New York run, most of Miranda's Spanish lyrics were cut and replaced with Sondheim's originals. "Audiences were getting the general idea of 'A Boy Like That,' but they weren't getting hammered by it," admitted Laurents. "The sheer power of 'A boy like that who'd kill your brother' has no real equivalent, and for people who don't understand Spanish, the impact was diluted."

Laurents always admitted that *West Side Story* had flaws. The allure of Bernstein's music and Robbins's choreography masks the ugliness of racism and violence that lies at the musical's core. "Many say *West Side* forever changed the American musical . . . because of dance and music," explained Laurents, "but what it really changed, what its real contribution to the American musical theatre was, was that it showed that any subject—murder, attempted rape, bigotry—could be the subject of a popular musical." This statement rings true when we look at the 2021 film version of *West Side Story*, created by Stephen Spielberg and Tony Kushner.

As in 1957, politics drove this version of *West Side Story*. Spielberg pitched the project to Kushner in 2016, and the increasing xenophobia that accompanied Donald Trump's arrival on the political stage that year convinced them that the show's message was still relevant. As Kushner explained, they both considered *West Side Story* "a masterpiece of Western dramatic art." Consequently, in creating their film, they "didn't want to make it feel like we were correcting it, or fixing it, or jimmying in an agenda of some kind." As Kushner explained, *West Side Story* had a message that was vitally important to contemporary audiences. "It's a tragedy, but it's also a political work of art and it's about racism. It's about xenophobia and it's about a sort of betrayal of the American dream by becoming reactionary and unwelcoming as opposed to expansive and welcoming and embracing. It's about poverty, and to some extent about gender."

New political issues were highlighted in the remake—gun violence, gentrification, gender identity, juvenile incarceration, drug addiction—but in each case, as Kushner explained, these were issues that were "latent" or "alluded to" in the original. The depiction of Anybodys is a good example. In previous versions, Anybodys is a tomboyish girl who wants to be accepted by the Jets but is marginalized for not fitting a traditional gender role. In Spielberg and Kushner's film Anybodys is a transgender boy. This shift in characterization came from a song that had been cut from the 1957 production. "I ain't like any other girl on Earth," sings Anybodys. "Don'cha see, I'm an accident of birth. . . . Why can't I be male, like everybody else?"

Even in its most recent version, *West Side Story* fails to adequately address the causes and effects of racial hatred and bigotry. Nor does it offer a realistic vision of New York or America. To be honest, it never did. Instead, the musical reflects the personal strife and struggles felt by its creative team. For Robbins, Laurents, Bernstein, and Sondheim, *West*

Side Story expressed the pain of being an outsider and a desire for acceptance. The musical's enduring presence, on stage and screen, should not be surprising. Through its various iterations over the course of nearly seven decades, one element has remained unchanged: Bernstein's music. As a composer, Bernstein held fast to the belief that *West Side Story* should be "poetry in music." No matter what one thinks of the show's take on politics, its music draws listeners in. The effect is emotional, one might even say philosophical. *West Side Story* challenges audiences to think about what it means to belong. At its core is an aspirational love song that describes a truth still elusive for too many in America: "There's a place for us. Somewhere, a place for us."

9

WHAT'S GOING ON?

·····

On the night of March 15, 1965, President Lyndon B. Johnson stood before a special joint session of Congress and addressed the nation: "I speak tonight for the dignity of man and the destiny of democracy," he began. "I urge every member of both parties, Americans of all religions and of all colors, from every section of this country, to join me in that cause."

Johnson was calling on Congress to pass the Equal Voting Rights Act. His speech was broadcast live, via television and radio, and over 70 million Americans tuned in as he outlined a new path towards justice. "At times history and fate meet at a single time in a single place to shape a turning point in man's unending search for freedom," he explained. "So it was at Lexington and Concord. So it was a century ago at Appomattox. So it was last week in Selma, Alabama."

Johnson was referring to the events of March 7, "Bloody Sunday," when state police and local law enforcement officers brutally assaulted several hundred peaceful protesters as they crossed the Edmund Pettus Bridge in Selma, Alabama. As Johnson explained, these "long-suffering men and women" were on their way to the state capital, Montgomery, to protest "the denial of their rights as Americans." Dozens suffered from the violent attack, and at least one man, a white Unitarian minister named James Reeb, died from his injuries.

"There is no cause for pride in what has happened in Selma," declared Johnson, "no cause for self-satisfaction in the long denial of equal rights of millions of Americans." The fight for civil rights was a fight for the nation's soul. "And should we defeat every enemy, should we double our wealth and conquer the stars, and still be unequal to this issue," explained Johnson, "then we will have failed as a people and a nation."

Passage of the Civil Rights Act the year before had been a step in the right direction, noted Johnson, but injustices still prevailed. "What happened in Selma is part of a larger movement which reaches into every section and state of America." The fight for equality affects more than black America, he explained. "Their cause must be our cause, too. Because it is not just Negroes, but really it's all of us who must overcome the crippling legacy of bigotry and injustice. And we shall overcome."

We shall overcome. These three words evoked a deep sense of racial unity among many Americans listening that evening. For well over a century, various versions of this affirmative phrase had been sung, first by black Americans, and then around the globe, as a call for freedom: freedom from racial oppression, freedom from unfair labor practices, freedom from political injustices. The folk singer and activist Pete Seeger once said: "The right song at the right time can change history." During Johnson's address, which came to be known as the "We Shall Overcome" speech, the truth of Seeger's claim seemed irrefutable. Music as peaceful protest had reached the president's ear. The seeds of the civil rights movement finally appeared to have taken root.

The origins of "We Shall Overcome" are hazy and convoluted. Historians of the song cite various milestones. In the nineteenth century, enslaved field workers sang "I'll be all right someday" under inhumane conditions. Reverend Charles Albert Tindley published a version of the tune in 1901 titled "I'll Overcome Someday." In the decades that followed, the song's themes of faith and perseverance spread from black churches to sharecropping communities and left-wing political rallies. For example, in 1945, striking female tobacco workers in South Carolina protested substandard wages by singing: "We will overcome, and we will win our rights someday." Two years later, the labor activist Zilphia Horton began teaching a version of the song to civil rights activists in New York and at the Highlander Folk School in Tennessee. That's where Seeger first encountered the tune. He adapted the lyrics and popularized the song at civil rights meetings and on college campuses. Seeger's version, "We Shall Overcome," imbued the song with a communal power that crossed racial lines. By 1965, when Johnson referenced the song in his speech, "We Shall Overcome" had become the anthem of a hopeful generation, ideologically committed to realizing the goals of America's blossoming civil rights movement. It had also become a profitable hit for the music industry, a reality that Seeger and Horton had both anticipated.

In 1960, Seeger, Horton, Guy Carawan, and Frank Hamilton copyrighted "We Shall Overcome." As Seeger later explained, the song's increasing popularity made it ripe for picking by the profit-seeking entertainment industry. "Our publishers said to us, 'If you don't copyright this now, some Hollywood types will have a version out next year—like 'come on baby, we shall overcome tonight.'" Seeger and his colleagues assigned all proceeds from the song to the Highlander Folk School, which distributed the funds to various initiatives in the black community. As Seeger later explained, they copyrighted the song to "protect its legacy" and to ensure that future profits from the song continued to support civil rights initiatives.

Seeger's intentions were laudable, but also a bit naïve. The corporate interests of America's music industry would not be stymied by activist concerns. In the 1960s and 1970s, as popular music became synonymous with protest, and civil rights issues merged with anger over Vietnam, America's music industry learned how to channel society's political frustrations into profits. The commercialization of protest music changed America's political landscape for a generation. And as many have argued, it all began with a singer songwriter from Hibbing, Minnesota, named Bob Dylan.

Dylan arrived in New York at age twenty-one with little more than his guitar and harmonica in hand. Like most impressionable youth of his era, he was drawn to a range of music, from rock and roll and rhythm and blues to traditional spirituals and folk songs. Dylan absorbed the music around him like a sponge, and when he came across something new, the effects of that exposure soon seeped into his own music. His early interest in folk music was driven by his admiration for Woody Guthrie, arguably one of the most important folk singers of the twentieth century. Guthrie's parents had named him after the twenty-eighth US president, Woodrow Wilson, and Guthrie spent the whole of his adult life fighting against the prejudice and social injustices that characterized his namesake's legacy. Guthrie's raw, gritty songs about hardship and resilience appealed to Dylan's rebellious nature and inspired his own songwriting. Dylan viewed Guthrie as a hero, even visiting him in the hospital during his final days battling Huntington's disease. But Guthrie wasn't the only folk legend who shaped Dylan's vision. Seeger's commitment to social justice and Phil Ochs's sharp, politically charged lyrics proved equally influential. Inspired by their successes, Dylan wrote songs that combined protest with poetry, and quickly became the voice of a new generation.

When Dylan arrived in Greenwich Village in 1961, America was at a crossroads. As the civil rights movement gained momentum, the nation was simmering with social unrest. It was in this charged atmosphere that Dylan began writing his own songs. One of them, "Blowin' in the Wind," would become a symbol of cultural change.

Legend has it that Dylan wrote "Blowin' in the Wind" in a matter of minutes, while sitting in a Greenwich Village café in April 1962. The song opens with a series of rhetorical questions, each one more poignant than the last: "How many roads must a man walk down, before he's called a man?" Dylan's words aren't heavy-handed or specific. Instead, they're abstract and universal: "How many seas must a white dove sail, before he sleeps in the sand?" The questions appear simple, yet they echo with complexity, evoking the search for meaning in a rapidly changing world. The open-ended quality of each line allows anyone listening to project their own struggles and frustrations onto it. The core of Dylan's song is its iconic refrain: "The answer, my friend, is blowin' in the wind. The answer is blowin' in the wind." It's an answer that is equally evasive and profound. The wind, after all, is something intangible yet ever-present. Dylan isn't prescribing solutions with his lyrics; he is simply reminding listeners that the answers are out there somewhere if they choose to look for them. This ambiguity gives the song its power, allowing it to speak to different people in different ways.

Dylan published "Blowin' in the Wind" in May 1962 on the front page of *Broadside*, a new folk music magazine committed to publishing songs that challenged the status quo. Throughout the summer, Dylan performed the song at union rallies and coffeehouses. To many, Dylan arrived on the scene like a prophet, and music journalists soon began to sing his praises. As Robert Shelton of the *New York Times* noted, Dylan resembled "a cross between a choir boy and a beatnik" with his "cherubic look and a mop of tousled hair." Wearing a "Huck Finn black corduroy cap" and clothes that "need a bit of tailoring . . . there is no doubt that he is bursting at the seams with talent." In October, "Blowin' in the Wind" was published again, this time in *Sing Out!*, a popular folk song magazine cofounded by Seeger in 1951. In the issue, Dylan was asked to explain the meaning of his song. His response was as evasive as the lyrics themselves:

> There ain't too much I can say about this song except that the answer is blowing in the wind. It ain't in no book or movie or T.V. show or discussion group. Man, it's in the wind—and it's blowing in the wind. Too many of these hip people are telling me where the answer is but oh I won't believe that. I still say it's in the wind and just like a restless piece of paper it's got to come down sometime . . . But the only trouble is that no one picks up the answer when it comes down so not too many people get to see and know it . . .

Society's biggest problem, according to Dylan, was the indifference of the older generation.

> I still say that some of the biggest criminals are those that turn their heads away when they see wrong and know it's wrong. I'm only 21 years old and I know that there's been too many wars . . . You people over 21 should know better . . . cause after all, you're older and smarter.

Dylan included "Blowin' in the Wind" on his second album, *The Freewheelin' Bob Dylan*, in 1963, but it didn't chart. Shortly thereafter, the popular folk group Peter, Paul, and Mary recorded a version, and the song caught fire. Their smooth, polished harmonies carried the song into homes across the nation. Even more impactful than their recording was the live performance they gave on August 28 at the March on Washington for Jobs and Freedom. "Blowin' in the Wind" became a rallying cry for the civil rights movement on that day. The questioning tone of the song's lyrics mirrored the movement's demands for justice and equality. As Mary later explained: "We started to sing, and I had an epiphany: Looking out at this quarter of a million people, I truly believed, at that moment, it was possible that human beings could join together to make a positive social change."

The highlight of the March on Washington, of course, was Martin Luther King Jr.'s "I Have a Dream" speech, delivered from the steps of the Lincoln Memorial, the same location where Marian Anderson had defied racial barriers with her groundbreaking concert in 1939. King's address occurred in the late afternoon, after a long day of speeches, performances, and demonstrations. Numerous celebrities kept the crowds entertained in the hours leading up to the official program, among them Charlton Heston, Burt Lancaster, Sidney Poitier, Tony Curtis, Billy Wilder, Marlon Brando, and Rita Moreno, who the year before had won an Oscar for her performance in *West Side Story*. Musicians performed for the marchers, too. In addition to Peter, Paul, and Mary, the singers at the morning rally held at the Washington Monument included Harry Belafonte, Sammy Davis Jr., Odetta, Joan Baez, and Bob Dylan. Camilla Williams, Marian Anderson, and Mahalia Jackson were the only musical performers who shared the stage with King during the official program.

Dylan sang several songs over the course of the day, the most memorable being "Only a Pawn in Their Game." Written in response to the murder of the civil rights activist Medgar Evers, this song, and Dylan's performance that day, was not without controversy. Although the lyrics reference the systemic roots of racism that led to Evers's death, the focus of the song is not Evers himself but his assassin, Byron De La Beckwith Jr. Instead of condemning De La Beckwith as a criminal, Dylan shifts the blame for the racially motivated killing to society in general. In Dylan's song, De La Beckwith is presented as the victim of an oppressive social system, nothing more than "a pawn in their game." At a gathering where the focus was on racial justice and the urgent need for accountability, the song's attempt to diffuse responsibility struck many of the marchers as tone-deaf.

In the months that followed, the conflict between Dylan the artist and Dylan the activist became increasingly noticeable. On December 13, 1963, the Emergency Civil Liberties Committee (ECLC), which had been founded in 1951, held its annual Bill of Rights Dinner at the Americana Hotel in New York City. The assassination of President Kennedy the month before cast a pall over the evening, which originally had been planned in celebration of King's successful March on Washington. Each year, the ECLC bestowed its prestigious Tom Paine Award on an individual who had made great strides in the fight for civil rights. In 1963, the honoree was Dylan, who was asked to give a speech.

As Dylan took his place at the podium, he looked nervous and a bit drunk. He wasn't comfortable at such a formal event. Wearing a wrinkled shirt and his usual denim blazer, he looked out at the room of distinguished attendees, most of whom were in black tie. Dylan began his speech—in truth, it was more of a rant—by differentiating himself from everyone else in the room.

> I consider myself young. And I'm proud of it. I'm proud that I'm young. And I only wish that all you people who are sitting out here today or tonight weren't here, and I could see all kinds of faces with hair on their head—and everything like that.

Dylan disparaged "the people that are governing me and making my rules." Like the members of the ECLC, they were old, and too concerned with issues of race:

> ... they talk about Negroes, and they talk about black and white. And they talk about colors of red and blue and yellow. Man, I just don't see any colors at all when I look out. I don't see any colors at all.... There's no black and white, left and right to me anymore; there's only up and down, and down is very close to the ground.

Dylan wasn't interested in the ground game of activism. As he told the audience: "I'm trying to go up without thinking about anything trivial such as politics." He was accepting the Tom Paine Award, but not as a spokesman for any specific cause or movement. "I'm not really accepting it in my name, and I'm not accepting it in any kind of group's name, any Negro group or any other kind of group." He then made a point of separating himself, again, from the attendees in the room and the activists he had encountered at the nation's capital.

> I was on the March on Washington up on the platform and I looked around at all the Negroes there and I didn't see any Negroes that looked like none of my friends. My friends don't wear suits. My friends don't have to wear suits. My friends don't have to wear any kind of thing to prove that they're respectable Negroes. My friends are my friends, and they're kind, gentle people if they're my friends. And I'm not going to try to push nothing over. So, I accept this reward—not reward—award in behalf of Phillip Luce.

Luce, a writer and activist with strong Communist leanings, had settled in New York around the same time Dylan had. In 1963, Luce led a series of illegal student trips to Cuba and was consequently called to testify before HUAC. Many in the audience that night considered Luce a troublemaker. Dylan didn't care. And as he went on to explain, he identified with Luce, just as he identified with President Kennedy's assassin, Lee Harvey Oswald.

> Phillip is a friend of mine who went to Cuba. I'll stand up and to get uncompromisable about it, which I have to be to be honest, I just got to be, as I got to admit that the man who shot President Kennedy, Lee Oswald, I don't know exactly where—what he thought he was doing, but I got to admit honestly that I too—I saw some of myself in him. I don't think it would have gone—I don't think it could go that far. But I got to stand up and say I saw things that he felt, in me.

At this point, the audience began to boo and hiss. "You can boo, but booing's got nothing to do with it," said Dylan. "I've got to tell you, man, this Bill of Rights is free speech."

News of Dylan's speech blew up in the press. In the days that followed, his supporters attempted to defend his comments by explaining that they had been misinterpreted. In an effort to clarify the situation, Dylan penned a long, rambling letter to the ECLC, wherein he doubled down on the content of his speech and offered to return the award if requested:

> ... I've heard I was misunderstood
>
> I do not apologize for myself nor my fears
> I do not apologize for any statement which led
> some t believe "oh my God! I think he's the one
> that really shot the president"
>
> I am a writer an a singer of the words I write
> I am no speaker nor any politician
> an my songs speak for me because I write them
> in the confinement of my own mind an have t cope
> with no one except my own self. I don't have t face
> anyone with them until long after they're done
>
> no I do not apologize for being me nor any part of me
>
> but I can return what is rightfully yours at any
> given time. I have stared at it for a long while
> now. it is a beautiful award ...
> yes thru all my flounderin wildness, I am, when it
> comes down to it, very proud that you have given this
> t me. I would hang it high, an let my friends see in
> it what I see, but I also would give it back if
> you wish. There is no sense in keepin it if you've
> made a mistake in givin it. for it means more'n any
> store bought thing an it'd only be cheatin t keep it

Dylan's speech at the ECLC dinner, and his refusal to apologize, shattered his image as a public activist. His rambling remarks alienated many civil rights leaders and tarnished his standing among some of his earliest supporters, most notably Pete Seeger and Joan Baez. But Dylan seemed not to care. He was a fiercely independent artist who refused to be boxed into any political or social movement. His Tom Paine speech became a defining moment in his career, marking his shift from protest bard to a more enigmatic, boundary-pushing celebrity.

As Dylan was actively shedding his identity as an artist/activist, a markedly different singer-songwriter, Nina Simone, was raising her voice in protest for the first time with a song titled "Mississippi Goddam."

Simone had been raised in Tryon, North Carolina, where she experienced both the joys of music and the pain of segregation. Trained in classical music from a young age, she dreamed of becoming a concert pianist, but racism thwarted her ambitions. After being rejected by the prestigious Curtis Institute of Music in Philadelphia—a rejection she believed was due to her race—Simone turned to singing and performing popular music to make a living. Despite her rising fame and critical acclaim in jazz, blues, and folk circles, the racism and inequality she saw around her remained a festering wound.

Simone did not attend the March on Washington, as she considered King's approach to confronting racial injustice generally ineffective. But in 1963, three events pushed her to a breaking point. The first was a series of violent attacks in May against John Lewis, leader of the anti-segregation Student Nonviolent Coordinating Committee (SNCC), during a series of peaceful protests in Nashville. The second was the murder of Medgar Evers in Mississippi in June. Then came the bombing on September 15 of the Sixteenth Street Baptist Church in Birmingham, Alabama, where four young black girls were massacred as they prepared for Sunday school. As Simone later explained, it was this final event that let loose within her a torrent of grief and anger.

> When the kids got killed being at church, that did it. First you get depressed and after that you get mad. And when these kids got bombed, I just sat down and wrote this song. And it's a very moving, violent song. Cause that's how I feel about the whole thing.

Simone was so shaken by the incident that her first instinct was to get a gun and exact revenge. "I was going to take one of them out, and I didn't care who it was." But then she realized her best weapon was her music. "When I sat down the whole song happened. I never stopped writing until the thing was finished. It was my first civil rights song, and it erupted out of me quicker than I could write it down."

Simone first performed the song a few days later during a set at the Village Gate in Greenwich Village. As Claudia Roth Pierpont noted in the *New Yorker*: "It wasn't 'We Shall Overcome' or 'Blowin' in the Wind': Simone had little feeling for the Biblically inflected uplift that defined the anthems of the era. It's a song about a movement nearly out of patience by a woman who never had much to begin with." "Mississippi Goddam" is a confrontational song, composed with the same anger and contempt as Charles Mingus's "Fables of Faubus." The audience at Village Gate embraced Simone's message; she was "singing to the choir," as the old saying goes. The true test came on March 21, 1964, during a concert at Carnegie Hall that was later released on her live album, *Nina Simone in Concert*. Even today, the performance is gut-wrenching. The audience wasn't expecting such a defiant act of protest, and you can hear it on the recording. Raw, direct, and incendiary, Simone's performance sends shockwaves through the mostly white audience.

The song begins with an upbeat vamp in the piano and drums. Simone announces to the audience: "The name of this tune is 'Mississippi Goddam.'" The audience laughs. Simone continues vamping, "and I mean every word of it." She then launches into the opening chorus:

> *Alabama's got me so upset.*
> *Tennessee made me lose my rest.*
> *And everybody knows about Mississippi, Goddam!*

The first verse names the psychological distress of recent events:

> *Can't you see it?*
> *Can't you feel it?*
> *It's all in the air.*

I can't stand the pressure much longer.
Somebody say a prayer.

After another rendition of the chorus, Simone addresses the audience directly: "This is a show tune, but the show hasn't been written for it yet." More laughter from the audience. At this point, Simone launches into a series of verses that outline the injustices of the past and the hopelessness of the present:

Hound dogs on my trail,
Schoolchildren sitting in jail,
Black cat across my path,
I feel every day's gonna be my last.

Lord have mercy on this land of mine.
We all gonna get it in due time.
I don't belong here.
I don't belong there.
I've even stopped believing in prayer.

Simone turns defiant:

Don't tell me.
I'll tell you.
Me and my people are just about due.

Without mincing words, Simone directly calls out the hypocrisy of white Americans who claim to support gradual change: "They keep on saying, 'Go Slow.' But that's just the trouble. 'Go Slow.'" Simone sings about the racist insults she's faced over the years, from comments about her looks and intelligence to hurtful stereotypes about black people in general. Between verses, she confronts the audience again: "I bet you thought I was kidding, didn't you?" No one laughs this time.

Simone concludes the song by describing the failures of the civil rights movement: "Desegregation ... Mass participation ... Reunification." Doing "things gradually" just brings "more tragedy."

> *Why don't you see it?*
> *Why don't you feel it?*
> *I don't know. I don't know.*

The song's final lines offer a rebuke to everyone in the audience:

> *You don't have to live next to me,*
> *Just give me my equality.*
> *Everybody knows about Mississippi.*
> *Everybody knows about Alabama.*
> *Everybody knows about Mississippi, Goddam!*

As the scholar Tammy Kernodle has noted, "In 'Mississippi Goddam,' we have Nina Simone pulling from the past and invoking it in the present—but also speaking to what was yet to come if America does not enact social change." As a critic for the *Philadelphia Tribune* explained it, to hear Simone sing was "to be brought into abrasive contact with the black heart and to feel the power and beauty which for centuries have beat there."

The cultural impact of "Mississippi Goddam" was immediate and far-reaching. Philips Records released the song as a single, "MISSISSIPPI *@!!?*@!," taking care not to print a curse word in the title. "Goddam" was also replaced with a sonic bleep on the recording. In the months that followed, "Mississippi Goddam" became an anthem for the civil rights movement. It captured the rage and frustration of black Americans who were tired of waiting for justice. Simone performed the song regularly at rallies and protests, including the Selma-to-Montgomery March in 1965, where her voice added power and urgency to the demand for voting rights and racial equality.

But while "Mississippi Goddam" resonated with civil rights activists, it also cost Simone dearly. The song's unapologetic message angered many, particularly in the South. Many radio stations refused to play the single, and some even returned copies of the record broken in half. Simone found herself blacklisted in parts of the music industry. Her outspokenness made her a target of both critics and former fans who preferred her earlier, less overtly political work.

Despite the backlash, Simone never wavered in her commitment to using her music as a tool for protest. Unlike Dylan, Simone embraced her identity as an artist–activist: "An artist's duty, as far as I'm concerned, is to reflect the times," she explained.

> That to me is my duty. And at this crucial time in our lives when everything is so desperate, when every day is a matter of survival, I don't think you can help but be involved. Young people, black and white, know this. That's why they're so involved in politics. We will shape and mold this country. I will not be molded and shaped at all anymore.

In the years that followed, Simone recorded Abel Meeropol's "Strange Fruit," made famous by Billie Holiday in 1939, and wrote more protest songs: "Four Women," "I Wish I Knew How It Would Feel to Be Free," "Backlash Blues," and "To Be Young, Gifted, and Black." She also continued to sing "Mississippi Goddam," and as new atrocities struck the black community, Simone kept the song relevant by updating the cities named in the chorus.

In 1969, Simone participated in the Harlem Cultural Festival. Spread over six weeks in Harlem's Mount Morris Park (now Marcus Garvey Park), this festival brought together iconic black musicians including Stevie Wonder, Sly and the Family Stone, Mahalia Jackson, and Gladys Knight and the Pips. One of the songs Simone performed was "To Be Young, Gifted, and Black," with lyrics drawn from the words of her departed friend Lorraine Hansberry, author of *A Raisin in the Sun*. Simone's performance resonated deeply with the audience. The emerging Black Power movement encouraged the same sense of self-determination and cultural reclamation. In addition to singing, Simone read aloud excerpts of black nationalist poetry. Her words, like those of other performers and speakers, echoed the sentiments of a community no longer asking for acceptance from the mainstream but instead celebrating its own identity and power.

Although more than 300,000 people attended the Harlem Cultural Festival, it received little attention from mainstream media. Organized by a local promoter named Tony Lawrence and supported by the New York City Parks Department, the free festival welcomed attendees of all ages. It was a community happening, designed to uplift Harlem's residents during a time of racial tension and political unrest.

More than a series of performances, the Harlem Cultural Festival was a deeply political event, rooted in the black community's ongoing struggle for civil rights and cultural recognition. Held just one year after the assassination of Martin Luther King Jr., the festival became a platform for celebrating black pride, resilience, and the rising influence of the Black Power movement. New York City mayor John Lindsay, a liberal Republican, lent his support and attended some of the performances. At a time when many politicians distanced themselves from events tied to Black Power, Lindsay's presence stood out. Many Harlem residents saw it as a gesture of solidarity.

The Harlem Cultural Festival's impact extended beyond the immediate community. It helped cement the role of music as a political tool in the black freedom struggle, blending art and activism in a way that inspired future generations. Yet for decades the festival was largely forgotten, overshadowed by the mythologized Woodstock. It wasn't until the release of the 2021 documentary *Summer of Soul*, directed by Ahmir "Questlove" Thompson, that America rediscovered this cultural milestone and recognized it as a moment when black culture and politics took center stage in a powerful, joyful expression of unity and resilience.

The Harlem Cultural Festival is often referred to as "Black Woodstock." Nothing could be further from the truth. Whereas the event in Harlem was a well-organized, free, weeks-long, all-ages celebration, the Woodstock Music and Art Fair was a poorly-planned, for-profit event aimed at America's youth that quickly spiraled into a chaotic mass gathering.

For many of the 400,000 young people in attendance, Woodstock symbolized a new cultural movement. It took place just months after the tumultuous events of 1968, which saw violent clashes at the Democratic National Convention in Chicago and the assassinations of Martin Luther King Jr. and Robert F. Kennedy. Even with severe overcrowding, food shortages, and torrential rain, the festivalgoers remained largely peaceful. This spontaneous coexistence offered a refutation of the negative "hippie" stereotype that had been perpetuated by mainstream media. But to many politicians and media voices, Woodstock initially seemed like another example of unruly, radical youth behavior. Some newspapers ran sensational headlines, describing the gathering as anarchy in a sea of mud and focusing on the use of drugs and the festival's apparent disorganization. The influx of young people to the small town was portrayed as a potential public health and safety hazard, and local authorities scrambled to deal with the enormous crowd.

Politicians were similarly divided. Some conservative voices saw Woodstock as emblematic of the moral decline they believed was afflicting the nation. New York governor Nelson Rockefeller reportedly considered sending in the National Guard to manage the situation. Vice President Spiro Agnew, known for his attacks on countercultural activities, used reports of the nude bathing and drug use at Woodstock to reinforce his claim that the youth of America were out of touch with traditional values.

Despite its legacy, Woodstock's performers were generally apolitical. Two notable exceptions were Joan Baez, who was dismayed by what she saw as a lack of political engagement among the audience, and Jimi Hendrix, whose performance of "The Star-Spangled Banner" on electric guitar transformed the national anthem into a chaotic soundscape filled with screeching feedback and bomb-like distortions. Equal parts protest and artistry, Hendrix's rendition turned the anthem into a visceral commentary on the nation's contradictions, leaving the crowd stunned and forever redefining what a patriotic performance could mean.

The wonder of Woodstock lives on in the collective memory of those who came of age in the 1960s. But looking back, one quickly realizes that it was only a fleeting moment of peace during an era rocked by violence and hate. Woodstock did not bring about political change. As Joan Baez noted years later, Woodstock was a "three-day hoo-ha." It was important, "but it was *not* a revolution." The only thing that made it revolutionary was the fact that "the cops put their guns away and smoked pot.... Nobody was really thinking about the serious issues." Woodstock's shared vision for a better world was a utopian dream, a glorious moment of drug- and music-induced escapism. Like Jimi Hendrix's electrified take on the "Star-Spangled Banner," it offered a vision of protest rooted in distortion.

In 1971, as America continued to grapple with war, civil unrest, and social upheaval, Marvin Gaye, Motown's smooth, soulful hitmaker, released a song that momentarily changed the landscape of popular music. "What's Going On" was more than just a hit single; it was a bold departure from the love songs and dance tunes that had defined Gaye's career up to that point. This introspective, socially conscious anthem spoke directly to the spirit of the times and marked Gaye's transformation from a pop star into a voice for social change. But the journey to the creation of this iconic song was anything but straightforward.

"What's Going On" began as a feeling of shock experienced by Renaldo "Obie" Benson, a member of the famed Motown group the Four Tops. While on tour in California in 1969, Benson witnessed a disturbing scene near the UC Berkeley campus. As his bus passed Prospect Park, Benson saw police attack a group of college students peacefully protesting the Vietnam War. At least thirty-five people were shot, and the brutality of the scene compelled Benson to write a protest song. When his colleagues in the Four Tops showed no interest in it, Benson shared what he had written with Gaye.

At the time, Gaye was facing personal and professional turmoil. His duet partner and dear friend, Tammi Terrell, had passed away in 1970 after battling brain cancer. Gaye was also encountering difficulties at Motown, where label founder Berry Gordy was pressuring him to churn out more love songs and feel-good hits. But Gaye was no longer interested in simply making music for romancing and dancing. He wanted to speak to the chaos and pain he saw unfolding around him.

The Vietnam War was raging, and images of young American soldiers fighting in a distant land filled television screens across the country. Gaye's own brother, Frankie, had just returned from three years in Vietnam, shaken by the horrors he had witnessed there. Gaye's personal turmoil weighed heavily on him. After hearing Benson's song, Gaye couldn't shake the probing question at its core: "What's going on?" This line captured everything Gaye had been feeling. He began reworking the song, shaping it into something deeply personal. Drawing from his brother's experiences in Vietnam and his own disillusionment with the violence and inequality in America, Gaye transformed the song into a plea for peace, love, and understanding. But this was no ordinary protest song.

Gaye's soulful, plaintive vocals, supported by a lush orchestration, offered a call for compassion that was both gentle and urgent.

"What's Going On" opens with the sounds of a party—friends talking and laughing, setting the stage for a conversation about the state of the world. Gaye's voice soon emerges, smooth and melodic, as he sings: "Mother, mother, there's too many of you crying / Brother, brother, brother, there's far too many of you dying." His lyrics are simple yet powerful, capturing the sense of despair and confusion that so many felt in the early 1970s. Instead of anger, Gaye's voice exudes sorrow and a yearning for change. The song is more a prayer for peace than a harsh indictment of the times.

The music itself was groundbreaking. Gaye, who had spent years mastering the Motown sound, pushed the boundaries of soul music with "What's Going On." The song blends jazz, funk, and classical influences, creating a rich, textured sound that was unlike anything Motown had ever released. Gaye worked closely with Motown's in-house band, the Funk Brothers, to craft a sound that was both elegant and raw, featuring strings, saxophones, and layered harmonies. The result was a song that was both lush and haunting, filled with emotional depth.

Despite the song's beauty and clear message, Gaye faced significant resistance from Gordy. Gordy thought Gaye's desire to tackle social issues was a mistake, and feared the song's political undertone would alienate Gaye's fans. Gordy famously called the song "the worst thing I've ever heard in my life" and refused to release it on the Motown label. But Gaye was determined. He threatened to quit Motown altogether if the song wasn't released, and Gordy finally relented. "What's Going On" was issued as a single in January 1971, and the response was immediate and overwhelming. "What's Going On" reached number two on the Billboard Hot 100. Critics and fans alike were stunned by its new sound and message. The song clearly resonated with a wide audience, from antiwar activists to civil rights leaders, and it became an anthem for a generation struggling with the trauma of war, violence, and social inequality.

"What's Going On" wasn't just a one-off success. The song soon became the centerpiece of an entire album, also titled *What's Going On*, which expanded on the themes introduced in the title track, exploring issues like child poverty, urban blight, environmental destruction, drug addiction, and police brutality. It was a concept album in every sense, a cohesive summary of the ills that plagued American society in the early 1970s.

One topic not covered in *What's Going On* was women's rights, an issue that was at a critical turning point in 1972. Fueled by the momentum of the feminist movement of the 1960s, landmark progress was being made in Congress, though significant challenges persisted. The year saw the passage of Title IX of the Education Amendments, which prohibited sex-based discrimination in federally funded educational programs. The Equal Rights Amendment, which sought to guarantee legal equality for all sexes, was also on the docket. Although it passed in the House and the Senate, the requisite number of states failed to ratify the amendment. Consequently, women found themselves still pushing against deeply entrenched barriers to equal pay and opportunities in the workforce. The Equal Pay Act of 1963 had been in effect for nearly a decade, but wage disparities persisted. Reproductive rights were also at the forefront, as 1972 also witnessed the Supreme Court decision in *Eisenstadt v. Baird*, which expanded access to contraception, granting unmarried individuals the same rights as married couples. This decision was a precursor to the monumental *Roe v. Wade* decision which would occur the following year.

As advocacy groups like the National Organization for Women fought for workplace equality and reproductive rights, Helen Reddy, an Australian-born singer who had relocated to the United States, lent her voice to the movement by writing the defiant anthem "I Am Woman."

Reddy's journey to creating this iconic song began with her own experience of sexism in the music industry. Born in 1941 into a family of performers, Reddy had always been surrounded by show business, but it wasn't an easy path. After winning a talent competition in Australia in 1966, she was promised a recording contract in the US, but upon arrival she was told the deal was off. Determined to make a name for herself, she remained in America, scraping by with nightclub gigs and recording small singles that garnered little attention. It wasn't until 1971 that she had her first major hit with "I Don't Know How to Love Him," from *Jesus Christ Superstar*.

Reddy often found herself marginalized as a woman, facing challenges that many male artists didn't have to face:

> For so many years, when I was an opening act for comics, you know, I would be working in some little club, and as I left the stage the comic would say, "Give her a big hand. There she goes. Take your clothes off and wait for me in the dressing room, Honey. I'll be right there." And you just die inside. I don't have to put up with that anymore. And I won't.

Reddy was dismayed by the music being pushed on her as a woman: "There were a lot of songs on the radio about being weak and being dainty and all of those sorts of things." Reddy didn't identify with this persona. "All the women in my family, they were strong women," she explained. "They worked, they lived through the Depression and a World War, and they were just strong women. I certainly didn't see myself as dainty." As a singer, Reddy wanted a song that represented who she was. "I was looking for songs that reflected the positive sense of self that I felt I'd gained from the women's movement," she said. "I couldn't find any. All I could find were these awful songs, like 'I am a woman, and you are a man. I am so weak, and you are stronger than.' So, I realized the song I was looking for didn't exist, and I was going to have to write it myself."

Drawing inspiration from the feminist literature she was reading at the time, particularly the works of Germaine Greer and Betty Friedan, Reddy began to jot down ideas. With the help of Australian musician Ray Burton, she crafted the lyrics and melody for "I Am Woman." The song is deceptively simple in its construction but profound in its message. The opening line—"I am woman, hear me roar, in numbers too big to ignore"—serves as the rallying cry of the track. It asserts both strength and solidarity. Reddy's voice, with its smooth yet commanding tone, carries the lyrics with a sense of quiet determination that grows into a powerful declaration by the time the chorus arrives:

Yes, I am wise,
But it's wisdom born of pain.
Yes, I've paid the price,
But look how much I've gained.
If I have to, I can do anything.
I am strong.
I am invincible.
I am woman.

The song promotes empowerment and resilience. As Reddy explained time and again, women had gained strength through hardship and struggle. Their time had come, and they weren't going to back down.

"I Am Woman" was first released in May 1971 on Reddy's debut album *I Don't Know How to Love Him*. It didn't garner much attention, but Reddy and her team believed in the song. She made a new recording, which was released as a single in May 1972. Slowly, word began to spread. Women who heard the song found it spoke directly to their own lives and struggles. As more listeners requested it, radio stations began to play the song more frequently. Eventually, "I Am Woman" climbed the charts, reaching number one on the Billboard Hot 100 in December 1972. The following year, Reddy won the Grammy Award for Best Female Pop Vocal Performance. In her acceptance speech, which was short and to the point, she thanked her collaborators and then famously declared: "And I'd like to thank God, because *She* makes everything possible."

The cultural impact of "I Am Woman" was enormous. As the feminist movement gained momentum, the song became a regular feature at rallies, marches, and consciousness-raising meetings. Its lyrics resonated with women across the country and beyond who were fighting for equal rights, reproductive freedom, and an end to workplace discrimination.

The United Nations declared 1975 International Women's Year, a groundbreaking initiative to spotlight women's issues and advance gender equality on a global scale. The year marked a coordinated effort to address disparities in education, employment, and political participation, as well as to combat violence against women. Culminating in the World

Conference on Women in Mexico City, the initiative set the stage for ongoing advocacy and the establishment of the UN Decade for Women. Pivotal to these efforts was "I Am Woman," which was selected as the International Women's Year anthem.

The political impact of "I Am Woman" deeply influenced the trajectory of Reddy's career. In 1974 she became an American citizen, primarily so that she could play a more active role in American politics. By 1976, she had established herself as a significant political force, raising millions of dollars for Democratic candidates, including California governor Jerry Brown, who appointed her a Commissioner of California's Parks and Recreation Department. When asked if she would ever consider running for public office herself, Reddy laughed. "Campaigning would be like being in show business," she said. "And if I'm going to do that, I'd like to be paid the enormous sums of money you get paid in show business."

As the years passed, Reddy continued to work for the causes that mattered to her: the environment, global peace, and especially women's rights and feminism. In 1989, she mobilized for the Women's Lives Rally. In 1996 she headed up the Feminist Expo, and in 2007 she was part of the Women's Leadership Conference. Each event was marked by at least one performance of "I Am Woman." In her later years, Reddy became a popular speaker at fundraising events, and used her skills as an entertainer when delivering a political message. In 2006, during a speech about the state of American politics, Reddy shared some insights that are still applicable today. She began by talking about the environment:

> I want to talk about the future, because I think we are at a very crucial period in the history of our planet. And we all have a great deal of work ahead of us, if we are going to make any sense out of all of it. A good friend of mine in California, a former governor, used to say that if you are in a canoe, going down stream, and you wanted to follow a straight course, you had to paddle to the right, and then to the left. To the right, and then the left. If you paddled only to the right or only to the left, you just went round and round in circles. And I think that what we are desperately in need of is some people paddling on the left.

She then moved on to the topic of contemporary global warfare:

> I look at the way the world was a hundred years ago. It was a very different place. First of all, a hundred years ago, ninety percent of the casualties in war were soldiers on the battlefield. Today, ninety percent of the casualties in war are civilians, many of them women and children being killed in their own homes. Obviously, war is not a feminine value.

Reddy experienced numerous ideological disappointments during her many years of political activism. Nonetheless, she soldiered on. One of her final performances occurred on January 21, 2017, at the Women's March in Los Angeles. Standing next to Jamie Lee Curtis and staring out at a massive crowd of women in pink hats, Reddy raised her voice in song, a final time, for women's rights. She was suffering from dementia by that point. She died in 2020, two years before the Supreme Court struck down *Roe v. Wade*, setting women's rights back a generation.

This final anecdote carries an important lesson about the power of protest songs. Pete Seeger claimed that "the right song, at the right time, can change history." I don't know if protest songs can change history, but they can, on occasion, motivate people to think about where they are in history and where they want to be. There is a general belief that protest songs, more than any other musical genre, have the power to influence politics and create positive change. But the power of protest songs is not so cut-and-dried. As the music discussed in this chapter reveals, the protest songs of the 1960s and 1970s made an impact on listeners. They created a sense of unity and belonging and, at times, they gave a voice to those who had been oppressed, marginalized, or silenced. But these songs rarely sparked debates in Congress. Now that a half century has passed, we must ask ourselves: Did the protest songs of the 1960s and 1970s have an enduring political impact? Did they really change America in a significant way?

Protest songs have a power, no doubt—but it's a fleeting power. During the civil rights era, the antiwar movement, and the sexual revolution, popular protest songs treated the symptoms of disaffection but they failed to provide long-term cures. Protest songs are an art form; they're created and sung as artistic acts. And in the 1960s and 1970s, when the gatekeepers of music were record labels and radio stations, distribution was dependent on a song's ability to speak to as broad an audience as possible. As Phil Ochs once confessed: "As bad as it may sound, I'd rather listen to a good song on the side of segregation than a bad song on the side of integration." In other words, the allure of the music is what draws listeners to a protest song. And when the music is really good, it can create a sense of change that is not a true reflection of reality.

SONIC SHIFT: WHEN POLITICS CHANGED MUSIC

▪ ▪ ▪ ▪ ▪

As the United States headed into the 1980s, many Americans felt rattled by the previous two decades of economic and political upheaval. This state of mind contributed greatly to Ronald Reagan's successful bid for president in 1980. Using the slogan "Let's Make America Great Again," Reagan pledged to be "a leader who will unleash [Americans'] great strength and remove the roadblocks government has put in their way." He promised a new era of prosperity, and many believed him. With Reagan at the helm, the soul-searching of the 1960s and 1970s came to an end. Many of those who had attended Woodstock as idealistic youth in 1969 now looked to music not so much as a means of rebellion but as a profitable industry. As Ken Kragan, a prominent music manager, told *Newsweek* reporters in 1985: "A lot of us who grew up in the '60s trying to change the establishment are now part of the establishment." Music promoter Bill Graham agreed. "The '80s learned from the '70s and '60s. Sooner or later you [realize] that a tent's not too comfortable, that it takes dollars to survive."

Congress and the nation's judiciary system took a deep interest in music in the 1980s. Innovations in technology—CDs, the internet, VCRs, and cable television—expanded the reach of music into everyday life. New revenue streams were created in the music industry, and this caught the attention of business leaders and politicians. As music spread more easily across an ever-expanding array of media, debates arose over access and profitability. On one side were the corporations and politicians who pushed for deregulation as a means of supporting capitalism. On the other were those who feared the consequences of putting big business in the driver's seat. The result was a tumultuous era of transformative decisions in Congress and the courts that significantly changed music in the United States.

One could argue that it all began in 1981, when Reagan established, by executive order, the President's Task Force on Regulatory Relief. Reagan firmly believed that the regulation of a wide range of industries (transportation, financial services, telecommunications, etc.) was best controlled by market forces, and he charged his new task force with finding the most effective means of trimming government regulations through legislative action.

The year 1981 also marked the debut of a new channel on cable television called MTV. "This is it!" promised video jockey Mark Goodman to the 800,000 viewers who tuned in for the first broadcast on August 1. "Welcome to MTV Music Television, the world's first 24-hour, stereo-video music channel.... Starting right now, you'll never look at music the same way again." Goodman was right. MTV pushed daring artists on the periphery of the music industry into the spotlight. It wasn't by accident that the first song aired on MTV was the Buggles' "Video Killed the Radio Star." On MTV, heavy metal bands like Judas Priest and Mötley Crüe took sex and violence mainstream. Pop stars like Cyndi Lauper highlighted female sexuality, and artists like Boy George and Annie Lennox challenged gender norms. The cable channel transformed America's popular music scene, and its effect on viewers' tastes was soon reflected in record sales. The week before MTV's launch, middle-of-the-road artists like Air Supply, Kenny Rogers, the Oak Ridge Boys, and Foreigner topped the Billboard charts. Two years later, high-visibility video artists like Prince, Madonna, Cyndi Lauper, and Billy Idol reigned supreme.

Meanwhile, in Washington, DC, several concerned parents began to take notice. Tipper Gore, wife of Tennessee senator Al Gore, bought her eleven-year-old daughter a copy of Prince's *Purple Rain* album in 1984. As the pair listened to the music together, Gore focused on the lyrics and was appalled to hear an explicit reference to female masturbation in the song "Darling Nikki." Around the same time, Susan Baker, wife of White House chief of staff Jim Baker, got a shock when she overheard her seven-year-old daughter singing along to Madonna's "Like a Virgin." Similarly, Pamela Howar, wife of real estate developer and Republican fundraiser Raymond Howar, noticed that an increasing number of the songs in her aerobics classes contained highly sexualized lyrics. Distraught by what they heard, these three women, together with Sally Nevius (wife of DC city councilman John Nevius) and Ethelyn Stuckley (wife of Georgia congressman Williamson Stuckley) founded the Parents Music Resource Center (PMRC).

The PMRC was a nonprofit organization committed to informing parents about the music their children were being exposed to on the radio, via recordings and videos, and at live concerts. Their central goal was to induce the recording industry to adopt "a rating system for music similar to the movie ratings system used by the Motion Picture Association of America." The PMRC wanted detailed warning labels placed on all records, cassette tapes, and CDs. They also demanded that "song lyrics be printed on the album covers, records with obscene covers be placed under the counters in record stores," and record companies "reconsider their contracts with performers who displayed sex or violence during [live] shows" or on music videos. Determined to make a difference, the PMRC conducted a pressure campaign throughout the summer of 1985. They published a monthly newsletter, grew their membership, and wrote letters to the National Association of Broadcasters and the Record Industry Association of America (RIAA), which represented roughly 85 percent of the nation's music industry. Most importantly, they pressured their well-connected spouses on Capitol Hill to support their efforts.

At first, the RIAA rejected the PMRC's demands, claiming that they amounted to censorship and were thus an affront to the First Amendment and musicians' freedom of speech. But as the pressure continued, the RIAA eventually caved. On August 5, Stanley Gortikov, then president of the RIAA, sent a letter to the PMRC agreeing to add a warning sticker on all future albums that contained songs with explicit content. But for Gore, Baker, and Howar, this wasn't enough. And on September 19, 1985, the Senate Committee on Commerce, Science, and Transportation hosted the Senate Hearing on Record Labeling (a.k.a. the "porn music hearing"), a five-hour event that was broadcast live on national television.

The hearing began with the committee chairman, Senator John Danforth (whose wife had also become affiliated with PMRC), describing the purpose of the hearing: to discuss, publicly, how songs promoting sex and violence were negatively impacting young listeners. In many ways, the event resembled the 1954 Senate hearing that blamed horror comic books for juvenile delinquency. In his opening statement, Danforth noted that "the reason for this hearing is not to promote any legislation . . . But simply to provide a forum for airing the issue itself, for ventilating the issue, for bringing it out in the public domain." Senator Gore agreed, stating that the goals of the PMRC were important but did not require legislative intervention to be realized. The music industry could regulate itself, much like the publishing industry had with the establishment of the Comics Code Authority. Other senators saw things differently. Senator Ernest Hollings noted in his statement that he would try his best to find "some constitutional provision" that would eliminate the "outrageous filth" of "music interspersed with pornography." Senator James Exon also advocated for legislative action.

Members of the PMRC offered the first round of testimony. Using an array of visual images and reciting the lyrics of songs they found especially offensive, they noted the growing influence popular music was having on America's youth and warned that the content found in contemporary lyrics could lead to physical and psychological damage in children. As Tipper Gore explained, "The issue here is larger than violent and sexually explicit lyrics. It is one of ideas and ideals, freedoms and responsibilities in our society. . . . Young minds are at stake." In her view, the recording industry needed to show "self-restraint." Gore and Baker even went so far as to suggest that the rising number of teen pregnancies, suicide, and rape could be attributed to the unregulated content of popular music. In support of these claims, the PMRC compiled a list of songs, the so-called Filthy Fifteen, which they had determined to be especially objectionable. These included "well-known and relatively obscure songs" by AC/DC, Black Sabbath, Def Leppard, Sheena Easton, Judas Priest, Cyndi Lauper, Madonna, Mary Jane Girls, Mercyful Fate, Mötley Crüe,

Prince, Twisted Sister, Vanity, Venom, and WASP. The PMRC discussed each song in detail, outlining the various allusions to what they deemed to be "filth" in the lyrics. These ranged from references to sexual acts and homosexuality to glorifications of violence and suicide. The genres represented were limited to pop and heavy metal. There were no offensive examples taken from country music or rap.

Next on the agenda were representatives from the music community, namely Frank Zappa, John Denver, and Dee Snider. Zappa went first. He began by reading the First Amendment aloud. He then described the PMRC's proposal as "an ill-conceived piece of nonsense which fails to deliver any real benefits to children, infringes on the civil liberties of people who are not children, and promises to keep the courts busy for years with the interpretational problems inherent in the proposal's designs." Declaring the PMRC's demands "equivalent to treating dandruff by decapitation," he called out the source of the complaints, which he said had been "whipped up like an instant pudding by the Wives of Big Brother." Zappa blamed a behind-the-scenes power play as the reason for the proceedings. He even went so far as to suggest that the RIAA and Congress had made a deal: RIAA would agree to use warning labels in exchange for passage of the Home Audio Recording Act (a.k.a. the blank tape tax), a piece of legislation that would "give royalties to the recording industry for the sale of tape recorders and blank tapes." As Zappa noted, the wife of Senator Strom Thurmond, chair of the committee responsible for the new legislation, was an active member of the PMRC.

John Denver spoke next. He began by recounting his own run-ins with music censorship. In 1972, when his song "Rocky Mountain High" began rising in the charts, it was "banned from many radio stations as a drug-related song." As Denver noted, to the laughter of those present, "this was obviously done by people who had never seen or been to the Rocky Mountains." Denver understood the PMRC's desire to keep children from harm, but he also believed in a strong democracy. The suppression of ideas and lyrics proposed by the PMRC, he noted, came dangerously close to the censorship practices that had existed in Nazi Germany. This is why "I am opposed to any kind of rating system, voluntary or otherwise," said Denver. "Even lewd and violent material should not be banned. That which is denied becomes desired. That which is hidden becomes interesting."

Dee Snider, of Twisted Sister, offered the most compelling testimony of the day. Snider began by stating that the PMRC was mistaken when they claimed that his songs contained references to sadomasochism, bondage, and rape. He backed up this statement with two examples. Earlier in the day, Susan Baker had submitted into evidence the music video for Snider's "We're Not Gonna Take It," claiming that it had incited violent behavior in children. Snider called this accusation "slanderous" and "little more than character assassination," and explained that the song was inspired by his favorite Looney Tunes cartoon character, Roadrunner. Similarly, Tipper Gore had claimed in her testimony that Snider's song "Under the Blade" was about a sadomasochistic rape. Snider rejected this interpretation, explaining that the song had been written for a friend who was anxious about an upcoming throat surgery. "Mrs. Gore was looking for sadomasochism and bondage, and she found it," Snider stated. "Someone looking for surgical references would have found those as well." In short, songs are subjective, and they can mean various things to various listeners.

Representatives from the Parents and Teachers Association (PTA) spoke next. Like the PMRC, they called for the implementation of a ratings system and cited the harm imposed on children through music lyrics. A musicologist and child psychologist offered "scientific" evidence of such claims, noting that heavy metal music offered the greatest cause for alarm.

After several hours of testimony, representatives of the music industry were finally given the opportunity to speak. RIAA President Gortikov noted the industry's willingness to create a uniform warning label for "explicit lyrics," but declared that the PMRC's other demands were unreasonable and impractical. Representatives of the broadcasting industry also testified. They acknowledged the growing concern over the explicit lyrics in some popular music and noted that station managers and disc jockeys took seriously their responsibility to protect young listeners. They also noted that they valued the First Amendment rights of musicians and worried that some of the demands made by the PMRC could be viewed as censorship.

In response to this testimony, Senator Paul Trible (whose wife was also a PMRC member) concluded the hearing with a short speech reprimanding the music industry:

> Probably the most important word in a democracy is "No." In a free society, not everything goes. Unbridled freedom leads to chaos and loss of freedom... And I would hope that in this industry there would be some measure of self-restraint. And I would encourage the leaders of this industry to respond responsibly to this very real national concern. Absent that, I would predict that there would be a response from the elected officials [here today]... who are very concerned about these kinds of activities and who have judged them destructive—destructive of lives, and destructive of our society.

Despite Trible's veiled threat, no legislation emanated from the hearing. But changes did come. The media coverage of the hearing planted the term "porn rock" in the public's consciousness, and over the next six weeks discussions continued in the press and behind closed doors. Gore and Snider made the rounds on talk shows and radio, as lobbyists and politicians brokered deals. A public poll taken shortly after the hearing revealed that 75 percent of Americans favored some sort of labeling system. On November 1, that system became a reality. The RIAA proposed the Parent Advisory Label (a.k.a. the PAL mark). This was a uniform, black-and-white sticker that was placed in the lower right corner of all records, cassette tapes, and CDs containing sexual or violent content. Its wording was direct: "Parental Guidance: Explicit Lyrics."

The impact of the PAL mark was immediate. Wal-Mart, which at the time was one of the largest retailers of recorded music in the United States, refused to stock recordings with the PAL mark. Radio stations began banning the music, too. Consequently, musicians were faced with three choices: self-censor to avoid the PAL mark, embrace the PAL mark, or create two versions of a song, one with "explicit lyrics," the other a sanitized version. Ironically, for some performers, including the heavy metal bands Mötley Crüe, Quiet Riot, and Poison, the PAL mark generated an unexpected boost in sales. As Nikki Stix of Mötley Crüe explained, "The sticker almost guaranteed your record would be bought by rebellious kids." The PAL mark served as a sign of danger and nonconformity to many young listeners in the 1980s. Unfortunately, it was this largely false association that caused legal problems for some artists in the years that followed.

In 1988, two civil cases involving the supposedly harmful effects of heavy metal music made national headlines: *McCollum v. CBS* and *Judas Priest v. Nevada*. In both cases, the families of young men who had committed suicide while listening to heavy metal music sued the artists and record companies for damages. In the first case, the parents of John McCollum claimed that Ozzy Osbourne and CBS were guilty of "negligence, product liability, and intentional misconduct" because the content of Osbourne's music had incited their son to shoot himself in 1984. In 1988 the Court of Appeals ruled that Osbourne's music, despite its explicit lyrics, was constitutionally protected free speech. The second case concerned the deaths of two young men who shot themselves in 1985 after six hours of drinking, smoking pot, and listening to Judas Priest's *Stained Glass* album on continuous repeat. The families of the men sued Judas Priest, but due to the outcome of the McCollum case, blamed not the lyrics but the subliminal messages supposedly embedded in the music. After two weeks of testimony, Judas Priest prevailed. The court found there were no "intentionally placed subliminal messages" in *Stained Glass*.

In both cases, the PAL mark included on the defendant's album covers contributed to the legal claim that their music was dangerous and resulted in mental and physical harm. This belief was not limited to heavy metal albums. In the late 1980s, a revolutionary new form of rap, dubbed by the music industry "gangsta rap," emerged from the urban landscape of South Central Los Angeles. Raw and unapologetic, the lyrics reflected the harsh realities faced by many black men in America: gun violence, governmental and family neglect, police brutality, and drug addiction. Growing out of the hard-core rap pioneered by artists like Schoolly D in Philadelphia and Run-DMC and LL Cool J in New York, gangsta rap presented listeners with a new reality. N.W.A. set the bar for gangsta rap, offering lyrics that were unflinchingly explicit and markedly different from the more lighthearted, party-driven themes that had dominated commercial hip-hop music in the mid 1980s.

Gangsta rap brought to the attention of mainstream America a litany of societal ills. Sparking conversations about systemic inequality, the genre provided a much-needed platform for marginalized voices and paved the way for future hip-hop artists who looked to rap as a form of social commentary. But the rise of gangsta rap was not without controversy. Critics accused it of glorifying violence, perpetuating negative stereotypes, and contributing to the deterioration of social values. N.W.A.'s foundational album, *Straight Outta Compton*, released in 1988, served as a rallying cry for disenchanted youth across America. The album offered unfiltered revenge narratives that critiqued the status quo. But with tracks like "Fuck tha Police," N.W.A. also drew unwanted attention from the justice system.

Shortly after the release of *Straight Outta Compton*, an assistant director for the FBI named Milt Ahlerich sent a threatening letter to Priority Records, N.W.A.'s label. "Advocating violence and assault is wrong," he wrote, "and we in the law enforcement community take exception to such action." Ahlerich then noted that more than six dozen police officers were "feloniously slain in the line of duty" in 1988, "and recordings such as the one from N.W.A. are both discouraging and degrading to these brave, dedicated officers." The letter concluded: "I wanted you to be aware of the FBI's position relative to this song and its message. I believe my views reflect the opinion of the entire law enforcement community."

When a description of the letter appeared in the press, public officials took notice. Representative Don Edwards of California declared: "The FBI should stay out of the business of censorship." Danny Goldberg of the American Civil Liberties Union (ACLU) agreed: "It is completely inappropriate for any government agency to try to influence what artists do.... It is completely against the American tradition of free speech and government non-interference for government agencies to criticize art, because such criticism carries with it an implied threat."

When asked why he wrote "Fuck tha Police," Ice Cube explained that he did it as a coping mechanism. "There is a lot of resentment of police because if you are black you get picked on a lot. They see you in a car or with a beeper and they assume you are a dope dealer. The song is a way to get out aggression." It should be seen as a "documentary" of "life in Compton, not a call for violence."

In the end, the FBI apologized for the letter, explaining that it represented the opinion of one man, not the agency as a whole. Ahlerich was reprimanded, and N.W.A. continued to tour the country. But there were consequences. Although N.W.A. eliminated "Fuck tha Police" from their concert playlist, several performances had to be canceled when local police refused to supply security at music venues.

Police outrage also occurred in 1992, when Ice-T and the heavy metal group Body Count released "Cop Killer." Law enforcement agencies across the country launched a grassroots campaign to get Ice-T's record label, Warner Bros. Records, to pull the album. Politicians got involved, too. Vice President Dan Quayle declared the song obscene, and President George H. W. Bush railed against the recording industry. Senators Daniel Patrick Moynihan, Lloyd Bentsen, and Al D'Amato withdrew from their scheduled participation in the Warner Bros. political comedy film *Dave*. Actor Charlton Heston railed against Ice-T's music at the Time–Warner Annual Shareholder's meeting as protesters picketed outside. In response to the turmoil, Ice-T defended the song as a work of fiction: "I'm singing in the first person as a character who is fed up with police brutality. I ain't never killed no cop. I felt like it a lot of times. But I never did it. If you believe I'm a cop killer, you believe David Bowie is an astronaut."

Warner Bros. eventually caved to the pressure; when the album was rereleased, "Cop Killer" was removed. Ice-T was distraught by what he viewed as corporate censorship, and in 1993 he left Warner Bros. Records. The company's chairman at the time, Mo Ostin, regretted the way things ended with the rapper. "Ice-T was a terrific artist who spoke the truth," said Ostin. "But the corporation got so thin-skinned after the incident at the shareholders' meeting. In the end, Ice-T decided to leave because he could not allow tampering with his work. And I can't blame him—considering the climate."

N.W.A. and Ice-T suffered losses due to the rejection of their lyrics by law enforcement, but those setbacks were minor compared to what other artists faced. In 1989, 2 Live Crew released their third album, *As Nasty As They Wanna Be*, along with a "sanitized" version, *As Clean As They Wanna Be*, that contained some of the same music but with different lyrics and titles. Several months after the record's release, the sheriff's office of Broward County, Florida, received complaints from private citizens about the explicit content on *As Nasty As They Wanna Be*. This prompted an investigation, and on February 26, 1990, a Broward County deputy sheriff entered a local record store, Sound Warehouse, and bought a cassette of *As Nasty As They Wanna Be*. Six of the album's songs were then transcribed and submitted to the Broward County Circuit Court as evidence of illegal distribution of obscene material. A local judge ratified the charge and on March 9 issued an order stating that the album was legally obscene. This ruling was then distributed to local retail stores carrying copies of 2 Live Crew's music, and within days sales of the album ceased. But this wasn't the end of the legal system's offensive. On February 8, police arrested Charles Freeman, the black owner of a Fort Lauderdale record store, for selling a copy of the album to an undercover policeman. Two days later, members of 2 Live Crew were arrested at a local nightclub for an "obscene, lewd performance." When the Broward County sheriff's office was asked to clarify what the "obscene, lewd performance" entailed, a representative explained, "They sang some songs from the album that Judge Gonzalez ruled was obscene" and were consequently "taken into custody." When the 2 Live Crew case went to trial in October, jurors found the defendants not guilty.

In response, Luther "Luke Skyywalker" Campbell, 2 Live Crew member and owner of Skyywalker Records, filed suit in a federal district court against the Broward County sheriff's office (*Skyywalker Records v. Navarro*). The judge ruled in favor of the sheriff's office, claiming that the record was "patently offensive" by "contemporary community standards," and that it lacked "serious literary, artistic, political, or scientific value." Campbell was shocked. "I was fighting, fighting for what we have today," he later explained. "It was like: 'This is really political. They really want to get rid of hip hop.'" Skyywalker Records appealed the ruling, stating that the judge had based his decision solely on his personal taste. It took two years, but eventually the United States Court of Appeals reversed the judge's decision, noting that he could not "determine relevant community standards" on his own and "should have relied on expert witnesses."

Skyywalker Records v. Navarro was one of the first instances when rap music was put on trial. Hip-hop culture had escaped mention during the PMRC hearing in 1985, primarily because it had not yet been fully commercialized by the music industry. In the mid-1980s, only a few songs, most notably "Rapper's Delight" (1979) by the Sugarhill Gang and Grandmaster Flash's "The Message" (1982) had broken into the Top 40. And only one rap video, Run-DMC's "Rock Box" (1984), had been broadcast on MTV. During its first decade of existence, rap music flew under the radar of the commercial music industry. Although the basic elements of the art form, MCs rapping and DJs mixing, sampling, and scratching, had coalesced during the 1970s, there were few rap albums in record stores. Instead, the music was generally experienced live, in clubs and at parties in the South Bronx and Harlem. When it first went mainstream, in 1979, the music had been sanitized into upbeat dance tunes, free of violent or sexually explicit lyrics. As Wonder Mike of the Sugarhill Gang noted: "It wasn't too heavy . . . It wasn't 'bash the police'—that was years later." Commercial rap music in 1984 was mostly about "guys having fun" and trying "to impress the chicks."

But by 1989, rap had found its voice in popular culture, and the PMRC took notice. In 1990, Tipper Gore published an op-ed in the *Washington Post* titled "Hate, Rape and Rap." One of her central concerns was the objectification of women in rap lyrics and the effect this was having on young listeners. So, while 2 Live Crew was fighting the obscenity charges brought against *As Nasty As They Want To Be*, Tipper Gore and the PMRC went after a track on *As Clean As They Want To Be*. The song in question was "Pretty Woman," a comedic takeoff on an old Roy Orbison tune. As Campbell explained:

> These people from the PMRC came. . . . Tipper Gore was rolling with this corps of girls, and they were hard core. They were calling everybody, trying to tear me down, limb by limb. The PMRC contacted the Roy Orbison Estate, and they said: "How could you let 2 Live Crew do a parody of 'Pretty Woman'? We're going to get people to boycott Roy Orbison's records. You need to stop the 2 Live Crew. You need to sue them."

In 1991, two significant copyright infringement cases involving music parodies were filed in court. The first, *Campbell v. Acuff-Rose Music, Inc.* involved 2 Live Crew's "Pretty Woman." The second, *Grand Upright Music Ltd v. Warner Brothers Records, Inc.*, went after a young rapper named Biz Markie. The results of both cases significantly influenced the production of popular music in the United States.

Discussing copyright is no easy task. This is especially true when it comes to music. Music is a self-referential art form. Musicians regularly perform works composed by others. They also often quote or allude to others' compositions when creating new works. Copyright law has attempted to accommodate these facts. Consequently, there are two basic types of music copyright: 1) the copyright of a composition, known as the publishing copyright, which is held by the songwriter/composer and/or music publisher, and 2) the copyright of a recording, known as the performance copyright, which is held by the performer and/or record label for a master sound recording. The two types of copyright are governed by different rules and regulations. For example, if a musician wants to record a song composed by someone else, he simply obtains a mechanical license (permission) and pays a fee to the holder of the publishing copyright. This is an automatic, compulsory process. The copyright holder cannot block the licensing, and the fee is the same for everyone. In 1991, the cost was set at 9.1 cents per composition or 1.75 cents per minute of composition used, whichever amount was larger. But what if a musician wants to change the content or structure of an existing composition? In this case, the changed version is called a derivative work, and a mechanical license is neither automatic nor compulsory. Except under rare circumstances, a derivative work cannot be created without first obtaining explicit permission from the holder of the publishing copyright. Legally, one of the only ways a musician can release a derivative composition without permission is if the new work is a parody; the "fair use" doctrine of the Copyright Act of 1976 states that derivative works do not require permission if they offer a critique or commentary on the original.

The licensing process surrounding performance copyright is noticeably different. If a musician wants to incorporate a recording by someone else in his own work, he must obtain a master license. This is not an automatic process; the fee must be negotiated, and the holder of a performance copyright has the legal power to deny licensing. For example, when Kanye West used a sample of Nina Simone's recording of "Strange Fruit" in his song "Blood on the Leaves," he obtained a mechanical license from Abel Meeropol's publisher (Edward B. Marks Publishing) and a master license from Universal Music Enterprises, which owns the copyright of Simone's master recording.

Article I, Section 8, Clause 8 of the Constitution grants Congress the power to define copyright law. Accordingly, over the past two centuries, as technological advances have transformed the way works are created, distributed, and sold, copyright law has changed, often in response to legal battles. In 1991, for example, the rules surrounding copyright law and licensing regulations were tested by the lawsuits brought against 2 Live Crew and Biz Markie. The final decisions in both cases were important: they established the copyright standards that future artists would be required to follow when creating works that parodied and/or sampled the songs and recordings by others—artistic practices that have been at the heart of rap music since the genre's beginning.

Encouraged by the PMRC, Acuff-Rose Music sued 2 Live Crew for copyright infringement two years after the release of *As Clean As They Want to Be*. The legal issue centered on whether 2 Live Crew's unauthorized use of Roy Orbison's song "Oh, Pretty Woman" as the basis for their own song "Pretty Woman" constituted copyright infringement or fell under the fair use doctrine.

In creating their song, 2 Live Crew had changed the lyrics of Orbison's original and constructed a markedly different song structure and musical arrangement. In the eyes of the law, their song was a derivative work, not a cover of Orbison's original. Consequently, lawyers for Acuff-Rose Music claimed that 2 Live Crew should have contacted the owner of the publishing copyright and requested a mechanical license. They also noted that if Acuff-Rose Music had been contacted about a mechanical license they would have blocked it, because they believed that 2 Live Crew's "Pretty Woman" hurt the commercial value of Orbison's original song.

The lawyers for Campbell and 2 Live Crew saw things differently. As they argued in court, "Pretty Woman" was indeed a derivative work, but because it was a parody, its creation fell under the fair use doctrine. The judge agreed with this line of defense, noting that 2 Live Crew's version was a parody, and that it was "extremely unlikely that 2 Live Crew's song could adversely affect the market for the original" because the "intended audience for the two songs [was] entirely different."

As with many legal cases, the dispute did not end there. Acuff-Rose Music petitioned for a review of the decision, which was reversed by the Court of Appeals. Campbell then appealed the appeal, and in 1994 the case got "kicked to the Supreme Court," where a landmark decision was reached in favor of Campbell and 2 Live Crew. "When they issued the ruling," Campbell later explained, "I was totally numb for the whole, entire day."

> I was like, "What just happened? Are you serious? Did I just win in the Supreme Court?" I actually went in the back room and started crying. It was emotional for me. If I would have lost that case, not only would it have affected hip hop, but it also would have affected shows like *Saturday Night Live*, and *Chappelle's Show*. All of them could have been sued. My case set precedent. It's the number one case that they use, right now today, for parodies on the internet.

Campbell v. Acuff-Rose Music, Inc. clarified that parodies were indeed protected under the fair use doctrine. As Campbell noted, the ruling opened the door for future creatives. In addition to sketch comedy artists like Kate McKinnon, Kenan Thompson, and Melissa Villaseñor on *Saturday Night Live*, musicians like Weird Al Yankovic and Randy Rainbow have benefited from the artistic freedom guaranteed by *Campbell v. Acuff-Rose Music, Inc.* Even the countless internet memes are protected thanks to the Supreme Court's decision.

But not all copyright infringement cases lead to greater artistic freedom. In fact, the opposite occurred in another groundbreaking lawsuit, *Grand Upright Music, Ltd v. Warner Brothers Records, Inc.* In December 1991, Biz Markie, affectionately dubbed by many hip hop's "clown prince," found himself sitting before Judge Kevin Thomas Duffy of the US Court for the Southern District of New York. The rapper had recently released his third album, *I Need a Haircut*, with Warner Bros. Records, and he was now in court for copyright infringement. The central dispute involved the 22-second audio sample from Gilbert O'Sullivan's 1972 hit "Alone Again (Naturally)" that Biz Markie had used in his parody song "Alone Again." It should be noted that, even though 2 Live Crew's "Pretty Woman" had sampled the distinctive bass lick from Orbison's master recording, the copyright of the recording was not debated in that case as Acuff-Rose Music was Orbison's publisher, not his record company. But in *Grand Upright Music, Ltd v. Warner Brothers Records, Inc.*, the owner of O'Sullivan's master recording, Grand Upright Music, Inc., was claiming damages for copyright infringement.

Lawyers for Biz Markie and Warner Bros. Records first argued that Grand Upright Music did not own the copyright needed to charge the defendants with copyright infringement. When this argument failed—the plaintiffs produced the necessary documents—the defense claimed that Biz Markie's unauthorized use of the audio sample was acceptable because sampling was an inherent element of the rap aesthetic and had become standard practice in recent years. This argument did not sit well with Judge Duffy, whose final ruling opened with a quote from the Ten Commandments:

> "Thou shalt not steal" has been an admonition followed since the dawn of civilization. Unfortunately, in the modern world of business, this admonition is not always followed. Indeed, the defendants in this action for copyright infringement would have this court believe that stealing is rampant in the music business, and for that reason, their conduct here should be excused. The conduct of the defendants herein, however, violates not only the Seventh Commandment, but also the copyright laws of this country.

Duffy did not simply declare Biz Markie guilty of copyright infringement; he accused the rapper and his label of felony theft, driven by financial greed:

> It is clear that the defendants knew that they were violating the plaintiff's rights as well as the rights of others. Their only aim was to sell thousands upon thousands of records. This callous disregard for the law and for the rights of others requires not only the preliminary injunction sought by the plaintiff but also sterner measures.

Specifically, Duffy referred the matter to the US Attorney General for felony prosecution.

Fortunately, felony charges were never filed. Still, the damage was done. Warner Bros. pulled "Alone Again" and paid O'Sullivan and Grand Upright Music $250,000. There was no appeal. Warner Bros. had no interest in throwing good money after bad, and Biz Markie's career hit a rough patch. Two years passed before he released another album. Titled *All Samples Cleared*, it featured a recreation of the Duffy courtroom on its cover, with the "clown prince" appearing as both judge ("The Honorable Biz Markie" in robe and white wig) and defendant (the distraught rapper in a striped prison uniform). Biz Markie might have "had the last laugh" with *All Samples Cleared*, but it came at a price. The "anything goes" era of sampling had come to an end.

Judge Duffy's designation of unauthorized sampling as theft changed the aesthetics of rap music overnight. In the years leading up to Duffy's ruling, many artists had begun to lay their raps over a dense collage of samples from multiple sources. For example, Public Enemy's "Night of the Living Baseheads" (1988) made use of twenty-three distinct samples, and in 1991 N.W.A. was producing songs with upwards of seventeen samples. As Chuck D of Public Enemy explained, the ruling in *Grand Upright Music, Ltd v. Warner Brothers Records, Inc.* dealt a severe blow to rappers' ability to practice their craft:

> Public Enemy's music was affected more than anybody's, because we were taking thousands of sounds. If you separated the sounds, they wouldn't have been anything—they were unrecognizable. The sounds were all collaged together to make a sonic wall. Public Enemy was affected because it is too expensive to defend against a claim. So, we had to change our whole style.

This change in style—the decreased use of multiple samples in a single song—affected the communicative power of rap. As Justin Williams explains in his book *Rhymin' and Stealin': Musical Borrowing in Hip Hop*, "the fundamental element of hip hop culture and aesthetics is the overt use of pre-existing material to new ends." Building a collage of sound using multiple samples creates various levels of intertextual meaning. Cultural historian Josh Kun has noted how sampling allows one to "combine without erasing," "to embrace the multitude, not the singular." It promotes the idea that "existence is coexistence." Following this point of view, one could even argue that sampling offers a new metaphor for the American experience. Instead of the "melting pot" image that had been promoted in connection with George Gershwin's blending of various styles and genres, sampling offers a mosaic, wherein the various ethnic and cultural elements form a cohesive whole without the sacrifice of each element's innate qualities. Sampling forces listeners to embrace "the other." It makes "the foreign familiar." Most importantly, perhaps, sampling "involves historical consciousness," because the creator needs an in-depth knowledge of the musical past before he can use it as the cornerstone for a musical future. In short, the artists who embraced the art of sampling in the early decades of hip-hop culture encouraged listeners to engage in "a new dialogue" that invited an array of "disparate voices." They were tapping into an aesthetic that had grown out of meaningful black traditions, like the practice of musical quotation in jazz. Judge Duffy chose to ignore these important precedents when he made his ruling. Discarding a century of black music practice, he declared Biz Markie's music sampling a criminal act.

Grand Upright Music, Ltd v. Warner Brothers Records, Inc. did not single-handedly kill sampling, but it did change the intrinsic meaning and effect of the sample. After 1991, the music industry became more litigious. Major labels dedicated additional staff and resources to licensing, and sample clearance fees skyrocketed. The result? For many up-and-coming rappers, even the use of a single sample became prohibitively expensive. As the twentieth century concluded, the sample took on new meaning. Like gold chains and fine champagne, the sample became a symbol of luxury and excess. And its link to rap's origins endowed it with authenticity.

The *Grand Upright Music, Ltd v. Warner Brothers Records, Inc.* ruling arose "in the midst of a moral panic surrounding hip hop music," and Duffy's decision to criminalize sampling added fuel to the fire. In the years that followed, state prosecutors began to take advantage of the perceived links between hip-hop culture and criminal behavior. Lyrics began to be introduced as evidence in the courtroom. This happened to rapper Andre "Mac Dre" Hicks in 1992, Snoop Dogg in 1996, McKinley "Mac" Phipps Jr. in 2000, Lil Boosie in 2012, Drakeo the Ruler in 2016, 6ix9ine in 2019, and Young Thug in 2022. Those are just the most prominent cases. Over the last three decades, hundreds of criminal cases have included rap lyrics as evidence of unlawful behavior. Some congressional leaders have taken an interest in this issue. In California, for example, the legislature passed a bill in 2022 that bans lyrics from being cited in court cases "unless prosecutors can illustrate that the words are directly relevant to the case in question" and don't "inject racial bias into the proceedings." Similar legislation (House Bill No. 475) passed in Louisiana in 2023. It's a start, but there is still work to be done.

Systemic bias is baked into the criminal justice system when it comes to rap. Although other genres use lyrics describing criminal behavior—just listen to Johnny Cash's "Folsom Prison Blues," Bob Marley's "I Shot the Sheriff," or Taylor Swift's "No Body, No Crime"—their creators are not subjected to the same judicial scrutiny. Taifha Natalee Alexander and other scholars have suggested that "this difference in treatment is, in part, a result of rap lyrics oftentimes being excluded from First Amendment protections." Others have noted the disparate ways that even unconscious racial biases have influenced discussions of song lyrics in court. As sociologist Amy Binder has shown, the discussions by "mainstream writers" of civil court cases in the 1980s citing heavy metal lyrics differ markedly from the discussions of criminal cases a decade later citing rap. In the former, the central concern was "the detrimental effects" that the "graphic" lyrics might have on "teen-aged listeners." In discussions of trials that quoted rap lyrics, reporters often focused on "the dangers" that "black youths posed to the society at large."

Before concluding this chapter, I'll return briefly to the topic of deregulation. Toward the end of his first term, President Bill Clinton signed into law the Telecommunications Act of 1996, a sweeping piece of legislation that was designed to fuel a new era of competition and innovation in the American media landscape. The event took place on a frigid February afternoon in the Reading Room of the Library of Congress. In attendance were Vice President Al Gore, top executives from an array of telecommunications companies, the director of the Federal Communications Commission (FCC), several leaders in the field of education, and members of the House and Senate who had sponsored the legislation, most notably House Speaker Newt Gingrich, representatives Thomas Bliley and John Dingell, and senators Ernest Hollings and Larry

Pressler. The Telecommunications Act of 1996 was an exceedingly complex piece of legislation that had been three years in the making. In many ways, it was an extension of the deregulation programs set in motion by President Reagan fifteen years earlier.

Enacted during a period of rapid technological advancement, the Telecommunications Act of 1996 implemented new guidelines for telephone, television, and radio. It was the first legislative action to address directly what Vice President Gore called "the information superhighway" (i.e., the internet). At the signing, Clinton and Gore both emphasized the myriad ways the new law would improve education, broaden access to resources, diversify media content, lower telephone bills, and give parents control over what their children watched on television. What they did not mention was a small provision buried deep within the behemoth piece of legislation: the new law eliminated the existing FCC limit on the number of radio stations a single entity could own nationally, and relaxed limits on the ownership of radio stations in a local market. As inconsequential as these details might have seemed at the time, they proved devastating to regional music ecosystems.

The deregulation of radio ownership triggered a wave of mergers and acquisitions. Almost overnight, the mosaic of diverse voices and musics that had characterized the auditory terrain of American broadcast radio since the 1920s disappeared. In its place arose Clear Channel Communications (now iHeartMedia), the colossus of America's new sonic landscape. To give a sense of the scale these changes wrought: Clear Channel went from owning approximately 60 stations in 1996 to over 1,200 in 2003.

The consolidation of broadcast radio led to the marginalization of local voices and music styles in favor of nationally syndicated content. Homogenized, risk-averse programming became the standard at most stations as large media companies cut costs by eliminating local programming. As these changes played out, the recording industry responded. Major labels exerted greater control over their artists, often restricting musicians' creative autonomy in favor of marketability. To get on the radio, musicians had to create music with national appeal.

It goes without saying that the consolidation of the radio industry made it increasingly difficult for independent and niche artists to reach new audiences. In the years that followed, consolidation swept through the recording industry, too. Warner Music Group, Universal Music Group, and Sony Music Entertainment took over nearly every independent record label. Independent musicians had few places to go until streaming services came on the scene. Strange as it may seem, many of the freedoms currently associated with online music streaming can be traced back to the way that the Telecommunications Act of 1996 treated the internet.

When Clinton and Gore described their vision for deregulation, they defined the internet as an essential service, like telephone and electricity, that should be accessible to everyone, "even rural and low-income areas." They argued that schools, libraries, hospitals, and clinics should "have access to advanced telecommunications services, and . . . be connected to the information superhighway." Their vision for the internet promoted an idea we now call net neutrality: the belief that internet service providers (ISPs) should treat all data on the internet equally and not discriminate or charge differently by user, content, website, platform, or application. Although most ISPs claim to abide by the tenets of net neutrality, there have been conflicts over their practices in the past. Net neutrality has been a contentious topic in the halls of Congress for nearly two decades, and it likely won't end anytime soon. Although a federal appeals court struck down the FCC's net neutrality rules in early January 2025, the chairwoman of the commission noted that the issue is not closed: "Consumers across the country have told us again and again that they want an internet that is fast, open, and fair. . . . It is clear that Congress now needs to heed their call, take up the charge for net neutrality and put open internet principles in federal law."

Politics has changed music on countless occasions, often without most of us even noticing. If there is a final message to this chapter, it is that we should all pay attention to the legislation going on around us. The influence of politics on music reaches far beyond the federal government. Noise ordinances, zoning laws, curricula reforms, and public transportation—decisions in these realms and countless others affect the health of local music ecosystems every day.

Music permeates our lives. Thanks to technology, it is always with us: via our smartphones, the radio, TV commercials, film scores, even the streamed music at stores and restaurants. Modern technology has made it easy for us to put music in the background. We owe it to future generations of artists and fans to bring it front and center again.

UNDER AFRICAN SKIES

On February 11, 1990, Nelson Mandela walked out of a South African prison after twenty-seven years of incarceration. Mandela had spent his entire adult life fighting against the racist policies of apartheid. His release, at age seventy-seven, was a global event. Newsreels showed crowds cheering and dancing with delight. As commentators noted, Mandela's newfound freedom was a sign of hope, the beginning of what promised to be a new era in South African history. In the United States, spontaneous celebrations also took place. Mandela's release represented a victory for democracy, living proof that "the arc of the moral universe" once described by Martin Luther King Jr. did indeed bend toward justice.

Mandela attributed his freedom to the years-long efforts of activists around the world. As he announced from the steps of Cape Town's City Hall:

> On this day of my release, I extend my sincere and warmest gratitude to the millions of my compatriots and those in every corner of the globe who have campaigned tirelessly.... Your mass marches, and other forms of struggle, have served as a constant source of strength to all political prisoners.... On this occasion, we thank the world. We thank the world

community for their great contribution to the anti-apartheid struggle. Without your support, our struggle would not have reached this advanced stage.

In the months that followed, Mandela traveled to various countries and connected with supporters. In June, he arrived in the United States, where he spent two weeks crisscrossing the country, always with the media in tow. Mandela visited schools and libraries. He spoke at fundraising events and met with politicians and anti-apartheid activists. The purpose of his travel was twofold: to express gratitude to the activists and to raise money for the African National Congress (ANC), the political party that represented black South Africans, so that his country could continue to move "from white domination to a democratically elected government." The highlight of Mandela's trip was his visit to Boston, where roughly 260,000 people gathered along the banks of the Charles River to hear him speak. Mandela shared the stage that day with various performers, including the South African vocal group Ladysmith Black Mambazo and the American singer-songwriter Paul Simon, musicians whose collaboration four years earlier had resulted in the groundbreaking album *Graceland*.

Mandela was a huge fan of *Graceland*. But there were some in South Africa, the United States, and Britain who did not share in his admiration. The problem wasn't the music. There was universal agreement that as a work of art, *Graceland* was a masterpiece. The problem was politics. Simon had recorded part of the album in South Africa, an act that was a violation of the comprehensive boycott that had been declared by the General Assembly of the United Nations in December 1980.

The UN's boycott of South Africa was meant to weaken the ruling Afrikaner National Party (ANP), which had implemented apartheid in 1948. Apartheid was based on the racist premise that people of African ancestry should live and work separately from those of European ancestry. In South Africa, this meant that white South Africans, who comprised roughly 10 percent of the population, controlled the nation's legal and political systems as well as most of the country's financial and natural resources. The majority black South Africans, many of whom had been relocated to Bantustans (so-called tribal homelands) and lived in poverty, were represented by the ANC and its offshoot the Pan Africanist Congress (PAC). In 1960, the ANP declared both the ANC and the PAC illegal entities, and many of their leaders, including Nelson Mandela, were eventually imprisoned or exiled.

Although boycotts against South Africa had been called for in the past, for example in 1968 by UNESCO, the country's racial strife had continued unabated. Consequently, the 1980 boycott declared by the UN was broader in scope. It called for a wide range of economic, political, military, and cultural sanctions—which meant that member states were encouraged to "prevent all cultural, academic, sporting, and other exchanges with South Africa." It urged "writers, artists, musicians, and other personalities to boycott South Africa" and "all academic and cultural institutions to terminate all links with South Africa." In short, it asked the world to cut off all contact with South Africa, to pretend it did not exist. As an artist, Simon thought this was unreasonable and wrong.

Simon's interest in South Africa began in 1984, when a fellow songwriter, Heidi Berg, gave him a homemade cassette tape labeled *Gumboots: Accordion Jive Hits, Volume II*. The bouncing, upbeat pulse and mix of instruments captivated Simon, and for several months he let the music wash over him as he drove around. "By the end of the summer I was scat-singing melodies over the tracks," he later recalled. "I thought that the group, whoever it was, would be interesting to work with." Simon heard in each tune an "almost mystical affection and strange familiarity." It was new, yet recognizable in a nostalgic sort of way, he explained.

> It sounded like very early rock & roll to me. Black, urban, mid-fifties rock & roll, like the great Atlantic [Records] tracks from that period. The rhythm was a fairly uptempo, 2/4 feel with a strange accordion in there. But the way they play the accordion, it sounds like a big reed instrument. It could almost be a sax.

The tape had come from South Africa, but Berg didn't know the musicians or the name of the band. As Simon explained, this was the beginning of his South African musical quest. "I went on a search to find out who they were, and where they came from." He soon learned that the instrumental tracks on *Gumboots: Accordion Jive Hits, Volume II* were examples of township jive, a type of street music popular in Soweto, a black township in Johannesburg.

Simon's desire to work with South African musicians was not surprising. As early as the 1970s, he had shown an interest in non-Western music with songs like "El Condor Pasa (If I Could)," his take on a Peruvian ballad that featured the Andean folk group Los Incas, and "Mother and Child Reunion," which he recorded in Jamaica with reggae and ska musicians Hux Brown and Jackie Jackson. Intent on connecting with the musicians on *Gumboots*, Simon reached out to Mo Ostin, chief executive of Warner Bros. Records. Ostin put him in touch with Hilton Rosenthal, a white South African record producer who knew the underground South African music scene well. Rosenthal tracked down the performers on the cassette tape—a group from Soweto called the Boyoyo Boys. Simon asked Rosenthal to reach out to the band and secure a better-quality recording of *Gumboots* and the required licenses to sample it. Rosenthal said he could do one better. If Simon was up for a trip to Johannesburg, a recording studio could be reserved and Simon could record with the Boyoyo Boys and other South African bands.

Simon jumped at the opportunity. To prepare for the trip, he did a deep dive into contemporary South African music. Rosenthal sent him "a package of about thirty albums covering different genres." The range of music was incredible, Simon later explained: There were "all different styles, like township jive from Soweto, which was an urban Zulu kind of music; Sotho music by the group Tao Ea Maysekha . . . [and] Shangan music by General Shirinda and the Gaza Sisters. . . . That's how I started off with those groups." Listening to the albums over the next few months gave Simon "a clear idea of what I liked, and what I wanted to record."

Simon wasn't the only musician showing an interest in Africa. In 1984, stars of the UK music scene formed the supergroup Band Aid and recorded the song "Do They Know It's Christmas?" to raise money for those suffering from the famine in Ethiopia. Written by Bob Geldof and Midge Ure, the song became a huge hit, and within a year the recording raised 8 million pounds. The project's success led to several spinoff charity recordings in the United States, the most notable being "We Are the World."

Simon participated in the "We Are the World" project. On January

28, 1985, he and four dozen other stars of the music industry gathered at A&M Studios in Los Angeles and recorded the song as the supergroup USA for Africa. Like the Band Aid single the year before, the purpose of "We Are the World" was to send humanitarian aid to those suffering from famine in Africa. When the record was released in March, it shot to the top of the charts. The recording received numerous awards, including four Grammys, and it raised over 63 million dollars.

Despite the spectacular success of "We Are the World," the project had its detractors. In October 1985, *Newsweek* published an article titled "Brother Can You Spare a Song?" that questioned the sincerity of the project's participants. "It is tempting to assume that such music augurs a deepening of social awareness," noted the article. "But the current upsurge of high-minded pop is marked by some curious paradoxes." For example, "while superstars have been joining hands to raise money for charities, senators on Capitol Hill have held a hearing on pornography in rock, creating pressure on record companies to censor themselves." Such "paradoxes" could not be accidental, noted *Newsweek*. "Far from deepening social awareness, much of the current craze for star-studded benefits seems calculated to make everybody—the stars, the fans, the corporate sponsors—feel a little better about themselves." In fact, some of the musicians listed in the PMRC's "Filthy Fifteen" had clamored to participate in the making of "We Are the World."

Despite the skepticism of some critics, Simon was glad to have participated in the project because it gave him the opportunity to consult with two musicians who had close connections to South Africa, namely Quincy Jones, a co-producer of "We Are the World," and Harry Belafonte, the artist–activist who had initiated the project. During the marathon recording session, Jones advised Simon that everything would be fine if he focused on the needs of the South African musicians. "Just make sure everybody gets paid," he said, "and that everybody likes you." Belafonte was more reserved in his response. "I thought it was an excellent idea," he later explained, "but I also suggested that he contact people directly involved with the boycott issue to explain the reasons for his trip." Specifically, Belafonte advised Simon to clear his plans with Oliver Tambo and other members of the ANC leadership before traveling to South Africa. Simon, who disliked the idea of asking politicians for permission to make music, asked his contact in South Africa, Hilton Rosenthal, if he needed permission. As Simon later explained, the answer was "No. I just needed a visa to get in. That's all I had to do."

Simon traveled to Johannesburg with recording engineer Roy Halee in February 1985. Once there, they met up with Rosenthal and a black South African producer named Koloi Lebona. Lebona was the one who had done the legwork—securing the studio and reaching out to local musicians—in preparation for Simon's visit. As Lebona later explained, he knew that Simon's plan to record with black South Africans might cause problems among the locals. "It was definitely a risk," he admitted, but an important risk. "Until then, South African music was regarded as third world music. I thought if our music gets a chance to be part of mainstream music, surely there can't be any harm. So, when Paul Simon came, I deliberately withheld some of the risks involved. I thought, 'What the heck? This is a chance in a million. We must do this!'"

One piece of information withheld from Simon was the pushback expressed by some musicians when they learned of Simon's plans. For example, a popular mbaqanga group, the Soul Brothers, told Lebona that a member of the ANC had advised them to decline Simon's offer. To avoid further conflict, Lebona reached out to the Musicians Union of South Africa, a group of several hundred black artists, and asked them to support Simon's visit. They took a vote, and as Simon later learned, "They decided that my coming would benefit them" because they wanted South African music to gain "a place in the international musical community similar to that of reggae."

Simon spent two weeks in South Africa in February 1985. Following Quincy Jones's advice, he paid the musicians well—three times the union scale in New York—and openly expressed his admiration for their music. During the first few days in the studio, Rosenthal and Lebona brought in one group at a time. The Boyoyo Boys were first, followed by Tao Ea Matsekha, then Stimela. As Simon later recalled, "It was very exciting to see the South African groups whose music I had already heard on records." But it took a day or two for everyone to get comfortable. "The feeling in the room was a little strained at first," noted Halee. "The musicians weren't sure of themselves or who Paul was, but he went about making them feel at ease." He let the performers bring their own sound to each session—for example, Forere Motloheloa's droning accordion, which had the pulse and timbre that first captivated Simon. By the end of the first week, Simon had formed a studio band with three of the musicians: Bakithi Kumalo (bass) from Tao Ea Matsekha, and Ray Phiri (guitar) and Isaac Mtshali (drums) from Stimela. With this core group in place, week two was "more of a traditional recording session," recalled Halee. "They would start grooving, just playing a vamp, waiting for something to come out. When Paul heard something he liked, he'd say, 'Let's build around that.'"

"We worked improvisationally," explained Simon. "While a group was playing in the studio, I would sing melodies and words—anything that fit the scale they were playing in." "It was fun," said Mtshali. "Paul said to us, 'Feel free. Play anything.' . . . At the end of the day, when we'd listen to the whole thing, we didn't believe it was us, because we weren't thinking about recording. It was like we were practicing—no pressure, no nothing." Kumalo agreed. "Paul was a godsend. The way he treated the musicians with dignity and made us believe that [we were] doing good. I was quiet most of the time, just smiling, thinking 'I have an engineer from America who was making my bass sound like heaven.' I was in heaven! It was joyful." "We were functioning in a magical world, just making music," said Simon. It was a "euphoric" experience. The barriers just seemed to fall away, he recalled—that is, as long as everyone remained in the studio. Outside, the dark shadows of apartheid were ever-present. "There was a surface tranquility," Simon explained, "but right below the surface there was all this tension." The biggest problem was getting the musicians home safely each night.

> They couldn't use public transportation. They [were] not allowed to be on the streets of Johannesburg after curfew. They would have to show papers, and it was something they clearly didn't want to have to do. So always around six or seven o'clock, there would be an uncomfortable time when the players couldn't concentrate until they knew there might be a car to take them home.

Kumalo noted the tension, too. But as he later explained, the difficulties he and the other musicians faced only strengthened their resolve to play well. "The struggle made me really creative.... I'd play strong to get out of this struggle... and it just happened. It was a great opportunity."

Toward the end of his second week in South Africa, Simon met Joseph Shabalala, leader of the ten-member male vocal group Ladysmith Black Mambazo. Today, Ladysmith Black Mambazo is an internationally revered group, but back in 1985 their contact with listeners outside of South Africa had been largely limited to an appearance in the 1979 BBC documentary *Rhythm of Resistance: The Music of South Africa*. As Simon later noted, he'd seen the film and found their sound to be mesmerizing. "The music was so unusual and so beautiful—all *a cappella*. I'd never heard anything like it." Shabalala was invited to attend one of Simon's last recording sessions in South Africa. "I didn't really know how I could possibly fit into their world or if they would want me to," explained Simon. Nonetheless, he couldn't leave South Africa without meeting them.

As Robert Hilburn has reported, Simon and Shabalala hit it off right away. "Shabalala was warm and gracious, and Simon was charmed when the singer gave him a bagful of Ladysmith tapes." Shabalala remembered fondly the events of their first encounter. "When I got the call, I went to meet Paul. He came to me like a child asking his father, 'Can you teach me something?' He was so polite." "Joseph is a very spiritual person," said Simon. "At the end of the session I finally said, 'Would you consider recording with me?'" Simon offered to write a song for Ladysmith Black Mambazo when he got back to the United States. Shabalala embraced Simon and said, "Please send a song." As he later admitted, "That was my first time to hug a white man."

Shortly after Simon's return from Johannesburg, he was contacted by Steven van Zandt (a.k.a. Little Steven), former guitarist for Bruce Springsteen's E Street Band. Van Zandt was organizing a new charity recording project designed to support the ANC and activist groups fighting apartheid repression. Since leaving Springsteen in 1984, Van Zandt had taken an interest in politics. In May, he released *Voice of America*, an album that one critic claimed "traffics in world politics" with an "angry urgency." Featuring songs like "Checkpoint Charlie," "Los Desaparecidos (The Disappeared Ones)," and the title song "Voice of America," the album offered a barbed protest of President Reagan's foreign policy. Despite airtime on MTV and a European tour, *Voice of America* did not sell well, prompting another critic to label Van Zandt "the political cartoonist of rock 'n' roll." By the time Van Zandt reached out to Simon, he had been booted from his record label, EMI, and was committed to establishing himself as a "Rock and Roll Ambassador." As the guitarist explained to Simon, his latest project would educate Americans about the atrocities of apartheid.

Like Simon, Van Zandt had firsthand experience of life in South Africa. In 1984, he traveled to the country on two separate occasions. The purpose of his first trip had been to promote *Voice of America* and hopefully arrange a multi-city tour. EMI had paid for the trip, and as Van Zandt later admitted, "Just by being there I was violating the boycott." Van Zandt "had wanted to play for integrated audiences in South Africa," but when those plans were criticized by members of the ANC, he "respected black leaders' wish" that he honor the boycott. Consequently, the goal of Van Zandt's second trip was markedly different. "I didn't feel particularly educated in America about South Africa," he admitted. "I was interested in finding out the truth." So, "like a journalist," he went to "see the situation for himself" and "research material on a street level for future songs."

> I met with everyone I could, from the labor unions to religious leaders and everybody in between. I met with Archbishop (then Bishop) Desmond Tutu.... While I was in Cape Town, my guides tried to arrange a meeting with Nelson Mandela, imprisoned on Robben Island, but the authorities wouldn't let me see him. And I couldn't get to the prime minister either.... We even managed a side trip to one of the so-called homelands ... Bophuthatswana, and its main attraction, the gambling resort of Sun City.

Bophuthatswana was one of ten Bantustans set up by the South African government as independent "tribal" states. Between 1960 and 1984, the ANP forcibly removed over 3.5 million black South Africans from their homes in the "white" regions of South Africa and relocated them to one of the Bantustans, stripping them of their rights as South African citizens. Van Zandt was angered by the injustices he witnessed in Bophuthatswana. Sun City was like "a Las Vegas gambling oasis built in the slums of Spanish Harlem," he declared. "Sun City was a con! ... one of the great cons of all time. It wasn't in a different country." It was just a bait and switch set up by the ANP to "fool everybody into thinking they were not violating the boycott by playing in Sun City." But even more upsetting to Van Zandt was America's complicity. Specifically, he blamed the Reagan administration's "constructive engagement" policy, which Van Zandt described as "little more than a bullshit way of maintaining the status quo in South Africa."

The UN's call for a comprehensive boycott of South Africa in 1980 coincided with the election of Ronald Reagan. When Reagan took office, many activists feared that he would be unwilling to join the fight against apartheid. In 1981, during a televised interview with Walter Cronkite, Reagan proved them right. In his conversation with Cronkite, Reagan linked his new domestic policies concerning deregulation to his unwillingness to adhere to the UN's boycott of South Africa. He argued that such measures were unnecessary, since slow and deliberate progress by "many people, black and white, in South Africa" was already being made "to remove apartheid." Like many right-wing politicians at that time, Reagan was wary of the ANC's Communist leanings and its alliance with the USSR. He prioritized America's economy and Cold War mindset over efforts to end human rights violations in South Africa. As he explained, his administration's pursuit of "constructive engagement" was based on the belief that by remaining engaged with South Africa's economy, the United States could improve conditions for those suffering under apartheid. As Reagan stated time and again, he believed the UN's comprehensive boycott would only "hurt the people we're trying to help."

Determined to "use the cultural boycott to jump-start the economic boycott," Van Zandt set his sights on exposing the fraud of Sun City. "Everyone I met [in South Africa] told me to go back [to the US] and tell people not to play Sun City," said Van Zandt. So, in the spring of 1985, he composed the protest song "Sun City" and pitched it to possible collaborators as "'We Are The World' against apartheid." "Our song targets Sun City," Van Zandt explained, "but we use Sun City as a symbol of the whole apartheid system.... Just as many of us sung out on behalf of the victims of Africa's famine, so we are singing out also for those hungry for freedom."

Van Zandt reached out to a wide array of performers as he assembled Artists United Against Apartheid (AUAA), the supergroup that would record his new song. In naming his group, Van Zandt linked his project to Artists Against Apartheid (AAA), an organization founded in the UK in 1983 by Jerry Dammers and Dali Tambo, son of ANC president Oliver Tambo. AAA functioned primarily as a presenting organization, arranging anti-apartheid concerts in Europe throughout the 1980s. "There were a lot of people like me who were politically involved but not really cut out to go around waving placards," explained Dali Tambo.

> We set out to popularise the liberation struggle, to pull in the youth by giving them something positive in return. We all need heroes and heroines, and kids loved the fact that it wasn't yet another politician droning on about apartheid, but someone up on their bedroom wall ... What we did was to give the whole thing a sense of style.

Van Zandt reached out to Dali Tambo and Dammers during the planning stage for "Sun City." He also connected with Simon, who was initially open to the idea of participating in Van Zandt's project. But when Simon heard the demo recording of "Sun City" that Van Zandt sent him in June, he changed his mind. The lyrics did more than just protest apartheid. They called out by name several American artists who had performed in Sun City, among them Simon's good friend Linda Ronstadt. Although Van Zandt eventually changed the lyrics, Simon still refused to take part in the project. He wasn't interested in contributing to such a blatantly political recording. But even more to the point, he was too deeply involved in his own South Africa project to take time out for Van Zandt's song.

During his two weeks in South Africa, Simon had recorded nearly one hundred hours of rough tracks that he hoped to use somehow in a series of songs. "The task was enormous," explained Halee. "There were no [finished] songs, no arrangements. We were looking at months of editing, editing, editing"—cutting and mixing. "Paul had to turn the tracks into songs, and then he had to put words to each one." The first step in that process was close listening, a sonic search for points of connection.

As Simon listened to the recordings, he found music linkages between the traditional music styles of South Africa and the US. For example, a rhythm track that Kumalo and Phiri had made reminded Simon of "a country rockabilly shuffle." He also heard similarities between Motloheloa's accordion in Soweto street music and Louisiana Cajun styles. Seeking a local musical link, Simon added more accordion/saxophone mixes to his album's instrumental tracks. In Lafayette, Louisiana, he recorded with the Zydeco band Rockin' Dopsie and the Twisters. In Los Angeles, he teamed up with the Mexican-American rock band Los Lobos. Excerpts from these recording sessions eventually found their place in the songs "That Was Your Mother" and "All Around the World or The Myth of Fingerprints."

What struck Simon most as he began working with the range of recordings he had made in Johannesburg, Lafayette, and Los Angeles was the distinctive sound of the South Africans' playing technique. "The guitar lines were different from American lines. That was something I didn't notice until I was back at home," he said. "I realized that the guitar part was playing a different symmetry than I had assumed, and the bass was doing something that was more important, and maybe I should follow that. That was the big jump—I really began to listen harder to rhythm." The harmonies were different, too, Simon explained.

> South African music is extraordinary in its vocal sounds and its three-chord harmonies. It's all in major keys for the most part. I began to think about what effect that would have on the lyrics, on the storytelling. That was the great gift that I received from making the trip to South Africa. It was like I had taken a master class working with really great musicians like Ray Phiri or Bakithi Kumalo. I began to raise the bar in my own writing.

In May, Phiri, Kumalo, and Mtshali came to New York for another recording session with Simon. Together, they recorded the tracks "Under African Skies" and "You Can Call Me Al." The first tune features Linda Ronstadt. The lyrics tell the story of two figures, one African, the other American, whose worlds are linked by "the roots of rhythm." The second song features a pennywhistle solo played by Morris Goldberg, a white

South African who was living in New York at the time. As ethnomusicologist Louise Meintjes explains, "You Can Call Me Al" brings together a unique mix of South African sounds. The pennywhistle comes from kwela, a black, urban genre of the 1950s and early 1960s that grew out of improvisational street music. Against this, Kumalo's bass guitar, with its call-and-response patterning and vocal glides, evokes mbube, the pre-industrial Zulu choral style associated with Ladysmith Black Mambazo. And the way the pennywhistle and bass "are combined is typical of mbaqanga," the township jive that Simon first fell in love with while listening to *Gumboots: Accordion Jive Hits, Volume II*.

Upon his return to South Africa, Phiri expressed to a reporter for *Pace*, a South African magazine with a predominantly black readership, the importance of the South Africans' work on *Graceland*: "We are aware of the role we have to play in a bid to make our kind of music accepted by the world. . . . Now that Simon is offering us an important platform, we have to use it properly in glorifying African music and making Americans aware that there are many good artists in this part of the world."

Simon waited until July to begin the process of writing lyrics. For most of the songs, he drew on his own life experiences. For example, "You Can Call Me Al" recounts a comical encounter Simon once had with the composer Pierre Boulez, and "Graceland" taps into a range of experiences, both real and fictional, connected to his search for redemption as a father, a husband, and an artist. As Simon later explained, "Graceland" wasn't about Elvis Presley's Memphis home; it was about the "spiritual connotation" of the name. The word Graceland, he said, became "a metaphor for the album."

> Eventually, I understood that the song is about why we are traveling to Graceland—to find how to get healed—and that's why I named the album *Graceland*. It seemed to be about finding something you could call a state of grace—the healing of a deep wound. And that's what was going on in South Africa. There was a deep wound, and then an attempt at a healing process.

Graceland is not a protest album. That said, some of Simon's encounters in South Africa, both joyful and disturbing, found their way into the songs. A perfect example is "Boy in the Bubble," a song that mixes the hopefulness and horror wrought on modern society by technology. Simon composed the song over the hypnotic drone of Motloheloa's accordion. As he later explained, "Boy in the Bubble" was the only song on the album with "any fragment of lyric" that came to him during his trip to South Africa.

> One night, I was falling asleep, somewhere on the edge of consciousness, and I thought, "The way the camera follows him in slo-mo, the way he smiled at us all." I had this image in my mind of the films of the Kennedy assassination, that slow-motion thing where you see it frame-by-frame, or the Reagan assassination attempt, where he's walking along and then all of a sudden everything drops out of the camera... I don't know why I had that image—maybe because there's so much underlying violence going on in that country that is unspoken about.

Simon also tapped into those South African experiences when writing the song "Homeless" for Ladysmith Black Mambazo. "With 'Homeless,' I didn't say 'I'm going to write a song with political implications for Ladysmith.' I just began to write." As Simon explained in his liner notes to the album, the song came into being like a musical conversation.

> The process began when I sent [Joseph Shabalala] a demo of "Homeless" with the melody and words: "We are homeless, homeless / moonlight sleeping on the midnight lake." In my note accompanying the cassette, I suggested that he make any changes in harmony or words that he wanted.

Shabalala wrote back. He liked the song, and he had some ideas about how it might be improved. So, a series of recording sessions was booked at Abbey Road Studios in London, where Simon and Ladysmith Black Mambazo converged in October 1985. "I had no idea what was in Joseph's mind when we met," explained Simon. "He was kind of mysterious to me." One of the singers, Albert Mazibuko, recalled what it was like when they entered the studio and initially met with Simon:

He greeted us and the microphones were set. We started to sing but the song didn't want to work that first day. We tried the song from two until six in the evening and Paul said, "Let's call it a day and we'll see tomorrow." We went back to our hotel very disappointed because usually Ladysmith Black Mambazo records twelve songs a day! . . . But this time we couldn't make one song.

Back at the hotel, Shabalala gathered the group together and asked them to pray. "It was a prayer we had learned when we started Mambazo," explained Mazibuko. "A prayer Joseph had heard in his sleep, asking for the blessing of heaven and that His glory shine on us in everything that we do." The men practiced the song until midnight.

The next day, Mambazo "showed me an introduction they'd worked on late into the night," recalled Simon. Shabalala told him that "the melody came from a traditional Zulu wedding song, but the new lyrics now told of people living in caves on the side of a mountain, cold and hungry, their fists used as pillows." We "wrote in English and Zulu," explained Simon, "starting the piece in the middle and working outwards to the beginning and end." The song's bridge is an adaptation of an existing Ladysmith recording, and the ending is "one that Joseph had used on many of his songs." A rough translation of the Zulu lyrics reads: "We would like to announce to the entire nation that we are the best at singing in this style."

As Simon and his collaborators continued to work on *Graceland*, often taking weeks to develop a single song, Van Zandt rushed feverishly forward with the "Sun City" project. Recording began at the end of July, with over fifty performers adding their talents to the song. Unlike "We Are the World," where everyone came together for a single multi-hour recording session, "Sun City" was created piecemeal, with musicians recording their own contributions in fifteen different studios across the US and the UK, using a single click track. Van Zandt wanted the music to be something listeners could dance to. "The beat is the first line of communication," Van Zandt later explained. "All around the world, everybody dances. We wanted the record to communicate at that level and let everybody absorb lyrics at their own pace." One of the highlights of "Sun City" is its mix of genres: rock, folk, jazz, R & B, and rap. Van Zandt was the first to bring together such a diverse group. As *Billboard* magazine noted, the song "showcases an overwhelming array of all-star voices, keeps up a blistering urban/dance tempo, and pulls no punches on the message."

"Sun City" was released as a single on October 16, 1985. The B side was "Revolutionary Situation," a collage of rhythm tracks and spoken-word excerpts from speeches given by Nelson Mandela, Bishop Desmond Tutu, and President Reagan, among others. On October 25, a complete album went on sale. This larger project had been pulled together quickly, which shows in the production values. All the songs are in the same tempo, and many share the same synthesizer and trumpet lines. In addition to two versions of the song "Sun City," and "Revolution Station," the album includes a group rap, "Let Me See Your I.D."; a free-form ballad, "No More Apartheid," by Peter Gabriel; a progressive jazz tune, "The Struggle Continues," featuring Herbie Hancock on keyboards, Ron Carter on bass, and Tony Williams on drums with previously recorded samples by Miles Davis on trumpet and Stanley Jordan on guitar; and a song by Bono, "Silver and Gold," accompanied by Keith Richards and Ron Wood of the Rolling Stones, which was written and recorded the day before the album went to press.

Promotion for *Sun City* drew on the album's political message. On October 30, the official release party was held at the UN's New York headquarters, where diplomats, politicians, and musicians gathered to celebrate Van Zandt's song and his support of the cultural boycott. Van Zandt made a speech, announcing that all royalties from *Sun City* would go to the Africa Fund, a charitable trust established in 1966 by the American Committee on Africa. The Africa Fund would then distribute the money to political prisoners and their families in South Africa, South African exiles, and anti-apartheid groups in the United States. In other words, the ANC and its supporters would be the primary beneficiaries of *Sun City* royalties.

The highlight of the evening was a screening of the "Sun City" music video, which featured a who's who of performers, from Afrika Bambaataa, Grandmaster Melle Mel, Fat Boys, and Run-DMC to Gil Scott-Heron, Miles Davis, Ravi Shankar, Lou Reed, Bob Dylan, Pat Benatar, Bruce Springsteen, Ringo Starr, and several dozen more. The video runs just over seven minutes and offers a compilation of contrasting imagery: graphic newsreel footage showing the horrors of racial violence in South Africa interspersed with upbeat shots of AUAA members singing and dancing in the streets of New York. Watching the video today, it is discomfiting to see how the graphic violence of the newsreel footage has been synchronized to align with the off-beat pulse of the music. Like a dance of death, the driving rhythm of the drum and guitar riffs accentuate the relentless beatings of black men and women. "Sun City" presents the worst of South Africa—the pain and suffering caused by apartheid—alongside triumphalist musicians proclaiming, "I ain't gonna play Sun City."

"Sun City" got a lot of press coverage when it was first released. *Village Voice* proclaimed it Best Single of the Year. But not everyone was a fan. Shortly after the release of "Sun City," Stevie Wonder released his own anti-apartheid song, "It's Wrong (Apartheid)." Like Simon, Wonder had declined Van Zandt's offer to participate in the "Sun City" project.

Van Zandt spent the final months of 1985 promoting "Sun City." He met with anti-apartheid activists and held press conferences around the country with prominent black figures like Mayor Tom Bradley in Los Angeles and Coretta Scott King in Atlanta. Despite months of heavy promotion, however, "Sun City" struggled to gain traction with young audiences. It peaked at number 38 on the Billboard charts in December 1985. As a fundraising project, the song paled in comparison to "We Are the World." A year after its release, barely 300,000 copies had been sold. In total, "Sun City" and the accompanying album, music video, and book had raised a little over $600,000—far less than the sum Van Zandt had predicted when the album was first released. But as Van Zandt explained, the money wasn't important. His primary goal was "to get people to be aware of apartheid."

As "Sun City" faded from view, Simon's *Graceland* became the talk of the town. Simon was in no hurry to release the album. He took his time composing and mixing each song and made sure that the album's launch was strategic and well-organized. To build interest in the album, he performed several songs in public before releasing any of the recordings. On May 10, 1986, Simon appeared as the musical guest on *SNL*. Breaking with the usual format, the cold open of this episode featured Simon singing

"You Can Call Me Al." An acoustic rendition of "Graceland" closed the show. In between, Ladysmith Black Mambazo joined Simon on stage for a performance of "Homeless." The response from the studio audience was overwhelming. "They loved it," explained Mazibuko. "They clapped and stomped, whistling—all those things!" Lorne Michaels, creator and producer of *Saturday Night Live* and Simon's close friend, agreed. "It wasn't like anything that was on the show before. You could feel the excitement in the studio." "Nobody had heard Ladysmith Black Mambazo sing," said Simon. "Nobody had ever seen *isicatimiya* dance." They had tapped into something special. A few days later, Simon and Ladysmith Black Mambazo returned to the studio to record another song, "Diamonds on the Soles of Her Shoes."

As he had in the creation of "Homeless," Simon asked Shabalala if he wanted to add some Zulu passages to the English lyrics. Shabalala took out a piece of paper and wrote down a few lines. "We were excited to see how things were changing [for us]," said Shabalala. "Before we could not sing with or hug a person who was white. . . . the jail was the next thing for you when you do that. That's why I wrote: O kodwa isondelisa namhlanje / Sibona kwenze ka kanjani," which roughly translates as "It's unusual, but in our days, we see these things happen."

Also in the studio that day was the Senegalese musician Youssou N'Dour. "He played the drums," said Simon, "and Ladysmith sang over it. It was truly world music because that kind of African percussion and South African *a cappella* singing had not been combined that way before." As Simon later explained, his goal that day was not to show the differences between Senegalese, South African, and American music, but rather to explore their similarities. "I wanted to say, 'Look, don't look upon this as something so strange and different—it actually relates to our world.'"

Graceland was released on August 25, 1986, to great acclaim. David Sly of the *Advertiser* wrote: "This album rocks and rolls, but more importantly it is a plaintive cry for help. By showcasing the talents of the many unheralded black musicians in South Africa, Paul Simon has removed another brick from the apartheid wall." Robert Christgau of the *Village Voice* was equally mesmerized by the album. He had been a fan of *Sun City*, but *Graceland* was something else entirely. "This is a pretty damn universal record," he proclaimed. "Within the democratic bounds of pop accessibility, its biculturalism is striking, engaging, unprecedented—sprightly yet spunky, fresh yet friendly, so strange, so sweet, so willful, so radically incongruous and plainly beautiful." In the *Village Voice*'s year-end poll, *Graceland* was voted Best Album of the Year. In the UK, Simon was named International Artist of the Year at the BRIT awards.

Despite these accolades, Simon was reportedly "feeling vulnerable" about the album's reception, and for good reason. As praise for *Graceland* increased, supporters of the cultural boycott began to speak out. Van Zandt criticized Simon for not clearing his project with the ANC, and the ANC deputy representative at the UN, Solly Semilane, told reporters that Simon was wrong to have recorded in South Africa. "The UN calls for comprehensive sanctions, that means that the lifeline to South Africa should be totally closed. Just spending money on a hotel and food is incorrect, because the country needs foreign currency to survive." In an interview with *New Musical Express*, Dali Tambo called for a boycott of Simon's album precisely because Simon had not consulted with the ANC before recording in South Africa.

> If you're going into [South Africa], then you must consult with the ANC... You consult with us so that we can put you wise about whether or not we think you will be used by apartheid, and about the effect of your cultural activities... If Paul Simon had come to us first and discussed this, none of this s*** would have happened.

Dammers agreed. "Who does [Simon] think he is? He's helping maybe thirty people, and he's damaging solidarity over sanctions. He thinks he's helping the cause of freedom, but he's naïve. He's doing far more harm than good."

On August 27, Warner Bros. Records invited reporters to a release party at the Mayfair Theatre in London. The event took a political turn when a reporter asked Simon why he had refused to engage with the ANC before traveling to South Africa. Simon responded angrily:

> I don't feel as an artist that I have to consult with anyone. I didn't ask for permission to do the project, nor did I want any

restriction on what I might think or say or write. Personally, I feel I'm with the musicians. I'm with the artists. I didn't ask the permission of the ANC. I didn't ask permission of [Mangosuthu] Buthelezi [founder of the National Cultural Liberation Movement], or Desmond Tutu, or the Pretoria government. And to tell you the truth, I have a feeling that when there are radical transfers of power on either the left or the right, the artists always get screwed. The guys with the guns say, "This is important," and the guys with guitars don't have a chance.

In the months that followed, Simon was accused of musical colonialism, cultural appropriation, and "white savior" exploitation by his critics. But his collaborators on the *Graceland* album painted a different picture: "We used Paul as much as Paul used us," said Phiri. "There was no abuse. He came at the right time, and he was what we needed to bring our music into the mainstream." Kumalo agreed. "Paul was a godsend.... He treated [us] musicians with dignity and made us believe that [we]'re doing good."

As the music industry continued to shine a light on South Africa, the US House of Representatives passed a comprehensive anti-apartheid bill in June 1986. Two months later, a watered-down version of the bill passed in the Senate, 84–14. In its final form, the Anti-Apartheid Act banned new US loans and corporate investments in South Africa. It also prohibited the importation of a long list of South African goods, from iron, steel, and uranium to textiles and farm products. Excluded from the new legislation, however, was any reference to the UN's call for a cultural boycott.

Reagan vetoed the Anti-Apartheid Act on September 26, calling it "economic warfare." Simon could never be called a Reagan ally, but his defiance of the UN's cultural boycott caused some of his adversaries, chief among them Van Zandt, Dammers, and Dali Tambo, to describe him that way in the press. On September 29, the House overrode the presidential veto. The Senate followed suit on October 2. Van Zandt claimed credit for the new sanctions, but in all fairness, *Graceland* was equally responsible. The album had instilled in listeners a newfound appreciation for South African music, and when Simon and Ladysmith Black Mambazo returned to the *Saturday Night Live* stage on November 22 for a performance of "Diamonds on the Soles of Her Shoes," they demonstrated how a cultural boycott of South Africa benefited no one. Oprah Winfrey was watching that night and "was overcome by the music." She had supported the idea of boycotting *Graceland*, but then she heard the music. As she later explained, the album "opened up a space" inside of her, so much so that her "deep and now abiding interest in South Africa was stirred by first listening to *Graceland*."

Graceland was nominated for four Grammy Awards in January 1987. Shortly after the announcement, Simon went on a speaking tour. Despite the success of the album and *SNL* performances, he was still getting pushback for recording in South Africa. During a visit with students at Howard University, the historically black university in Washington, DC, Simon was accused of "exploiting South African musicians" and appropriating their music. As Jon Pareles, a music journalist for the *New York Times*, explained: "There was a lot of talk about the cultural boycott and colonialism, of going to some impoverished Third World place, stealing their cultural resources, making a big hit out of them." The "intensity and ubiquity of the criticism" caught Simon off guard. He needed to find a better way to communicate with his critics.

On January 30, Simon held a press conference in London to announce the launch of an international *Graceland* tour. Over the next six months, he would travel across the US, Europe, and Africa with two dozen South African musicians. The Grammy Award nominations had caused the UN's Anti-Apartheid Committee to rethink their response to *Graceland*, and they had removed Simon's name from the UN's blacklist of performers. Even so, the ANC called for a boycott of the *Graceland* tour, a message amplified by Dali Tambo, Van Zandt, and Dammers. The primary criticism now was Simon's failure to write songs that confronted apartheid directly, as Van Zandt and Dammers had done with "Sun City" and "(Free) Nelson Mandela." As a reporter for the *Washington Post* explained:

> Part of the controversy surrounding *Graceland* seems to be the fact that Simon et al. didn't turn the project into an angry political diatribe against the evils of the South African system—or fill his videos with scenes of blacks being beaten or blasted with rubber bullets.

Instead, continued the reporter, *Graceland* offers a "universal message of cooperation and hope," which he found more persuasive than overt protest music. "Simon's album transcends politics, the way the most enduring art always has," he noted. "It's when I listen to the spirited words and music of Simon and Ladysmith Black Mambazo that the future seems the clearest: that oppressors can never trample the human spirit—and that the blacks in South Africa ultimately will win."

Hugh Masekela, a jazz musician who had been exiled from South Africa since 1961, found a similar sense of hope in *Graceland*. "South African music has been in limbo because of apartheid," he explained. "Exile and the laws have parted us and caused a lack of growth." Masekela joined the *Graceland* tour, as did Miriam Makeba, another exiled South African. Consequently, the *Graceland* tour expanded into a celebration of South African and American unity. Only half of the songs at each concert came from the *Graceland* album. The rest were traditional South African songs, like "Jikele Maweni (The Retreat Song)" and original works by Masekela and Shabalala.

On Valentine's Day, the musicians performed two concerts at an outdoor stadium in Harare, Zimbabwe, the closest the tour came to the border of South Africa. Despite the distance (roughly 1,000 miles), most of the 20,000 cheering fans were South Africans. Black and white fans stood side by side. The concerts were a sign of what was possible, politically. Looking back at the videos of the event, three performances stand out. One is Masekela's "Bring Him Back Home," a song he wrote in 1986 that cries: "Bring back Nelson Mandela / Bring him back to Soweto. / We want to see him walking down the streets / Of South Africa tomorrow!" Equally moving, but in a markedly different way, is a performance of "Under African Skies" featuring Makeba and Simon. Simon had originally recorded the song with Linda Ronstadt; the lyrics tell the story of two figures, one African, the other American, whose worlds are linked by "the roots of rhythm." For the tour, Simon revised the lyrics. Makeba now sang of her own musical origins, while Simon sang, as he had on the album, of a spiritual figure named Joseph, a reference to both the biblical character and his close friend and colleague Joseph Shabalala. As Simon explained, "on the surface" it was "apolitical," but on a deeper level, it "was the essence of the anti-apartheid movement in that it was a collaboration between blacks and whites to make music that people everywhere enjoyed." The tour proclaimed that "there were no inferiors or superiors, just an acknowledgement of everybody's work as a musician. It was a powerful statement." The concert concluded with a performance of "N'kosi Sikelele iAfrica" (God Bless Africa), a liberation hymn banned in South Africa. One of the percussionists on the tour, Okeyama Asante, recalled the performance: "blacks and whites on the field were mixed together, fists clenched in the black power salute and singing the anthem. I looked at the audience, how they were singing together and tears started falling from my eyes. And across the border this is a song that if you sing it you go to jail."

Ten days after the concert in Zimbabwe, *Graceland* was named Best Album of the Year at the 29th annual Grammy Awards. In his acceptance speech, Simon highlighted the global, collaborative effort behind *Graceland*. He thanked those from his part of the world, but the bulk of his speech expressed his "deep admiration and love for the singers and musicians from South Africa . . . particularly Isaac Mtshali, Bakithi Kumalo, and Ray Phiri from Stimela; and Joseph Shabalala from Ladysmith Black Mambazo."

> They live along with other South African artists and their countrymen under one of the most repressive regimes on the planet today, and still, they are able to produce music of great power and nuance and joy, and I find that just extraordinary, and they have my great respect and love. Thank you.

One year later, at the 30th Annual Grammy Awards, *Graceland* was honored once again, when the title song was named Record of the Year. Ladysmith Black Mambazo also won a Grammy that year for *Shaka Zulu*, an album released in conjunction with the *Graceland* tour.

The *Graceland* tour changed some minds about the effectiveness of a cultural boycott. For example, Harry Belafonte noted the power of seeing "the physical presence of Africans and whites and the mix of races and cultures . . . come together and the songs and wonderful words that Paul wrote. The music that influenced him and that he influenced. That was a supreme moment regardless of what motivated it."

Nelson Mandela was released from prison in February 1990. Although numerous musicians performed alongside Mandela as he traveled from city to city, Van Zandt was not among them. The cultural boycott had come to be seen as a sincere but misguided effort. "Sun City" was excluded from the various celebrations. Such was not the case for Paul Simon and the other musicians associated with *Graceland*. Ladysmith Black Mambazo joined Simon for a lunch with Mandela in New York a few days before the outdoor performance in Boston. In the months that followed, Mandela publicly declared Ladysmith Black Mambazo "South Africa's cultural ambassadors." Mandela invited Simon to perform in South Africa, and in 1992 he returned for a multi-city tour, this time with the full endorsement of the ANC. However, protests did not disappear completely—a small extremist group called the Azanian People's Organization criticized the ANC and its endorsement of Simon's tour as being "about business, not liberation." When a concert promoter's office in Johannesburg was bombed, Simon contemplated ending the tour. He asked the South African musicians what they wanted to do. They wanted to continue. Change was happening. They'd come too far to turn back now. Nelson Mandela celebrated their decision to continue by declaring an end to the cultural boycott: "Artists are now free to come to our country!"

The 1992 *Graceland* tour of South Africa served as a symbol of Mandela's unifying political spirit. And in the months that followed, the soundtrack for that spirit was supplied by Ladysmith Black Mambazo. In 1993, the ensemble accompanied Mandela to Oslo, Norway, where he was awarded the Nobel Peace Prize. They also sang at Mandela's presidential inauguration on May 10, 1994.

The enduring power of *Graceland* shaped the reputation of Simon as well. In 2006, *Time* magazine included him in its list of "100 People Who Shaped the World." One year later, Simon became the inaugural recipient of the Library of Congress's Gershwin Prize for Popular Song. The award was created to "recognize the profound and positive effect of popular music on the world's culture." In the press release for the award, Librarian of Congress James H. Billington wrote: "Few songwriters have had a broader influence or contributed more to song genres than Paul Simon. Because of the depth, range and sheer beauty of his music, as well as its ability to bridge peoples and cultures, he is the perfect first recipient of this prestigious award."

Graceland showed Americans that cultural boycotts may silence art, but they rarely solve conflict. In contrast, musical exchange and collaboration offer powerful responses to strife—connecting people across borders and cultures. Under African skies, Simon and his South African colleagues found common ground in rhythm and sound. Together, they demonstrated that music can do what politics so often can't: build trust, spark joy, and shift perspectives.

WHO TELLS OUR STORY?

·····

On May 12, 2009, President Barack Obama and First Lady Michelle Obama hosted "An Evening of Poetry, Music, and Spoken Word" in the East Room of the White House. This was a new event, designed "around the theme of dialogue." The goal was to "ensure that all voices are heard" in art as well as politics. The audience included members of Congress, White House staff, and students from local universities. Among the various poets, actors, and musicians was the twenty-nine-year-old composer–performer Lin-Manuel Miranda. At the time, Miranda was best known for his Tony Award-winning musical *In the Heights*, which featured themes the Obamas wanted to celebrate, like "the vibrancy of the Latino community." So, when Miranda took the stage as the final act of the evening, most assumed he would perform a song from his musical or one of the Spanish numbers he had written for the recent revival of *West Side Story*. But as Miranda explained, in a voice brimming with nervous energy, he had something else in mind:

> I'm thrilled the White House called me tonight, because I am actually working on a hip-hop album. It's a concept album about the life of someone I think embodies hip-hop: Treasury Secretary Alexander Hamilton.

The audience chuckled. Miranda continued, undeterred.

> You laugh, but it's true! He was born a penniless orphan in St. Croix of illegitimate birth, became George Washington's right-hand man, became Treasury Secretary, caught beef with every other founding father, and all on the strength of his writing. I think he embodies the word's ability to make a difference. So, I'm going to be doing the first song from [the album] tonight.

With that, Miranda launched into a mesmerizing performance of what would become, six years later, the opening song of *Hamilton: An American Musical*.

> *How does a bastard, orphan, son of a whore and a*
> *Scotsman, dropped in the middle of a forgotten*
> *Spot in the Caribbean by providence, impoverished, in squalor*
> *Grow up to be a hero and a scholar?*

These four lines drive the plot of Miranda's musical. The story begins with Hamilton's arrival in New York as an ambitious immigrant and follows his rise to prominence as a close aide to George Washington during the American Revolution. Hamilton later plays a key role in drafting the Constitution and proves indispensable in shaping the nation's financial system. But there is more to the man than just his historic achievements. The musical explores Hamilton's complex relationships: his marriage to Eliza Schuyler, his rivalries with Thomas Jefferson and Aaron Burr, and his controversial affair with Maria Reynolds. Hamilton's relentless ambition results in both remarkable professional achievements and personal tragedy. The story culminates with Hamilton's death in his infamous duel with Aaron Burr.

Miranda first got the idea for *Hamilton* while reading Ron Chernow's 2004 biography of the Founding Father. Chernow concludes his study with a description of Hamilton's widow, Eliza, and her efforts to preserve her husband's legacy. Eliza dedicated the remaining fifty years of her life to organizing Hamilton's papers, defending his reputation against critics, and working tirelessly to ensure his story was not forgotten. Miranda ends *Hamilton* in a similar way. The final song emphasizes Eliza's steadfast commitment to cementing Hamilton's place in American history after his death. It asks the question: "Who lives, who dies, who tells your story?"

When Miranda performed at the White House in 2009, he was interested in telling a story that blended social commentary and contemporary music. His father, Luis Miranda Jr., was a prominent community advocate and Democratic strategist who had immigrated from Puerto Rico in 1971. Miranda's breakout success, *In the Heights*, a musical about immigrant experiences in a Latino neighborhood in Manhattan, drew praise for its progressive message from many of his father's colleagues. Representative Charles Rangel even went so far as to read into the Congressional Record a "Tribute to a Puerto Rican–American Success Story—Composer, Lyricist and Actor Lin-Manuel Miranda" for "all of his marvelous accomplishments."

> I want to give thanks to this exceptional constituent for sharing his vision and talents with the world for all to enjoy. . . . His claim to fame comes from writing and starring as Usnavi in the Broadway musical *In the Heights*, which opened on Broadway at the Richard Rodgers Theater in 2008. . . . With his creativity and determination, he was able to take an idea and catapult it into success. He took a risk and believed in his dream as well as himself. We can all learn from this fine example and believe in ourselves, especially when no one else will. We should all have the courage to live out our dreams, while inspiring others.

Based on Miranda's own life experiences, *In the Heights* features a cast of Latino performers and a musical mix of salsa, pop, traditional Broadway ballads, and rap. Miranda wasn't the first to make use of hip-hop music on the Broadway stage. That honor goes to *Bring in 'da Noise, Bring in 'da Funk* (1996), a musical revue by George C. Wolfe and Savion Glover that chronicles black history, from the Middle Passage and slavery to the civil rights movement and contemporary urban life.

In the Heights was the first show to use rap as a genre, instead of a signifier for black culture. The music reflects the popular styles that make up the sonic landscape of the musical's setting—Washington Heights in the twenty-first century. As producer Jeffrey Seller explained, *In the Heights* was promoted as a "rap musical." That was a mistake, he believes. "We were saddled in some ways with perceptual difficulties with rap music and racism.... It became known as 'the hip-hop musical,' and that unfortunately limited the audience. It deserved to run longer, and I believe it would have if not for that issue." Consequently, *Hamilton* was promoted as an "all-American" show. As Seller explained: "We don't want this to be a show that lasts for four years and everybody says, 'That was nice.' We want people who come to New York to say: 'I want to see the Statue of Liberty, go to the top of the Empire State Building, walk in Central Park. And I want to see *Hamilton.*'" Rap was not the show's focus, but rather the vehicle for telling the story of America's founding, when "the word's ability to make a difference" was all-important. As Oskar Eustice, artistic director of the Public Theater in New York, explained, Miranda's use of rap was a turning point in theatrical language, as Shakespeare's prose was four centuries earlier.

> What Lin is doing is taking the vernacular of the streets and elevating it to verse. That is what hip-hop is, and that is what iambic pentameter was. Lin is telling the story of the founding of his country in such a way as to make everyone present feel they have a stake in their country. In heightened verse form, Shakespeare told England's national story to the audience at the Globe and helped make England England—helped give it its self-consciousness. That is exactly what Lin is doing with *Hamilton*.

As Miranda began developing the plot for *Hamilton*, he linked the lead characters to his favorite performers. "I always imagined George Washington as a mix between Common and John Legend; Hercules Mulligan was Busta Rhymes; and Hamilton was modeled after my favorite polysyllabic rhyming heroes, Rakim, Big Pun and Eminem." Rap enabled Miranda to include considerably more narrative content than pop or Broadway ballads ever could. This was especially important in tunes like "Rap Battle #1" and "#2," when the intricacies of policy debates over national debt and foreign policy had to be expressed in a clear, concise manner. Miranda used rap to tell a story that, on its surface, had nothing to do with hip-hop culture. This was the genius, and the immense challenge, of *Hamilton*. Getting it right took six years and a team of committed collaborators.

After the performance at the White House in 2009, Miranda put his Hamilton project on a back burner. He was overcommitted and in high demand. Nonetheless, as he moved from one project to the next, he plugged away at "My Shot," the second song in his Hamilton narrative. Jeremy McCarter recalled that the song emerged in bits and pieces. Miranda "wrote and rewrote, trying to capture Hamilton's sprawling ambition in beats and rhymes. It took more than a year to get right." Miranda eventually premiered "My Shot" in June 2011 at a benefit concert with his improv hip-hop group Freestyle Love Supreme. In the audience that night was Tommy Kail, Miranda's close friend and collaborator. Kail had served as director of *In the Heights*, and when he heard "My Shot," he knew Miranda had the makings of another groundbreaking musical. As he told his friend after the performance, the time had come to "get serious about developing the Hamilton project," and he wanted to be a part of it.

Over the next six months, Miranda diligently filled out Hamilton's life story with a dozen more songs. On January 11, 2012, the 255th anniversary of Hamilton's birth, a sneak preview of Miranda's work in progress was presented as part of Lincoln Center's popular "American Songbook" series. Publicity for the event described Miranda's work as "a hip-hop song cycle about the life and death of American founding father Alexander Hamilton." On the night of the performance, which featured ten singers and a six-piece band, every seat in the house was filled. Many "friends and collaborators were in the crowd," explained McCarter, "but so were members of the press and some heavyweights of New York theater." It was a make-or-break moment for the future of the project.

Miranda opened the concert with a tribute to the rappers who encompassed what he described as "the DNA of my brain"—namely, Big Pun, Jay-Z, The Notorious B.I.G., Pharcyde, Talib Kweli, and Eminem. As *New York Times* theater critic Stephen Holden explained in his review of the event, the audience was confused and charmed in equal measure. Although no one could figure out what Miranda's composition was supposed to be—"A future Broadway musical? A concept album? A multimedia extravaganza in search of a platform?"—it didn't really matter. *Hamilton* was "hot," and the audience wanted more.

The Lincoln Center concert engendered growing enthusiasm for Miranda's project. To producer Jeffrey Seller, the future of *Hamilton* "became crystal clear to everyone in the room... It was a Broadway show," he explained. "Even in concert format, the story was taking shape."

By 2013, a large team of collaborators had committed to bringing *Hamilton* to the stage, and over the next two years they transformed Miranda's vision of American history into a reality. As McCarter explained, *Hamilton*'s success depended on everyone's willingness to compromise and collaborate: "A bunch of people from a bunch of backgrounds had to come together to make the show work"—much like what it takes to make a nation work.

Alex Lacamoire worked most closely with Miranda. His genius as orchestrator and music director elevated the score, as he seamlessly blended the diverse set of music styles Miranda envisioned—rap, R & B, and Broadway ballads—into a cohesive work. The different musical styles reflect each character's personality, motivations, and relationships, creating a rich tapestry of sound that enhances the storytelling. The contemporary hip-hop style associated with Hamilton reflects both his status as a disruptor and his relentless pursuit of success. Intricate, rapid-fire verses convey his sharp intellect as they articulate his ideas and ambitions. In contrast, Aaron Burr's songs have smooth, deliberate melodies; the jazz-infused style of "Wait for It" and "Dear Theodosia" reflects his cautious, wait-and-see philosophy. George Washington's gravitas and leadership are characterized by songs, like "Right Hand Man" and "One Last Time," that combine elements of classic rap and soul, using powerful, steady rhythms to underscore his authority and wisdom. Similarly, the sophistication of Angelica, Eliza, and Peggy Schuyler is captured in pop and R & B styles. When the trio is first introduced in the upbeat "The Schuyler Sisters," modern feminist themes mix with a playful tone. As the show progresses, however, the sisters' distinct personalities become more obvious: complex rap lines underscore Angelica's sharp wit in "Satisfied," just as Eliza's heartfelt ballads, "Helpless" and "Burn," reveal her emotional depth and vulnerability.

The presentations of Thomas Jefferson and King George III provide comic relief. Jefferson is flamboyant, confident, and charming. In "What'd I Miss?," his grand entrance is accompanied by a jazz-infused funk number featuring a swing rhythm and lively brass. The theatricality of the song mirrors Jefferson's larger-than-life persona, just as the playful, almost vaudevillian style underscores his flair for the dramatic. King George's song, "You'll Be Back," is a parody of the British Invasion style associated with groups like the Beatles. A sense of detachment in King George's character is created by a mix of harpsichord riffs, bouncy melodies, absurdly polite lyrics, and menacing threats. The ridiculousness of his character effectively emphasizes his distance from the chaos of the revolution happening on the far side of the Atlantic.

Hamilton presents the Founding Fathers as a group of scrappy young men relentlessly pursuing their individual visions of a new nation. As in politics, the show is comprised of winners and losers. Hamilton was no stranger to rejection—an experience that every artist and politician faces when trying to make their way in the world. As Miranda explained, he tried to capture this reality sonically with the musical's opening note: "I wanted the sound of a door slamming as the downbeat, and in my computer music program I grabbed a sound file called 'Door Wood Squeak.' The sound of the wood squeak was so compelling I set it to notes. Hence the opening riff."

There is no dialogue in *Hamilton*. Instead, the plot unfolds in a series of songs and visual tableaux, dynamically staged by Thomas Kail, the director. An ensemble of dancers surrounds the main characters; their innovative, kinetic movement was choreographed by Andy Blankenbuehler. Like Jerome Robbins in *West Side Story*, Blankenbuehler worked "to ground his choreography in the dramatic motivation of the character." "There are very few times when I really want the audience to look at dance," he said. "Dance is just meant to be a framing device that matches emotionally what I want the audience to feel."

The stage design and costumes are equally effective in creating the mood and advancing the story. David Korins's minimalist set uses a dual-level wooden scaffolding structure, exposed brick, and ropes to evoke a sense of eighteenth-century architecture. The centerpiece is a rotating stage, which enhances the storytelling by fluidly shifting scenes, creating the illusion of motion and emphasizing the passage of time and the intensity of pivotal moments.

Paul Tazewell's costumes reflect the musical approach, giving the eighteenth century a modern flair. Tazewell's rule was "Period from the neck down, modern from the neck up." Thus, the clothing and accessories are period-appropriate, while the hair and makeup adhere to familiar twenty-first-century styles. As Tazewell explained, he wanted "to keep the world [of *Hamilton*] feeling youthful and sexy."

On February 17, 2015, after a few weeks of previews, *Hamilton: An American Musical* opened off-Broadway at the Public Theater. The response was enthusiastic. The *New York Times* announced that in *Hamilton*, "Lin-Manuel Miranda forges democracy through rap." The *Washington Post* called it "History as you've never seen it before." And Jesse Green, in *Vulture*, went so far as to claim that those who disliked "Miranda's new hip-hop biomusical" must "dislike the American experiment." Green described the show as a metaphor for the nation: "The conflict between independence and interdependence is not just the show's subject but also its method: It brings the complexity of forming a union from disparate constituencies right to your ears." The *Wall Street Journal* called it "the hottest ticket in New York."

When Miranda was asked what he thought was the driving force behind *Hamilton*'s success, he replied: "This is a story about America then, told by America now." When asked to elaborate, Miranda explained that he and his collaborators had worked hard "to eliminate any distance between a contemporary audience and this story." What he didn't say was that one of the methods he used to bridge the gap between the past and present was to reframe the narrative of the Founding Fathers along the ideological lines of the Democratic Party in the age of Obama.

After Obama was reelected in 2012, the Democratic Party's focus began to shift away from the economic liberalism of the twentieth century to an ideology focused on racial and sexual identity. Consequently, party leaders in states across the nation began a subtle process of scrubbing references to figures whose biographies had become problematic, namely Thomas Jefferson and Andrew Jackson. As Andrei Cherney, a Democratic advisor and former speechwriter for Bill Clinton, noted in 2015: "Jefferson and Jackson and the ideas they stood for, spreading economic opportunity and democracy, were the beginnings of what was the Democratic Party. That is what unified the party across regional and other lines for most of the last 200 years." But these men also actively participated in the nation's greatest sins. Jefferson enslaved over six hundred people over the course of his lifetime, and relied on enslaved labor to build the structures and till the land on his Virginia estate, Monticello. Andrew Jackson was an enslaver, too, and he did not appear to "wrestle with the morality of slavery" the way Jefferson occasionally had. As president, Jackson drove thousands of American Indians from their homelands in the Southeast, forcing them to migrate westward on a brutal journey now known as the Trail of Tears.

As Alana Samuels noted in *The Atlantic* shortly after *Hamilton* opened, the nation's founding, as told by Miranda, echoed the contemporary political scene. While Hamilton represents everything appealing—"he's an immigrant" and "a self-made man"—Jefferson, the "slave-owning aristocrat," embodies everything Democrats are against. He is the primary villain, "a well-dressed dandy" who traveled to France to avoid fighting in the war. As Samuels explains, "for a man who wrote the phrase 'all men are created equal,' [Jefferson] holds hypocritical positions about slave ownership and women's rights."

The perception of *Hamilton* as a parable of contemporary politics was solidified on August 6, 2015. That night, while *Hamilton* made its official Broadway debut at the Richard Rodgers Theatre, the first Republican presidential debate of the 2016 election cycle aired nationwide on Fox News. The political symbolism of this historic double bill was not lost on the press. The *New York Times* compared the Republican candidates to the characters in *Hamilton*, noting that in our twenty-four-hour news cycle, politics has become more about performance than policy. "Donald Trump has become like one of those star actors hired by theater producers to gin up ticket sales to a famous old play. . . . Audiences already have a sense of the plot . . . yet they come anyway to watch a Trump chew the scenery and make them laugh and wince before the climax (Election Day)."

Miranda embraced the comparisons. He was no fan of Donald Trump: "This is no working-class hero," he famously quipped. In the weeks that followed, as *Hamilton* "attracted breathless reviews and a steady procession of celebrity and politician fans," Miranda readily admitted, when asked, that the underlying message in *Hamilton* was a product of his own political beliefs.

> *Hamilton* is more autobiographical than *Heights* for me—not in the sense that I feel like I'm Hamilton, but in terms of how I feel about life and our country. My feelings about what this country is and can be are all in this show. When Eliza Hamilton sings, "Look around at how lucky we are to be alive right now," that's true. I say that to myself every day.

From the beginning, Miranda felt a connection not just to the story of Alexander Hamilton but to that of Barack Obama, too.

> When I was asked to do a song from *In the Heights* at the White House in 2009, I chose instead to do "Alexander Hamilton" because I felt like I was meeting a moment. This was a president that I had worked hard to help elect, and I wanted to show something about the American experience and do something new there because I felt like I was part of something. And now, with the show opening as Obama's presidency is winding down, it feels very fitting and full circle. I don't know what his legacy will be. I do know that the thing that Hamilton and Obama have in common is that they're totally improbable stories—except they happened.

Miranda's music turned Alexander Hamilton into a national hero. And the ripple effects of the Founding Father's new status soon made their way into political discourse.

On June 15, 2015, the Treasury Department announced that the image of Alexander Hamilton on the ten-dollar bill would soon be replaced with a portrait of the black abolitionist and social activist Harriet Tubman. This proposed change was accepted with little comment from politicians—that is, until the *Hamilton* fan base got wind of the decision. Why is the government canceling Hamilton? they asked. Isn't there someone else who could step aside for Harriet Tubman? Democratic lawmakers soon offered a solution: perhaps "the more controversial, slave-owning President Jackson could be removed from the twenty-dollar bill instead?" If nothing else, replacing Jackson's image with that of a female fighter for racial freedom would be an act of ironic justice. In response to public outcry, the Treasury Department changed course. To use a quote from Miranda's show, Hamilton would remain "the ten-dollar founding father" in perpetuity.

"*Hamilton: An American Musical* has cut an exuberant swath through American culture," noted a reporter in 2016. "Like the Continental light infantry swarming over the redoubts at Yorktown, the show and its creator, Lin-Manuel Miranda, have laid successful siege to a battery of prestigious awards." These include eleven Tony Awards including Best Musical, a Grammy for Best Musical Theater Album, a MacArthur "Genius" grant, and the Pulitzer Prize for Drama. The key criterion for this last award is that the drama depict aspects of the American experience. The prize committee described *Hamilton* as "a landmark American musical about the gifted and self-destructive founding father whose story becomes both contemporary and irresistible."

The popularity of *Hamilton* made it a powerful political tool during the 2016 election season. The musical became the driving engine behind multiple fundraisers, including one for the Democratic Hope Fund in November 2015, attended by the Obamas. Miranda was a strong Clinton supporter. He considered Trump's popular appeal nothing more than "an illusion," and he was eager to expose it.

On July 12, 2016, Miranda scheduled a special matinee performance of *Hamilton* as a fundraiser for the Clinton campaign. The Hillary Victory Fund purchased all 1,300 seats in the Richard Rodgers Theater, and donors paid between $2,700 and $100,000 per ticket. Clinton emailed supporters encouraging them to attend the show, which she said spoke to her as both a national symbol and a great work of art: "It's an incredible feat of storytelling about the fight for the heart and soul of our very nation. It's a look at history that feels immediately relevant today. It's a beautiful piece of art with empathy to spare."

Miranda did not perform at the fundraiser. Instead, he sat in the audience and interacted with donors. He also served as the event's emcee, introducing Clinton to the sold-out crowd as the "45th president of the United States." Miranda explained that the differences between Clinton and Trump could not be starker. "Are you going to vote for the guy who's channeling your fears? Who's acting on your fears?" he asked. Or for the woman who's "acting toward your hopes? Are you going to vote for the guy who wants to build a wall? Or for someone who's building bridges?"

When Clinton got up to speak, she linked the musical to her own campaign message. "As Washington tells us, history's eyes are on us," she said. "So, I want to thank all of you for supporting our vision of the kind of America that does try to keep moving us toward that more perfect union." Clinton described *Hamilton* as an encapsulation of the Democratic Party's mission. "America's best years are still ahead of us," she claimed. "Our Founders were not perfect people, but they were united in their conviction that they could build this new country from nothing, and with all the fits and the starts that we have endured over the course of our history, we are still going strong."

Clinton then referred to her rival, the presumptive Republican nominee Donald Trump. "We cannot be detoured by those who would play to the worst of our feelings, who would divide us, who would scapegoat us," she said. "We have to keep that vision in front of us." She concluded her speech with a rallying cry, drawn from Miranda's musical: The time has come. We have a choice. "Let's not throw away our shot!" Two weeks later, at the Democratic National Convention, Clinton concluded her acceptance speech as the party's presidential nominee with another paraphrase from *Hamilton*: "Though we may not live to see the glory, let us gladly join the fight."

The morning after Donald Trump was elected the forty-fifth president of the United States, Miranda and the *Hamilton* cast went into mourning. "It was a soul-crushing day," explained Seller. But that didn't stop Miranda from pushing forward. "We had to get up and say, now our play is more important than ever before, and we need to tell this story that embodies our greatest values as a country, as a democracy."

Ten days before Obama's second term came to an end, Miranda and members of the original *Hamilton* cast returned to the White House for a final performance. "As we prepare for President Barack Obama's final days in office," said Miranda, "we celebrate the profound legacy he leaves behind." He and Christopher Jackson, who played George Washington in the original cast, performed "One Last Time," the *Hamilton* tune based on Washington's farewell address, published in 1796.

> Though, in reviewing the incidents of my administration, I am unconscious of intentional error, I am nevertheless too sensible of my defects not to think it probable that I may have committed many errors. I shall also carry with me the hope that my country will view them with indulgence. And that after forty-five years of my life dedicated to its service with an upright zeal, the faults of incompetent abilities will be consigned to oblivion, as I myself must soon be to the mansions of rest. I anticipate with pleasing expectation that retreat in which I promise myself to realize, the sweet enjoyment of partaking, in the midst of my fellow citizens, the benign influence of good laws under a free government, the ever-favorite object of my heart, and the happy reward, as I trust, of our mutual cares, labors, and dangers.

This is the speech Hamilton penned for Washington as he left office in 1796. Sung by Miranda and Jackson, it became the parting sentiment of Barack Obama. "One last time," goes the final chorus:

> *Teach 'em how to say good bye.*
> *You and I,*
> *Going home.*
> *History has its eyes on you.*
> *We're gonna teach 'em how to say goodbye! . . .*
> *Say goodbye!*
> *One last time!*

After the performance, Obama approached the stage and shook Jackson's hand. "Thank you for teaching me how to say goodbye," he said. Jackson later confessed that he was so overwhelmed by the encounter that he broke down in tears.

A lesson to be learned from *Hamilton* is how stories harden into history. It matters who tells the stories. It matters who is listening. On November 18, 2016, vice president-elect Mike Pence attended a performance of *Hamilton*. As he entered the theater, many members of the audience booed. A few cheered. During the show, a joyful roar erupted from the audience after Lafayette and Hamilton proclaimed: "Immigrants, we get the job done!" By the end of the show, tensions were high. To address the elephant in the room, Brandon Victor Dixon, the actor playing Vice President Aaron Burr, returned to the stage with the full cast behind him. He had been asked by Miranda to read a statement that he and the production team had written. Dixon motioned for the audience to stop clapping, and then announced: "You know, we have a guest in the audience this evening. And Vice President–elect Pence, I see you walking out, but I hope you will hear us just a few more moments."

When several audience members reacted to Pence's presence, Dixon responded: "There's nothing to boo here, ladies and gentlemen, there's nothing to boo here. We're all here sharing a story of love." Dixon encouraged everyone "to pull out your phones and tweet and post because this message needs to be spread far and wide." He then addressed Pence directly:

> We have a message for you, sir. We hope that you will hear us out. Vice President-elect Pence, we welcome you, and we truly thank you for joining us here at *Hamilton: An American Musical*. We really do. We, sir, we are the diverse America who are alarmed and anxious that your new administration will not protect us, our planet, our children, our parents, or defend us and uphold our inalienable rights, sir. But we truly hope this show has inspired you to uphold our American values and work on behalf of all of us. All of us. Again, we truly thank you for seeing this show, this wonderful American story told by a diverse group of men and women of different colors, creeds, and orientations.

It's unclear if Pence remained long enough to hear the complete statement. If he didn't hear it in the theater, he most definitely heard it later. The curtain-call speech made headline news as President-elect Trump went on a Twitter rampage. "The cast of *Hamilton* was very rude last night to a very good man, Mike Pence. Apologize!" Judge Jeanine Pirro lambasted the cast on her Fox News show, *Justice*: "The treatment of Vice President-elect Mike Pence last night in New York City—where he was booed on the way into the play *Hamilton* and lectured from the stage on his way out—was both outrageous and embarrassing," she noted. "What happened in that theater—one block from here—was out-and-out reverse racism, and teed up hate for a man who has done nothing to deserve this inappropriate and disgusting behavior." It should be noted that Pence saw nothing wrong in the curtain-call speech. During an interview two days later, on *Fox News Sunday*, he said, "I can tell you I wasn't offended by what was said."

Over the next several days, commentators in the media argued over the pros and cons of the statement read by Dixon. Charles McNulty of the *Los Angeles Times* agreed with the actors' sentiment, but not the way it was delivered. "The most eloquent case that can be made for the pluralistic values endorsed by *Hamilton*," he noted, "is the musical itself."

> What happened during the curtain call involved artists, yet it wasn't really about art. It was about theater etiquette and those moments when the democratic imperative of speaking out overrides all other considerations. I don't see the incident as an egregious breach of decorum myself. But nor do I think this is the occasion to get on our high horses and preach to one another in our echo chambers about the nobility of our artistic mission. The constitutional stakes are too high for sanctimony.

Miranda was unfazed by the accusations that his politicization of *Hamilton* was ill-advised. Vocal about his political views, particularly regarding Trump's immigration policies and his attitude toward Puerto Rico, Miranda continued to use his art as a political tool for liberal causes. On June 28, 2017, the music video for "Immigrants (We Get the Job Done)" from *The Hamilton Mixtape* (an album that reimagines songs from the musical through the lens of contemporary artists) was released. The goal was to shine a light on the nation's treatment of immigrants under the Trump administration. The video's release occurred one week before the Supreme Court heard testimony in *Hawaii v. Trump*, a case that questioned the constitutionality of Trump's proclamation restricting entry into the United States for nationals of several Muslim-majority countries. The video, which lasts a little more than six minutes, pulses with powerful imagery, shifting from immigrants meticulously stitching American flags to Snow Tha Product delivering fiery verses in front of the very symbol they create. Scenes of workers laboring under the sun, picking fruit in vast fields, intertwine with Riz MC's electrifying rap in the dim glow of a New York City subway car. The crescendo builds to a haunting finale, as immigrants are torn from their homes in the dead of night by border patrol agents, amplifying the song's poignant message of struggle and resilience. As Priscilla Frank noted on *Huffington Post* the day it was released, the video's "lyrics and visuals powerfully describe the dire conditions facing refugees attempting to immigrate to, and make lives in, America today. It also highlights the immeasurable contributions immigrants have made to a country that continues to dehumanize them." There was no hiding the political intentions of the video. As Miranda himself explained: "This election cycle has brought xenophobia and vilification of immigrants back to the forefront of US politics. This is a musical counterweight."

On July 3, 2020 a filmed version of *Hamilton* began streaming on Disney+. The original plan had been to release the film in theaters in October 2021, but when the Covid-19 pandemic led to shutdowns across the nation, including Broadway, Disney decided to move up the release date, allowing millions of Americans to experience *Hamilton* in the confines of their homes.

The initial response was predictably enthusiastic. As *Forbes* and *Variety* noted shortly after the release, *Hamilton* "dominated streaming platforms," where viewership for the musical was "far bigger than anything on Netflix in July . . . almost three times the number that watched the second widest-reaching title of the month," *Unsolved Mysteries*.

Despite its popularity, the streaming of *Hamilton* presented some major challenges for the production team, especially Miranda. Increased familiarity with the show led to mounting criticism. Several weeks earlier, on May 25, George Floyd had been killed in Minneapolis during an encounter with police, when a now-former officer knelt on Floyd's neck for over nine minutes, despite Floyd repeatedly stating that he could not breathe. This incident, captured on video, sparked widespread protests and a global movement advocating for racial justice and police reform. "Black Lives Matter" became a new call for justice that "laid bare the racism at the heart of many American institutions." When Miranda was called out on social media for not responding to Floyd's death, he quickly posted a video apology on Twitter:

> We spoke out on the day of the Pulse shooting. We spoke out when Vice President Mike Pence came to our show ten days after the election. And that we have not yet firmly spoken the inarguable truth of Black Lives Matter and denounced systematic racism and white supremacy from our official *Hamilton* channels is a moral failure on our part. As the writer of the show, I take responsibility and apologize for my part in this moral failure. I'm sorry for not pushing harder and faster for us to speak these self-evident truths under the *Hamilton* banner, which has come to mean so much to so many of you.

From the beginning, there had been criticism of Miranda's supposed erasure of slavery in *Hamilton*, mostly in academic journals and obscure newsletters, but prior to 2020 its impact had been negligible. As protests related to the Black Lives Matter movement reached fever pitch, the criticisms of *Hamilton* went mainstream. A "Cancel *Hamilton*" campaign erupted on social media, prompting many of the cast to speak out in support of Miranda. Leslie Odom Jr., the original Aaron Burr, had defended the musical for years by noting how Miranda "made these dead white guys make sense to a bunch of, you know, black and brown people. He's made them make sense in the context of our time, with our music." But Odom also separated the message of *Hamilton* from the real-life struggles of black America, noting that he had fought hard with the studio to be paid a fair wage for his work on the *Hamilton* film. "If my black life matters, make sure I can take money home to feed my children."

Throughout Trump's first term as president, Miranda continued his commitment to political activism. In response to Hurricane Maria's devastation in 2017, he spearheaded the release of "Almost Like Praying," a charity single that rallied numerous artists to raise funds for Puerto Rico's recovery. He also championed immigrant rights, notably supporting the Deferred Action for Childhood Arrivals (DACA) program and participating in initiatives like the "Found/Tonight" charity single in 2018, which benefited the March for Our Lives movement against gun violence. Miranda's commitment to civic engagement was evident in his collaborations with organizations like When We All Vote. Like his father, Miranda worked behind the scenes to get Joe Biden elected president in 2020. In the years that followed, the Democrats continued to look to Miranda as a unifying voice of the party. On January 6, 2022, Miranda was invited to participate in a congressional event marking the one-year anniversary of the January 6 attack on the US Capitol. After an introduction by Nancy Pelosi stressing the importance of American democracy, Miranda called for unity in a prerecorded speech that referenced the ideals he had highlighted in *Hamilton*:

> A new year brings hope for the future, new energy to face the tasks ahead of us, and a renewed promise to strengthen the foundations of our democracy. . . . We are all stewards of the American experiment, working to pass down to our children and our grandchildren a more perfect union that treats all its citizens with fairness and equity. . . . We should never take our rights and liberties for granted, and we must remain committed to finding a way forward together. That's what I wrote about in . . . *Hamilton*.

Miranda concluded his speech with a call to action: "I believe no challenge is worth abandoning our efforts to unite as Americans. We will keep working, generation after generation, until we reach that someday."

During the Biden presidency, Miranda's impact on progressive politics continued unabated. As Vinson Cunningham of the *New Yorker* wrote, by the time Kamala Harris was nominated as the Democratic presidential candidate in 2024 her party's platform had become "the *Hamilton* theory of political action," which represented "an entire school of center-left, post-civil-rights thought, a well-trodden path forward after the great emotional and legislative heights of the fifties and sixties." The "principal thing" is to be the one in power, Cunningham explained, "to be in the room where it happens," as Miranda's song goes.

On November 1, Miranda co-authored, with Ricky Martin and Rita Moreno, an article in the *New York Times* titled "Puerto Ricans' Votes

Won't Be a Reaction to Racist Jokes." They were responding to the comedian Tony Hinchcliffe's recent description of Puerto Rico as "a floating island of garbage" at a Trump rally held in Madison Square Garden. "Puerto Ricans will not be throwing away their shot," they noted, and their vote "won't be a reaction to racist jokes." Instead, it will be a vote "for the future of a country that could be majority-minority by midcentury."

> The United States is changing, as it always has: changing what it looks like, what it listens to, what it eats.... The country's changing sense of self is unsettling for some, and their backlash is part of our American tradition, too.

Miranda, Martin, and Moreno urged readers to reject the "willful ignorance" of racism and rise to the challenge of a new era in American history.

> Our capacity to change is our American superpower—the core energy that drives our entrepreneurs, our artists, our visionaries. It's a beautiful, creative force and it comes from a people who are young at heart, seeking new ideas and questioning old ways.

"Never mind the noise," they urged. "Listen to the harmony. Because history has its eyes on us." Four days later, Donald Trump was elected president for a second time.

The story of Miranda's failure (twice) to get a woman elected president might cause one to ask: Was the vision of America outlined in *Hamilton* just a mirage? Has music lost its power as an agent of political change in the United States? I doubt it. During the 2024 election cycle, politicians abandoned the use of music as an agent of change. While Trump gaslit liberals by dancing to progressive pop songs like the Village People's "YMCA" and Bruce Springsteen's "Born in the USA" at his rallies, Harris sought the endorsements of celebrities like Miranda, Beyoncé, and Taylor Swift. In 2024, America stopped listening to what music could say. Moving forward, we need to start listening again.

Henry Cabot Lodge, an early editor of Hamilton's writings, once noted: "The dominant purpose of Hamilton's life was the creation of a national sentiment, and thereby the making of a great and powerful nation from the discordant elements furnished by thirteen jarring states." *Hamilton: An American Musical* offers a similar sentiment, in a moment even more discordant and jarring. As Miranda has said, time and again, our work as a nation is still incomplete. Unity and justice are ideals worth pursuing, and music can help us imagine them. If there is one message that I hope readers take away from this book, it is this: We all need to spend more time listening to the world around us. If we do, we might just find the music that tells *our* story.

Acknowledgments

This book took much longer to complete than I initially imagined. Part of the delay was practical—life, as it often does, had its own timeline. But more than anything, it was the world itself that kept shifting. The political landscape was in constant flux, and at times it seemed as though the stories I was tracing through history were changing shape as I tried to pin them down. Writing *On the Record: Music that Changed America* meant not just chronicling the past but staying attentive to the present. It was often difficult to find the right balance. I'm not sure I did, but I am deeply grateful to those who helped me stay the course.

First, I am profoundly indebted to the many scholars whose work paved the way for mine. Their rigorous research, passionate storytelling, and unwavering commitment to historical truth offered both guidance and inspiration. Their voices resonate on every page of this book. I have learned much from their scholarship and hope that *On the Record* stands as a worthy continuation of the conversations they began. Though they are too many to name individually, I must mention Dora Apel, Nancy Kovaleff Baker, Harvey G. Cohen, Elizabeth B. Crist, Mathieu Deflem, Jennifer DeLapp-Birkett, Annegret Fauser, Marc Ferris, Paul Laird, Beth Levy, Frances Negrón-Muntaner, David C. Paul, Imani Perry, Howard Pollack, Shana Redmond, Jan Swafford, Judith Tick, Brooks Tolliver, and Penny Von Eschen.

Before there was a manuscript, there was the spark of an idea that might easily have remained just that had it not been for the encouragement of Michael Bracy, Maribeth Payne, and Steven Schragis. Their early belief in the project encouraged me to pursue it in earnest.

I am equally grateful to the students at Peabody Conservatory who shared my journey over these past few years, especially Nya Angel, Jonah

Askew, Emerson Borg, Sam Broomell, Sophie Clarke, Lance Fisher, Eugene Han, Jacob Heacock, Kaitlyn Heit, Celine Mogielnicki, Maia Schmidt. Marjorie Sheiman, Andrea Simon, Sebastian Suarez-Solis, Ben Vinh Tran, Andrea Velasquez, Taylor Wang, Sean Webster, and Nicholas Wynn. Teaching and writing are deeply intertwined pursuits, and I could not have asked for a more engaged and inspiring group of interlocutors. They brought fresh eyes and thoughtful critiques to the early versions of these chapters, and their questions pushed me to think more clearly, more critically, and more expansively. I am especially indebted to my graduate research assistant, Yuval Tessman-Bar-On, for her close reading and thoughtful insights.

To my colleagues who over the years generously read drafts of individual chapters, offered wise counsel, or provided encouragement when I needed it most—thank you, Michael Beckerman, Paul Bratcher, Mark Clague, Soyica Colbert, Benjamin Harbert, Valerie Hartman, David Hildebrand, Maurice Jackson, Tammy Kernodle, Meryl Lauer, Chandra Manning, Jill Rogers, Anicia Timberlake, and Kristen Turner. Your insights sharpened my arguments, your questions deepened my thinking, and your support sustained me through the inevitable periods of doubt. It is a privilege to be part of such a generous intellectual community.

I also owe tremendous thanks to the librarians and archivists who assisted me in my research: Tonika Berkley, Sam Bessen, Lyn Conway, Sandra Garcia-Myers, Jane Parr, Billy T. Smith, Paul Allen Sommerfeld, Scott Taylor, LuLen Walker, and Raynetta Wiggens-Jackson. Their expertise, patience, and unfailing generosity made the daunting task of navigating collections not only manageable but often joyful. In a time when access to archives and physical materials was sometimes complicated or limited, their commitment to helping scholars mattered more than ever. I also thank Robert Meeropol, who took the time to talk with me about his father's life and work.

To my editor at W. W. Norton, Chris Freitag, I extend my heartfelt appreciation. From our first conversation, you understood the vision for this book and challenged me to make it sharper, more honest, and more compelling. Your careful editing, strategic wisdom, unending patience, and unwavering belief in the project made all the difference. I also offer gratitude to the entire editorial and production team, especially Allegra

Huston, whose keen editorial eye, thoughtful queries, and unwavering commitment to clarity and precision have strengthened this book at every turn, and Derek Thornton, whose cover design is proof that a picture is indeed worth 1000 words. Warmest thanks also to Jennifer Lanchart of Syncalicious Music for her assistance in acquiring the print licenses for various song lyrics.

On a more personal level, I thank my family: my parents, Ann and Rupert, who read drafts of the early chapters; my sister Mary, who was always there with an encouraging word; and my mother- and sister-in-law, Nancy and Mary, who cheered me on in the final stages. Thanks for never being afraid to ask how the book was coming along.

Finally, I dedicate this book to my husband, Chris: words cannot capture what I wish to say. Your love, patience, encouragement, and steadfast belief in this book—and in me—carried me through the long stretches when this project felt interminable. You accompanied me every step of the way and cheered the loudest when we crossed the finish line!

There is no such thing as a truly solitary endeavor. This book is the product of countless conversations, collaborations, and acts of kindness. To everyone who contributed along the way, whether through a recommendation, a conversation, a word of encouragement, or simply by asking the right question at the right time—thank you. I am deeply, humbly grateful.

Notes

Preface

xi **"It is with the greatest hope"**: "Stevie Wonder's Surprise Performance at Johns Hopkins Commencement," May 23, 2024, YouTube.

xii **"Show me the money... granted"**: "Johns Hopkins Commencement 2024—Stevie Wonder Performance," May 23, 2024, YouTube.

xii **"What I came here for"**: "Johns Hopkins Commencement 2024—Stevie Wonder Performance," comments.

1: Land of the Free, Home of the Brave

1 **"I am not going to stand up"**: Steve Wyche, "Colin Kaepernick explains why he sat during the national anthem," nfl.com, August 27, 2016.

3 **watched the progress of the ensuing strike**: Kate Van Winkle Keller, *Music of the War of 1812 in America* (Colonial Music Institute, 2011), 114.

3 **"The awful stillness"**: Marc Ferris, *Star-Spangled Banner: The Unlikely Story of America's National Anthem* (Johns Hopkins University Press, 2014), 17–18.

3 **"our morning gun was fired"**: Lonn Taylor, Kathleen M. Kendrick, and Jeffrey L. Brodie, *The Star-Spangled Banner: The Making of an American Icon* (Smithsonian Books, 2008), 27.

4 **"the greatest levity and vulgar obscenity"**: Richard John Samuel Stevens, *Recollections of R. J. S. Stevens: An Organist in Georgian London*, edited by Mark Argent (University of Southern Illinois Press, 1992), 25.

5 **"When the warrior"**: Mark Clague, *O Say Can You Hear?: A Cultural Biography of The Star-Spangled Banner* (W. W. Norton, 2022), 58–59.

6 **"a distinct and inferior race"**: Ferris, *Star-Spangled Banner*, 34.

9 **"Oh, say do you hear"**: E. A. Atlee, "A New Version of the National Song," *Liberator* (1844), quoted in Ferris, *Star-Spangled Banner*, 30–31.

9 **"a racist, nativist newspaper"**: Ferris, *Star-Spangled Banner*, 29.

9   **popular dime novels**: Harry Hazel [Justin Jones], *Big Dick, the King of the Negroes, or, Virtue and vice contrasted: a romance of high and low life in Boston* (Boston: Star-Spangled Banner, 1843) and *The Brigand, or, The mountain chief: a romance of the War of 1812* (T. B. Peterson & Brothers, 1864).

9   **Order of the Star-Spangled Banner**: Tyler Anbinder, *Nativism and Slavery: Northern Know-Nothings and the Politics of the 1850s* (Oxford University Press, 1992), 20–21.

10 **"attachment to the Stars and Stripes"**: Ferris, *Star-Spangled Banner*, 40.

11 **"When our land is illumined"**: Additional Verse for "The Star-Spangled Banner," Star-Spangled Banner Foundation. Starspangledmusic.org.

11 **"at concerts, declaimed"**: "The Star-Spangled Banner," *Dwight's Musical Journal* 19, no. 5 (May 4, 1861): 39.

11 **"National Anthem of Secession"**: "Dixie's Land," *Daily Dispatch* 19, no. 70 (March 25, 1861): 2.

12 **"fire your patriotism"**: James Homer Kennedy, *Star-Spangled Banner Poems, Consecrated to Union and Liberty* (J. H. Kennedy, 1862), vi, inside cover.

12 **"cannabis, chloroform and alcohol"**: Ferris, *Star-Spangled Banner*, 61–62.

12 **"the strains of an old, familiar tune"**: A Richmond Lady [Sallie A. Brock Putnam], *Richmond During the War: Four Years of Personal Observation* (G. W. Carleton, 1867), 367.

12 **"Never before did I hear"**: George Templeton Strong, *Diary of George Templeton Strong: The Civil War, 1860–1865*, edited by Allan Nevins and Milton Halsey Thomas (MacMillan, 1952), 574–75.

13 **"still those passions"**: Anna Celenza, "A Jesuit University in the New World: Music's Cultural Mission at Georgetown University (1789–1930)," in *Music as Cultural Mission: Explorations of Jesuit Practices in Italy and North America*, edited by Anna Celenza and Anthony DelDonna (St. Joseph's University Press, 2014), 174.

13 **chorus of 20,000**: Ferris, *Star-Spangled Banner*, 64.

13 **"All persons present"**: US Department of the Navy, General Order No. 374, issued by B. F. Tracy, Secretary of the Navy, July 26, 1889. The same order commands "Hail, Columbia" to be played at the lowering of the flag.

14 **"If an American"**: Louis Charles Elson, *The National Music of America and Its Sources* (L. C. Page, 1899), 155.

14 **"Of all the songs"**: Nicholas Smith, *Stories of the Great National Songs* (Young Churchman, 1899), 44, quoted in Ferris, *Star-Spangled Banner*, 111.

15 **"The spirit of the poem had taken"**: James Weldon Johnson, *Along This Way* (1933; Penguin, 2008), 154.

15 **"sent a copy"**: Johnson, *Along This Way*, 155.

15 **"respectfully dedicated"**: James Weldon Johnson and J. Rosamond Johnson, "Lift Every Voice and Sing," (Jos. W. Stern & Co., 1900), notated music, Library of Congress item 2021561009.

16 **"went on with other work"**: Johnson, *Along This Way*, 155.

17 **"The song had ... devil himself"**: Quoted in Julian Bond and Sondra Kathryn Wilson, eds., *Lift Every Voice and Sing: A Celebration of the Negro National Anthem 100 Years, 100 Voices* (Random House, 2000), 13–16.

17 **"who was a beautiful ... bombast"**: Quoted in Imani Perry, *May We Forever Stand: A History of the Black National Anthem* (University of North Carolina Press, 2018), 178.

18 **"It was a song that resisted"**: Perry, *May We Forever Stand*, 178.

19 **"We do not believe that"**: "Baltimore's Star-Spangled Banner Ordinance Unpopular," *New York Times*, September 3, 1916.

19 **passed similar laws**: Ferris, *Star-Spangled Banner*, 144.

19 **"Though Congress is a powerful body"**: Ferris, *Star-Spangled Banner*, 90.

20 **"Any man who refuses"**: "Send Dr. Muck Back, Roosevelt advises: Would Have Those Who Refuse to Play Our Anthem Pack Up and Go Away," *New York Times*, November 3, 1917, 22.

20 **"The man who"**: Quoted in "America's Greatest Musical Opportunity," *Etude*, January 1919, 9.

20 **Margaret got involved**: Ferris, *Star-Spangled Banner*, 124.

20 **ceremony at Mount Vernon**: George Creel, *How We Advertised America* (MacMillan, 1920), 200–06.

21 **Johnson blended "Dixie"**: Tom Davin, "Conversations with James P. Johnson, 1912–1914," *Jazz Review* 2, no. 6 (July 1959): 13.

21 **"the mental poison"**: Kitty Cheatham, *Words and Music of "The Star-Spangled Banner" Oppose the Spirit of Democracy which the Declaration of Independence Embodies: A Protest by Kitty Cheatham* (Kitty Cheatham, 1918), 49.

21 **"All the perfumes"**: "Wet Origin of 'Star-Spangled Banner,'" *New York World*, May 12, 1921, quoted in Ferris, *Star-Spangled Banner*, 147.

21 **"sacred shrine of American"**: "President Harding Extols Francis Scott Key And The 'Star-Spangled Banner'," *Baltimore American*, June 15, 1922, 1.

22 **"to throw mud ... get up again"**: Quoted in Ferris, *Star-Spangled Banner*, 150.

22 **"Believe It or Not"**: Robert L. Ripley, "Believe It or Not, America Has No National Anthem!," *Lexington Herald*, November 3, 1929, 28.

23 **"could represent the nation"**: Shana L. Redmond, *Anthem: Social Movements and the Sound of Solidarity in the African Diaspora* (NYU Press, 2013), 91.

25 **Subcommittee on the Constitution**: House Committee on the Judiciary, "Examining the History and Importance of 'Lift Every Voice and Sing,'" February 4, 2022, YouTube.

2: The Unanswered Question

27 **"Mr. Speaker, just less"**: *Congressional Record – House*, vol. 105, no. 15 (September 11, 1959), H19185 (statement by Rep. Donald J. Irwin).

27 **"a significant first step"**: Alan Gevinson, "Leonard Bernstein at the National Press Club, October 13, 1959," National Audio-Visual Conservation Center, Library of Congress.

27 **"rousing demand . . . translated them into music"**: "A Tribute to an American Composer."

29 **"a musical genius"**: James Burkholder, *Charles Ives and His World* (Princeton University Press, 1996), 6.

29 **"partly serious and partly in fun"**: Charles Ives, letter to Richard Dana, December 1949, quoted in James B. Sinclair, *A Descriptive Catalogue of the Music of Charles Ives* (Yale University Press, 1999), 248.

29 **"almost as fun"**: Jan Swafford, *Charles Ives: A Life with Music* (W. W. Norton, 1996), 63.

30 **"the little son of G. E. Ives"**: *Danbury News*, June 2, 1880.

30 **"all Danbury loves music"**: "Danbury's Delight Is All for Music," *New York Herald*, January 5, 1890, quoted in Swafford, *Charles Ives*, 61.

30 **"brought together in cacophonous conflict"**: "Biography: Charles Ives, 1874–1954," Library of Congress, item 200035714.

31 **"it made the boys laugh . . . dissonances"**: Charles Ives, *Memos*, edited by John Kirkpatrick (Calder & Boyars, 1973), 115, 131.

32 **"an original relation"**: *Ralph Waldo Emerson*, edited by Richard Poirier (Oxford University Press, 1990), 3.

33 **"Parker was a composer"**: Ives, *Memos*, 115.

33 **"not about something"**: Quoted in Swafford, *Charles Ives*, 251.

33 **"What we want is Honest Money"**: Charles Ives, "William Will: A Republican Campaign Song," with lyrics by Susan Benedict Hill (Willis Woodward and Company, 1896).

34 **"resigned as a nice organist"**: Ives, *Memos*, 57.

35 **first of several heart attacks**: Vivian Perlis, *Charles Ives Remembered: An Oral History* (Yale University Press, 1974), 12.

35 **"the silences of the Druids"**: Charles Ives, foreword to *The Unanswered Question* (Southern Music Company, 1953).

37 **the social virtue of life insurance**: Stephen Budiansky, *Mad Music: Charles Ives the Nostalgic Rebel* (ForeEdge, 2014), 5.

37 **"the soul and mind"**: Quoted in Swafford, *Charles Ives*, 194.

37 **"To an insurance man"**: Quoted in Swafford, *Charles Ives*, 209.

37 **"tragedy, nobility, meanness"**: Henry Bellaman, "Charles Ives: The Man and His Music," *Musical Quarterly* 19, no. 1 (January 1933): 47.

38 **"Often when a mass"**: Quoted in Stuart Feder, *Charles Ives: "My Father's Song": A Psychoanalytic Biography* (Yale University Press, 1992), 235.

38 **"emblematic of the fight"**: Tom Owens, ed., *Selected Correspondence of Charles Ives* (University of California Press, 2007), 294.

39 **"can call forth a tear"**: Philip Foner, ed., *The Life and Writings of Frederick Douglass* (International Publishers, 1950), 356–57.

39 **"debasements and imitations"**: W. E. B. Du Bois, *The Souls of Black Folk: Essays and Sketches* (A. C. McClurg, 1903), 256–57.

39 **"sadness for the slaves"**: Owens, *Selected Correspondence of Charles Ives*, 295.

40 **direct democracy**: Judith Tick, "Charles Ives and the Politics of Direct Democracy," in *Ives Studies*, edited by Philip Lambert (Cambridge University Press, 1997), 134.

41 **"It is discouraging"**: Charles Ives, "Concerning a Twentieth Amendment," in *Essays Before a Sonata and Other Writings* (W. W. Norton, 1962), 209.

42 **"Leaving the office"**: Ives, *Memos*, 92–93.

44 **debate ended in failure**: Tick, "Charles Ives," 135.

45 **recipients of his musical efforts**: David C. Paul, *Charles Ives in the Mirror: American Histories of an Iconic Composer* (University of Illinois Press, 2014), 10.

46 **"clean house"**: Charles Ives, "Postface," *114 Songs* (G. Schirmer, 1922).

48 **"I suspect that the works"**: Lou Harrison, "The Music of Charles Ives," *Listen* 9 (November 1946): 7–9.

48 **"9/11 and all the loss"**: Daniel Colvard, "John Adams Discusses *On the Transmigration of Souls*," in *The John Adams Reader: Essential Writings on an American Composer*, edited by Thomas May (Amadeus Press, 2006), 198.

48 **"I realized right up front ... thoughts"**: Tom Huizenga, "John Adams' Memory Space: *On The Transmigration Of Souls*," *Deceptive Cadence*, NPR, September 10, 2011.

49 **"It's there. It's a ghost"**: Colvard, "John Adams Discusses *On the Transmigration of Souls*," 198.

3: The Search for an American Sound

52 **"In 1790, the first Congress . . . introduce today"**: *Congressional Record – Senate*, vol. 141, no. 39 (March 2, 1995), S3391–2 (statement by Sen. Orrin Hatch).

52 **"The monetary part"**: Dinitia Smith, "Immortal Words, Immortal Royalties? Even Mickey Mouse joins the Fray," *New York Times*, March 28, 1998, B7.

53 **"Who does not know"**: *Congressional Record – Senate*, vol. 79, part 12 (August 6, 1935), S12563 (statement by Sen. Robert F. Wagner).

53 **"concert to be given"**: "Whiteman Judges Named: Committee Will Decide 'What is American Music,'" *New York Tribune*, January 4, 1924, quoted in Robert Wyatt and John Andrew Johnson, eds., *The George Gershwin Reader* (Oxford University Press, 2004), 44–45.

53 **"It was on the train"**: Merle Armitage, ed., *George Gershwin* (Longmans, Green, 1938), 188.

55 **"It spoke to me"**: George Gershwin, "Jazz is the Voice of the American Soul," in *Gershwin in His Time: A Biographical Scrapbook, 1919–1937*, edited by Gregory R. Suriano (Gramercy, 1998), 47–48.

56 **"represent the soul"**: "Tales of Tin Pan Alley: 'Swanee' and Its Author," *Edison Musical Magazine*, October 1920, 9.

58 **"the most dismal"**: Quoted in Kevin Jackson, *Constellation of Genius: 1922: Modernism Year One* (Farrar, Straus & Giroux, 2012), 235.

58 **"association with Whiteman"**: Walter Rimler, *George Gershwin: An Intimate Portrait* (University of Illinois Press, 2009), 48.

59 **"All the years"**: Paul Whiteman, "George and the Rhapsody," in Armitage, *George Gershwin*, 25.

62 **"Segregation is not a humiliation"**: William Loren Katz, *Eyewitness: The Negro in American History* (Pitman, 1967), 389–90.

63 **"We were awed"**: Duke Ellington, *Music is My Mistress* (Doubleday, 1973), 36.

63 **"It was a good place"**: Ellington, *Music is My Mistress*, 36.

63 **"We sang anything"**: Harvey G. Cohen, *Duke Ellington's America* (University of Chicago Press, 2010), 20.

64 **Ellington's first response to Gershwin's *Rhapsody in Blue***: Mark Tucker, *Ellington: The Early Years* (University of Illinois Press, 1991), 199.

64 **"an authentic record"**: Duke Ellington, "The Duke Steps Out," *Rhythm*, March 1931, 61.

65 **"the seed from which"**: Ellington, *Music is My Mistress*, 82.

66 **"And was the picture true"**: Duke Ellington, "Beige," 3–4, *Black, Brown,*

and *Beige* typescript, Smithsonian Archives of the National Museum of American History, Ellington Collection, 301, series 4, box 3, folder 7.

69 "[My *Symphony in Black*] was true": Quoted in Krin Gabbard, *Jammin' at the Margins: Jazz and the American Cinema* (University of Chicago Press, 1996), 170.

70 "You can say anything": Richard O. Boyer, "How Duke Ellington Dealt with Jazz Critics and Jim Crow," *New Yorker*, June 30, 1944.

70 "engaged with the work": Ryan Raul Bañagale, *Arranging Gershwin: Rhapsody in Blue and the Creation of an American Icon* (Oxford University Press, 2014), 75.

70 "root and branch exploration": Bañagale, *Arranging Gershwin*, 75.

70 "The great tragedy": Quoted in Bañagale, *Arranging Gershwin*, 74.

71 "You can cut": Leonard Bernstein, "Why Don't You Run Upstairs and Write a Nice Gershwin Tune?" in *The Joy of Music* (Simon & Schuster, 1959), 58.

72 "pseudo-Lisztian pastiche": Eric Larrabee, "Jazz Notes," *Harper's* 225 (July 1962): 96.

72 "traditional music dressed in jazz": Neil Leonard, *Jazz and the White Americans: The Acceptance of a New Art Form* (University of Chicago Press, 1962), 84.

4: Saving the American Landscape

73 "Mr. [Jerome] Kern": George Gershwin, letter to J. C. Rosenthal, August 18, 1928, quoted in Ryan Raul Bañagale, *Arranging Gershwin: Rhapsody in Blue and the Creation of an American Icon* (Oxford University Press, 2014), 14.

74 **Conservation—the act of protecting a resource**: Brooks Tolliver, "Ecoing in the Canyon: Ferde Grofé's *Grand Canyon Suite* and the Transformation of Wilderness," *Journal of the American Musicological Society* 57, no. 21 (2004): 325–67.

75 "itchy feet": Quoted in Jim Farrington, "Ferde Grofé: An Investigation Into His Musical Activities and Works" (Master of Music thesis, Florida State University, 1985), 13.

75 "I first saw it at dawn": Quoted in Don Rayno, *Paul Whiteman: Pioneer in American Music*, vol. 2 (Scarecrow Press, 2009), 45–46.

75 "made frequent visits": Ferde Grofé, "Story of the *Grand Canyon Suite*," *Arizona Highways* 14, no. 12 (December 1938): 8.

76 "In those days": Grofé, "Story of the *Grand Canyon Suite*," 8.

76 **"It became an obsession"**: Ferde Grofé, "And Then I Wrote . . . American Music," *Musical Courier* 153, no. 2 (January 15, 1956): 5.

76 **"On that occasion"**: Grofé, "Story of the *Grand Canyon Suite*," 8.

77 **"I was thinking of giving . . . meditation"**: Rayno, *Paul Whiteman*, 46–47.

78 **"I went again to memories"**: Grofé, "Story of the *Grand Canyon Suite*," 9.

78 **"I thought a lot of colors"**: Quoted in Rayno, *Paul Whiteman*, 47.

79 **"a natural wonder . . . be wronged"**: Theodore Roosevelt, "Presidential Address at the Grand Canyon," May 6, 1903, quoted in *Coconino Sun* 20, no. 19 (May 9, 1903): 1.

80 **"a few savage hunters"**: Kathleen DuVal, "Enough with the Land Acknowledgments," *New York Times,* January 5, 2025.

81 **"Indian Offences"**: Office of Indian Affairs, Department of the Interior, Segments from the Circular No. 1665 and Supplement to Circular No. 1665, April 26, 1921, and February 14, 1923, University of Idaho website.

81 **"On the Trail" and "Cloudburst"**: Rayno, *Paul Whiteman*, 47–49.

82 **"almost see it"**: Rayno, *Paul Whiteman*, 46.

82 **"invited listeners"**: Beth Levy, *Frontier Figures: American Music and the Mythology of the American West* (University of California Press, 2012), 17.

83 **"portrayal of nature's moods . . . couple of minutes"**: Rayno, *Paul Whiteman*, 51.

83 **"Ferde Grofé has been"**: "Music: Grofé's Canyon," *Time* 18, no. 22 (November 30, 1931): 22.

83 **"Ghost Writer of Jazz"**: Earl Sparling, "Ghost Writer of Jazz," *Scribner's Magazine* 90, no. 6 (December 1931): 594–600.

83 **"I was able at last"**: Liner notes to *Grofé: Grand Canyon Suite*, performed by Leonard Bernstein and the New York Philharmonic, CBS Records, 1963.

84 **arrangement of the work for solo piano**: Ferde Grofé, *Grand Canyon Suite*, arranged for piano by D. Savino (Robbins Music Corp., 1932).

85 **"I treasure my recollections"**: Grofé, "Story of the *Grand Canyon Suite*," 7.

85 **"This composition was born"**: Mary Dell Jenkins, "Musical Paintings," Library of Congress Blogs, NLS Music Notes, July 28, 2016.

89 **"to conserve the irreplaceable . . . refreshed"**: "Remarks by Cornelius W. Heine, Special Assistant to the Director (National Park Service), U.S. Department of the Interior, at the Arizona Travel Workshop, Flagstaff, Arizona, September 22, 1966," in [*Addresses*] (Government Printing Office, ND): 2–4. Currently held at the Northern Regional Library Facility of the Berkeley Library, University of California. Catalogue number SB482.A1A4 A4.

- 90 **"In sanctifying... in that land"**: Environmental Quality Education Act of 1970, 91st Congress, House Select Subcommittee on Education of the Committee on Education and Labor, April 7, 1970 (Washington, DC: Government Printing Office, 1970), 174–80.
- 91 **"burros came... five years"**: *Congressional Record – Senate*, vol. 123, part 13 (May 20, 1977), S15818 (statement by Sen. Charles Mathias Jr.).
- 92 **"'Sunrise'—birth"**: Lisa Schiavone, "Profile: Ferde Grofé's *Grand Canyon Suite*," *Weekend Edition*, NPR, October 29, 2000.
- 92 **"Only to the white man"**: Luther Standing Bear, *Land of the Spotted Eagle* (Boston: Houghton Mifflin, 1933), xix.
- 92 **national parks don't just preserve places**: David Treuer, "Return the National Parks to the Tribes: The Jewels of America's Landscape Belong to America's Original Peoples," *The Atlantic*, May 2021, 43.

5: Witness for the Prosecution

- 95 **"it was over 100 years ago"**: "Remarks by President Biden at Signing of H.R. 55, the Emmett Till Anti-Lynching Act," March 29, 2022, White House website.
- 96 **"lynch carnivals"**: Dora Apel, *Imagery of Lynching: Black Men, White Women, and the Mob* (Rutgers University Press, 2004), 15.
- 99 **the central identity of Dewitt-Clinton**: Gerard J. Pelisson and James A. Garvey, *The Castle on the Parkway: The Story of New York City's Dewitt-Clinton High School and Its Extraordinary Influence on American Life* (Hutch Press, 2021), 65.
- 99 **the Scottsboro case**: B. D. Amis, *They Shall Not Die!: The Story of Scottsboro In Pictures: Stop the Legal Lynching!* (Workers' Library, 1932).
- 100 **"What is the reason"**: *New Masses* 10, no. 2 (January 9, 1934): 6.
- 100 **"Lynch law took"**: *New Masses* 10, no. 2 (January 9, 1934): 6.
- 101 **"a union of art and propaganda"**: *The Crisis* 42, no. 4 (April 1935): 106.
- 101 **"pendant mass of silvered realism"**: M. M., "Review of *Art Commentary on Lynching*," *Art News*, February 23, 1935, 13.
- 101 **detailed description of the sculpture**: "Noguchi 'Sculpture,'" *New Masses* 14, no. 12 (March 19, 1935): 29.
- 102 **"threatening and frightening"**: Apel, *Imagery of Lynching*, 40.
- 102 **"Do not look at the Negro"**: NAACP flier, 1935, 2, Yale University Library, item 10834052.
- 103 **"in the early thirties"**: Lewis Allan, "The Strange Case of 'Strange Fruit,'" *Broadside* 122, no. 1 (1973): 6.

104 "**Laura Duncan**": Allan, "The Strange Case of 'Strange Fruit,'" 6.

104 "**by four young Black men**": Lewis Allan [Abel Meeropol], letter to Linda Kuehl, July 28, 1971, Johns Hopkins University Libraries, Billie Holiday Collection.

105 "**to serve as the voice**": TAC Manifesto, quoted in Michael L. Greenwald, "Actors as Activists: The Theatre Arts Committee Cabaret 1938–1941," *Theatre Research Journal* 20, no. 1 (1995): 20, 27.

105 "**a record that has no equals**": Henry Johnson [John Hammond II], "Music," *New Masses* 20, no. 12 (September 15, 1936): 27.

105 "**I had been to Europe**": Whitney Balliett, "Night Clubs," *New Yorker*, October 9, 1971, 75–76.

106 "**To be perfectly frank**": Quoted in David Margolick, *Strange Fruit: Billie Holiday and the Biography of a Song* (Ecco, 2001), 28.

106 "**I was doing agitprop ... burned with it**": Quoted in Kitty Grime, *Jazz Voices* (Quartet, 1983), 166.

106 "**There wasn't even a patter**": Billie Holiday with William Dufty, *Lady Sings the Blues* (1956; Penguin, 1992), 84.

106 "**She gave a startling**": Lewis Allan [Abel Meeropol], letter to Linda Kuehl, July 28, 1971.

107 "**It was incredible**": Quoted in Margolick, *Strange Fruit*, 43.

107 "**[she] was putting into words**": Julia Blackburn, *With Billie: A New Look at the Unforgettable Lady Day* (Pantheon, 2005), 111.

107 "**I have to sing it**": Quoted in Margolick, *Strange Fruit*, 45.

108 "**so that we will**": Emanuel Levin, "Strange Fruit on Southern Trees—The Fight for the Anti-Lynch Bill," *Fraternal Outlook*, March 1939, 4–5.

108 "**This is about a phonograph**": Quoted in Margolick, *Strange Fruit*, 53.

109 "**no expert record collector**": Ted Le Berthon, quoted in Margolick, *Strange Fruit*, 64.

109 "**buxom blues singer**": "Billie Holiday Records First Song About Lynching Evils," *Atlanta Daily World*, June 19, 1939, 2.

109 "**the first phonograph recording**": Quoted in Margolick, *Strange Fruit*, 73–74.

109 "**By all means ... marketing device [for Holiday]**": Quoted in Margolick, *Strange Fruit*, 61.

109 "**When [Holiday] recorded it**": Quoted in Margolick, *Strange Fruit*, 7.

110 **Gavagan Anti-Lynching Bill**: *Congressional Record – House*, vol. 86, part 1 (January 10, 1940), 253.

110 "**America is a nation**": "TAC Sends 'Strange Fruit' to Congress in Anti-Lynching Move," *TAC* 2, no. 6 (March 1, 1940): 16.

110 **a haunting instrumental version**: Victor refused to release the recording during Bechet's lifetime. The recording sat in storage until 2013.

111 **"The dance begins"**: Barbara Cohen-Stratyner, "Pearl Primus in 'Strange Fruit,'" New York Public Library blog, August 29, 2016.

111 **"In America's bosom"**: Richard C. Green, "(Up)Staging the Primitive: Pearl Primus and 'the Negro Problem' in American Dance," in *Dancing Many Drums: Excavations in African American Dance*, edited by Thomas F. DeFrantz (University of Wisconsin Press, 2002), 107.

111 **"I wrote 'Strange Fruit'"**: Quoted in Nancy Kovaleff Baker, "Abel Meeropol (a.k.a. Lewis Allan): Political Commentator and Social Conscience," *American Music* 20 (Spring 2002): 53.

112 **"an era of repression"**: Abel Meeropol, letter to Dalton Trumbo, December 26, 1970, quoted in Baker, "Abel Meeropol," 63.

112 **"like she was singing . . . existence"**: Vernon Jarret, quoted in Margolick, *Strange Fruit*, 43.

113 **"You allow me to sing"**: Rebecca Ferguson @RebeccaFMusic, Twitter post, January 2, 2017.

113 **"felt like they were not"**: Soraya Nadia McDonald, "There's more to Nina Simone than just 'Strange Fruit,'" *Andscape*, February 28, 2017, andscape.com.

114 **"I rise today to recognize"**: *Congressional Record – Extensions of Remarks*, vol. 167, no. 34 (February 23, 2021), E157 (statement by Rep. Eddie Bernice Johnson).

114 **"'Strange Fruit,' written by Abel"**: Kweisi Mfume, "The Emmett Till Anti-Lynching Act: Why Is It Important?," *Afro News*, April 8, 2022.

6: A New Vision for America

117 **"YOU ARE HEREBY"**: Telegram from Senator Joseph McCarthy to Aaron Copland, reproduced in Aaron Copland and Vivian Perlis, *Copland Since 1943* (St. Martin's Press, 1989), 190.

117 **"hard-working fellow-travelers"**: "Dupes and Fellow Travelers Dress Up Communist Fronts," *Life* 26, no. 14 (April 4, 1949): 42–43.

119 **"No one to my knowledge"**: Julia Smith, *Aaron Copland* (E. P. Dutton, 1953), 41.

119 **"It was wonderful"**: Aaron Copland and Vivian Perlis, *Copland 1900–1942* (St. Martin's Press, 1984), 64.

119 **"Gershwin is serious"**: Melissa de Graaf, "Aaron Copland and the Composers' Rorum-Laboratory: A Post-Concert Discussion, February 27,

1937," in *Aaron Copland and His World*, edited by Carol J. Oja and Judith Tick (Princeton University Press, 2005), 399.

120 **"I got the feeling"**: David King Dunaway, *How Can I Keep from Singing: The Ballad of Pete Seeger* (Villard, 2008), 38.

120 **"the wasteland of dehumanizing machines"**: Adnan Morshed, "Flying to the World of Tomorrow: The Ascension Theme at the 1939 New York World's Fair," in *Meet Me at the Fair: A World's Fair Reader*, edited by Laura Hollengreen, Celia Pierce, Rebecca Rouse, and Bobby Schweizer (ETC Press), 505.

121 **"This is a fight"**: Henry A. Wallace, *The Century of the Common Man* (Reynal & Hitchcock, 1943).

122 **"a legend of living . . . rope swing"**: Martha Graham, "House of Victory" script, May 16, 1943, Library of Congress, Aaron Copland Collection, item 200154130.

122 **"I think I have my first"**: Aaron Copland, letter to Harold Spivacke, June 8, 1943, Library of Congress, Aaron Copland Collection.

122 **"religious communism"**: Daryl Chase, *The Early Shakers: An Experiment in Religious Communism* (University of Chicago Press, 1936).

122 **"ideal for Martha's scenario"**: Copland and Perlis, *Copland Since 1943*, 33.

123 **"the matriarch . . . up to you"**: Graham, "House of Victory" script.

123 **"revitalize the native past"**: Helge Normann Nilsen, "Hart Crane's Indian Poem," *Neuphilologische Mitteilungen* 72, no. 1 (1971): 127.

124 **"There is no reason . . . white person's Indian"**: Martha Graham, script for *Appalachian Spring*, May 29–July 10, 1943, 2–3, Library of Congress, Aaron Copland Collection.

124 **disagreement over the monument's message**: Russel Lawrence Barsch, "An American Heart of Darkness: The 1913 Expedition for American Indian Citizenship," *Great Plains Quarterly* 13 (Spring 1993): 94–100.

125 **"This could have the feeling"**: Graham, script for *Appalachian Spring*.

125 **"was almost done"**: Quoted in Annegret Fauser, *Aaron Copland's Appalachian Spring* (Oxford University Press, 2017), 40.

125 **"The music is so knit . . . give them great joy"**: Martha Graham, letter to Aaron Copland, August 5, 1944, Library of Congress, Aaron Copland Collection.

126 **"a new town"**: Graham, script for *Appalachian Spring*.

126 **"farmyard was suggested"**: Copland and Perlis, *Copland Since 1943*, 40.

126 **"a real breakthrough"**: Quoted in Copland and Perlis, *Copland Since 1943*, 39.

127 **"Part and parcel of our lives"**: Quoted in Elizabeth B. Crist, *Music for the*

Common Man: Aaron Copland During the Depression and War (Oxford University Press, 2005), 170.

127 **"music composed"**: Quoted in Howard Pollack, *Aaron Copland: The Life and Work of an Uncommon Man* (Henry Holt, 1999), 393.

127 **"Appalachian Spring became"**: Fauser, *Aaron Copland's Appalachian Spring*, 90.

128 **"We all had such wonderful hope"**: Quoted in Copland and Perlis, *Copland Since 1943*, 40.

129 **Pulitzer Prize in music**: pulitzer.org/winners/william-schuman.

129 **"The first movement is a kind"**: Steve Swayne, *Orpheus in Manhattan: William Schuman and the Shaping of America's Musical Life* (Oxford University Press, 2011), 139.

129 **"Since I cannot serve"**: Fauser, *Aaron Copland's Appalachian Spring*, 238.

130 **"Aaron Copland has written"**: John Martin, "Graham Dancers in Festival Finale," *New York Times*, November 1, 1944, 19.

130 **"subtle communistic touches"**: Karl F. Cohen, *Forbidden Animation: Censored Cartoons and Blacklisted Animators in America* (McFarland, 2004), 169–70.

131 **"a comic opera"**: "Dupes and Fellow Travelers Dress Up Communist Fronts," *Life* 26, no. 14 (April 4, 1949): 40.

131 **"I am here . . . of other nations"**: Aaron Copland, "Effect of the Cold War on the Artist in the U.S. (1949)," in *Aaron Copland: A Reader, Selected Writings 1923–1972*, edited by Richard Kostelanetz (Routledge, 2003), 128–31.

132 **"As I have but a passing knowledge . . . Activities"**: *Congressional Record – Appendix*, vol. 99, part 9 (January 16, 1953), A169–71.

134 **"discredit"**: Pollack, *Aaron Copland*, 455.

134 **"McCarthy: Mr. Copland, have you"**: *State Department Teacher-Student Exchange Program*, 83rd Congress, Senate Permanent Subcommittee on Investigations of the Committee on Government Operations, May 26, 1953 (Government Printing Office, 2003), 1267–90.

136 **"My impression is that McCarthy"**: Quoted in Alex Ross, "Appalachian Autumn," *New Yorker*, August 27, 2007.

137 **"insufficient evidence"**: Bill Morelock, "Conscience vs. McCarthy: the political Aaron Copland," Minnesota Public Radio, May 3, 2005.

137 **"firmly defended him"**: Pollack, *Aaron Copland*, 459.

137 **"We thank Aaron"**: Quoted in Copland and Perlis, *Copland Since 1943*, 44.

138 **"the incomparable contributions"**: Public Law 99–418, passed by the 99th Congress, September 23, 1986.

138   **"The idea of two fellows"**: Anna Kisselgoff, "Dance: Graham with Baryshnikov, Nureyev and Plisetskaya," *New York Times*, October 7, 1987, C23.

7: America's Secret Sonic Weapon

139   **"Our country has come through"**: Dwight D. Eisenhower, "Annual Message to Congress on the State of the Union," February 2, 1953, Eisenhower Presidential Library.

140   **"Throughout the world"**: "1954 – Colour & B/W, Cold War, USA: U.S. Overseas Information Program Pt. 1 of 2," Footage Farm, item 220540.

140   **"The contribution which"**: *Foreign Relations of the United States, 1952–1954*, vol. 2, pt. 2, document 365. "The President to the President of the Senate, July 27, 1954." See also Lisa Davenport, "Jazz and the Cold War: Black Culture as an Instrument of American Foreign Policy," in *Crossing Boundaries: Comparative History of Black People in Diaspora*, edited by Darlene Clark Hine and Jacqueline McLeod (Indiana University Press, 1999), 286; and Penny M. Von Eschen, *Satchmo Blows Up the World: Jazz Ambassadors Play the Cold War* (Harvard University Press, 2004), 4.

141   **first Music Advisory Panel**: Danielle Fosler-Lussier, *Music in America's Cold War Diplomacy* (University of California Press, 2015), 23.

141   **"counteract Russian propaganda"**: Minutes of Music Panel Meeting, October 26, 1954, quoted in Davenport, "Jazz and the Cold War," 287.

141   **"show tunes and folk music"**: Minutes of Music Advisory Panel Meeting, November 15, 1955, quoted in Fosler-Lussier, *Music in America's Cold War Diplomacy*, 23.

142   **"defenses of US foreign policy"**: Von Eschen, *Satchmo Blows Up the World*, 15–16.

142   **"Jazz is a classical parallel"**: Quoted in Nicholas J. Cull, *The Cold War and the United States Information Agency: American Propaganda and Public Diplomacy, 1945–1989* (Cambridge University Press, 2008), 107–08.

142   **"no American problem"**: Comments by Senator Henry Cabot Lodge and unnamed State Department official, in the minutes of meeting of US delegation to UN, November 10, 1950, quoted in Michael Sy Uy, "Performing Catfish Row in the Soviet Union: The Everyman Opera Company and Porgy and Bess, 1955–56," *Journal of the Society for American Music* 11, no. 4 (2017): 476.

143   **"to Moscow . . . governments"**: "U.S. Will Not Pay for 'Porgy' Visit," *New York Times*, September 28, 1955, 70.

143 **"I not only hope"**: *The Jazz Ambassadors: The Untold Story of America's Coolest Weapon in the Cold War*, film directed by Hugo Berkeley, PBS, 2018.
144 **"most effective ambassador"**: Felix Belair Jr., "United States Has Secret Sonic Weapon—Jazz," *New York Times*, November 6, 1955.
145 **"It's the first thing I said"**: "They Cross the Iron Curtain to Hear American Jazz," *U.S. News & World Report*, December 2, 1955, 54–62.
145 **"Jazz has come to represent"**: Quoted in Davenport, "Jazz and the Cold War," 282.
145 **"the legislation of jazz"**: Minutes of the Music Advisory Panel, November 15, 1955, 2, University of Arkansas at Fayetteville, Bureau of Educational and Cultural Affairs Historical Collection, J. William Fulbright Papers, ser. 5, box 12, fol. 12; and Von Eschen, *Satchmo Blows Up the World*, 58.
145 **"We've just decided"**: *The Jazz Ambassadors*.
146 **"I took it as an honor"**: Dizzy Gillespie, *To Be or Not . . . to Bop* (1979; University of Minnesota Press, 2009), 414.
146 **"the Eisenhower administration's conception"**: Von Eschen, *Satchmo Blows Up the World*, 32.
147 **"We had a complete"**: Gillespie, *To Be or Not . . . to Bop*, 414.
147 **"They priced the tickets"**: Gillespie, *To Be or Not . . . to Bop*, 418.
147 **"Dizzy almost turned white"**: *The Jazz Ambassadors*.
147 **"You know, I'm always"**: Gillespie, *To Be or Not . . . to Bop*, 419.
148 **"I have never heard"**: Von Eschen, *Satchmo Blows Up the World*, 40.
148 **"plot to mongrelize America"**: Von Eschen, *Satchmo Blows Up the World*, 26.
148 **President's Special International Program**: Ross Parmenter, "U.S. Helps Out: Bill Passed to Make Cultural Tours a Branch of Our Foreign Policy," *New York Times*, August 5, 1956, 7.
149 **"strengthened the impression"**: Von Eschen, *Satchmo Blows Up the World*, 47.
150 **"The noise and the clamor"**: Anna Celenza, catalogue for *Jazz Ambassador Louis Armstrong, Ghana 1956*, Georgetown University Special Collections online exhibit, 2016.
150 **"I must state here"**: Benjamin Fine, "Militia Sent To Little Rock; School Integration Put Off," *New York Times*, September 3, 1957, 1.
151 **"gutless . . . any country"**: "Louis Armstrong, Barring Soviet Tour, Denounces Eisenhower and Governor Faubus," *New York Times*, September 19, 1957, 23.
151 **"ruining our foreign policy"**: "Memorandum of a Telephone Conversation Between the Secretary of State and the Attorney General (Brownell),

Washington, September 24, 1957, 2:15 p.m.," *Foreign Relations of the United States, 1955–1957*, vol. 9, document 208.

151 **"Jazz, the music"**: Dizzy Gillespie and Ralph Ginsberg, "Jazz Is Too Good for Americans," *Esquire*, June 1957, 55.

151 **"this lionizing of American jazzmen"**: Gillespie and Ginsberg, "Jazz Is Too Good for Americans," 140.

152 **"I see the audience"**: Dave Brubeck, program note, quoted in Marek Kepa, "Take 12: Dave Brubeck's Unforgettable 1958 Tour of Poland," *Culture* (Poland), November 7, 2018.

152 **"No dictatorship can tolerate jazz"**: Penny Von Eschen and Curtis Sandberg, "Dave Brubeck: The Timing Was Right," catalogue for *Jam Session: America's Jazz Ambassadors Embrace the World*, photography exhibition, Meridian International Center website.

152 **"the rhythmic pattern"**: "Jam Session: America's Jazz Ambassadors Embrace the World—Dave Brubeck," Meridian International Center website.

153 **"These sketches of Eurasia"**: Dave Brubeck, liner notes to the Dave Brubeck Quartet, *Jazz Impressions of Eurasia*, Columbia Records, 1958.

153 **"The entire jazz community was elated"**: Iola Brubeck, liner notes to Dave Brubeck, *The Real Ambassadors*, featuring Louis Armstrong et al., Columbia Records, 1962.

154 **"high salaries to outstanding artists"**: Harvey G. Cohen, *Duke Ellington's America* (University of Chicago Press, 2010), 423–34.

154 **tour was canceled**: Cohen, *Duke Ellington's America*, 411–13.

154 **"it was the propaganda"**: Reinhold Wagnleitner, *Coca-Colonization and the Cold War: The Cultural Mission of the United States in Austria after the Second World War* (University of North Carolina Press, 1994), 210.

155 **"When we think"**: Richard Nixon, "Remarks on Presenting the Presidential Medal of Freedom to Duke Ellington," April 29, 1969, American Presidency Project website.

156 **question the financial commitment**: Von Eschen, *Satchmo Blows Up the World*, 249.

156 **"superb representatives"**: Penny Von Eschen and Curtis Sandberg, "Enter the Newport Jazz Festival," catalogue for *Jam Session* exhibition.

156 **"Politics is everybody's business"**: William Raspberry, "A New PAC for Blacks," *Washington Post*, December 18, 1981.

157 **"an indigenous American music"**: For a detailed discussion of the Jazz Preservation Act of 1987, see Jeff Farley, "Jazz as a Black American Art Form: Definitions of the Jazz Preservation Act," *Journal of American Studies* 45, no. 1 (2011): 113–29.

157 **jazz as strictly African American**: Michael Eugene Crutcher, *Tremé: Race and Place in a New Orleans Neighborhood* (University of Georgia Press, 2010), 87–89.

157 **"myth of jazz's African origins"**: Quoted in Crutcher, *Tremé*, 88.

158 **California Desert Protection Act**: Amendment 1626, "To establish the New Orleans Jazz National Historical Park in the State of Louisiana," to Senate bill S. 21, "California Desert Protection Act of 1994."

158 **"indigenous to the United States"**: "H.Con.Res.501—Honoring the life and work of Duke Ellington, recognizing the 30th anniversary of the Duke Ellington School of the Arts, and supporting the annual Duke Ellington Jazz Festival," 108th Congress, introduced September 28, 2004.

158 **African American contribution to jazz**: H.Con.Res.363 (2002), S.Con.Res.101 (2002), H.Con.Res.144 (2003), H.Res.778 (2004), H.Con.Res.501 (2004), H.Con.Res.300 (2005), H.Res.894 (2009), H.Res.641 (2012), H.Res 839 (2015).

159 **"What you brought"**: Fred Kaplan, "When Ambassadors Had Rhythm," *New York Times*, June 29, 2008.

8: There's a Place for Us . . . Somewhere

161 **"an active partner"**: John F. Kennedy, "Remarks Upon Signing the Juvenile Delinquency and Youth Offenses Act," September 22, 1961, American Presidency Project website.

161 **"national emergency"**: Michael W. Flamm, *Law and Order: Street Crime, Civil Unrest, and the Crisis of Liberalism in the 1960s* (Columbia University Press, 2005), 40.

162 **Adam Yarmolinsky**: Neil A. Lewis, "Adam Yarmolinsky Dies at 77; Led Revamping of Government," *New York Times*, January 7, 2000.

162 **three-word response**: Transcript of the Poverty and Urban Policy Conference, Brandeis University, June 16–17, 1973, 49, Kennedy Presidential Library. Quoted in Flamm, *Law and Order*, 195.

162 **"noble idea: a modern version"**: Leonard Bernstein, "Excerpts from a West Side Log," *Playbill*, September 30, 1957, 47; reprinted in Leonard Bernstein, *Findings* (New York: Simon & Schuster, 1982), 144.

162 **"was conceived as taking place"**: "Landmark Symposium: *West Side Story* [1985]," *Dramatist* 11 (February 2008): 21.

162 **"undergo local renovation"**: Louis Calta, "'Romeo' to Receive Musical Styling," *New York Times*, January 27, 1949, 19.

163 **"great American opera"**: Nigel Simeone, ed., *The Leonard Bernstein Letters* (Yale University Press, 2013), 250.

163 **"I want to make one thing clear"**: Misha Berson, *Something's Coming, Something Good: West Side Story and the American Imagination* (Applause, 2011), 23.

164 **"Dear Lenny, I'm sorry"**: Simeone, *Leonard Bernstein Letters*, 255.

165 **"much good stuff"**: Bernstein, "Excerpts from a West Side Log," entry for April 15, 1949.

165 **"I remember receiving"**: Quoted in Nigel Simeone, *Leonard Bernstein: West Side Story* (Routledge, 2016), 19.

165 **"an old Commie-chaser"**: Simeone, *Leonard Bernstein Letters*, 309.

165 **"improperly exploited"**: Simeone, *Leonard Bernstein Letters*, 305.

166 **homosexuality would be exposed**: See Deborah Jowitt, *Jerome Robbins: His Life, His Theater, His Dance* (Simon & Schuster, 2004), 231.

166 **alleged "perverts"**: "126 Perverts Discharged; State Department Reports Total Ousted Since Jan. 1, 1951," *New York Times*, March 26, 1952, 25.

166 **"immoral," "sexual perversion"**: Executive Order 10450: "Security Requirements for Government Employment," National Archives website.

166 **"You were a shit"**: Lucy E. Cross, "Arthur Laurents," *Masterworks Broadway*, Masterworksbroadway.com.

167 **"You are a homosexual"**: Simeone, *Leonard Bernstein Letters*, 294.

167 **"Jerry brushed us aside"**: Arthur Laurents, *Original Story By: A Memoir of Broadway and Hollywood* (Alfred A. Knopf, 2000), 334.

167 **"from their idea bank"**: Lewis Funke, "Rialto Gossip," *New York Times*, June 19, 1955, X1.

167 **"My reaction was"**: "Landmark Symposium: *West Side Story* [1985]."

167 **"the barest of skeletons . . . specific city"**: Simeone, *Leonard Bernstein Letters*, 343.

168 **"As a nation"**: "Senators to Hold Teen Age Hearings: Subcommittee Plans Sessions Here and in 19 Other Cities—Local Assistance Sought," *New York Times*, September 19, 1953, 16.

168 **"The truth is, that delinquency"**: Peter Kihiss, "No Harm in Horror, Comics Issuer Says," *New York Times*, April 22, 1954, 1.

168 **"deadliest of teen war areas"**: Charles Grutzner, "Bronx is Deadliest of Teen War Areas," *New York Times*, May 10, 1950, 44.

169 **"there are historical connotations"**: Simeone, *Leonard Bernstein Letters*, 345.

169 **"on two teen-age gangs"**: Bernstein, "Excerpts from a West Side Log," entry for August 25, 1955.

169 **"Lenny said: 'What about doing it'"**: "Landmark Symposium: *West Side Story* [1985]."

169 **newspaper headlines**: Quoted in Lorrin Thomas, "Displacement and Sur-

vival in Puerto Rican New York: Broken Promises in Lincoln Square," January 30, 2023. *Legacies of San Juan Hill*, online exhibit, lincolncenter.org.

169 **"the slums of Harlem"**: Charles Abrams, "How to Remedy our 'Puerto Rican Problem,'" *Commentary* 19 (February 1955): 121, 123.

169 **"many families packed"**: Dan W. Dodson, *Between Hell's Kitchen and San Juan Hill—A Survey* (Human Relations Studies, 1952), 10, 16.

170 **"The streets are darker"**: Courtney Escoyne, "#TBT: How West Side Story Created a Broadway Revolution," *Dance Magazine*, May 6, 2020.

170 **"We visited a gym"**: Al Kasha and Joel Hirschorn, *Notes on Broadway: Conversations with the Great Songwriters* (Contemporary, 1985), 15.

170 **"I can't do the show"**: Alberto Sandoval, "*West Side Story*: A Puerto Rican Reading of 'America,'" *Jump Cut* 39 (1994): 65.

171 **"in possession of the area"**: Norris Houghton, ed., *Romeo and Juliet / West Side Story* (Dell, 1965), 137.

171 **"Them PRs are the reason"**: Houghton, *Romeo and Juliet / West Side Story*, 140–41.

171 **"These PRs are different"**: *West Side Story*, film directed by Jerome Robbins and Robert Wise, United Artists, 1961.

172 **"I had conceived an idea"**: Mel Gussow, "*West Side Story*: The Beginnings of Something Great," *New York Times*, October 21, 1990, section 2, 5.

173 **"an expansiveness and mood"**: Howard Taubman, "Music: The Duke Jumps. Ellington and Band Join Symphony of the Air," *New York Times*, March 17 1955, 29.

173 **reading a comic book**: Houghton, *Romeo and Juliet / West Side Story*, 169.

174 **"an experiential, quasi-psychoanalytical approach"**: Berson, *Something's Coming*, 20.

174 **"Policemen along the 52nd St. beat"**: Dorothy Kilgallen, "What's in a Name? Sid Finds Out," *Washington Post*, July 24, 1957.

174 **"Everyone's coming"**: Simeone, *Leonard Bernstein Letters*, 272.

174 **"He was a little disconcerted"**: Maxine Cheshire, "Composer Bernstein Tells Capitalites: *West Side Story* is 'Poetry,'" *Washington Post*, August 20, 1957.

175 **"tremendously moved"**: Richard L. Coe, "'West Side' Has That Beat," *Washington Post*, August 20, 1957.

175 **"immigrant Puerto Ricans"**: Paul Hume, "Minor Musical Touch-Ups Can Make *West Side Story* a Long-Run Hit," *Washington Post*, August 21, 1957.

175 **"In *West Side Story*, four men"**: Richard L. Coe, "Musical at National Is a Triumph," *Washington Post*, September 1, 1957.

175 **"[DC] Commissioner [Robert E.] McLaughlin"**: "Musical's Authors Get Key to Capital," *New York Times*, August 31, 1957, 18.

175 **"I don't want to see the *West Side Story*"**: James Clayton, "Commissioners Asked to Restore $44,000 Trim," *Washington Post*, September 14, 1957.

176 **"the boot camps"**: Flamm, *Law and Order*, 40.

176 **"the show would be picketed . . . not picketed"**: "Landmark Symposium: West Side Story [1985]," 31.

176 **rife with tropical diseases**: Howard A. Rusk, MD, "The Facts Don't Rhyme: An Analysis of Irony in Lyrics Linking Puerto Rico's Breezes to Tropic Diseases," *New York Times*, September 29, 1957, 83.

176 **"The Puerto Rican Adapts Remarkably"**: Rev. David W. Barry, "The Puerto Rican Adapts Remarkably," *Washington Post*, March 8, 1959.

176 **"tragic intolerance"**: Henry Raymont, "Señalan el exito West Side Story," *El Mundo*, September 9, 1957, quoted in Julia Foulkes, *A Place For Us: West Side Story and New York* (Chicago University Press, 2016), 83.

176 **"hired a public relations firm"**: Benjamin Lapidus, *New York and the International Sound of Latin Music 1940–1990* (University of Mississippi Press, 2021), 275.

177 **"The Cherubs Are Rumbling"**: Walter Bernstein, "The Cherubs Are Rumbling: A Club Dance with a Teen-Age Street Gang," *New Yorker*, September 13, 1957.

177 **"shook-up generation"**: Harrison E. Salisbury, "Youth: On the Streets, in the Schools. Pt. 1: 'Gangs That Plague the City Take Toll in Talents,'" *New York Times*, March 24, 1958, 7.

177 **"bopping (fighting) street gangs"**: Harrison E. Salisbury, "Youth Gang Members Tell of Lives, Hates and Fears; City's 'Shook-Up' Youth: Their Lives Are Found Lacking in the Basic Securities," *New York Times*, March 25, 1958, 1.

178 **"For most New Yorkers"**: Harrison E. Salisbury, "Lethargy of Public Found at Root of Youth Problem," *New York Times*, March 30, 1958, 1.

178 **"The show did not"**: *50 years of West Side Story*, part 3, "Broadway to Hollywood—and Beyond," NPR, September 26, 2007.

178 **"playing straight man"**: George Dixon, "Washington Scene . . . Tips to the American Theater," *Washington Post*, April 22, 1958.

179 **Bernstein greeted President Eisenhower**: Barry Seldes, *Leonard Bernstein: The Political Life of an American Musician* (University of California Press, 2009), 83.

179 **"a mighty influence for peace"**: "President Turns Earth to Start Lincoln Center," *New York Times*, May 15, 1959, 1.

179 **"There is no single American cultural product"**: Frances Negrón-

Muntaner, "Feeling Pretty: *West Side Story* and Puerto Rican Identity Discourses," *Social Text* 18, no. 2 (2000): 83.

179 **"is the most powerful piece"**: R. Domínguez, letter to Robert Wise, October 31, 1961, USC Cinematic Arts Library, Robert Wise Papers, box 34, f. 5.

180 **"a Disneyfied version"**: Quoted in Simeone, *Leonard Bernstein: West Side Story*, 3.

180 **"Film is either realistic or surreal"**: *50 years of West Side Story*, part 3, "Broadway to Hollywood—and Beyond."

180 **"lend itself to exploitation"**: Quoted in Foulkes, *A Place For Us*, 180.

181 **"When you're a Red"**: William Gaines, "East Side Story," *Mad Magazine* 78 (April 1963): 5.

182 **"today's gangs are not the bands"**: *Congressional Record – Senate*, vol. 142, no. 54, (April 24, 1996), S1700 (statement by Senator Dianne Feinstein).

182 **"we must not excuse the behavior"**: *School Violence: What is Being Done to Combat School Violence? What Should Be Done?*, 106th Congress, House Subcommittee on Criminal Justice, Drug Policy, and Human Resources of the Committee on Government Reform, May 20, 1999 (Government Printing Office, 2000), 75.

182 **"Gangs in America are no longer"**: *Combating Gang Violence in America: Examining Effective Federal, State and Local Law Enforcement Strategies*, 108th Congress, Senate Committee on the Judiciary, September 17, 2003 (Government Printing Office, 2004), 1.

183 **"My biggest challenge"**: Quoted in Josh Getlin, "*West Side Story* with a Spanish accent," *Los Angeles Times*, March 18, 2009.

183 **"As a piece of art"**: David Montgomery, "A *West Side Story* That Finally Speaks to Latinos," *Washington Post*, January 3, 2009.

183 **"It was a tall order"**: "Lin-Manuel Miranda, the 'West Side Story' interpreter," *New York Daily News*, March 17, 2009.

183 **"He killed your brother!"**: Colleen Rua, "El Poder y Educación: Bilingualism and Translation in the American Musical," *Delos: A Journal of Translation and World Literature* 35, no. 1 (Spring 2020): 45–61.

183 **"It gave the show a new life"**: Getlin, "*West Side Story* with a Spanish accent."

183 **"Audiences were getting the general idea"**: Patrick Healy, "Some 'West Side' Lyrics Are Returned to English," *New York Times*, August 26, 2009.

184 **"Many say *West Side*"**: Arthur Laurents, *Mainly on Directing: Gypsy, West Side Story, and Other Musicals* (Alfred A. Knopf, 2009), 145.

184 **"a masterpiece of Western dramatic art"**: Geri Cole, "Tony Kushner, *West Side Story*," *OnWriting: A Podcast of the Writers Guild of America East*.

9: What's Going On?

184 **"I ain't like any other girl on Earth"**: Library of Congress, "Salute to *West Side Story*," 2007, YouTube.

187 **"I speak tonight"**: Lyndon B. Johnson, "Special Message to the Congress: The American Promise," March 15, 1965, American Presidency Project.

188 **"The right song"**: David Dunaway, *How Can I Keep from Singing? The Ballad of Pete Seeger* (Villard, 2008), 427.

189 **"Our publishers said to us"**: Pete Seeger, *Where Have All the Flowers Gone: A Singer's Stories, Songs, Seeds, Robberies* (Sing Out, 1993), 33–34.

191 **"a cross between"**: Robert Shelton, "Bob Dylan: A Distinctive Folk-Song Stylist," *New York Times*, September 29, 1961, 31.

191 **"I still say that some"**: Bob Dylan, "Blowin' in the Wind," *Sing Out!* 12, no. 4 (October–November 1962): 4.

192 **"We started to sing"**: "Peter Paul & Mary Talk about The March On Washington & Sing Songs 1963," YouTube.

193 **"I consider myself young . . . free speech"**: Bob Dylan, speech at the ECLC Bill of Rights dinner December 13, 1963, AllDylan.com.

196 **"When the kids got killed"**: *What Happened, Miss Simone?*, film directed by Liz Garbus, Netflix, 2015.

197 **"I was going to take"**: Nina Simone, *I Put a Spell on You: The Autobiography of Nina Simone* (Da Capo Press, 1993), 90–91.

197 **"It wasn't 'We Shall Overcome'"**: Claudia Roth Pierpont, "A Raised Voice," *New Yorker*, April 11–18, 2014.

199 **"In 'Mississippi Goddam,' we have Nina Simone"**: "How It Feels to Be Free," *American Masters*, PBS, January 18, 2021.

199 **"to be brought into abrasive contact"**: Quoted in Pierpont, "A Raised Voice."

200 **"An artist's duty"**: Quoted in Liz Fields, "The story behind Nina Simone's protest song, 'Mississippi Goddam,'" *American Masters*, PBS, January 14, 2021.

202 **"three-day hoo-ha"**: Rob Tannenbaum, "Joan Baez on 3 Days of Pregnancy and Priggishness," *New York Times*, August 11, 2019, F15.

206 **"For so many years"**: "Iconic feminist Helen Reddy's must see interview | 60 Minutes Australia," 1979, YouTube.

206 **"There were a lot . . . see myself as dainty"**: Mark Caro, "Helen Reddy to Roar Again," *Chicago Tribune*, March 13, 2013.

206 **"I was looking for songs"**: Fred Bronson, *The Billboard Book of Number 1 Hits* (Billboard, 2003), 324.

207 **"And I'd like to thank God"**: "Watch Helen Reddy Win Best Female Pop Vocal Performance In 1973 | GRAMMY Rewind," YouTube.

208 **"Campaigning would be like"**: Robert Windeler, "I Am Woman," *People*, January 23, 1978.

208 **"I want to talk about the future"**: Helen Reddy, speech at Parliament House, September 18, 2006, YouTube.

210 **"As bad as it may sound"**: Mark Kemp, "Phil Ochs: Song of a Soldier," *DailyKemp*, July 8, 2022.

10: Sonic Shift: When Politics Changed Music

211 **"a leader who will"**: Ronald Reagan, "Official Announcement of His Campaign for President of the United States," November 13, 1979, 4president.org.

211 **"A lot of us who grew up"**: Jim Miller, Pamela Abramson, Peter McAlevey, and Abigail Kuflik, "Brother Can You Spare a Song?," *Newsweek*, October 28, 1985.

212 **"This is it!"**: "Watch the First Two Hours of MTV's Inaugural Broadcast (August 1, 1981)," *Open Culture* website.

213 **"a rating system"**: Mathieu Deflem, "Popular Culture and Social Control: The Moral Panic on Music Labeling," *American Journal of Criminal Justice* 45 (2020): 7.

214 **Senate Hearing on Record Labeling**: C-Span broadcast, September 19, 1985.

214 **"well-known and relatively obscure songs"**: Zach Schonfeld, "Parental Advisory Forever: An Oral History of the PMRC's War on Dirty Lyrics," *Newsweek*, September 19, 2015.

217 **"The sticker almost guaranteed"**: *Heavy: The Story of Metal*, episode 3, directed by Michael John Warren, VH-1, 2006.

218 ***McCollum v. CBS* and *Judas Priest v. Nevada***: Deflem, "Popular Culture and Social Control," 10–11.

219 **"Advocating violence and assault"**: Steve Hochman, "Compton Rappers Versus the Letter of the Law: FBI Claims Song by N.W.A. Advocates Violence on Police," *Los Angeles Times*, October 5, 1989.

220 **declared the song obscene**: Erik Nielson and Andrea L. Dennis, *Rap on Trial: Race, Lyrics, and Guilt in America* (New Press, 2019), 46–47.

220 **"I'm singing in the first person"**: Matthew McKinnon, "Hang the MC. Blaming hip hop for violence: a four-part series," *CBC News*, February 7, 2006.

220 **"Ice-T was a terrific artist"**: Robert Hilburn and Chuck Philips, "Quotations from Chairman Mo," *Los Angeles Times*, December 11, 1994.

220 **"sanitized" version**: Deflem, "Popular Culture and Social Control," 11.

221 **"They sang some songs"**: Steve Hochman, "Two Members of 2 Live Crew Arrested After X-Rated Show," *Los Angeles Times*, June 11, 1990.

221 **"patently offensive"**: Quoted in Deflem, "Popular Culture and Social Control," 12.

221 **"I was fighting"**: Quoted in "Luke Skyywalker Goes to the Supreme Court," directed by Jim Fitzgerald, part 1 of *The Complete History of Rap*, VH-1, 2016.

221 **"determine relevant community standards"**: Deflem, "Popular Culture and Social Control," 12.

222 **"It wasn't too heavy"**: Elizabeth Blair, "'Rapper's Delight': The One-Take Hit," *Morning Edition*, NPR, December 29, 2000.

222 **"These people from the PMRC"**: Quoted in "Luke Skyywalker Goes to the Supreme Court."

224 **"extremely unlikely"**: *Acuff–Rose Music Inc. v. Campbell*, 972 F.2d 1429 (6th Cir., August 17, 1992).

225 **"When they issued"**: Quoted in "Luke Skyywalker Goes to the Supreme Court."

226 **"'Thou shalt not steal'"**: *Grand Upright Music Ltd. v. Warner Brothers Records, Inc.*, 780 F. Supp. 182; LEXIS 18276 S.D.N.Y. 16 (December 17, 1991).

227 **"had the last laugh"**: Oliver Wang, "20 Years Ago Biz Markie Got the Last Laugh," *The Record*, NPR, May 6, 2013.

227 **"Public Enemy's music"**: Claire E. A. McLeish, "Hip-hop sampling aesthetics and the legacy of *Grand Upright v. Warner*," *Popular Music* 42, no. 1 (2023): 79.

227 **"the fundamental element"**: Justin Williams, *Rhymin' and Stealin': Musical Borrowing in Hip Hop* (University of Michigan Press, 2013), 1.

227 **"combine without erasing . . . disparate voices"**: Josh Kun and J. Period, "The Art of the Crossfade," November 2013, YouTube.

228 **"in the midst of a moral panic"**: McLeish, "Hip-hop sampling aesthetics," 103.

228 **Lyrics began to be introduced as evidence**: Taifha Natalee Alexander, "Hip-hop on trial: When can a rapper's lyrics be used as evidence in a criminal case?," *The Conversation*, September 27, 2023.

229 **hundreds of criminal cases**: Nielson and Dennis, *Rap on Trial*.

229 **"unless prosecutors can illustrate"**: Alexander, "Hip-hop on trial."

229 **"this difference in treatment"**: Alexander, "Hip-hop on trial."

229 **"mainstream writers"**: Amy Binder, "Constructing Racial Rhetoric: Media Depictions of Harm in Heavy Metal and Rap Music," *American Sociological Review* 58, no. 6 (December 1993): 753–67.
229 **"the dangers" that "black youths"**: Nielson and Dennis, *Rap on Trial*, 91.
230 **"the information superhighway"**: "President Clinton Signs the Telecommunications Act of 1996," February 8, 1996, National Archives.
231 **"even rural and low-income"**: "President Clinton Signs the Telecommunications Act of 1996."
231 **"Consumers across the country"**: Cecilia Kang, "Appeals Court Strikes Down Net Neutrality," *New York Times*, January 3, 2025, B1.

11: Under African Skies

233 **"the arc"**: Martin Luther King Jr., "Remaining Awake Through a Great Revolution," speech given at the National Cathedral, Washington DC, March 31, 1968.
233 **"On this day"**: "11 February 1990: Nelson Mandela's First Speech After Being Released From 27 Years in Prison," Nelson Mandela Foundation.
234 **The purpose of his travel was twofold**: Dolores Handy, "Why Nelson Mandela Came to Boston in 1990," WBUR, December 6, 2013.
235 **"prevent all cultural, academic"**: UN Resolution 35/206, December 16, 1980.
235 **"By the end of the summer"**: Stephen Holden, "Paul Simon Brings Home the Music of Black South Africa," *New York Times*, August 24, 1986, section 2, 1.
235 **"almost mystical affection"**: Paul Simon, "Remembering Days of Miracle and Wonder," *New York Times*, December 14, 2013, C1.
235 **"It sounded like"**: David Fricke, "Paul Simon: African Odyssey," *Rolling Stone*, October 23, 1986.
235 **"I went on a search"**: Holden, "Paul Simon Brings Home."
236 **"a package ... wanted to record"**: *Graceland: 25th Anniversary Edition*, commemorative book (Sony Music Entertainment, 2012), 12.
237 **"It is tempting"**: Jim Miller, Pamela Abramson, Peter McAlevey, and Abigail Kuflik, "Brother Can You Spare a Song?," *Newsweek*, October 28, 1985.
237 **"Just make sure ... reasons for his trip"**: Robert Hilburn, *Paul Simon: The Life* (Simon and Schuster, 2018), 253.
238 **"No. I just needed"**: Charles M. Young, "Paul Simon—the Soweto factor," *Sunday Times* (UK), August 24, 1986.
238 **"It was definitely a risk"**: Hilburn, *Paul Simon*, 254.
238 **"They decided that my coming"**: Holden, "Paul Simon Brings Home."

238 "It was very exciting... build around that": *Graceland: 25th Anniversary Edition*, 15–16.
239 "We worked improvisationally": Holden, "Paul Simon Brings Home."
239 "It was fun": *Graceland: 25th Anniversary Edition*, 19.
239 "Paul was a godsend": Mark Beaumont, "Graceland at 35: How Paul Simon recorded a masterpiece in apartheid South Africa," *Independent* (UK), August 24, 2021.
239 "We were functioning": Beaumont, "Graceland at 35."
239 "They couldn't use public transportation": Fricke, "Paul Simon: African Odyssey."
240 "The struggle made me": Beaumont, "Graceland at 35."
240 "I didn't really know": *Graceland: 25th Anniversary Edition*, 27.
240 "Shabalala was warm": Hilburn, *Paul Simon*, 256.
240 "When I got the call": *Graceland: 25th Anniversary Edition*, 27.
240 "Joseph is a very spiritual person": Hilburn, *Paul Simon*, 256.
240 "That was my first time": *Graceland: 25th Anniversary Edition*, 27.
240 "traffics in world politics": Larry McShane, "Mixing Rock 'n' Roll With Politics," Associated Press, November 12, 1985.
241 "the political cartoonist of rock 'n' roll": McShane, "Mixing Rock 'n' Roll With Politics."
241 "Rock and Roll Ambassador": Danny Schechter, "Human Rights: Musician Steven Van Zandt Sees Rock as a 'Political Force,'" Inter Press Service, February 26, 1985.
241 "Just by being there": Steven Van Zandt, *Unrequited Infatuations* (New York: Hachette, 2021), 173.
241 "had wanted to play": Frank Spotnitz, "Musicians Unite Against Apartheid," United Press International, October 25, 1985.
241 "I didn't feel particularly educated": Schechter, "Human Rights."
241 "I met with everyone": Van Zandt, *Unrequited Infatuations*, 173.
241 "a Las Vegas gambling oasis": Schechter, "Human Rights."
242 to "fool everybody": Van Zandt, *Unrequited Infatuations*, 176.
242 "little more than a bullshit": Van Zandt, *Unrequited Infatuations*, 172.
242 "many people... trying to help": "Excerpts from an Interview with Walter Cronkite of CBS News," March 3, 1981, Reagan Presidential Library.
242 "use the cultural boycott": Van Zandt, *Unrequited Infatuations*, 179.
242 "Everyone I met": Schechter, "Human Rights."
242 "'We Are The World' against apartheid": "Rock Stars Slam Apartheid in Song," *Toronto Star*, October 4, 1985.
242 "Our song targets": Dave Marsh, *Sun City By Artists United Against*

Apartheid. *The Struggle for Freedom in South Africa. The Making of the Record* (Penguin, 1985), 10.

243 **"We set out to popularise"**: Yolanda Groenwald, "Brother with Perfect Timing," *Mail & Guardian* (Zambia), January 14, 1994.

243 **"There were no [finished] songs"**: Hilburn, *Paul Simon*, 256–57.

244 **"a country rockabilly shuffle"**: Hilburn, *Paul Simon*, 258.

244 **"The guitar lines"**: Hilburn, *Paul Simon*, 262.

244 **"I realized that the guitar"**: *Graceland: 25th Anniversary Edition*, 24.

244 **"South African music"**: Hilburn, *Paul Simon*, 262.

245 **pennywhistle and bass "are combined"**: Louise Meintjes, "Paul Simon's *Graceland*, South Africa, and the Mediation of Musical Meaning," *Ethnomusicology* 34, no. 1 (Winter 1990): 44.

245 **"We are aware of the role"**: "Paul Simon Teams Up with Stimela," *Pace*, June 1985, 87.

245 **"Eventually, I understood"**: Hilburn, *Paul Simon*, 259.

246 **"One night, I was falling"**: Fricke, "Paul Simon: African Odyssey."

246 **"With 'Homeless,'"**: Fricke, "Paul Simon: African Odyssey."

246 **"The process began"**: *Graceland: 25th Anniversary Edition*, 48.

247 **"He greeted us ... everything that we do"**: *Graceland: 25th Anniversary Edition*, 27–28.

247 **"showed me ... in this style"**: *Graceland: 25th Anniversary Edition*, 48–49.

247 **"All around the world"**: Jon Pareles, "'Sun City' Gets a Range of Authority," *New York Times*, October 21, 1985, C17.

248 **"showcases an overwhelming array"**: "Singles," *Billboard*, October 26, 1985, 79.

248 **a complete album went on sale**: Artists United Against Apartheid, *Sun City*, Manhattan/Capitol Records, 1985.

249 **Best Single of the Year**: Robert Christgau, "Pazz and Jop Critics Poll," *Village Voice*, February 16, 1986.

249 **a little over $600,000**: Africa Fund records, Sun City: correspondence and financial records, 1980–85, 744; Amistad Research Center, box 162, folder 6.

249 **"to get people to be aware"**: Joan Mower, "Musicians Come To Capitol Hill To Promote Anti-Apartheid Album," Associated Press, December 5, 1985.

250 **"They loved it"**: *Graceland: 25th Anniversary Edition*, 28.

250 **"It wasn't like anything"**: Hilburn, *Paul Simon*, 272.

250 **"Nobody had heard"**: *Graceland: 25th Anniversary Edition*, 28.

250 "We were excited": *Graceland: 25th Anniversary Edition*, 28, 31.
250 "He played the drums": *Graceland: 25th Anniversary Edition*, 31.
250 "I wanted to say": Beaumont, "*Graceland* at 35."
250 "This album rocks and rolls": Hilburn, *Paul Simon*, 276.
251 "feeling vulnerable": Young, "Paul Simon—the Soweto factor," 42.
251 "The UN calls for": Young, "Paul Simon—the Soweto factor," 42.
251 "If you're going into": Beaumont, "*Graceland* at 35."
251 "Who does [Simon] think": Robin Deneslow, "Paul Simon's *Graceland*: The Acclaim and the Outrage," *Guardian*, April 19, 2012.
251 "I don't feel as an artist": Deneslow, "Paul Simon's *Graceland*."
252 "We used Paul . . . doing good": Beaumont, "*Graceland* at 35."
253 "was overcome by the music": *Under African Skies*, film documentary, directed by Joe Berlinger, Radical Media, 2012.
253 "There was a lot of talk": *Graceland: 25th Anniversary Edition*, 31.
253 "Part of the controversy": William K. Knoedelseder Jr., "The Misguided Controversy over *Graceland*," *Washington Post*, January 18, 1987.
254 "South African music": Deneslow, "Paul Simon's *Graceland*."
254 "on the surface": Beaumont, "*Graceland* at 35."
255 "blacks and whites on the field": *Graceland: 25th Anniversary Edition*, 36.
255 "They live along with": Album of the Year presentation at the 1987 Grammy Awards, YouTube.
255 "the physical presence": *Graceland: 25th Anniversary Edition*, 36.
256 "South Africa's cultural ambassadors": "Adam Boulton Meets Ladysmith Black Mambazo," *Sky News*, 1999.
256 "about business . . . our country!": Christopher S. Wren, "Paul Simon Begins South Africa Concerts," *New York Times*, January 13, 1992, C11.
256 "Few songwriters have had": Library of Congress, "Paul Simon To Be Awarded First Annual Gershwin Prize for Popular Song by Library of Congress," press release, July 2, 2007.

12: Who Tells Our Story?

259 "An Evening of Poetry": Jesse Lee, "Poetry, Music and Spoken Word," White House press release, May 12, 2009.
259 "the vibrancy of the Latino community": Lin-Manuel Miranda and Jeremy McCarter, *Hamilton: The Revolution* (Grand Central, 2016), 14.
259 "I'm thrilled the White House called": "Lin-Manuel Miranda Performs at the White House Poetry Jam," May 12, 2009, YouTube.
261 "Tribute to a Puerto Rican–American": *Congressional Record - Exten-*

sions of Remarks. vol. 157, no. 101 (July 8, 2011), E1276 (statement by Representative Charles Rangel).

262 **"rap musical"**: Michael Sokolove, "The C.E.O. of 'Hamilton' Inc.," *New York Times Magazine*, April 10, 2016, 34.

262 **"What Lin is doing"**: Cheryl L. Keyes, "Long Live Hip-Hop: *Hamilton* and the Death (and Rebirth) of Hip-Hop," in *Dueling Grounds: Revolution and Revelation in the Musical* Hamilton, edited by Mary Jo Lodge and Paul R. Laird (Oxford University Press, 2021): 195.

262 **"I always imagined George Washington"**: Quoted in Frank DiGiacomo, "'Hamilton's' Lin-Manuel Miranda on Finding Originality, Racial Politics (and Why Trump Should See His Show)," *Hollywood Reporter*, August 12, 2015.

263 **"wrote and rewrote"**: Miranda and McCarter, *Hamilton*, 21.

263 **"get serious about developing"**: Miranda and McCarter, *Hamilton*, 21.

263 **"a hip-hop song cycle"**: Andrew Gans, "American Songbook Season Kicks Off Jan. 11 with Lin-Manuel Miranda's *The Hamilton Mixtape*," *Playbill*, January 11, 2012.

263 **"friends and collaborators"**: Miranda and McCarter, *Hamilton*, 46.

263 **"the DNA of my brain"**: Miranda and McCarter, *Hamilton*, 46.

263 **"A future Broadway musical?"**: Stephen Holden, "Putting the Hip-Hop in History as Founding Fathers Rap," *New York Times*, January 13, 2012, C4.

264 **"became crystal clear"**: Miranda and McCarter, *Hamilton*, 46.

264 **"A bunch of people"**: Miranda and McCarter, *Hamilton*, 14.

265 **"I wanted the sound of a door"**: Miranda and McCarter, *Hamilton*, 16.

265 **"to ground his choreography"**: Larry Stemple, *Showtime: A History of the Broadway Musical Theater* (W. W. Norton, 2010), 587.

265 **"There are very few times"**: Dustyn Martincich, "Revolutionary Movement: 'Non-Stop' Ensemble Choreography at Work," in *Dueling Grounds*, 150.

266 **"Period from the neck down"**: Miranda and McCarter, *Hamilton*, 113.

266 **"to keep the world"**: Ella Hawkins, "Telling the Story of *Hamilton* in the Twenty-First Century: The Layering of Historical and Modern Aesthetics Through Costume Design," in *Dueling Grounds*, 168.

266 **"Lin-Manuel Miranda forges"**: Ben Brantley, "Lin-Manuel Miranda Forges Democracy Through Rap," *New York Times*, February 18, 2015.

266 **"History as you've never"**: Peter Marks, "History as You Have Never Seen It Before," *Washington Post*, February 17, 2015.

266 **"The conflict between independence"**: Jesse Green, "Lin-Manuel Miranda's *Hamilton* Is Worth Way More Than $10," *Vulture*, February 17, 2015.

266 **"the hottest ticket in New York"**: Stephanie Cohen, "'Hamilton' Is the Hottest Ticket in New York," *Wall Street Journal*, February 6, 2015.

266 **"This is a story about America"**: Edward Delman, "How Lin-Manuel Miranda Shapes History," *The Atlantic*, September 29, 2015.

266 **"Jefferson and Jackson"**: Jonathan Martin, "Democrats Sever Ties to Founders of Party," *New York Times*, August 12, 2015, A12.

267 **"he's an immigrant"**: Alana Semuels, "How *Hamilton* Recasts Thomas Jefferson as a Villain," *The Atlantic*, August 19, 2015.

267 **"a well-dressed dandy...women's rights"**: Semuels, "How *Hamilton* Recasts Thomas Jefferson."

267 **"Donald Trump has become"**: Patrick Healy, "Political Theater vs. Political Theatrics," *New York Times*, August 2, 2015, SR7.

267 **"This is no working-class hero"**: Mark Hensch, "*Hamilton* creator: Trump no 'working-class hero,'" *The Hill*, Blog Briefing Room, August 14, 2015.

267 **"attracted breathless reviews"**: Quoted in DiGiacomo, "'Hamilton's' Lin-Manuel Miranda."

269 **"*Hamilton: An American Musical* has cut"**: Alison L. LaCroix, "The Rooms Where It Happened," *New Rambler*, May 23, 2016.

269 **"It's an incredible feat"**: Nick Romano, "Hamilton: Hillary Clinton fundraiser performance announced for July 12," *Entertainment Weekly*, June 25, 2016.

269 **"45th president of the United States"**: CNN, "Hillary Clinton's full DNC speech (Entire speech)," YouTube.

270 **"Though we may not live"**: James Poniewozik, "Her Shot: Hillary Clinton Shares a Vision of America Out of *Hamilton*," *New York Times*, July 29, 2016.

270 **"It was a soul-crushing day"**: Sophie Gilbert, "Hamilton's Peaceful Protest," *The Atlantic*, June 29, 2017.

270 **"As we prepare"**: "'One Last Time' – Hamilton At The White House #ObamaLegacy," YouTube.

271 **"One last time," goes the final chorus**: Miranda and McCarter, *Hamilton*, 210–11.

271 **"Thank you for teaching me"**: "Jonathan Groff Takes on Serial Killers in *Mindhunter*," *The Last Magazine*, reproduced at JGroffDaily.tumblr.

272 **"You know, we have a guest"**: Gilbert, "Hamilton's Peaceful Protest."

272 **"The cast of *Hamilton* was very rude"**: Gilbert, "Hamilton's Peaceful Protest."

272 **"The treatment of Vice President-elect"**: Carl Lamarre, "Judge Jeanine Pirro Slams 'Hamilton' Cast Following Mike Pence Remarks: 'What Happened in That Theater Was Reverse Racism,'" *Billboard*, November 21, 2016.

273 **"The most eloquent case"**: Charles McNulty, "Let the power of 'Hamilton' speak louder than a Twitter feud," *Los Angeles Times*, November 20, 2016.

274 **"lyrics and visuals powerfully describe"**: Priscilla Frank, "Immigrants, They Get the Job Done in Amazing New 'Hamilton Mixtape' Video," *Huffington Post*, June 28, 2017.

274 **"dominated streaming platforms"**: Alison Durkee, "*Hamilton* Boosts A Struggling Disney As Broadcast Dominated Streaming Platforms In July," *Forbes*, August 10, 2020.

274 **"far bigger than anything"**: Kevin Tran, "*Hamilton* Far Bigger than Anything on Netflix in July, Audience Data Reveals," *Variety*, August 10, 2020.

274 **"laid bare the racism"**: Mary Jo Lodge and Paul R. Baird, "Introduction: Revolution and Liminality in the Musical *Hamilton*," in *Dueling Grounds*, 8–9.

275 **"We spoke out"**: Quoted from Lexy Perez, "Lin-Manuel Miranda and 'Hamilton' Producer Apologize for Silence on Protests," *Hollywood Reporter*, May 31, 2020.

275 **"made these dead white guys"**: "60 Minutes Presents: A Front Row Seat," CBS, February 5, 2017.

275 **"If my black life matters"**: Leslie Odom Jr. in conversation with Dax Shepard, *Armchair Expert* podcast, August 3, 2020.

276 **"A new year brings hope"**: Harper Lambert, "Lin-Manuel Miranda Helps Congress Mark Jan. 6 Anniversary with Speech, 'Hamilton' Performance," *The Wrap*, January 6, 2022.

276 **"the *Hamilton* theory"**: Vinson Cunningham, "The Kamala Show," *New Yorker*, August 26, 2024.

276 **"Puerto Ricans' Votes"**: Ricky Martin, Rita Moreno, and Lin-Manuel Miranda, "Puerto Ricans' Votes Won't Be a Reaction to Racist Jokes," *New York Times*, November 1, 2024, A22.

277 **"The dominant purpose"**: Miranda and McCarter, *Hamilton*, 11.

Credits

ALEXANDER HAMILTON
Words and Music by LIN-MANUEL MIRANDA
© 2015 5000 BROADWAY MUSIC (ASCAP)
All Rights Administered by WC MUSIC CORP.
All Rights Reserved
Used by Permission of ALFRED MUSIC

BLOWIN' IN THE WIND
Words and Music by Bob Dylan
Copyright © 1962 UNIVERSAL TUNES
Copyright Renewed
All Rights Reserved Used by Permission
Reprinted by Permission of Hal Leonard LLC

I AM WOMAN
Words by Helen Reddy
Music by Ray Burton
Copyright © 1971 IRVING MUSIC, INC. and BUGGERLUGS
    MUSIC CO.
Copyright Renewed
All Rights Administered by IRVING MUSIC, INC.
All Rights Reserved Used by Permission
Reprinted by Permission of Hal Leonard LLC

JET SONG from *West Side Story*
Composed by Leonard Bernstein
Text by Stephen Sondheim

© 1956, 1957, 1958, 1959 Amberson Holdings LLC and Stephen Sondheim.
Copyright Renewed.
Leonard Bernstein Music Publishing Company LLC, publisher.
Boosey & Hawkes, agent for rental.
Reproduced by permission of Boosey & Hawkes

MISSISSIPPI GODDAM
Words and Music by NINA SIMONE
© 1964 (Renewed) WC MUSIC CORP.
All Rights Reserved
Used by Permission of ALFRED MUSIC

ONE LAST TIME
Words and Music by LIN-MANUEL MIRANDA
© 2015 5000 BROADWAY MUSIC (ASCAP)
All Rights Administered by WC MUSIC CORP.
All Rights Reserved
Used by Permission of ALFRED MUSIC

STRANGE FRUIT
Words and Music by Lewis Allan
Copyright © 1939 (Renewed) by Music Sales Corporation
All Rights outside the United States Controlled by Edward B. Marks Music Company
International Copyright Secured All Rights Reserved
Used by Permission
Reprinted by Permission of Hal Leonard LLC

WHAT'S GOING ON
by Alfred Cleveland, Marvin Gaye, and Renaldo Benson.
© 1971 FCG Music, Jobete Music Co Inc, MGIII Music, NMG Music, and Stone Agate Music.
All rights administered by Sony Music Publishing (US) LLC, 1005 17th Avenue South, Suite 800, Nashville, TN, 37212.

All rights reserved. Used by permission.
Territory: United States

WHAT'S GOING ON
by Alfred Cleveland, Marvin Gaye, and Renaldo Benson.
© 1971 Jobete Music Co Inc and Stone Agate Music.
All rights administered by Sony Music Publishing (US) LLC, 1005 17th Avenue South, Suite 800, Nashville, TN, 37212.
All rights reserved. Used by permission.
Territory: World excluding United States

Index

A&M Studios, Los Angeles, 237
Abbey Road Studios, London, 246–47
Abie's Irish Rose (A. Nichols), 167
Abrams, Charles, 169
Academy Awards (Oscars), 89, 109, 122, 181, 192
Acuff-Rose Music, Inc., 222–26
"Adams and Liberty" (campaign song), 5, 7
Adams, John (composer), 48–49. *See also On the Transmigration of Souls*
Adams, John (politician), 5, 7
Adams, Sherman, 174
Afghanistan, 152, 154
Africa
　American music in, 142–46
　Louis Armstrong on tour in, 149–50, 153–54
　and the origins of jazz, 157–58
　See also Republic of the Congo; Ethiopia; Ghana; Liberia; Senegal; South Africa; Sudan; USA for Africa; Zimbabwe
Africa Fund, 248
African National Congress (ANC), 234–35, 237–43, 248, 251–53, 256
Afrikaner National Party (ANP), 234–35, 241–42
Agnew, Spiro, 202
Ahlerich, Milt, 219–20
Aida (Verdi), 62
Alexander, Taifha Natalee, 229

Algar, James, 87
"All Around the World or The Myth of Fingerprints" (Simon), 244
"All For You, Louis, All For You!" (E. T. Mensa), 149
"All the Things You Are" (Kern), 152
Allan, Anne. *See* Meeropol, Anne
Allan, Lewis. *See* Meeropol, Abel
"Almost Like Praying" (Miranda), 275
"Alone Again" (Biz Markie), 225–27
"Alone Again (Naturally)" (O'Sullivan), 225–27
Ambassador Billiard Parlor, NYC, 53
"America the Beautiful" (Bates), 14
"America" (contrafactum). *See* "My Country Tis of Thee"
"America" (Bernstein), 176
American Academy of Arts and Letters, 137
American Civil Liberties Union (ACLU), 219
American Committee on Africa, 248
American culture
　the American dream, 175, 184
　the American experiment, 266, 276
　counterculture, 201–2
　cultural appropriation, 252
　democracy, 40–44, 111, 140, 180–81, 215, 250–51

　diversity, 147, 158–59, 230, 248, 264, 230, 272
　Fourth of July celebrations, 20–21, 29
　free speech, 8–9, 213, 215–16, 218, 229
　gatekeepers of, 45–46, 210
　"hippies," 201–2
　the landscape of America, 73–93
　"melting pot," 54, 69, 71, 228
　New England culture, 28–29, 40, 46, 97
　See also American music
American Federation of Teachers, 90
American in Paris, An (G. Gershwin), 83
American Legion, 137
American music, xi–xiv, 2, 51–72
　American folk traditions, 120
　American identity and the national anthem, 1–25
　big band music, 149
　blues, 53–54, 59, 64–65, 68, 105, 108, 109, 189, 196
　conservatories and music schools, 44–45, 47, 48
　country music, 215
　heavy metal, 212, 215–20, 229
　hip hop, 218–22, 225–29, 259, 261–66
　klezmer music, 55, 60–61, 64, 71
　ragtime, 19, 29, 55, 56, 64, 72
　rap, 215, 218–30, 248, 261

American music (*continued*)
  Zydeco, 244
  See also jazz; pop music; protest music
American National Theatre and Academy (ANTA), 141–42, 174
American Society of Composers, Authors, and Publishers (ASCAP), 73
"American Songbook" Lincoln Center series, 263–64
Amsterdam News, 109
Anacreontic Society, 4–5
Anderson, Marian, 109–10, 192
Antheil, George, 60
Anti-Apartheid Act of 1986, 252
anti-Catholic nativism, 9
anti-lynching legislation, 66, 95–100, 110–11, 107
Antiquities Act of 1906, 79–80
anti-Semitism, 98, 162–63
Appalachian Spring (Copland), 118, 121–38
  American presidents and, 137–38
  composition of, 121–26
  politicization and Cold War anxiety, 131–37
  Pulitzer Prize in Music, 129–30
  reception of, 126–37
Arizona, 75–79, 82, 87, 126
Armstrong, Louis, 144–51, 153–54. *See also The Real Ambassadors*
Armstrong, William W., 35
Army–McCarthy hearings, 136–37
arrangements, 5, 15, 23, 60, 74, 76, 84, 104, 147, 224, 241
Arranging Gershwin (Bañagale), 70
Art Commentary on Lynching (exhibition), 101–2
Artists Against Apartheid (AAA), 243
Artists United Against Apartheid (AUAA), 243, 249
As Nasty As They Wanna Be (2 Live Crew), 220–22, 224
Asante, Okeyama, 255

Asia, American music in, 142–46, 148, 152–53, 156
Astaire, Fred, 63
Atlanta Daily World (newspaper), 109
Atlanta, GA, 249
Atlantic Records, 235
Atlantic, The (magazine), 267
Atlee, E. A., 9
Audubon Society, 87
Australia, 205–6
Avakian, George, 149
Azanian People's Organization, 256

Baez, Joan, 192, 195–96, 202
Baker, Anita, 24
Baker, Jim, 213
Baker, Josephine, 57
Baker, Susan, 213, 214, 216
Baldwin, James, 98
"Ballad of Ozie Powell" (Copland), 128
ballads, 56, 141–42, 236, 261, 262, 264
"Ballet for Martha." *See Appalachian Spring* (Copland)
ballets, 118, 121–38, 163, 172
Baltimore Afro-American (newspaper), 109
Baltimore, MD, 2–4, 6–7, 18–19
Bañagale, Ryan, 70
Band Aid (supergroup), 236–37
Badung Conference of 1955, 143–44
Bangladesh, 154
Bantustans (tribal homelands) of South Africa, 234, 241
Baraka, Amiri, 17
Barbary Coast War, 5
Barris, Kenya, 113
Barry, David W., 176
Baryshnikov, Mikhail, 138
Basie, William "Count," 145, 158
Bates, Katharine Lee, 14, 14
Batiste, Jon, 24
"Battle Cry of Freedom, The" (Root), 38
BBC, 240
bebop, 72, 146, 171, 173
Bechet, Sidney, 110

Belafonte, Harry, 192, 237–38, 255
Belair, Felix, Jr., 144–45
Bellamy, Francis, 13. *See also* Pledge of Allegiance
Bellamy salute, 13–14
Benson, Renaldo "Obie," 203. *See also* "What's Going On"
Benton, Thomas Hart, 101
Bentsen, Lloyd, 220
Berg, Heidi, 235
Bernstein, Leonard, 27, 118, 162–76, 179, 180, 183–85
  accused of communism, 118, 165–66
  Conch Town, 173
  Fancy Free, 63
  revival of Gershwin's *Rhapsody in Blue*, 70–72
  See also West Side Story
Beyoncé, 24, 277
Biden, Joseph, 95, 276
big band music, 149
Big Pun, 262, 263
Bigard, Barney, 64–65, 68
Billboard (magazine), 212, 249
Billboard Hot 100, 204, 207
Billington, James H., 256–57
Billy the Kid (Copland), 120
Binder, Amy, 229
Biz Markie, 222–28
Bizet, Georges, 166
"Black and Blue" (Waller), 150
Black History pageants, 62, 110
Black Lives Matter, 24, 113–14, 274–75
"Black March" (C. Ives), 37–40, 43, 46
Black Power movement, 200–201, 255
"Black Woodstock." *See* Harlem Cultural Festival of 1969
Black, Brown, and Beige (Ellington), 70
Blackboard Jungle (film), 167
blackface, 11, 56–58, 65, 72. *See also* minstrel shows
black-ish (TV series), 113
blacklisting, 112, 118, 166, 169, 199
Blake, Eubie, 18, 57

"blank tape tax." *See* Home Audio Recording Act
Blankenbuehler, Andy, 265
Bliley, Thomas, 229–30
"Blood on the Leaves" (West), 223
"Bloody Sunday" (March 7, 1965), Selma, AL, 187–88
"Blowin' in the Wind" (Dylan), 189–96
Blue Bells of Harlem (Ellington), 65
Blue Monday (G. Gershwin), 57–58, 69
blues, 53–54, 59, 64–65, 68, 105, 108, 109, 189, 196
Blutopia (Ellington), 65
Body Count (heavy metal group), 220
Boggs, Lindy, 157
Bolshoi Ballet, 178
"Bonnie Blue Flag" (H. McCarthy), 10
Bono, from U2, 248
Bono, Sonny, 51
Boothby, Homer, 65–66
Bophuthatswana, South Africa, 241
"Born in the USA" (Springsteen), 277
Boston, MA, 9, 13, 53, 234, 256
  Great National Peace Jubilee of 1869, 13
Boston Common, 37–38, 39, 46
Boston Symphony Orchestra, 141
Botkin, B. A., 81
Boulanger, Nadia, 118–19
Boulez, Pierre, 245
Boy George, 212
"Boy in the Bubble" (Simon), 245–46
Boyd, Frederick S., 20
Boyoyo Boys (group), 236, 238
Brackett, Joseph, 122
Bradley, Tom, 249
Brahms, Johannes, 60
"Brandenburg Gate" (D. Brubeck), 152
Brando, Marlon, 192
Breen, Robert, 142–43

Brewster Methodist Church, NY, 28, 31
Bridge, The (Crane), 123–24, 126–27
Bright Angel Trail in the Grand Canyon, 79, 81
"Bring Him Back Home" (Masekela), 254
Bring in 'da Noise, Bring in 'da Funk (musical), 261
BRIT awards, 251
Britain, 20, 149, 262
  the British Invasion, 265
  English immigrants, 2, 28–29
  "God Save the King," 8, 28
  in the War of 1812, 2–4, 6, 20
Broadside (folk music magazine), 190
Broadway musicals. *See* musicals
Brooks, Harry, 150
Brooks, Henry Anderson, 30
Broward County, FL, 220–21
Brown v. Board of Education (1954), 142
Brown, Hux, 236
Brown, Jerry, 208
Brown, Lawrence, 72
Brownell, Herbert, 151
Brubeck, Dave, 152–54, 159. *See also The Real Ambassadors*
Brubeck, Iola, 152, 153. *See also The Real Ambassadors*
Brunswick (record label), 64
Bryant's Minstrels (blackface minstrel troupe), 11
Buggles (band), 212
Bureau for American Ideals, 22
Burma (now Myanmar), 148, 156
Burr, Aaron, 260, 264, 272, 275
Burton, Ray, 206
Busbey, Fred E., 132–33
Bush, George H. W., 220
Busta Rhymes, 262
Buthelezi, Mangosuthu, 252

Caesar, Irving, 56
Café Society, NYC, 105–8, 111–12

Cain, James M., 166
"Calcutta Blues" (Brubeck), 153
California, 87, 156–58, 182, 203, 208–9, 219, 229
call-and-response, 5, 245
Cambodia, 148
Cameron, James, 97
Camp Unity, Berkshires, MA, 98
Campbell v. Acuff-Rose Music, Inc., 222–26
Campbell, Luther "Luke Skyywalker," 221–26
Canada, 2
Capital Theater Orchestra, 83
capitalism, 99, 119–20, 122, 212
Carawan, Guy, 189
Carmen (Bizet), 166
Carnegie Hall, 55, 60, 70, 112, 149, 197
Carney, Harry, 72
Carr, Thomas, 6–7
Carter, Elliott, 47
Carter, Jimmy, 137–38
Carter, Ron, 248
Carter, Rosalynn, 137
Cash, Johnny, 229
Catholics, 9, 162, 167
CBS, 83–84, 128, 145, 149, 218
celebrities, 54, 192, 267, 277
Central Park in the Dark (C. Ives), 47
"Century of the Common Man" (speech), 121
Ceylon (now Sri Lanka), 152, 154
"Change is Gonna Come, A" (Cooke), 113
Chaplin, Charles, 118
Charles H. Raymond Agency, 34
charts, the. *See* pop music
Cheatham, Kitty, 21
Cherney, Andrei, 266
Chernow, Ron, 260
Chicago World's Fair of 1893, 56
Chopin, Frédéric, 152
Christgau, Robert, 250–51
Chuck D, 227
City, The (documentary), 120
civil rights
  anti-lynching legislation, 66, 95–100, 110–11, 107
  Black Power, 200–201, 255

civil rights (*continued*)
  "Bloody Sunday" (March 7, 1965), Selma, AL, 187–88
  "A Change is Gonna Come" (Cooke), 113
  "Lift Every Voice and Sing" (J. W. Johnson), 14–18, 21, 23–25, 57, 100
  March on Washington for Jobs and Freedom (1963), 192–94, 196
  "Mississippi Goddam" (Simone) 196–200
  segregation of public schools, 15, 142, 150–51
  "We Shall Overcome" (freedom song), 187–89, 197
  See also "Strange Fruit" (Meeropol)
Civil Rights Act of 1964, 188
Civil War, 19, 29–30, 37–40, 46, 125, 127
Civilian Conservation Corps (CCC), 86, 176
classical music, 57, 61, 64, 66, 110, 118, 141–44, 196, 204. *See also* conservatories and music schools; *specific titles, composers, and performers*
Clay, Henry, 38
Clear Channel Communications. *See* iHeartMedia
Clef Club Orchestra, 62
Clinkscales, Marietta, 61
Clinton, Bill, 51, 138, 229–31
Clinton, Hillary, 269–70
Clyburn, James E., 24–25
Coachella music festival, 24
Coe, Richard L., 175
Cohen, Harvey G., 154
Cohn, Roy, 134–36
Cold War, 131–32, 165, 242
  Badung Conference of 1955, 143–44
  jazz in the war against communism, 139–59
  the Red Scare at home, 112–13, 117–18, 133–37, 139, 141, 144, 165–66, 194
  Vietnam War, 156, 189, 203–4
  See also communism

Cole, Bob, 62
Coleridge-Taylor, Samuel, 62
College Art Association, 101
Colorado River, 84, 88
Colorado, 14, 19, 24, 100
Columbia Records, 47, 108, 109, 149, 153
Columbia University, 47–48
Comden, Betty, 170
comic books, 168, 173, 181, 214
comics and comedians, 206, 277
Comics Code Authority (CCA), 168, 214
commercialization
  of American landscapes, 79
  of hip hop, 218, 221–22, 224
  the "Latin Craze," 171
  of patriotism, 12
  promotion of an "American sound," 54, 56
  of protest music, 189
  royalties, 60, 108, 215, 248
  streaming services, 231, 274
  See also radio
Committee on Public Information, 20
Commodore Records, 108
Common (rapper), 262
Commoner, Barry, 90
communism
  alternatives to, 122, 143–44
  anthems, 119–20, 136
  anti-lynching movement, 101–2
  "fellow travelers," 117, 165
  House Un-American Activities Committee (HUAC), 112–13, 117, 133, 165–66, 194
  jazz in the war against, 139–59
  McCarthyism, 117–18, 134–37, 139, 141, 144
  in New York public schools, 98–99, 111–13
  Pierre Degeyter Club, 119–20
  protests of the 1960s, 194
  in South Africa, 242
  West Side Story and Cold War anxieties, 165–66, 179, 180–81, 194, 242
  See also Cold War

Communist Party of the United States of America (CPUSA), 45–46, 98–99, 105–6, 117–20, 126, 130–37
Composers' Collective, 119–20
composition
  arrangement, 5, 15, 23, 60, 74, 76, 84, 104, 147, 224, 241
  ballads, 56, 141–42, 236, 261, 262, 264
  contrafacta, 2–3, 5, 8, 28
  experimentation and, 29, 32–35, 58–60, 63–65, 74, 168, 266, 276
  as response, 64, 223
  as solitary art, 29
  traditional study and, 32–33, 118–20
  See also dance
Conch Town (Bernstein), 172
Concord Sonata (C. Ives), 47
Confederate States of America (CSA), 10–12, 38, 63
Congress, xiii–xiv
  declaring a national anthem, 1–25
  January 6 attack on the US Capitol, 276
  legislation of jazz, 157–59
  President's Special International Program, 148
  Senate Hearing on Record Labeling, 213–17, 237
Congressional Record, 261
Conover, Willis, 141–42
conservation, of jazz, 157–59
conservation, of the Grand Canyon, 74, 86–89, 92
conservatories and music schools, 44–45, 47, 48
Constitution of the United States, 41, 43–44, 99, 142, 214, 218, 260, 273.
  First Amendment to the US Constitution, 8–9, 213, 215–16, 218, 229
  Seventeenth Amendment to the US Constitution, 41
  Nineteenth Amendment to the US Constitution, 43
  See also Congress; legislation

contrafacta, 2–3, 5, 8, 28
Conyers, John, Jr., 156–57, 158
Cook, Will Marion, 61
Cooke, Sam, 113
Coolidge, Elizabeth Sprague, 121, 126
Coons, Philip, 180–81
Copland, Aaron, 60, 117–21
   accused of communism, 118–19, 131–37
   Appalachian Spring, 118, 121–38
   Billy the Kid, 120
   early life and career, 119–21
   El Salón México, 120, 171–72
   enter Martha Graham, 121–28
   Fanfare for the Common Man, 118, 121, 138
   Lincoln Portrait, 118, 120, 132, 137
   Music for the Theatre, 119
   in New York, 119
   in Paris, 118–19
   Piano Concerto, 119
   Presidential Medal of Freedom, 137
   Rodeo, 118, 120–21
copyright, 15, 18, 21, 23, 51–53, 189
   Copyright Act of 1976, 52, 223–24
   derivative works, 223–24
   fair use, 221–26
   master licenses/recordings, 223–26
   master vs. mechanical licenses, 223–24
   open copyright status, 23
   parody, 222–26
   public domain, 23, 52, 72, 214
   sampling, 222, 223–29, 236, 248
   Sonny Bono Copyright Term Extension Act of 1998, 51–53
CORE (Congress of Racial Equality), 155
Costigan, Edward, 100–101
Cotton Club, NYC, 63, 64
Counterattack (journal), 118
country music, 215

cover songs, 224
Covid-19 pandemic, 24, 274
Cowell, Henry, 47
Crane, Hart, 123–24, 126–27
Cranston, Alan, 157
Crawford, Traverse, 104
Creole Rhapsody (Ellington), 64–65, 68, 119
Crisis, The (newspaper), 99, 101, 104, 125
Cronkite, Walter, 242
Cuba, 171–72, 194
Cuban Love Song, The (film), 171
Cuban Overture (G. Gershwin), 171
Cullen, Countee, 98, 99–100
Cultural and Scientific Conference for World Peace, 131
cultural diplomacy, 139–45
   Badung Conference of 1955, 143–44
   boycott of South Africa, 234–35, 237, 241–43, 248, 251–57
   Cultural Presentations Program, 140–41, 144–45
   exchanges with the Soviets, 178–79
   Jazz Ambassadors program, 145–56, 179
   Porgy and Bess on tour, 142–43
   Voice of America (VOA), 141–42
Cunningham, Evelyn, 109
Cunningham, Vinson, 276
Curtis Institute of Music, Philadelphia, 196
Curtis, Jamie Lee, 209
Curtis, Tony, 192

D'Amato, Al, 220
Dammers, Jerry, 243, 251, 252, 253
dance, 17, 30, 62, 66, 67, 68, 69, 111, 122, 140, 143, 177, 222, 247
   ballet, 118, 121–38, 163, 172
   dance band, 20, 75, 76
   in *Hamilton*, 265
   isicatimiya dance, 250

   Tin Pan Alley dance tunes, 56–58
   in *West Side Story*, 162–63, 170–72, 184
"Dance, The" (poem by Crane), 123.
Danforth, John, 214
Daniels, Ron, xi–xii
"Darling Nikki" (Prince), 212–13
Darnton, Charles, 58
Dave (film), 220
Dávila, Arlene, 182
Davis, Jefferson, inauguration of, 11
Davis, Miles, 155, 158, 248
Davis, Sammy, Jr., 192
De La Beckwith, Byron, Jr., 192
Dean, James, 167
Decatur, Stephen, Jr., 5
Dee Snider, 215, 216, 217
"Defence of Fort M'Henry, The" (Key), 4, 6–7. *See also* "Star Spangled Banner"
Deferred Action for Childhood Arrivals (DACA) program, 275
Degeyter, Pierre, 119–20
Deming, Edward Andrews, 122, 125, 122
democracy, 40–44, 111, 140, 180–81, 215, 250–51
Democratic Party, 44, 100–101, 133, 134, 201, 266, 276, 225
Denver, John, 215–16
deregulation, 212, 229–31, 242
derivative works, 223–24
deSaulles, Charles, 33
Desmond, Paul, 152
DeSylva, B. G. "Buddy," 53, 56
"Diamonds on the Soles of Her Shoes" (Simon), 250, 252–53
Dingell, John, 229–30
direct democracy, 40–44
Disney Corporation, 51, 87–93, 274
Disney, Walt, 87, 92, 130
Disneyland, Anaheim, CA, 87
"Dixie" (Emmett), 10–11, 21
Dixon, Brandon Victor, 272, 273

Dixon, Dean, 118
Dixon, George, 178
"Do They Know It's Christmas?" (charity single) 236–37
Domínguez, R., 179–80
Double Indemnity (Cain), 166
Douglass, Frederick, 37–39, 98
Down Argentine Way (film), 171
Drakeo the Ruler, 228
Du Bois, W. E. B., 39, 62, 96
Duffy, Kevin Thomas, 225–28
Duke Ellington and His Orchestra, 66, 154–55
Duke Ellington Jazz Festival, Washington, DC, 158–59
Dulles, John Foster, 151
Duncan, Laura, 104, 110, 112
Dwight's Musical Journal, 11
Dyer, Leonidas, 100
Dylan, Bob, 189–96, 200, 248
Dynasty of Dust and Other Poems, The (Meeropol), 98
"Dziekuje" (Brubeck), 152

East Side Story, 162–67. *See also West Side Story*
Edmund Pettus Bridge in Selma, AL, 187–88
education
    ecology lesson plans, 90
    jazz appreciation and education, 151–52, 156–59
    segregation of public schools, 15, 142, 150–51
    See also Environmental Quality Education Act of 1970; Title IX of the Education Amendments
Edward B. Marks Music Co., 15, 18, 21, 23, 223
Edwards, Don, 219
Edwin M. Stanton School, Jackson, FL, 14–16
Egypt, 62, 152, 153
Einstein, Albert, 118
Eisenhower, Dwight D., 132, 139–40, 143–51, 165, 166, 174, 179
Eisenstadt v. Baird (1972), 205
"El Condor Pasa (If I Could)" (Simon), 236

El Mundo (newspaper), 176
El Salón México (Copland), 120, 171–72
Ellender, Allen J., 148, 151
Ellington, Edward Kennedy "Duke," 60
    Creole Rhapsody, 64–65, 68, 119
    early life and career, 61–63
    on Gershwin's *Porgy and Bess*, 69–70
    jazz ambassador, 154–56
    in *Murder at the Vanities*, 65–68
    Presidential Medal of Freedom, 155–56
    Rhapsody in Blue arrangement, 60–69, 72
    Symphony in Black, 67–69, 105, 119
    See also Duke Ellington and His Orchestra; Duke Ellington Jazz Festival
Elson, Louis C., 14
Emergency Civil Liberties Committee (ECLC), 193–96
Emerson, Ralph Waldo, 32, 37, 45
EMI (record label), 241
Eminem, 262, 263
Emmett Till Anti-Lynching Act, 95, 114–15, 142
Emmett, Daniel Decatur, 11
England. *See* Britain
Entertainment Comics, 168
Environmental Quality Education Act of 1970, 89–90
Equal Pay Act of 1963, 205
Equal Rights Amendment, 205
Equal Voting Rights Act, 187
Esquire (magazine), 151
Essays Before a Sonata (C. Ives), 45
Ethiopia, 236
Europe, James Reese, 18, 21, 62. *See also* Harlem Hellfighters of WWI
Eustice, Oskar, 262
Evers, Medgar, 192, 196
Evolution of the Negro in Picture, Song and Story, The (pageant), 62
Ewing, Alexander, 43

Exon, James, 214
"Experiment in Modern Music" (concert series), 58–63, 65, 74

"Fables of Faubus" (Mingus), 197
Faddis, Jon, 158
Fancy Free (Bernstein), 163
Fanfare for the Common Man (Copland), 118, 121, 138
fascism, 14, 99, 104, 105, 110, 112, 129
Faubus, Orval, 150–51, 197
Fauser, Annegret, 127
FBI (Federal Bureau of Investigation), 112, 117, 132, 137, 165, 219–20
Feather, Leonard, 142
Federal Communications Commission (FCC), 229–31
federal government. *See* Congress; legislation; presidency; US Supreme Court
"Federalist Song, The" (Hopkinson), 7
Feinstein, Dianne, 182
"fellow travelers," 117, 165
female sexuality, 206, 212–13
Feminist Expo, 208
Ferguson, Rebecca, 113
Festival Productions, 156
"Filthy Fifteen," 214–15, 237
First Amendment to the US Constitution, 8–9, 213, 215–16, 218, 229
Flores, Juan, 182
Florida, 14–16, 102, 220–21
Floyd, George, 114, 274–75
"Folsom Prison Blues" (Cash), 229
Forbes (magazine), 274
Ford, Gerald, 24
Fort McHenry, Baltimore, MD, 6, 21–22
Foster, Stephen, 39, 43, 56, 61, 64, 89
    "Massa's in de Cold Grave," 39, 43
    "My Old Kentucky Home," 43
    "Old Black Joe," 39

"Found/Tonight" (charity single), 275–76
Four Tops, 203
Fourth of July celebrations, 20–21, 29
Fox News, 267, 272–73
Frank, Priscilla, 274
Frankenstein, Alfred, 141
Frankfurter, Felix, 174
Fraternal Outlook (magazine), 107
free speech, 8–9, 213, 215–16, 218, 229
Freeman, Charles, 221
Freestyle Love Supreme (improv hip-hop group), 263
Freewheelin' Bob Dylan (Dylan), 191
Friedan, Betty, 206
"Fuck tha Police" (N.W.A/Ice Cube), 219–20
Fulbright, J. William, 174

G. Schirmer (music publisher), 45
Gabler, Milt, 108
Gabriel, Peter, 248
Gaines, Otho Lee, 104
Gaines, William, 181
Gains, William, 168
Gang Violence Act of 1996, 182
gangsta rap, 218–19
Gavagan Anti-Lynching Bill, 110
Gaye, Frankie, 203
Gaye, Marvin, 203–5
Geldof, Bob, 236
gender, 184, 207, 212
General M. D. Shirinda and the Gaza Sisters (South African music group), 236
George III of Britain, 264–65
George White's Scandals of 1922 (musical revue), 57
Germany, 6, 14, 20, 125, 152, 215
Gershwin Family Trust, 51, 52
Gershwin Prize for Popular Song, 256
Gershwin, George
  An American in Paris, 83
  Blue Monday, 57–58, 69
  criticisms of, 60, 119
  Cuban Overture, 171
  death of, 70
  early life and career, 54–56
  Porgy and Bess, 52, 69–70, 105, 142–43
  Rhapsody in Blue, 51–72
  "Swanee," 52, 56–57
Gershwin, Ira, 53, 56, 60
Gershwin, Marc, 52
Gettysburg, Battle of, 29–30
Ghana, 149–50
Gift to Be Simple, The (Deming), 122
Gillespie, Dizzy, 145–49, 151–52, 154–55
Gilmore, Patrick, 13
Gingrich, Newt, 229–30
Gladys Knight and the Pips, 200
Glover, Savion, 261
Gluck, Alma, 53
"God Save the King" (UK national anthem), 8, 28
Gold Coast, *see* Ghana
gold standard, 33–34
Goldberg, Danny, 219
Goldberg, Morris, 244–45
Golden Gate Ballroom, NYC, 110
"Golden Horn, The" (Brubeck), 152
Gone with the Wind (film), 109
Gonsalves, Paul, 72
Goodman, Benny, 148–49
Goodman, Mark, 212
Gordon, Max, 104–5
Gordon, Robert H., 105–6
Gordy, Berry, 203, 204
Gore, Al, 212, 214, 229, 230, 231
Gore, Tipper, 212–17, 222
Gortikov, Stanley, 213, 216
Graceland (Simon), 233–57
  accolades and awards, 255–56
  inspiration for, 235–36
  international tour, 253–55
  production of, 236–40, 243–47, 249–50
  release and reception of, 250–56
  South Africa under apartheid, 233–35
  Steven van Zandt and, 240–41, 247–49
Grafton, Samuel, 108
Graham, Bill, 211
Graham, Martha, 121–28. See also *Appalachian Spring*
Grammy Awards, 207, 237, 253, 255, 269
Grand Canyon, 80–81, 86, 87
  Bright Angel Trail in, 79, 81
  conservation of, 74, 86–89, 92
  Disney-fication of the, 87–89, 90–93
  environmentalism in education, 89–90
  indigenous people of the Grand Canyon, 77–82, 85, 91
  preservation of, 87–89, 92
  the wild horses and burros of the, 91–92
Grand Canyon Suite (Grofé), 73–93
  composition of, 76–78, 81–83
  Disney-fication of, 87–89
  early performance of, 83–86
  impact on environmental legislation, 86–87; 89–91
Grand Upright Music Ltd v. Warner Brothers Records, Inc., 222–28
Grandmaster Flash, 221
Granniss, Robert, 34, 35
Graves, Denyce, 24
Great Depression, 2, 46, 96, 98
Great Migration, 57
Great National Peace Jubilee of 1869, 13
Great Seal of the United States, 19
Greece (ancient), 4, 60
Greece (modern), 146, 148, 154
Green, Adolph, 170
Green, Jesse, 266
Greer, Germaine, 206
Grofé, Ferde, 73–93
  early life and career, 74–75
  orchestrations of *Rhapsody in Blue*, 60, 63, 71, 73
  visiting the Grand Canyon, 75–76, 79
  See also *Grand Canyon Suite*

Gullah community of South Carolina, 69
Gumboots: Accordion Jive Hits, Volume II (mixtape), 235–36, 245
Guthrie, Woody, 189–90

"Hail, Columbia" (Hopkinson), 7–8, 14. *See also* "President's March, The"
Halee, Roy, 238–39, 243
Hall, Adelaide, 57
Hamilton: An American Story (Miranda), 259–78
   "Cancel Hamilton" campaign, 275
   opening and reception of, 266–68
   production of, 259–63, 264–66
   recent presidential elections, 269–78
   streaming on Disney+, 274
   and the ten-dollar bill, 268–69
   VP Mike Pence at, 271–73, 275
Hamilton, Frank, 189
Hamilton, Jimmy, 72
Hammerstein, Oscar, II, 170
Hammond, John, 105, 148
Hampton, Lionel, 148–49, 156, 158
Hancock, Herbie, 248
Hansberry, Lorraine, 200
Hanson, Howard, 130, 141
"Happy Birthday" (Wonder), xiii
Harare, Zimbabwe, 254–55
Harding, Warren G., 21–22, 44
Harlem, 54–55, 58, 63, 69, 222
   Cotton Club, 63, 64
   Golden Gate Ballroom, 110
   Mount Morris Park (now Marcus Garvey Park), 200
   rent parties in, 63
   Spanish Harlem, 169, 241
Harlem Cultural Festival of 1969, 200–201
Harlem Hellfighters of WWI (369th regiment), 21
Harper's Magazine, 71–72
Harris, Kamala, 114, 276, 177

Harrison, Lou, 48
Harrison, William Henry, 9–10
Hart, Lorenz, 171
Hatch, Orrin, 51–52
Havasupai people, 78–82, 85, 91
Hawaii v. Trump (2018), 273
Hawkins, Erick, 126, 128
Heath, Gordon, 111
heavy metal, 212, 215–20, 229
Heifetz, Jascha, 53
Heine, Cornelius W., 89
Hendricks, Jon, 155
Hendrickson, Robert, 168
Hendrix, Jimi, 202
Hernández, Carmen Dolores, 182
Herrmann, Bernard, 47
Heston, Charlton, 192, 220
Hewitt, James, 7
Hicks, Andre "Mac Dre," 228
Highlander Folk School, TN, 188–89
Hilburn, Robert, 240
Hill, John, 22
Hinchcliffe, Tony, 277
hip hop, 218–22, 225–29, 259, 261–66. *See also* rap.
"hippies," 201–2
Hitler, Adolf, 14
Holden, Stephen, 263–64
Holiday, Billie, 68, 95–115
Hollings, Ernest, 214, 229–30
Hollywood blacklisting, 112, 118, 166, 169, 199
Hollywood Bowl, Los Angeles, CA, 169
Holmes, Oliver Wendell, Sr., 11
Home Audio Recording Act ("blank tape tax"), 215
Home of the Brave (Laurents), 163, 169
"Homeless" (Simon, Shabalala), 246, 250
homosexuality, 166–67, 215
Hong Kong, 148
Hoover, Herbert, 1, 23
Hoover, Herbert, Jr., 143
Hopi people, 77–82, 85, 91
Hopkinson, Joseph, 7
Horn, Shirley, 158
Horne, Lena, 107, 158

Horne, Marilyn, 138
Horton, Zilphia, 188, 189
"House I Live In, The" (Meeropol), 111–12
"House of Victory" (ballet script), 123–24, 126
House Un-American Activities Committee (HUAC), 112–13, 117, 133, 165–66, 194
Howar, Pamela, 213–14
Howar, Raymond, 213
Howard University, Washington, DC, 61–62, 253
Huffington Post (website), 274
Hughes, George, 97, 101–2
Hughes, Langston, 118, 128
Hull, William, 2
Hume, Paul, 175
Humphrey, Hubert, 175–76
Hungarian Rhapsodies (Liszt), 60–61, 65–66
Hunting Wild Horses and Burros on Public Lands Act, 91
Hurricane Maria, 275

"I Don't Know How to Love Him" (A. L. Webber), 206
"I Have a Rendezvous with Life" (Cullen), 98
"I Shot the Sheriff" (Marley), 229
Ice Cube, 219
Ice-T, 220
iHeartMedia, 230
"Immigrants (We Get the Job Done)" (Miranda), 273
immigration
   Deferred Action for Childhood Arrivals (DACA) program, 275
   German immigrants, 14
   Irish immigrants, 9, 168
   Italian immigrants, 168, 178
   Jewish immigrants, 54, 56, 118, 162, 167–69
"improvements," 80
"In Flanders Field," 43, 44
In the Heights (Miranda), 283, 259–63, 268
India, 152, 153, 154

Indians. *See* indigenous people of America
Indiana, 96–97, 102, 103–4
indigenous people of America
  of the Grand Canyon, 77–82, 85, 91
  "powwows," 75–76, 80–81
  on the Trail of Tears, 267
  the vanishing "Indian Girl," 123–24, 126–28
  See also National American Indian Memorial
Interior Department Appropriation Act, 81
International Labor Defense, 101, 106
International Workers Organization, 107–8
"Internationale, The" (Communist anthem), 119–20
internet, 211, 225, 230–31
"Into the Streets, May 1st" (Copland), 119, 136
Iran, 146, 152, 154
Iraq, 152, 154
Irwin, Donald J., 27–28
Israeli–Palestinian conflict, xi–xii
"It's Wrong (Apartheid)" (Wonder), xiii, 249
Ives, Charles, 27–49
  belief in direct democracy, 40–44
  "Black March," 37–40
  education and early career, 28–34
  his proposed Twentieth Amendment, 43
  and the insurance industry, 34, 36–37
  "The Masses," 41–42
  in New York, 34–35
  "Nov. 2, 1920" or "The Election," 44
  publication of his works, 44–47
  "Tom Sails Away," 43
  The Unanswered Question, 27–28, 35–38, 46–49
  Variations on "America," 28–29
  "Vote for Names," 41
  Yale–Princeton Football Game, 33

Ives, George, 29–32
Ives, Isaac, 31

Jackson, Andrew, 6, 80, 266–69
Jackson, Christopher, 270–71
Jackson, Jackie, 236
Jackson, James Thomas, 17–18
Jackson, Mahalia, 192, 200
Jamaica, 236
January 6 attack on the US Capitol, 276
Japan, 148
Japanese Americans, 126
Jarret, Vernon, 107
Javits, Jacob K., 174
Jay-Z, 263
jazz, 24, 55, 76, 77, 119
  an American export, 141–56, 159, 179
  appreciation and education, 151–52, 156–59
  bebop, 72, 146, 171, 173
  the legislation of, 156–59
  politicization and Cold War anxiety, 139–40
  See also specific titles, composers and performers
Jazz Ambassadors program, 145–56, 159, 179
Jazz Club USA (radio show), 142
Jefferson, Thomas, 260, 264–67
Jefferson, William L., 158
Jerome H. Remick Music Company, 55
"Jerusalem, The Golden" (Ewing), 43
Jesus Christ Superstar (A. L. Webber), 206
"Jesus Loves Me" (hymn), 46
Jewish songs, 63. *See also* klezmer music
"Jikele Maweni, The Retreat Song" (Makeba), 254
Jim Crow, 17, 62–63, 99
Johannesburg, South Africa, 236, 238, 239, 240, 244, 256
John Birch Society, 137
John Reed Club, 101
Johnson, Eddie Bernice, 114
Johnson, J. Rosamond, 62

Johnson, James P., 21, 61, 64
Johnson, James Weldon, 14–18, 21, 23–25, 57, 100
Johnson, Lyndon B., 137, 187–89
Johnston, J. Bennett, 157, 158
Jolson, Al, 56
Jones, Justin, 9
Jones, Quincy, 147, 237, 238
Joplin, Scott, 18, 56, 61
Jordan, 154
Jordan, Stanley, 248
Josephson, Barney, 105–6, 107, 112
Josephson, Leon, 106, 112
Judas Priest, 212, 214–15, 218
Julliard School, NYC, 47
Justice for Victims of Lynching Act, 114
juvenile delinquency, 161–62, 167–70, 173–79, 182, 184, 214

Kaepernick, Colin, 1–2, 24
Kahn, Gus, 84
Kail, Tommy, 263, 265
Katims, Milton, 141
Kennedy Center, Washington, DC, 137
Kennedy, James Homer, 12
Kennedy, John F., 137, 154, 161–62, 181, 193, 194, 246
Kennedy, Robert F., 52–53, 161, 201
Kennedy, Sheelagh, 110
Kenton, Stan, 145
Kentucky Club, NYC, 63
Kern, Jerome, 152
Kernodle, Tammy, 199
Ketcham, Orman W., 175
Key, Francis Scott, 2–18, 20, 172
King, Coretta Scott, 249
King, Eddie, 81
King, Martin Luther, Jr., xiii, 24, 156–57, 192, 193, 201
Kirkpatrick, John, 47
klezmer music, 55, 60–61, 64, 71
Knickerbocker Press, 45
Konstantin, Stanislavski, 174
Korea, Republic of, 139
Korean War, 139

Korins, David, 265
Kragan, Ken, 211
Krupa, Gene, 148–49
Kumalo, Bakithi, 239–40, 244–45, 252, 255
Kun, Josh, 227–28
Kushner, Tony, 184
kwela (street music of South Africa), 245
Kweli, Talib, 263

La Prensa (newspaper), 176
Lacamoire, Alex, 264
Ladysmith Black Mambazo (South African male choral group), 234, 240, 245–47, 250, 252–56. See also Shabalala, Joseph
Lancaster, Burt, 192
Lander, Eric, 65, 66
Lang, Paul Henry, 47
Lang, Pearl, 137–38
Larrabe, Eric, 71–72
Lauper, Cyndi, 212, 214
Laurents, Arthur, 162–72, 175, 180, 182–86. See also West Side Story
Lavender Scare, 166
Lawrence, Tony, 201
League of Struggle for Negro Rights (LSNR), 99–101
Lebanon, 146, 154
Lebona, Koloi, 238
Lee, Canada, 105
Lee, Peggy, 155
Legend, John, 262
Legislation, xiii, 19, 40, 51–52, 86, 100–02, 105, 117, 145, 156–57, 214–17
  Anti-Apartheid Act of 1986, 252
  anti-lynching legislation, 66, 95–100, 110–11, 107, 114
  Antiquities Act of 1906, 79–80
  California Desert Protection Act of 1994, 158
  Civil Rights Act of 1964, 188
  Copyright Act of 1976, 52, 223–24
  Emmett Till Anti-Lynching Act, 95, 114–15, 142
  Environmental Quality Education Act of 1970, 89–90
  Equal Pay Act of 1963, 205
  Equal Rights Amendment, 205
  Equal Voting Rights Act of 1965, 187
  Gang Violence Act of 1996, 182
  Gavagan Anti-Lynching Bill, 110
  Home Audio Recording Act ("blank tape tax"), 215
  Hunting Wild Horses and Burros on Public Lands Act, 91
  Interior Department Appropriation Act, 81
  Justice for Victims of Lynching Act, 114
  Juvenile Delinquency and Youth Offenses Control Act, 161–62
  National Park Service Organic Act, 80
  New Orleans Jazz National Historic Park Act, 158
  Sonny Bono Copyright Term Extension Act, 51–53
  Telecommunications Act of 1996, 229–30, 231
  Title IX of the Education Amendments, 205
  See also Congress; Constitution
Leipzig, Germany, 74–75
Lennox, Annie, 212
Leonard, Neil, 72
Levin, Emanuel, 107–8
Lewis, Harry, 104
Lewis, John, 196
Liberia, 153
Library of Congress, 15, 113, 121–22, 162, 229, 256
Life (magazine), 117, 165
"Lift Every Voice and Sing" (J. W. Johnson), 14–18, 21, 23–25, 57, 100
Lil Boosie, 228
"Lincoln and Liberty" (campaign song), 10
Lincoln Center for the Performing Arts, NYC, 179, 263–64
Lincoln Memorial, Washington, DC, 63, 110, 192
Lincoln Portrait (Copland), 118, 120, 132, 137
Lincoln, Abraham, 10, 12–15, 37–38, 59, 192
Lindsay, John, 201
Linthicum, John, 23
Listen (magazine), 48
Liston, Melba, 147
Liszt, Franz, 60–61, 65–66, 72
Little Rock, AR, 150–51
"Little Steven." See van Zandt, Steven
Lodge, Henry Cabot, 277–78
London, UK, 4, 246, 251–52, 253
Los Angeles, CA, 169, 218, 244, 249
Los Angeles Daily News, 109
Los Angeles Symphony Orchestra, 74, 75
Los Angeles Times, 169, 273
Los Incas (folk group), 236
Los Lobos (band), 244
"Lost My Man Blues" (Ellington), 68
Lower East Side, NYC, 55, 162–67
Luce, Phillip, 194
Lusitania (ship), 42
lynchings, 21, 57, 66, 95–115, 126, 142

MacArthur "Genius" grant, 269
Mad Magazine, 181
Madame Butterfly (Puccini), 14
Madison Square Garden, 104, 277
Madonna, 213
Mailer, Norman, 118
Makeba, Miriam, 254. See also "Jikele Maweni"
Malaya, 148
Mali, 153
Mandela, Nelson, 233–35, 241, 248, 253–56
Mann, Thomas, 118
March for Our Lives (2018), 276
March on Washington for Jobs and Freedom (1963), 192–94, 196

"Marching through Georgia" (Clay), 38
Marie, René, 24
Marín, Luis Muñoz, 176
Marley, Bob, 229
Martin, John, 22, 130, 277
Martin, Ricky, 276–77
Martín-Rodríguez, Manuel M., 182
"Massa's in de Cold Grave" (Foster), 39, 43
Massachusetts 54th Regiment, 37–40, 46. *See also* "Black March"
"Masses, The" (C. Ives), 41–42
master licenses/recordings, 223–26
Mathias, Charles, Jr., 91
Mayfair Theatre, London, 251–52
Mazibuko, Albert, 246–47, 250
mbaqanga (South African music genre), 235–36, 238, 245
mbube (South African choral genre), 245
McCarter, Jeremy, 263, 264
McCarthy, Joe, 117–18, 134–37, 139, 141, 144
McClellan, George, 12
McCollum v. CBS (1988), 218
McCollum, John, 218
McCormack, John, 21
McCurdy, Richard A., 35
McDaniel, Hattie, 109
McInerney, James, 165
McKinley "Mac" Phipps Jr., 228
McKinley, William, 33–34
McLaughlin's Tavern, Washington, DC, 5
McNulty, Charles, 273
McRae, Carmen, 113
mechanical licenses, 223–24
Meeropol, Abel
early life and career, 97–99, 102
enter Billie Holiday, 105–10
enter Countee Cullen, 98, 99–100
The Dynasty of Dust and Other Poems, 98
as "Lewis Allan," 95, 104, 108–9, 111, 148

"The House I Live In," 111–12
See also "Strange Fruit"
Meeropol, Anne, 98–99, 104, 112
Megel, Carl J., 90
Meintjes, Louise, 245
"melting pot," 54, 69, 71, 228
Mendelssohn, Felix, 64
"Message, The" (Grandmaster Flash), 221
Metropolitan Opera House, 74, 83, 141
Mexican Hayride (Porter), 171
Mfume, Kweisi, 114–15
Michaels, Lorne, 250
Michigan, 19, 156
Mickey Mouse, 51
Middle East, 142, 154–56. *See also* Iran; Iraq; Israeli-Palestine conflict; Jordan; Syria; United Arab Republic
Middleton, Velma, 153
Miller, Elmaurice, 104
Mills, Florence, 57
Mingus, Charles, 156, 197
Minneapolis, MN, 274
Minnesota, 19, 189
minstrel shows, 11, 30. *See also* blackface
Miranda, Lin-Manuel
Hamilton: An American Story, 259–78
In the Heights, 283, 259–63, 268
Lincoln Center's "American Songbook" series, 263–64
performances at the White House, 259–60, 263
revival of *West Side Story*, 182–85
Miranda, Luis, Jr., 261
"Mississippi Goddam" (Simone), 196–200
Moiseyev, Igor, 178
Moiseyev Dance Company, 178
Montealegre, Felicia, 167
Monterey Jazz Festival of 1962, 154
Montgomery, AL, 142, 187, 199

Moore, Melba, 24
Morello, Joe, 152
Moreno, Rita, 179, 181, 192, 276–77
"Mother and Child Reunion" (Simon), 236
Motion Picture Alliance for the Preservation of American Ideals (MPA), 130
Mötley Crüe, 212, 214–15, 217–18
Motloheloa, Forere, 239, 244, 246
Moton, Robert Russa, 63
Motown, 203–4
Moynihan, Daniel Patrick, 220
Mtshali, Isaac, 239, 244, 255
MTV, 212, 222, 240–41
Mulligan, Hercules, 262
Munroe, Isaac, 3
Murder at the Vanities (film), 65–68
Murrow, Edward R., 149
Music Advisory Panel to the Cultural Presentations Program, 141, 145, 147
music awards. *See* prizes and awards
music industry
deregulation and the, 212, 229–31, 242
gatekeepers of culture, 45–46, 210
litigiousness of, 221–28
rise of popular music, 211–31
royalties, 60, 108, 215, 248
sheet music, 6–7, 55, 108, 110
Tin Pan Alley, 39, 55, 56, 60, 62, 63
See also copyright; *specific publishers and record labels*
Music USA (radio program), 141–42
Musical Courier (magazine), 45
musicals, 34, 53, 55, 57–58, 63–64, 274. *See also specific musicals*
Musicians Union of South Africa, 238

Muslim travel ban, 273
Mussolini, Benito, 14
Mutual Life Insurance Company, 34–35
"My Country 'Tis of Thee" (Smith), 8, 28–29, 31
"My Old Kentucky Home" (Foster), 43
"My Shot" (Miranda), 263
Myrick, John, 36

N.W.A., 218–20, 227
N'Dour, Youssou, 250
"N'kosi Sikelele iAfrica" (hymn), 255
NAACP (National Association for the Advancement of Colored People), 100–102, 109, 126
   Art Commentary on Lynching (exhibition), 101–2
   The Crisis newspaper, 99, 101, 104, 125
   "Lift Every Voice and Sing," 17, 21, 23, 57, 100
Nance, Ray, 72
National American Indian Memorial (proposed), 124
National Association of Broadcasters, 213
National Cultural Liberation Movement, 252
National District Attorneys Association, 182
National Endowment for the Arts, 156
National Guard, 150–51, 202
National Museum of African American History and Culture, Washington, DC, 24
National Negro Congress, 110
National Organization for Women (NOW), 205
National Park Service Organic Act, 80
National Park Service, 80–81, 86–87, 89, 91, 157
National Recording Registry, Library of Congress, 113
National Theatre, Washington DC, 174
National Urban League, 99

Native Americans. *See* indigenous people of America
Nazi Germany, 14, 215
NBC, 83, 173
Negro in American Life, The (pageant), 110
Negrón-Muntaner, Frances, 179, 182
net neutrality, 231
Nevius, Sally, 213
New England, 28–29, 40, 46, 97
New Masses (newspaper), 99–102, 104, 105
New Mexico, 19
New Music (journal), 47
New Musical Express (magazine), 251
New Orleans, 11, 64, 157–58
New Orleans Jazz National Historic Park Act, 158
New Theatre League, 108
"New Version of the National Song, A" (Atlee), 9
New York Age (newspaper), 109
New York City
   Ambassador Billiard Parlor, 53
   Brooklyn, 54, 118, 170, 177
   Café Society, Greenwich Village, 105–8, 111–12
   Carnegie Hall, 55, 60, 70, 112, 149, 197
   Dewitt–Clinton High School, 97–99, 102, 111–12
   Julliard School, 47
   Lincoln Center for the Performing Arts, 179, 263–64
   Lower East Side, 55, 162–67
   Madison Square Garden, 104, 277
   Metropolitan Opera House, 74, 83, 141
   the Puerto Rican community of, 143, 168–83, 259–78
   San Juan Hill neighborhood, 98, 169–70, 176
   Sound Money Parade of 1896, 34
   Tin Pan Alley, 39, 55, 56, 60, 62, 63

   Winter Garden Theater, 176
   World's Fair of 1939, 120
   See also musicals; Harlem; immigration
New York Herald (newspaper), 30
New York Philharmonic, 27, 48, 70–71, 141, 163
New York Post (newspaper), 108
New York Teacher (magazine), 104
New York Times, 20, 83, 129, 130, 138, 144
   on Bob Dylan, 191
   on *Hamilton*, 263, 266, 267, 276–77
   on South Africa, 253
   on *West Side Story*, 162–63, 167–68, 173, 175–77, 180
New York World, 21, 58
New York World's Fair of 1939, 120
New Yorker (magazine), 105, 107, 177, 197, 276
Newport Jazz Festival, 70, 156
Newsweek (magazine), 211, 237
Night Creatures (Ellington), 173
9/11 terrorist attacks, 48–49
Nineteenth Amendment to the US Constitution, 43
Nixon, Richard, 137, 155, 161, 174
Nkrumah, Kwame, 150
"No Body, No Crime" (Swift), 229
Nobel Peace Prize, 256
Noguchi, Isamu, 101, 126, 138
   Appalachian Spring set design, 126, 138
   Death (Lynched Figure) sculpture, 101, 126
non-Western music. *See* world music
Norman, Jessye, 138
North Carolina, 45, 196
North Star, The (film), 125
Norton, Eleanor Holmes, 158, 159
"novelty songs," 56
nuclear arms race, 139, 174
Nureyev, Rudolf, 138

O'Sullivan, Gilbert, 225–27
Obama, Barack, 183, 259, 266–71
Obama, Michelle, 259
obscenity, 213, 220–22
Ochs, Phil, 190, 210
Odetta, 192
Odom, Leslie, Jr., 275
"Oh, Pretty Woman" (Orbison), 222–26. *See also* "Pretty Woman"
"Old Black Joe" (Foster), 39
Olympics Games of 1924, 22
On the Town (Bernstein), 163
"On the Trail" (Grofé), 81–84, 88, 91–92
On the Transmigration of Souls (J. Adams), 48–49
"One Last Time" (Miranda), 264, 270–71
"Only a Pawn in Their Game" (Dylan), 192
Opportunity: Journal of Negro Life, 99, 101, 104
Orbison, Roy, 222–26
Orozco, José Clemente, 101
Osbourne, Ozzy, 218
Ostin, Mo, 220, 236
Oswald, Lee Harvey, 194
Our Town (film), 122
Owens, Jesse, 145

Pace (South African magazine), 245
Pakistan, 146–48, 152, 154
Pallone, Frank, Jr., 158
Pan Africanist Congress (PAC), 235
Paramount Studios, 65, 67–68
Pareles, Jon, 253
Parent Advisory Label (PAL mark), 217–18. *See also* warning labels for "explicit lyrics"
Parents and Teachers Association (PTA), 216
Parents Music Resource Center (PMRC), 213–16, 221–24, 237
Parker, Horatio, 32–33
Parker-Coltrane Political Action Committee, 156–57
Parks, Rosa, 142

parodies, 8, 9, 56, 181, 222–26, 265
Paul Whiteman and His Orchestra, 59, 82–83
Paul, Rand, 114
Pearl Harbor, 126
Pelosi, Nancy, 276
Pence, Mike, 271–73, 275
Pendleton, George, 12
Perry, Imani, 18
Persip, Charlie, 147
Peruvian ballads, 236
Peter, Paul, and Mary (folk group), 191, 192
Phelps, William Lyon, 32
Philadelphia, PA, 7, 196, 218
Philadelphia Tribune, 199
Phile, Philip, 7
Philips Records, 199
Phiri, Ray, 239, 244, 245, 252, 255
Pierpont, Claudia Roth, 197
Pierre Degeyter Club, 119–20
Pirro, Jeanine, 272–73
Pittsburgh Courier, 109
Pledge of Allegiance, 13–14
Plessy v. Ferguson (1896), 15
PMRC (Parents Music Resource Center), 213–16, 221–24, 237
pogroms, 98
Poison (band), 217
Poitier, Sidney, 167, 192
Poland, 143, 152
politics
  Democratic Party, 44, 100–101, 133, 134, 201, 266, 276, 225
  Hollywood blacklisting, 112, 118, 166, 169, 199
  lobbying, 51, 217
  musicians and fundraisers, 137, 269–70
  Progressive Party, 41, 131
  Republican Party, 10, 17, 33, 41, 44, 114, 117, 132–34, 267, 270
  right-wing politicians and media, 112, 118, 130–31, 137, 242
  See also communism; protest music; Socialist Party; *specific branches and agencies of government*

"Poodle Dog Rag" (Ellington), 62
pop music, 55, 56, 211–31
  Billboard Hot 100, 204, 207, 212, 249
  the Top 40, 221
  See also specific songs and performers
Popular Front, 105, 118
Porgy and Bess (G. Gershwin), 52, 69–70, 105, 142–43
"porn music hearing." *See* Senate Hearing on Record Labeling
Porter, Cole, 171
Postman Always Rings Twice, The (Cain), 166
Poston Internment Camp, AZ, 126
Powell, Adam Clayton, Jr., 118, 143–46
Preservation of Jazz Commission, 157
presidency
  Dizzy Gillespie's run for the, 154–55
  elections, 9–10, 12, 41, 44, 154–55, 242, 267, 276
  executive orders, 19–21, 40, 166, 212
  inauguration music, 7, 10, 11, 34, 113, 132–33, 137–38
  performances at the White House, 259–60, 263
  President's Special International Program, 148
  Presidential Medals of Freedom, 137, 155–56
  Task Force on Regulatory Relief, 212
"President's March, The" (Phile), 7
Pressler, Larry, 229–30
"Pretty Woman" (2 Live Crew), 222–26. *See also* "Oh, Pretty Woman" (Orbison)
Primus, Pearl, 111, 112, 115
Prince, 212–13
Prince, Hal, 178
Priority Records, 219
prizes
  Academy Awards (Oscars), 89, 109, 122, 181, 192

prizes (*continued*)
  BRIT awards, 251
  Duke Ellington Festival Lifetime Achievement Award, 159
  Gershwin Prize for Popular Song, 256
  Grammy Awards, 207, 237, 253, 255, 269
  Presidential Medals of Freedom, 137, 155–56
  Pulitzer Prizes, 47–48, 129–30, 269
  Tom Paine Award, 193–96
  Tony Awards, 183, 259, 269
Progressive Party, 41, 131
Prohibition, 21
protest music, 187–210
  "Blowin' in the Wind" (Dylan), 189–95
  "Bring Him Back Home" (Masekela), 254
  "I Am Woman" (Reddy), 204–9
  "Into the Streets, May 1st" (Copland), 119, 136
  "It's Wrong (Apartheid)" (Wonder), xiii, 249
  "Mississippi Goddam" (Simone), 196–200
  "Nov. 2, 1920" or "The Election" (C. Ives), 44
  "We Shall Overcome" (freedom song), 187–89
  "What's Goin On" (Gaye), 203–5
  See also "Strange Fruit" (Meeropol)
Psycho (film), 47
public domain, 23, 52, 72, 214
Public Enemy, 227
publishers. *See* music industry
Puccini, Giacomo, 14
Puerto Rican community, 143, 168–83, 259–78
  negative portrayal in *West Side Story*, 170–72, 176, 179–80, 182, 183–84
Pulitzer Prizes, 47–48, 129–30, 269
Purple Rain (Prince), 212–13
Putnam, Sallie, 12

Quayle, Dan, 220
Questlove (Ahmir Thompson), 201
Quiet Riot (heavy metal band), 217

raag (in traditional Pakistani music), 148
race and racism
  anti-Semitism, 98, 162–63
  blackface, 11, 56–58, 65, 72
  Japanese American internment during WWII, 126
  Jim Crow, 17, 62–63, 99
  "melting pot" image, 54, 69, 71, 228
  Red Summer of 1919, 21, 56–57, 62–63, 96
  See also civil rights movement; lynchings; Red Summer; segregation; slavery; *West Side Story*
Rachmaninoff, Sergei, 53, 72
radio, 21–22, 131, 133, 187
  CBS, 83–84, 128
  the business of, 230
  diplomacy through the, 140–42
  protest and, 206, 207, 210
  refusing to play songs, 199, 213, 215, 217, 220, 222
ragtime, 19, 29, 55, 56, 64, 72
Raisin in the Sun, A (Hansberry), 200
Rakim, 262
Rangel, Charles, 158, 261
rap, 215, 218–30, 248, 261. *See also* hip hop
Rapp–Coudert Commission, 111
"Rapper's Delight" (Sugarhill Gang), 221
Raymond, Charles H., 34, 35
Raymond, Robert, 149–50
Razaf, Andy, 150
RCA, 84
Reagan, Ronald, 211–12, 240, 242, 248, 252
  assassination attempt on, 246
  deregulation, 212, 229–31, 242
  inauguration of, 138

Real Ambassadors, The (Brubeck/Armstrong), 154
"Real American Folk Song (is a Rag)" (Gershwin), 56
Rebel Without a Cause (film), 167
Record Book (magazine), 109
Record Industry Association of America (RIAA), 213–17
Red Channels report, 118, 165
Red Scare, 112–13, 117–18, 133–37, 139, 141, 144, 165–66, 194
Red Summer of 1919, 21, 56–57, 62–63, 96
Reddy, Helen, 205–9
Reeb, James, 187
reggae, 236, 238
Republic of the Congo, 153
Republican Party, 10, 17, 33, 41, 44, 114, 117, 132–34, 267, 270
"Revolutionary Situation" (Artists United Against Apartheid), 248
Reynolds, Maria, 260
Rhapsody in Blue (G. Gershwin), 51–72
  Bernstein's revival of, 70–72
  enter Duke Ellington, 60–69, 72
  origins of, 53–54, 58–60
  premiere of, 119
  the sounds of multicultural New York, 54–55
Rhythm of Resistance: The Music of South Africa (documentary), 240
Richard Rodgers Theater, 261, 267, 269
Richards, Keith, 248
Richmond, VA, 11–13
right-wing politicians and media, 112, 118, 130–31, 137, 242
"Rio Pakistan" (Gillespie), 147
Ripley, Robert L., 22–23
Rivera-Servera, Ramón, 182
Riz MC, 274
Roach, Max, 109, 155
Robbins Music Corporation, 84
Robbins, Jerome, 162–71, 174–75, 179–80, 265. *See also West Side Story*

Roberts, Lucky, 18
Robeson, Paul, 57, 109, 110, 165–66
Robinson, Earl, 104
Rockefeller, Nelson, 202
Rockin' Dopsie and the Twisters (zydeco band), 244
"Rocky Mountain High" (Denver), 215
Rodeo (Copland), 118, 120–21
Roe v. Wade (1973), 205, 209
Rogers, Richard, 171
Romeo and Juliet (Shakespeare), 162, 168–69, 177
Romney, Mitt, xi
Ronstadt, Linda, 243, 244, 254
Rooney, John, 148, 151, 166
Roosevelt, Franklin Delano, 86, 99, 128
Roosevelt, Theodore, 20, 41, 79–80
Root, George F., 38
Rose, Al, 157
Rosenthal, Hilton, 236, 238
Rosenthal, J. C., 73
Run-DMC, 218, 222, 248
Rusk, Howard A., 176
Ryan, Paul, 114

sadomasochism, 216
Saga of the Prairie (Copland), 128
Saint-Gaudens, Augustus, 37
  The Shaw 54th Regiment Memorial 37–38, 39, 46
Salisbury, Harrison E., 177–78
"Salt Peanuts" (Gillespie), 155
sampling, 222, 223–29, 236, 248
Samuels, Alana, 267
San Juan Hill neighborhood, NYC, 98, 169–70, 176
Santa Fe Railway, 87
Satchmo the Great (documentary), 149–50
Saturday Night Live (SNL), 225, 249–50, 252–53
Saturday Review, 47
"Schirmer's Library of Musical Classics," 45
Schoolly D of Philadelphia, 218
Schuman, William, 129–30, 141

Schuyler, Eliza, 260, 264
Scott, Hazel, 144
Scottsboro Nine, 99–100, 128
Scribner's (magazine), 83
"Secret World of Plants, The" (Wonder), xiii
Secular Cantata No. 2: *A Free Song* (Schuman), 129–30, 141
See It Now (TV show), 149
Seeger, Charles, 120
Seeger, Pete, 120, 188–89, 190, 191, 195, 209
segregation, 15, 21, 38, 54–55, 62, 139
  of audiences, 105–6, 241
  Jim Crow, 17, 62–63, 99
  of public schools, 15, 142, 150–51
Seller, Jeffrey, 262, 264, 270
Selma, AL, 187–88, 199
Semilane, Solly, 251
Senate Hearing on Record Labeling, 213–17, 237
Senegal, 153, 250
Serenade (Bernstein), 167
Sessions, Jeff, 182
Seventeenth Amendment to the US Constitution, 41
Shabalala, Joseph, 240, 246–47, 250, 254–55
Shaffer, Anne. *See* Meeropol, Anne
Shaka Zulu (Ladysmith Black Mambazo), 255
Shaker community, 122, 125, 138
Shakespeare, William, 162, 168–69, 177, 262
Shaw, Robert Gould, 37–38, 39, 46
Shelton, Robert, 191
Sherman's March to the Sea (1864), 38
Shipp, Tom, 96–97, 102, 103–4
Shuffle Along (Blake and Sissle), 57–58, 62
Sierra Club, 87
Sierra Leone, 153
Simon, Paul, 233–57. *See also* Graceland
Simone, Nina, 113, 196–200, 223. *See also* "Mississippi Goddam"

"Simple Gifts" (hymn), 122, 125, 138
Sinatra, Frank, 112
Sing Out! (folk song magazine), 191
Sing Out the News (H. J. Rome), 104–5
Singapore, 148
Sissle, Noble, 57
Sixteenth Street Baptist Church, Birmingham, AL, 196–97
ska, 236
Skyywalker Records v. Navarro, 221
slavery, 6, 8–11, 17, 20, 30, 38–39, 121, 123, 127–29, 188, 266–68, 275
Sleeping Beauty (film), 89
Sly and the Family Stone (band), 200
Sly, David, 250
Smith, Abe, 96–97, 102, 103–4
Smith, John Stafford, 4, 5
Smith, Layton F., 18–19
Smith, Samuel Francis, 28
Smith, Willie "The Lion," 110
Smithsonian Museum of American History, 63
Snoop Dogg, 228
Snow Tha Product, 274
social media, 24, 95, 275
Socialist Party (US), 119
"Somewhere" (Bernstein), 170, 185
Sondheim, Stephen, 170, 172–73, 175, 176, 180, 183, 184–85. *See also* West Side Story
Sonny Bono Copyright Term Extension Act, 51–53
Sons of the American Revolution, 18
Sony Music Entertainment, 231
Soul Brothers (mbaqanga group), 238
Sound Warehouse record store, FL, 221
Sousa, John Philip, 19, 20
South Africa, xiii, 233–57
  apartheid in, 233–57
  African National Congress (ANC), 234–35, 237–43, 248, 251–53, 256

South Africa (*continued*)
  Afrikaner National Party (ANP), 234–35, 241–42
  Azanian People's Organization, 256
  Paul Simon recording in, 238–40
  Paul Simon on tour in, 256
  Steven Van Zandt in, 241–42
  See also Bantustans; Johannesburg; United Nations boycott of
South Carolina, 10, 69, 188
  Gullah community of, 69
South Korea, 148
Southern Christian Leadership Conference., 155
Southern Democrats, 100–101, 225
Soviet Union, 138, 139, 143, 150, 181
  criticisms of American race relations, 140, 142–44, 146–47, 149
  cultural exchanges, 27, 178, 178
  nuclear arms race with the, 139, 174
  See also Cold War; communism
Spielberg, Stephen, 184
spoken-word poetry, 248
"Spring Song" (Mendelssohn), 64
Springsteen, Bruce, 240, 248, 277
Sri Lanka, 152, 154
Stacy, Rubin, 102, 104
Standing Bear, Luther, 92
Star of Ethiopia (pageant), 62
"Star Spangled Banner, The" (Key), 1–25
  alternatives to, 7–8, 14–18
  in the civil rights movement and beyond, 23–25
  during the Civil War, 10–13
  composition of, 2–7
  in Congress, 18–23
  criticism of, 2, 21–22
  the meaning of, 8–10
  rituals arising around, 1–2, 13–14, 24
  See also "Defence of Fort M'Henry, The"

Stearns, Marshall, 145, 147
Stern, Joseph W., 15, 18
Stetson, Augusta, 22
Stevens, R. J. S., 4
Stewart, Charles, 5
Still, William Grant, 58
Stimela (band), 238, 239, 255
Stix, Nikki, 217
Stock Market Crash of 1929. *See* Great Depression
Stowe, Harriet Beecher, 123
Straight Outta Compton (NWA), 219
"Strange Fruit" (Meeropol), 95–115
  composition of, 95–96, 102–5
  enter Billie Holiday, 105–10
  lynchings, 95–100
  publisher Edward B. Marks Music Co., 15, 18, 21, 23, 223
  recent revivals of, 113–15
  streaming services, 231, 274
Streibert, Theodore, 140, 143
Struggle for Negro Rights (exhibition), 101–2
Stuckley, Ethelyn, 213
Stuckley, Williamson, 213
Studebaker Theater, Chicago, 82–83
Student Nonviolent Coordinating Committee (SNCC), 196
subliminal messages, 218
Sudan, 153
suffrage for women, 9, 20, 43
Sugarhill Gang (hip hop group), 221, 222
Summer of Soul (documentary), 201
"Summertime" (G. Gershwin), 105
Sun City (Artists United Against Apartheid), 241–43, 247–50, 253–54, 256
"Swanee River Rhapsody" (Ellington), 64
"Swanee" (G. Gershwin), 52, 56–57
"Sweet By-and-By, The" (gospel hymn), 43
Sweet Little Devil (G. Gershwin), 53

Swift, Taylor, 229, 277
Symphony in Black (Ellington), 67–69, 105, 119
Symphony of the Air Orchestra, 173
Syria, 146, 154

TAC. *See* Theatre Arts Committee (TAC)
Taft, William Howard, 41, 124
Tambo, Dali, 243, 251, 253
Tambo, Oliver, 237, 243
Tao Ea Maysekha (Sotho music group), 236, 238, 239
Tazewell, Paul, 266
Telecommunications Act of 1996, 229–30, 231
television, 136, 187, 203, 211–14, 230
  CBS, 145, 149, 218
  Fox News, 267, 272–73
  MTV, 212, 222, 240–41
Tennessee, 188–89, 197, 212
Terrell, Tammi, 203
Texas, 98, 101–2, 114
Thailand, 148
The Notorious B.I.G., 263
Theatre Arts Committee (TAC), 99, 104–5, 110–12
Thompson, Ahmir "Questlove," 201
Thomson, Virgil, 60, 141
Thurmond, Strom, 215
Till, Emmet, 95, 114–15, 142
Time (magazine), 60, 70, 83, 101, 108–9, 113, 131, 256
Tin Pan Alley, 39, 55, 56, 60, 62, 63
Tindley, Charles Albert, 188
Title IX of the Education Amendments, 205
"To Anacreon in Heaven" (J. S. Smith), 4–6
"To Be Young, Gifted, and Black" (Simone), 200
Tom Paine Award, 193–96
"Tom Sails Away" (C. Ives), 43
Tomlinson, Ralph, 4
Tony Awards, 183, 259, 269
Too Many Girls (musical), 171
Toscanini, Arturo, 84

"township jive," 235–36, 238, 245
Trail of Tears, 267
Transcendentalism, 32, 36
Treuer, David, 92
Trible, Paul, 216–17
Trilling, Lionel, 98
Trotter, William Monroe, 62
Truman, Harry S., 165
Trump, Donald, 113–14, 184, 267, 269–75, 277
Tubman, Harriet, 268
Turkey, 146, 152, 154
Tuskegee Institute, 100
Tutu, Desmond, 241, 248, 252
Twisted Sister (heavy metal band), 215, 216, 217
2 Live Crew (hip hop group), 220–26

US Department of Agriculture, 86
US Department of Labor, 86
US Department of State
 cultural diplomacy, 139–45
 Jazz Ambassadors program, 145–56, 159, 179
 Lavender Scare in the, 166
 passport control, 112, 137, 165, 166
 Red Scare in the, 134–37
 West Side Story and, 174, 178–81
US Department of the Interior, 81, 86, 157
US Department of the Treasury, 259–60, 268–69
US Department of War, 86
U.S. News and World Report, 145
US Supreme Court, 8–9, 15, 142, 205, 209, 218, 221–28, 273
 Brown v. Board of Education (1954), 142
 Campbell v. Acuff-Rose Music, Inc., 222–26
 Eisenstadt v. Baird (1972), 205
 Hawaii v. Trump (2018), 273
 Plessy v. Ferguson (1896), 15
 Roe v. Wade (1973), 205, 209

Unanswered Question, The (C. Ives), 27–28, 35–38, 46–49
Uncle Tom's Cabin (Stowe), 123
"Under African Skies" (Simon), 244–45, 254, 257
"Under the Blade" (Snider), 216
UNESCO, 235
United Arab Republic, 153, 154
United Artists, 149
United Kingdom. *See* Britain
United Nations, 178, 181
 boycott of South Africa, 234–35, 237, 241–43, 248, 251–57
 International Women's Year and Decade for Women, 207–8
United States Information Agency (USIA), 140–43, 150
United States Information Service (USIS), 140
United States, xi–xiv
 Constitution of the United States, 41, 43–44, 99, 142, 214, 218, 260, 273
 as a democracy, 40–44, 111, 140, 180–81, 215, 250–51
 free speech in the, 8–9, 213, 215–16, 218, 229
 gold standard, 33–34
 after World War II, 121
 See also Congress; Presidency; Supreme Court; specific groups and subcultures
Universal Music Enterprises, 223–24, 230–31
University of California, Berkeley (UC Berkeley), 203
Unsolved Mysteries (TV show), 274
Ure, Midge, 236
USA for Africa (supergroup), 236–37, 242, 247, 249
USSR. *See* Soviet Union

van Zandt, Steven (a.k.a. Little Steven), 240–43, 247–54, 256

Variations on "America" (C. Ives), 28–31
Variety (magazine), 83, 274
vaudeville, 11, 55–56
Verdi, Giuseppe, 62
Victor Records, 64–65, 81, 84, 110
Victorian parlor songs, 61
"Video Killed the Radio Star" (music video), 212
Vietnam War, 156, 189, 203–4
Village People, 277
Village Voice, 249, 250–51
violence
 lynchings, 21, 57, 66, 95–115, 126, 142
 murder of Medgar Evers, 192, 196
 political assassinations, 13, 154, 193, 194, 201, 246
 race riots, 8, 21
 Red Summer of 1919, 21, 56–57, 62–63, 96
 Sixteenth Street Baptist Church, Birmingham, AL, 196–97
 See also lynchings; warfare
Vocalion Records, 108
Vodery, Will, 58
Voice of America (van Zandt), 240–41
Voice of America radio broadcast (VOA), 141–42
Von Eschen, Penny, 146
"Vote for Names" (C. Ives), 41
Voting Rights Act of 1965, 187
Vulture (website), 266

Wagner, Robert F., 52–53, 100–101
Wagnleitner, Reinhold, 154
Walker, Gary L., 182
Wall Street Journal, 266
Wallace, Henry, 121, 128, 131
Waller, Thomas "Fats," 98, 150
Walt Disney's Grand Canyon (documentary), 87–89
Warner Bros. Records, 220, 222–28, 230–31, 236, 251–52
warning labels for "explicit lyrics," 213, 215–18
Warsager, Hyman, 100
Warsaw, 143, 152

Warwick, Dionne, 24
Washington Post, 174, 175, 178, 222, 253, 266
Washington, Booker T., 15
Washington, DC, 8, 158–59, 253
    Shaw neighborhood (formerly Uptown), 61–64
Washington, Dinah, 158
Washington, Fredi, 57
Washington, George, 7, 260, 262, 264, 270
Watts Stax concert of 1972, 24
"We Are the World" (charity single), 236–37, 242, 247, 249
"We Shall Overcome" (freedom song), 187–89, 197
"We're Not Gonna Take It" (Twisted Sister) 216
Wein, George, 156
West Side Story (Bernstein), 161–85
    Broadway revival, 182–85
    composition of, 161–74
    film versions of, 179–82, 184–85
    negative portrayal of the Puerto Rican community, 170–72, 176, 179–80, 182, 183–84
    original Broadway run, 174–79
    politicization and Cold War anxieties, 165–66
West, Kanye, 223
"What's Going On" (Benson/Gaye), 203–5
When We All Vote (organization), 276

White Citizens Council of Alabama, 148
White, Clarence Cameron, 61
White, George Henry, 95
White, George, 104
White, Josh, 110–12, 115, 118
White, Walter, 100–101, 109
Whiteman, Paul, 53–54, 58–60, 63–65, 74–78, 82–84
wild horses and burros, 90–92
Wilder, Billy, 192
Wilder, Thornton, 122
"William Will" (C. Ives), 33–34
Williams, Bert, 18
Williams, Camilla, 192
Williams, Justin, 227
Williams, Tony, 248
Wilson, Margaret, 20
Wilson, Robert C., 156
Wilson, Teddy, 148–49
Wilson, Woodrow, 19–21, 41, 42, 62, 80, 190
Winfrey, Oprah, 253
Winter Garden Theater, NYC, 176
Wise, Robert, 179–81
Wolfe, George C., 261
women
    an anthem for the women's movement, 205–9
    female sexuality, 212–13
    first African American woman winning an Oscar, 109
    objectification of women in music industry, 206, 222
    suffrage, 9, 20, 43
Women's Leadership Conference, 208

Women's Lives Rally (2017), 208–9
Wonder Mike (Michael Anthony Wright), 222
Wonder, Stevie, xi–xiv, 24, 200, 249
Wood, Natalie, 167
Wood, Ron, 248
Woodstock Music and Art Fair, 201–3, 211
Workers' Music League, 119
world music
    from Africa, 235–36, 238, 245, 247, 250, 255
    Peruvian ballads, 236
    reggae, 236, 238
    traditional Pakistani ragas, 148
World War I, 19, 21, 43, 56–57, 105
World War II, 47, 70, 121, 126, 128, 129, 141, 166, 206
Wright, Eugene, 152

X-Factor UK (TV show), 113

Yale–Princeton Football Game (C. Ives), 33
"Yankee Doodle" (traditional song), 3, 8, 14
Yarmolinsky, Adam, 162
"YMCA" (Village People), 277
"You Can Call Me Al" (Simon), 244–45, 249–50
Yugoslavia, 146, 154

Zappa, Frank, 215
Zimbabwe, 254–55
Zimbalist, Efrem, 53
Zydeco, 244